AI Frameworks Enabled by Blockchain

Creating Trustworthy and Responsible AI Using Distributed Ledger Technology

Vikram Dhillon
David Metcalf
Max Hooper

Apress®

AI Frameworks Enabled by Blockchain: Creating Trustworthy and Responsible AI Using Distributed Ledger Technology

Vikram Dhillon
Apartment 215
Detroit, MI, USA

David Metcalf
UCF Inst for Simulation & Training
Orlando, FL, USA

Max Hooper
Merging Traffic Inc. & Global Blockchain Ventures
Orlando, FL, USA

ISBN-13 (pbk): 979-8-8688-1401-3
https://doi.org/10.1007/979-8-8688-1402-0

ISBN-13 (electronic): 979-8-8688-1402-0

Copyright © 2025 by Vikram Dhillon, David Metcalf, Max Hooper

This work is subject to copyright. All rights are reserved by the Publisher, whether the whole or part of the material is concerned, specifically the rights of translation, reprinting, reuse of illustrations, recitation, broadcasting, reproduction on microfilms or in any other physical way, and transmission or information storage and retrieval, electronic adaptation, computer software, or by similar or dissimilar methodology now known or hereafter developed.

Trademarked names, logos, and images may appear in this book. Rather than use a trademark symbol with every occurrence of a trademarked name, logo, or image we use the names, logos, and images only in an editorial fashion and to the benefit of the trademark owner, with no intention of infringement of the trademark.

The use in this publication of trade names, trademarks, service marks, and similar terms, even if they are not identified as such, is not to be taken as an expression of opinion as to whether or not they are subject to proprietary rights.

While the advice and information in this book are believed to be true and accurate at the date of publication, neither the authors nor the editors nor the publisher can accept any legal responsibility for any errors or omissions that may be made. The publisher makes no warranty, express or implied, with respect to the material contained herein.

   Managing Director, Apress Media LLC: Welmoed Spahr
   Acquisitions Editor: Shivangi Ramachandran
   Desk Editor: James Markham
   Editorial Project Manager: Gryffin Winkler

Cover designed by eStudioCalamar

Cover Photo by Shubham Dhage on Unsplash

Distributed to the book trade worldwide by Springer Science+Business Media New York, 1 New York Plaza, New York, NY 10004. Phone 1-800-SPRINGER, fax (201) 348-4505, e-mail orders-ny@springer-sbm.com, or visit www.springeronline.com. Apress Media, LLC is a Delaware LLC and the sole member (owner) is Springer Science + Business Media Finance Inc (SSBM Finance Inc). SSBM Finance Inc is a **Delaware** corporation.

For information on translations, please e-mail booktranslations@springernature.com; for reprint, paperback, or audio rights, please e-mail bookpermissions@springernature.com.

Apress titles may be purchased in bulk for academic, corporate, or promotional use. eBook versions and licenses are also available for most titles. For more information, reference our Print and eBook Bulk Sales web page at http://www.apress.com/bulk-sales.

Any source code or other supplementary material referenced by the author in this book is available to readers on GitHub. For more detailed information, please visit https://www.apress.com/gp/services/source-code.

If disposing of this product, please recycle the paper

Table of Contents

About the Authors xi

About the Technical Reviewer xv

Acknowledgments xvii

Chapter 1: The Era of Artificial Intelligence 1
   Traditional Application Stack 3
   Blockchain Application Stack 6
   AI Integration Stack 11
   Safety and Responsible Design in AI 16
   Designing Guardrails for AI Models 24
   Constitutional AI 26
   Secure Machine Learning 28
   Open Source AI Models 30
   Blockchain-Based Governance for AI 40
   Consensus-Based Alignment 46
   Summary 48
   Bibliography 49

Chapter 2: Building Up to Large Language Models (LLMs) 53
   Introduction 53
   RNN with Attention 57
   The Transformer 59
   BERT Transformers 61

TABLE OF CONTENTS

    T5 Architecture 63

    Generative Pre-trained Transformer (GPT) 63

    Model Alignment Research 72

        InstructGPT 72

        Constitutional AI (CAI) 73

        Self-Generated Instruction 73

        Sparks of Artificial General Intelligence 75

    Scaling Research 75

        Kaplan's Scaling Laws 75

        Chinchilla Scaling Laws 77

        Low-Rank Adaptation 78

        Parameter-Efficient Finetuning 79

        FlashAttention 80

        One GPU and One-Day Training 82

    Bibliography 83

Chapter 3: Behold the Dreamers 89

    Paradigm Shift 90

    Technology Stack 93

    Next Generation of Dreamers 99

    Mood of the Investors 101

    Blockchain and AI Integration 104

    Mood of the "AI Doomers" 104

    Regulatory Landscape 107

    Summary 108

    Bibliography 108

TABLE OF CONTENTS

Chapter 4: The Gold Rush in Bitcoin and AI 111
Reaching Consensus 111
Mining Hardware 119
Startup Stories 123
New Consensus 125
AI Hardware 126
Memory Considerations 129
Performance Metrics 130
AI Energy Crisis 131
AI Copyrights 133
Summary 136
Bibliography 136

Chapter 5: Foundations of the Future: Blockchain and Large Language Models 139
Transaction Workflow 140
    Components of a Transaction List 144
Simple Payment Verification (SPV) 151
A Real-World Analogy for Merkle Trees 153
Blockchain Forks 156
    Transformer Architecture 157
    Tokenization 158
    Embeddings 159
    Attention Mechanisms 161
    Layer Normalization and Residual Connections 165
    Activation Functions 167
    Decoder 169
Summary 170
Bibliography 171

TABLE OF CONTENTS

Chapter 6: Inference, Fine-Tuning, and Retrieval-Augmented Generation 173

Retrieval-Augmented Generation 174

Fine-Tuning 176

When to Use RAG versus Fine-Tuning? 179

Example Use Cases 180

    Use Case 1: RAG—Customer Support Knowledge Base 180

    Use Case 2: Fine-Tuning—Medical Diagnosis Assistant 181

Inference 183

Decoding 185

Attention 187

Inference Metrics 193

Request Batching 196

Summary 197

Bibliography 198

Chapter 7: Unpacking Ethereum 201

Overview of Ethereum 202

    Accounts in Ethereum 206

    State, Storage, and Gas 209

Ethereum Virtual Machine 215

    Solidity and Vyper Programming Languages 218

    Developer Resources 224

    World Computer Model 225

    Layer 2 Upgrades 230

    Blockchain-as-a-Service 238

Decentralized Applications 240

TABLE OF CONTENTS

    Geth and Mist 242

    Ethereum Upgrades 244

    Upcoming Proposals 252

Summary 254

Bibliography 255

Chapter 8: Physics of Large Language Models 257

Part 0: Prelude 258

Part 3: Knowledge in Language Models 263

Part 2: Reasoning in Language Models 277

Part 1: Language Structures in Language Models 290

Conclusion 297

Chapter 9: Contemporary Decentralized Organizations 299

The Public DAO: Inception and Collapse 300

Technical Foundations of a DAO 304

Governance Models 316

Use Case for DAOs: Decentralized Science (DeSci) 323

Automated Market Makers (AMMs) and Real-World Asset (RWA) Protocols 328

Regulatory Landscape and Future Directions 330

Summary 334

Bibliography 335

Chapter 10: Biological Large Language Models 337

DNA Language Models 341

RNA Language Models 346

Protein Language Models 353

    ESM-3 356

    AlphaFold 357

vii

TABLE OF CONTENTS

scGPT 360
Evo 361
Drug Discovery with LLMs 363
Public Health with LLMs 365
Clinical Foundational Models 367
Reducing Physician Burnout with LLMs 376
AI and LLMs Powering Mental Health Services 380
Summary 384
Bibliography 386

Chapter 11: Blockchain in Scientific Reproducibility 389

Blockchain Properties and Reproducibility 390
Reproducibility Crisis 391
Clinical Trials 398
Reputation System 407
Pharmaceutical Drug Tracking 413
    Updates in Blockchain for Science 416
Summary 427
Bibliography 427

Chapter 12: Large Reasoning Models 431

Test-Time Compute 432
DeepSeek Architecture 435
    Mixture of Experts (MoE) Architecture 435
    Floating-Point 8 Quantization 437
    Multi-head Latent Attention (MLA) 438
    Multi-token Prediction 440
    Stage 1: Cold Start with Supervised Fine-Tuning (SFT) 442
    Stage 2: Reinforcement Learning and Policy Evolution 444

Stage 3: Rejection Sampling and Expanded Supervised Fine-Tuning 447
　　Stage 4: Secondary Reinforcement Learning 448
　　Distillation 450
　　Training Costs 452
　Summary 452
　Bibliography 453

Chapter 13: Technological Revolutions and Financial Capital Markets 457
　Blockchain 459
　Large Language Models 461
　AI Models as Smart Contracts 463
　ICOs 464
　Regulatory Updates for Blockchain Platforms in 2025 468
　Summary 481
　Bibliography 481

Chapter 14: Blockchain-as-a-Service 483
　Updates on BaaS Providers 484
　BaaS Providers in 2025: A Decision Tree Approach 494
　　Step 1: Core Business Requirements Assessment 494
　　Step 2: Technical Architecture Requirements 495
　　Step 3: Infrastructure and Integration 497
　　Step 4: Operational Considerations 498
　　Step 5: Compliance and Governance 499
　　Use Case Summary 500
　Security in BaaS 500
　Summary 504
　Bibliography 504

TABLE OF CONTENTS

Chapter 15: Lean Blockchain and AI 507
Lean Methodology 508
Business Model Canvas 519
Applying Lean Methodology to AI Startups 522
AI-Specific MVP Considerations 524
Business Model Canvas 527
AI-Specific Success Factors 529
Common Pitfalls in AI Startups 532
Summary 533
Bibliography 534

Chapter 16: Beyond Large Language Models and Blockchain 537
Agentic AI 537
Large Concept Models 541
Model Context Protocol 543
LLM-Powered Robotics 547
Nuclear-Powered Data Centers 549
Sparks of AGI 551
Bibliography 554

Index 557

About the Authors

Vikram Dhillon is a Hematology and Oncology fellow in Houston. Vikram finished his internal medicine residency training at Wayne State University and holds a Doctor of Osteopathic Medicine degree and an MBA from Nova Southeastern University. He was previously a research fellow at UCF's Institute for Simulation and Training while completing his BSc in Molecular Biology. His research focus includes AI in healthcare as well as clinically meaningful translation of AI. Over the years, he has had several peer-reviewed scientific publications in the areas of bioinformatics and computational biology. He gained invaluable entrepreneurial experience through the National Science Foundation's Innovation Corps program, where he studied customer discovery and high-risk startup commercialization. A long-standing member of the Linux Foundation, Vikram has been an active contributor to open source projects over the last decade. He regularly attends national and international conferences bridging the worlds of healthcare, technology, and innovation.

ABOUT THE AUTHORS

Dr. David Metcalf, PhD, is General Partner and Managing Director at Global Blockchain Ventures and is a technology specialist. Dr. Metcalf has over 20 years' experience in the design and research of web-based and mobile technologies converging to enable learning and healthcare. Since 2005, Dr. Metcalf has served as Director of the Mixed Emerging Technology Integration Lab (METIL) at UCF's Institute for Simulation and Training, formerly held lead research roles for NASA, and was a consulting executive and investor. Dr. Metcalf co-authored *Blockchain Enabled Applications* (2017), *Blockchain in Healthcare* (2019), *Blockchain Enabled Applications* (2021), and *ABC: AI, Blockchain, and Cybersecurity for Healthcare* (2024).

Dr. Metcalf has worked globally on many projects in and out of the United States in enterprise, education, healthcare, and other areas. Dr. Metcalf has a long history working in simulation, AI, mobile, learning, visualization systems, and quantum cybersecurity applications. Dr. Metcalf frequently presents at industry and research events shaping business strategy, discussing the use of technology to improve learning and human performance, and serves on multiple boards of directors that work to impact global problems.

ABOUT THE AUTHORS

Max Hooper, PhD, is the chief executive officer of Merging Traffic and co-founder of Global Blockchain Ventures. He is responsible for these companies' management and growth strategy while also serving as the corporate liaison to the financial services industry and various capital formation groups. Prior to starting the company, he was the co-founder of Equity Broadcasting Corporation (EBC), a media company that owned and operated more than 100 television stations across the United States. He was responsible for activities in the cable, satellite, investment banking, and technology industries, and during his tenure it grew to become one of the top ten largest broadcasting companies in the country. A lifelong learner, Hooper has earned five doctorate degrees, including two PhDs, two DMins, and a ThD, from a variety of institutions. Hooper studied financial technology with cohorts at MIT and cryptocurrency and business disruption with cohorts at the London School of Economics. Hooper is the co-author of three books about blockchain-enabled applications and has taken several companies public on NASDAQ. As an avid runner, he has completed more than 100 marathons and an additional 20 ultra-marathons, which are 50- or 100-mile runs. He has completed the Grand Slam of Ultra Running. Hooper is committed to his family and is a husband, father to five children, and grandfather to seven grandsons. He is active in many organizations and serves on various boards of directors. He works globally with several ministries and nonprofit aid groups and was honored to speak at the United Nations in New York in 2015.

About the Technical Reviewer

Prasanth is a Blockchain Certified Professional, Professional Scrum Master, and Microsoft Certified Trainer who is passionate about helping others learn how to use and gain benefits from the latest technologies. He is a thought leader and practitioner in blockchain, cloud, and Scrum. He also handles the Agile methodology, cloud, and blockchain technology community initiatives within TransUnion through coaching, mentoring, and grooming techniques.

Prasanth is an adjunct professor and a technical speaker. He was selected as a speaker at China International Industry Big Data Expo 2018 by the Chinese government and also at the International Blockchain Council by the governments of Telangana and Goa. He also received accolades for his presentation at China International Industry Big Data Expo 2018 by the Chinese government. Prasanth has published his patent titled "Digital Educational Certificate Management System Using IPFS Based Blockchain."

He is a globally recognized blockchain and GenAI expert, empowering over 50,000 students with cutting-edge technology skills through professional training and innovative community initiatives. He's a celebrated speaker and prolific trainer, significantly advancing technological education and digital transformation.

Acknowledgments

I would like to dedicate this work to Aaron Swartz, whose unwavering commitment to the free and open exchange of knowledge continues to inspire a generation of technologists and activists. Your vision of a more accessible and equitable digital world guides those who follow in your footsteps. To my parents, who nurtured my curiosity and supported my dreams without hesitation. Your sacrifices and unconditional love have made every achievement possible. To my brother, my first friend and constant ally, whose support and friendship have been an anchor through life's challenges and celebrations. I would like to thank the Burroughs Wellcome Fund, as part of this work was supported by the Burroughs Wellcome Fund Physician Scientist Institutional Award to the Texas A&M University Academy of Physician Scientists.

—Vikram Dhillon

I would like to thank Katy, Adam, and Andrew for their patience during the extended hours and effort while putting the book together and colleagues and students at UCF and through the NSF I-Corps program who identified the power of voice technology years ago and shared their knowledge and future strategies that inspired us to pursue this area of research early. Thank you to my co-authors and our outside collaborators and contributors and of course to God for the wisdom, ability, and grit to bring this effort to life.

—David Metcalf

ACKNOWLEDGMENTS

I would like to thank my co-authors and colleagues at UCF/METIL. I extend a special thanks to Mindy Hooper for her help and support. Additionally, I would like to thank God for His inspiration, guidance, direction, and wisdom. I would like to acknowledge His leadership.

—Max Hooper

CHAPTER 1

The Era of Artificial Intelligence

The year 2023 has been transformational for deployment of artificial intelligence (AI) in nearly every domain of human inquiry. Robust, resilient, and reliable models trained on an unprecedented volume of high-quality training data have enabled rapid advancements in natural language processing (NLP), computer vision, and general AI capabilities. Advancements in GPU design and novel architectural approaches are paving the way for state-of-the-art (SOTA) AI models that are increasingly more interpretable, practical, and semi-autonomous. This renaissance-like period in AI has largely been shaped by the emergence of foundational models: general-purpose, pre-trained representations of our world, learned from different modalities (structured, semi-structured, and unstructured) and sources of data (images, text, code, etc.). Foundational models extract fundamental patterns in data and encode the relationship between text, images, and code in terms of entities, concepts, and their interactions within the data.

A key defining feature of foundational models is self-supervised learning wherein a model creates labels from input data without any human intervention. The model is presented with a task (for instance, predicting a missing word in a sentence) and a dataset that has not been explicitly labeled for that task. Then, the model is trained to predict some parts of the data from other parts. Throughout the training process, the model generates

CHAPTER 1   THE ERA OF ARTIFICIAL INTELLIGENCE

its own supervisory signals and learns rich and nuanced representations of underlying training data. This also allows the model to capture complex structures and relationships within the data and perform well on unseen tasks. Imagine giving someone a puzzle with some missing pieces and asking them to figure out what's missing just by looking at the rest of the picture. That's what self-supervised learning does: it hides part of the data (like a missing word in a sentence or a patch in an image) and trains the model to predict the missing piece based on the context. Using this process, a foundational model can generalize knowledge across various domains, and after completing the training phase, it can be further fine-tuned to solve domain-specific tasks. Foundational models also significantly reduce the amount of data needed for task-specific fine-tuning and deployment of specialized models. Bommasani et al. from the Center for Research on Foundation Models (CRFM) describe two necessary features of foundational models: emergence and homogenization. Emergence implies that the characteristics and behavior of a system arise from interaction among the constituent parts rather than intentionally built into the system. For instance, how an AI model performs on an unseen task and in-context learning can be considered an emergent phenomenon. Homogenization refers to the standardization and convergence of outputs across models derived from the same foundational model. For instance, all models fine-tuning an existing foundational model (e.g., Llama or Mistral) will respond very homogeneously to standard input tasks. In other words, homogenization means making your data more consistent and comparable, so the model can understand patterns more easily. It's like cleaning up and organizing things before learning from them. We will begin this chapter by discussing the components of a traditional application stack, novel functionalities enabled by distributed ledger technology, and the prospective gradation of AI infrastructures. We subsequently explore the principles of safe and responsible AI design, as well as the concepts of secure machine learning (ML). Additionally, we investigate the use of oracles and zero-knowledge proofs (ZKPs) to augment the reliability of artificial intelligence models. Finally, we will conclude with a discussion on extending blockchain-based decentralization to AI governance via consensus protocols and whether the next-generation consensus mechanisms can guide model alignment.

Traditional Application Stack

In an attempt to simplify contemporary web application stacks, we can decompose them into the following eight layers:

1. **Front-end (client-side) layer:** This layer is responsible for creating the user interface (UI) and user experience (UX) of the web application. It includes HTML, CSS, JavaScript, and various front-end frameworks such as React, Angular, Vue.js, and Ember.js. These technologies allow developers to create interactive client-side functionality, handle user input, and communicate with the back-end server.

2. **Back-end (server-side) layer:** This is the language used for building server-side logic, handling data storage, and managing business logic and adherence to application rules. Popular choices include Python (with Django or Flask), Ruby (with Rails), Java (with Spring or Struts), C# (with .NET Core), PHP (with Laravel or Symfony), and Node.js (using Express). Most of these frameworks provide a scaffold to organize back-end development, making it easier to manage routes, controllers, views, and models. To make the development process more seamless, software stacks for back-end and front-end development have recently gained more popularity, for instance, the MEAN (MongoDB + Express.js +

Angular + Node.js) stack and the MERN (MongoDB + Express.js + React + Node.js) stack.

3. **Database layer**: Databases play a crucial role in storing and retrieving structured data needed for applications. Relational databases like MySQL, PostgreSQL, Oracle, and Microsoft SQL Server are commonly used for storing structured data, while NoSQL databases like MongoDB, Cassandra, and Redis are used for unstructured or semi-structured data. An object-relational mapper simplifies communication in modern web applications where a developer writes code to interact with objects derived from the database. Examples include SQLAlchemy for Python, Doctrine for PHP, Hibernate for Java, and Sequelize for Node.js.

4. **Web server layer**: The web server layer is responsible for serving the web application, and frequently used web servers include Apache HTTP Server and Nginx. This layer concomitantly provides security against threats such as SQL injections, cross-site scripting (XSS), and denial of service (DoS). The web server works in conjunction with a load balancer to scale the application across multiple back-end servers for incoming traffic. Amazon Elastic Load Balancer and Google Cloud Load Balancer are among the popular choices.

5. **Caching layer**: A layer designed to reduce latency associated with database queries by storing frequently accessed data in a temporary location closer. Tools like Redis and Memcached are commonly used. Similarly, Content Delivery Networks (CDNs) such

as Cloudflare and Akamai are also a type of caching mechanism to serve static assets such as images and videos close to a user's location and significantly reduce page load times.

6. **API layer**: In modern web applications, APIs are a necessary component for making application functionality available to external clients. An API gateway is an entry point for API calls, and it provides direct communication between an application service and external client. API gateways like AWS API Gateway and Azure API Management also provide policy enforcement for request rate limitation and security.

7. **Monitoring layer**: Any production-grade app needs close monitoring and effective logging. This allows for early identification of critical issues, troubleshooting errors and optimizing performance. Frameworks like New Relic, Prometheus, and Splunk enable granular logging for sysadmins.

8. **Deployment layer**: Finally, this layer focuses on tools that help deploy an app and critical code updates to production. From source control with Git to automated testing with Jenkins and Chef, these tools standardize the deployment of new changes and trigger safety checks to catch potentially fatal errors from affecting a production environment. Another aspect of the deployment layer is containerization, and platforms like Docker help standardize container deployment.

These eight layers are an oversimplification in the context of large-scale web applications; however, this introduction lays the groundwork for exploring blockchain application stacks and, furthermore, AI-based application stacks leveraging the blockchain.

Blockchain Application Stack

A blockchain application stack is a collection of protocols that enable the deployment of a decentralized application (dApp) to a blockchain network. Building on a traditional application stack, the following are the layers of a blockchain stack:

1. **Foundation layer**: The blockchain itself is the foundation layer for all dApp stacks, providing the underlying infrastructure that enables smart contracts, secure and transparent transactions, tamper-proof data storage, and a virtual runtime environment for managing complex dApps. Popular blockchain platforms include Ethereum, Cardano, and Polkadot.

2. **Consensus layer**: On a blockchain, for transactions to propagate throughout the network, consensus must be reached. Consensus algorithms help validate transactions and reach agreement on the state of a blockchain. Different implementations rely on different consensus mechanisms. Popular algorithms include proof of work (PoW), proof of stake (PoS), delegated proof of stake (DPoS), Byzantine fault tolerance (BFT), and leader-based consensus.

The consensus layer also encompasses peer-to-peer (P2P) communication between nodes on a blockchain without the need for a central authority. This communication commissions conflict resolution (often regarding transaction order or forks in the chain) and exchange of transaction verification data, ultimately producing a more resilient network.

3. **Contract layer**: Smart contracts are self-executing contracts that live on the blockchain and encode the terms of agreement between two parties, or users of the contract. They automate the enforcement of business logic and application rules on the blockchain without the need for an intermediatory. Most dApps use one or multiple smart contracts to provide a service to users. Smart contracts are typically written in contract-oriented programming languages such as Solidity (for Ethereum) or Chaincode (for Hyperledger Fabric).

4. **Executable layer**: Smart contracts need to be compiled into executable bytecode that can be deployed in a safe environment that interacts with the blockchain to execute any underlying logic. On Ethereum, this runtime environment is called the Ethereum Virtual Machine (EVM), and the executables are created by the Solidity compiler (Solc). Similarly, other blockchain protocols use a set of build and monitor tools for the executable layer to deploy dApps.

5. **Storage layer:** For dApps to store user parameters as well as internal state without creating bloat on the blockchain, a storage protocol can distribute data in a peer-to-peer manner rather than relying on a central authority. InterPlanetary File System (IPFS) is a decentralized storage protocol that can be used seamlessly with blockchain platforms. IPFS provides a unique identifier for users (or smart contracts in this case) to store and retrieve files across a decentralized network with very low friction.

6. **Tokenization layer:** Most blockchain platforms have a native digital currency (called a token) that facilitates payments within the network. For instance, the Ethereum blockchain uses ether (ETH) to cover transaction fees and runtime costs for smart contracts, access to digital assets, and other services within the ecosystem. This token is usually well-integrated into a dApp and enables new monetization models for developers, including microtransactions and subscription fees for additional dApp features.

7. **Blockchain explorer:** A graphical user interface for anyone to explore the transactions occurring on the network in real time. It can be immensely useful for viewing the transaction history of a particular address or group of addresses, examining the contents of individual blocks (including the transactions they contain and mining information), searching for specific transactions or addresses, and viewing statistics related to that blockchain's activity (transactions per day or total volume). Popular blockchain explorers include Etherscan (for Ethereum) and Blockchair (for Bitcoin and others).

8. **Front-end layer:** The most successful user interfaces make the back-end blockchain component invisible to an end user, and popular frameworks like React, Angular, or Vue.js provide the tools and libraries for building applications that can communicate with smart contracts on a blockchain. Of note, blockchain explorers are one such example of a front-end interface.

9. **Identity layer:** More complex dApp features also require user role groups and identity management where only authorized addresses or parties can execute particular portions of a contract (for instance, withdrawal using a smart contract). Self-sovereign platforms like uPort allow users to control what information they want to share and manage their own digital identifies that can be connected to a blockchain.

10. **Deployment layer:** Cloud platforms such as Amazon Web Services (AWS) and Azure offer managed Blockchain-as-a-Service (BaaS) that simplify doing prototyping on a blockchain as well as deploying dApps on the chain. Similarly, auditing frameworks such as Embark and Hardhat provide the tools for testing smart contracts to detect memory leaks and any areas where exploits can be applied. Data analysis tools such as Prometheus and Geth help with continued monitoring and metrics to optimize dApps and have reliable metrics to track.

11. **Regulatory layer**: A well-defined regulatory framework is crucial for any blockchain implementation to survive in the long term. Organizations and groups can encode the regulatory logic as part of an application to prevent any malicious actors from jeopardizing the app. Governance frameworks like DAOstack and Aragon provide the necessary tools to implement best practices and often have to be supplemented by domain-specific knowledge.

In this chapter, the term *model* will be used frequently, so let's define it. An AI model is a mathematical construct that implements one aspect of intelligent behavior. This behavior is often generated by machine learning algorithms, where the parameters (or weights) of a model are iteratively updated based on observation to minimize a defined loss function. Large language models (LLMs) are a class of AI models specialized in handling natural language processing tasks and rely on sequences of tokens (words and characters). LLMs are essentially deep neural networks with several layers of nodes connected to map token sequences to vector representations. These models are built on transformer architecture, which utilizes a self-attention approach to weight the relevance of a token in the context of the previous word. In the training phase, LLMs optimize for a loss function related to predicting the next token, and in this manner, LLMs can generate meaningful responses. Multimodal LLMs (MLLMs) extend traditional LLMs to new streams of data such as images, videos, and audio. MLLMs use specialized transformers for each source to compile information in a meaningful manner for training and then optimize for the next token. One prominent example of this is Google's DeepMind, an advanced MLLM combining vision, language, and speech in a unified framework and that can create long-form content without human input.

CHAPTER 1   THE ERA OF ARTIFICIAL INTELLIGENCE

AI Integration Stack

New programming languages and frameworks are paving the way for more sophisticated software stacks. With increased accessibility to trained AI models and access to infrastructure for deployment, AI models are being integrated into new verticals daily. Just as blockchain extended the traditional application stack, AI models, due to their platform agnosticism, will extend both traditional and blockchain stacks. Let's review two use cases enabled by such an integration. Currently, access to specialized AI models for scientific research is prohibitive for individual researchers or startups. A blockchain-based platform can host a decentralized marketplace where researchers can upload their own domain-specific AI models, form collaborations with other researchers, and trade computation time using the marketplace: rent or lease AI models with a given computational time that is compensated by the currency native to the blockchain. Smart contracts on the marketplace blockchain can dictate payment schemes and democratize access to the next generation of research tools. In a similar note, traditional supply chains are inundated with inefficiencies due to lack of transparency, potential for fraud, and unpredictable logistics. Sourcing AI models trained on time-series forecasting can allow for more accurate predictions of delivery time and reduce waste. By analyzing historical data in the domain-specific supply chain, an AI model can predict demand, re-route goods based on worsening weather conditions, and even respond to real-time market fluctuations. In this example, the blockchain can enable tracking of raw material to delivery and product authenticity and combat counterfeiting. Data-driven decisions from AI models can enhance a supply chain's efficiency and lead to more reliable daily operations. These are just two examples of new domains enabled by integrating AI models into a blockchain stack; the potential for new applications in domains of healthcare and personalization is immense. We postulate that an AI stack will inherit layers from any foundational stack it builds upon, whether traditional or blockchain-based, and will have the following additional new layers:

1. **Model deployment layer**: An isolated, containerized layer that would host the AI models necessary for a blockchain implementation. Once AI models are trained, they need to be deployed to a secure environment that can interact with a smart contract without creating new security risks—essentially, a wrapper mechanism that benefits from the security features provided by the underlying blockchain and allows for secure communication between an end user and the trained model. In order to containerize this layer, we can use Docker to package the models into smart contracts. Frameworks like OpenZeppelin that provide pre-built templates for creating and managing smart contracts on Ethereum can be extended to include instructions or queries to the AI model, filtered by the smart contract.

2. **Interfacing layer**: To make the AI models more accessible, a real-time message-passing protocol layer is necessary. This layer will provide a standard, secure interface for other components of the ecosystem to interact with the model layer. For instance, using a custom messaging protocol built on gRPC or GraphQL, a dApp can send and receive communication from the model, track the processing time and computational costs, and bill the end user in microtransactions for using the model.

CHAPTER 1   THE ERA OF ARTIFICIAL INTELLIGENCE

3. **Contract layer**: Smart contracts running on an AI-enabled blockchain will benefit from new features and upgraded business logic due to the domain-specific and generalized models integrated into the blockchain protocol. Smart AI contracts with enhanced programmatic access to models allow for the contract terms to adapt based on changing market conditions, user behavior, or other predefined external factors. This self-updating mechanism keeps the contract relevant and effective over time. Programming languages like Solidity will have new data structures and routines to query the models within a contract and update the contract based on response. New dApps built on top of next-generation responsive contracts will also implement new monetization schemas for model access, on-chain computation time, and model response latency. In domain-specific use cases (for instance, scientific research and simulation), smart AI contracts may serve an instance of the AI model to an end user as a dApp.

4. **Model development layer**: In this layer, new and experimental models and model marketplaces can be developed and tested in a high-risk, high-reward manner. This allows any blockchain-based ecosystem to thoroughly test new models or markets by exposing them only to part of a blockchain and assessing the response. Libraries like OpenMined provide tools for developing decentralized, transparent, explainable, and privacy-preserving AI models that can be used in computer vision, natural language processing

13

tasks, and financial modeling. Using this toolkit, developers can deploy AI models on blockchain infrastructure, and presently, there is integration support for Ethereum and Polkadot. Decentralized AI marketplaces built on top of OpenMined can facilitate exchange of AI assets such as models and model weights, training data (through IPFS), and even computing resources, in a secure and transparent manner. Federated learning in the model training layer supports multiple parties to train machine learning models without sharing sensitive data, and by preserving data privacy, this collaborative effort ultimately gives rise to better models.

5. **Oracle layer**: An oracle is an intermediary service that provides external data to a smart contract. Oracles are necessary because smart contracts are designed such that no external data sources outside a blockchain can be accessed. Data oracles, event oracles, time oracles, and identity oracles are the four general types of oracles implemented on a blockchain. Using AI techniques can enhance the security of oracles, for instance, using anomaly and outlier detection and robust aggregation, AI-powered oracles can guarantee tamper-resistant integration of external data streams into smart contracts for decision-making. Two oracle networks (Tellor and Oraichain) are currently using AI-based reputation scales to select honest reports and incentivize honest reporting such that the data delivered to a smart contract is of the highest quality.

CHAPTER 1   THE ERA OF ARTIFICIAL INTELLIGENCE

6. **Off-chain tracking layer**: In certain domain-specific tasks, a dApp may need to perform more intensive computations, and although the blockchain can handle on-chain computing, heavy processing can impede network performance. To overcome limitations imposed by blockchain computational constraints, off-chain computation frameworks allow complex calculations to occur outside the chain and the results reported back to the end user. In this manner, the end user can rent hardware via a smart contract and obtain the results. Machine learning algorithms can inform a smart contract on management of resource allocation, predict workload patterns, and dynamically adjust parameters according to changing environmental factors. These improvements can yield greater efficiency, lower latency, and reduced costs for off-chain computations. One such example is TensorFlow Serving by Google Research designed to facilitate provisioning and monitoring of off-chain computations.

7. **Privacy layer**: With AI embedded into a blockchain protocol, advanced user privacy measures can be implemented, for instance, homomorphic encryption, secure multi-party computations, differential privacy, and zero-knowledge proofs can preserve identity when deploying a blockchain-based consortium with sensitive data.

CHAPTER 1   THE ERA OF ARTIFICIAL INTELLIGENCE

The three stacks are visually depicted in Figure 1-1. Now that we discussed the layers of an AI-powered application stack, let's narrow our focus to how a blockchain can enhance safe and responsible model design in AI.

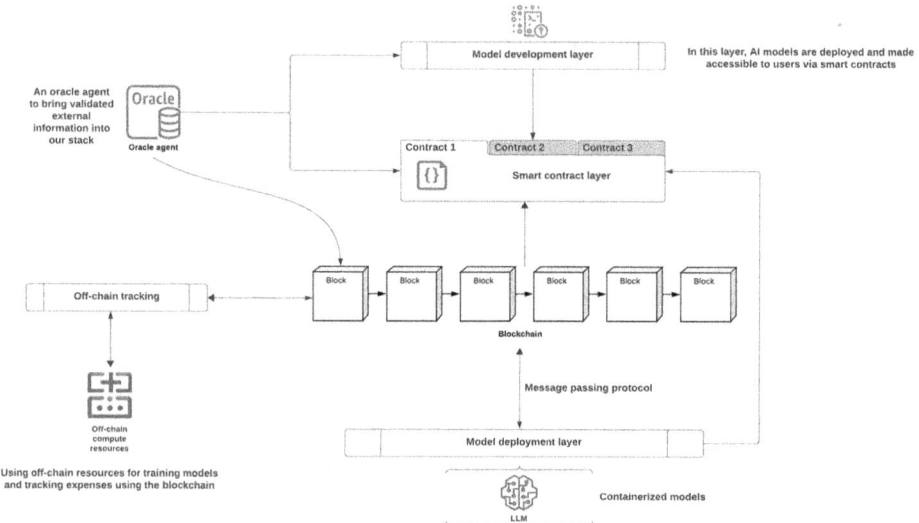

Figure 1-1. *Illustrating a blockchain–AI application stack with all the major players*

Safety and Responsible Design in AI

With growing amounts of high-quality training data, upcoming AI models will be increasingly more capable, and therefore, establishing safe and responsible design of new models is paramount. We broadly propose the following ten principles of safe and responsible model design (illustrated in Figure 1-2).

CHAPTER 1   THE ERA OF ARTIFICIAL INTELLIGENCE

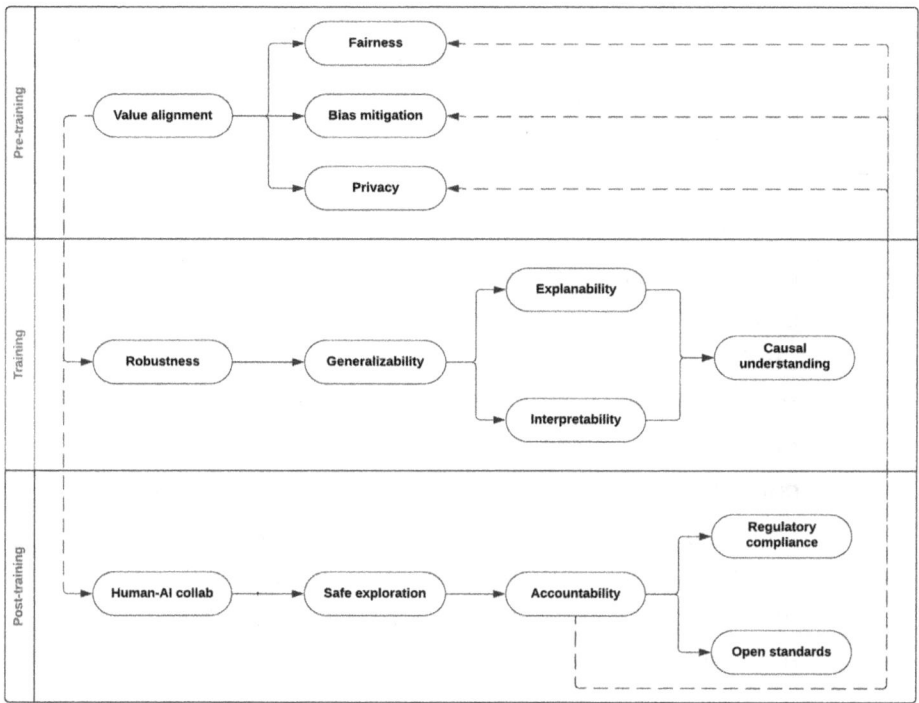

Figure 1-2. *Illustrating the principles of safe and responsible design for AI models across the lifespan of a model*

While each principle can be subject to a very nuanced and lengthy discussion, we will only focus on the most pertinent points:

1. **Value alignment**: Alignment of AI models is an incredibly complex problem, and the complexity increases as we build more sophisticated models. When tackling a task, aligning AI goals with human values and norms is the paramount principle of safe and responsible design. The famous paperclip maximizer problem by Nick Bostrom illustrates this concept: a super-intelligent AI model is tasked with finding the most optimal approach to manufacture

17

paperclips. In searching a solution space, the model may inevitably determine that human existence is impeding the model's primary objective by diverting resources to sustain the civilization and eliminating humanity may liberate resources for manufacturing. This thought experiment highlights the need for an AI model to interpret the presented task in the context of societal norms and ethical principles. Statistical methods such as value sensitivity analysis and reinforcement learning (RL) can help identify areas of potential misalignment and present acceptable corrections. Ultimately, mechanisms for creating and enforcing representations of moral principles during training and fine-tuning phases may pave the way for embedding a degree of alignment in model behavior beyond the typical reward learning.

2. **Fairness and bias mitigation**: AI models must be designed intentionally such that all individuals and groups are treated without any discrimination based on sensitive attributes such as gender, age, race, or socioeconomic status. This process is iterative and active throughout the lifecycle of an AI model, beginning from preprocessing and careful auditing of training data to ensure appropriate encapsulation and representation of a broader population to post-processing and deployment where adversarial debiasing can mitigate majority of underlying biases. Representation learning is a very active area of research with numerous statistical and algorithmic advances such as equalized odds post-processing and learning fair representations approach.

3. **Explainability and interpretability**: AI models must be designed to provide clear and simple explanations of their decision-making process, making it transparent to users, or at least highlight the model weights (training data) that generated the decision. Novel approaches to interpretability such as SHAP (SHapley Additive exPlanations), LIMFE, or DeepLIFT algorithms can make increasingly interpretable models that elevate a user's trust and reduce the "black-box"-like manifestation of AI models.

4. **Robustness and generalizability**: AI models must be designed to handle unexpected input and edge cases while maintaining peak performance. Perturbations to the model can be managed with techniques such as error handling protocols, adversarial attacks, input validation, and continuous monitoring. Monitoring and updating models after deployment is crucial to maintaining reliability and preventing concept drift (where the strength of association between input and output variables decreases). In addition, the model should retain consistent performance when generalized to adjacent domains for unseen tasks. Concept drift can be measured using Kullback–Leibler divergence or Hellinger distance, whereas robustness can be tracked dynamically using weighted moving averages.

5. **Causal understanding**: Traditional machine learning approaches focus on identifying correlational patterns in training data and apply the trained search patterns when presented with new data. When such a model

is applied to new domains, it can be misguided by the data, even after normalization, and lead to unreliable predictions. To enhance alignment and safety, AI models need to be causally aware. Causal reasoning enables a model to recognize the cause-and-effect relationship between variables instead of merely identifying correlations, giving rise to more reliable predictions, with a higher degree of explainability and ease in adapting to new domains while retaining accuracy. Measuring causal understanding between variables in AI models encompasses three challenges: representation, identification, and estimation. Representation refers to the process of encoding causal knowledge in formal mathematical frameworks such as structural equation models or directed acyclic graphs. This encoding process creates unambiguous description of the causal relationships for systematic analysis. Identification is the task of determining the necessary assumptions for statistically estimating causal structure from either observational or experimental data. Given a set of observed variables and their defined correlations, identification entails pinpointing the assumptions required to ascertain which variable exerts a causal influence over the other. Lastly, estimation is focused on quantifying the magnitude of causal effects (i.e., how much each cause influences its effect) between variables after they've been identified. Estimation is done by applying propensity score matching or regression analysis onto the observed data while taking into account confounding factors and potential bias. These statistical methods enable AI models to

CHAPTER 1   THE ERA OF ARTIFICIAL INTELLIGENCE

capture complex causal effects and generate more reliable explanations. Moreover, causally aware AI models display greater transferability to adjacent domains given their ability to detect true causes among noise, discard weak features, and ultimately yield models more resilient to perturbations.

Note   The term "understand" is used frequently in this chapter when referring to an AI model. The concept of whether an AI model "understands" a concept or an idea and generates output in response versus stochastic outputs that fit a probability distribution generated by a model's learned weights is an area of ongoing debate within the field.

---

6. **Accountability**: Developer groups and organizations designing AI models must take responsibility for unsafe actions of the model and provide clear mechanisms to report such events. Every organization that releases an AI model must have an accountability team with well-defined roles and responsibilities. Moreover, whenever feasible, disclosure of incident response plans should be encouraged. On a larger scale, legal frameworks need to expand their scope and encapsulate AI tech and safeguard consumers from potential harm.

7. **Human–AI collaboration**: Incorporating human expertise, surveillance, and intervention during an AI model training is necessary to develop safe models that align with human values. Human oversight into early phases of model training can be immensely

helpful in monitoring and validating the training process and stop bias from mitigating further into model weights, as well as intervening when necessary to offer corrections. Ultimately, AI models should be designed to work synergistically with humans and, as a collaborative, make well-informed decisions in solving a problem. A human–agent teaming framework is becoming increasingly popular for coordinating decisions between human operators and AI agents.

8. **Privacy and security**: AI models must prioritize the privacy and safety of end users across three complementary dimensions: First and foremost, a model must be designed to prevent unintentional leakage of training data via the model's responses. This is crucial as training data may have personal or sensitive information and risk re-identifying a user. Second, any prompting techniques and requests that probe for sensitive data should be subject to stringent screening, and finally, rigorous protections against prompt injections (a hidden injected message within a seemingly normal prompt that causes a model to operate outside its safeguards) must be designed. This requires designing privacy measures suitable to each stage for the entire lifecycle of a model such that any sensitive information can be processed securely while maintaining utility. Cryptographic protocols, differential privacy with controlled noise, and federated learning techniques are among the most commonly used methods of enhancing user privacy.

We will look at a few blockchain-specific privacy enhancing measures later in this chapter as well. The implemented privacy measures must also comply with local regulations.

9. **Safe exploration and ethical considerations**: When an AI model interacts with new data in a novel domain, safe exploration techniques prevent the model from being fixated on exploring unsafe states and minimize potential risks from uncertain outcomes. All AI models must be designed with mechanisms to detect unsafe states and steer away from them during the training and exploration phases. Exploratory analysis must strike a balance between cautious exploration and violating predefined safety rules. Some mechanisms to accomplish this include probability matching methods, risk exposure using quantile regression forests, and skill chains to support long-term planning. Deployed models need to be under regular monitoring and auditing to detect response deviations and, if deviations do occur, have established feedback loops for continuous improvement. As AI models become more heavily integrated into our social fabric, we need to establish institutional review boards (IRBs) and ethics committees to systematically assess how social norms and behaviors are evolving in response to AI models. IRBs can establish new informed consent protocols for studying AI models and set up rules of ethical conduct involving participant recruitment as well as

results reporting. Publishing negative results along with model weights and hyperparameters can help us quickly eliminate hypothesis of undesired outcomes from AI.

10. **Regulatory compliance and open standards**: Finally, all AI models must comply with the relevant statutory guidelines; however, the dynamic adaptability of foundational models poses a distinctive challenge in crafting oversight policies for both the base model and the respective industries it operates in such as finance or healthcare. Cross-discipline collaboration between regulatory agencies and standardization efforts by groups such as IEEE will lead to development of common vocabulary and evaluation criteria for safe and responsible model design. Collaborative endeavors involving regulatory agencies and standardization bodies (for instance, IEE) will lead to development of safety frameworks with common vocabulary and evaluation criteria that can be used to benchmark safe, ethical, and responsible design practices for AI models.

It must be noted that meeting the standards exemplified by each principle is more important than attaining them during a particular stage.

Designing *Guardrails* for AI Models

Foundational AI models are already being trained and implemented in sensitive domains such as healthcare, and creating barriers to confine the unintended consequences from foundational models is essential. Designing blockchain-enabled AI models for clinical workflows is a very challenging endeavor due to the delicate nature of patient care. This problem is compounded by hallucination-induced hidden biases that LLMs may introduce when interacting with clinical data. When deploying AI models in live environments for healthcare, it is prudent to develop *guardrails*, protective measures that can discard dangerous model actions or responses before ever reaching an end user. Burns et al. offered a very interesting and generalizable solution to this problem: use a smaller LLM as a *supervisory model* to fine-tune and *refresh* the guardrails already intrinsic to the foundational model. A weak supervisory model is not expected to teach new capabilities to the foundational model; however, it can elicit and strengthen the protective measures intrinsic to the foundational model. For instance, a foundational model for healthcare can be further fine-tuned for reading radiology reports, clinical guidelines, and laboratory investigations. Once an acceptable level of performance on domain-specific tasks has been achieved, a second round of fine-tuning with a weaker model can rescue the guardrails residual to the prime model's training. A more sophisticated approach would be to use Mixture of Experts (MoE) where discrete LLMs trained to identify sources of bias help fine-tune a healthcare-specific foundational model and minimize additional clinical disparities introduced by the LLM. A gated-interaction protocol can be implemented for live environments wherein an independent LLM serves as a gatekeeper, evaluating all recommendations generated by the foundational model before dissemination to the end user. Flagged responses would be regenerated by the foundational model and also become a part of future fine-tuning. Ultimately, such a dual-model architecture holds great promise in making safe and responsible AI models available to sensitive domains like healthcare.

CHAPTER 1   THE ERA OF ARTIFICIAL INTELLIGENCE

Constitutional AI

Anthropic has implemented this multi-layer method, called Constitutional AI (CAI), into Claude, their flagship LLM. The primary LLM (called the Constitutional Model) is trained on a *constitution* encompassing human behavior, preferences, and societal norms. This model generates an instruction set that dictates the actions of a smaller model (called the Policy Model). The Policy Model is smaller and more agile (in comparison to the primary LLM), designed for real-time decision making and user interactions. This design ensures that the responses generated by the Policy Model, when interacting with end users, align with the societal and ethical guidelines set up by the *constitution*. This smaller model is continually supervised and iteratively adjusts based on feedback from the Constitutional Model, and this feedback loop allows for refinement of the Policy Model behavior longitudinally, ensuring persistent alignment (with the constitutional principles) even when exposed to new data. Implementing this structure maintains the relevance and effectiveness of safeguards on model actions and ultimately assures that they remain beneficial to humanity and within ethical boundaries, as established in the *constitution*.

CAI as a broader concept relies on AI feedback provided in two stages, an initial supervised learning (SL) stage followed by a reinforcement learning (RL) stage. The initial stage involves prompting a LLM with "Red Teaming" prompts that are designed to elicit potentially harmful output. Model responses are subjected to a critique phase where they undergo evaluation for alignment with the ethical and safety standards established in the AI's *constitution*. This identifies areas of weakness from AI responses and where deviations from desired outcomes may occur. After the critique, the model undergoes a revision process. This process involves adjusting the AI's response generation mechanism to address the identified issues. The revision phase is crucial for iteratively refining the AI's behavior, ensuring that it not only avoids harmful outputs but also progressively

CHAPTER 1   THE ERA OF ARTIFICIAL INTELLIGENCE

aligns more closely with the constitutional guidelines. The final responses here are collected as part of a synthetic dataset and used to fine-tune the underlying LLM to generate responses that align closely with the *constitution*. Here, we end up with a Supervised Learning CAI (SL-CAI) model.

The second stage of AI feedback involves fine-tuning of a SL-CAI model into a reward model used to continually reinforce behaviors that align with the *constitution*. We start with a SL-CAI model obtained from stage 1 and prompt with the same "Red Teaming" prompts, multiple times to collect multiple replies. The responses are presented again to the SL-CAI model as a multiple-choice question with an objective of selecting the response that most closely follows the *constitution*. Here, the best-chosen answers become a second synthetic dataset for training a reward model (different from the baseline model or SL-CAI model) to do reinforcement learning. This reward model (called the Fine-tuned Preference Model (PM)) becomes a supervisor to the SL-CAI model to reinforce desired behavior and punish dangerous outcomes, reinforcing the *constitution* and yielding the final RL-CAI model. This whole process is visually depicted in Figure 1-3.

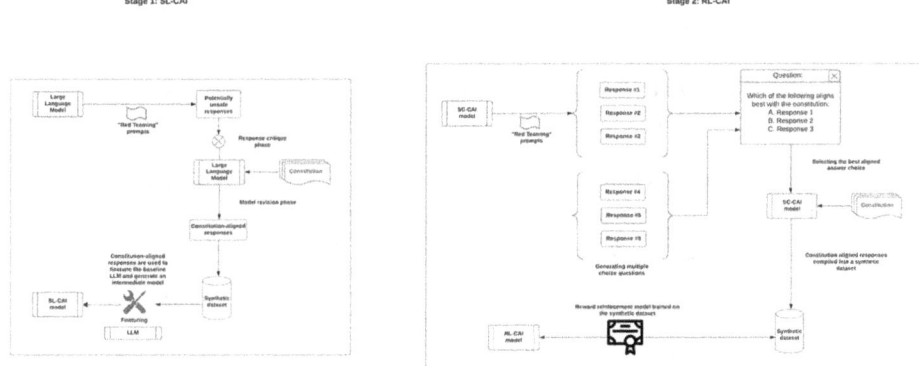

Figure 1-3. *SL-CAI training and RL-CAI training approaches*

27

CHAPTER 1   THE ERA OF ARTIFICIAL INTELLIGENCE

Secure Machine Learning

Secure machine learning (SML) is defined by Xiong et al. in a recent survey of literature as a security-aware approach to developing machine learning methods and technologies that includes threat modeling, attack vectors, and potential defense mechanisms. The paper emphasizes the importance of understanding where potential attacks may surface in the ML training and how threat modeling can be used to categorize attacks based on the attacker's goal, knowledge, and strategy. In addition, the paper provides various methodologies of attacks (gradient descent attack, label-flipping, and mimicry) as well as specific examples of attach types such as poisoning attacks, evasion attacks, and adversarial sampling. Poisoning attacks aim to compromise model training by introducing malicious data, whereas evasion attacks seek to deceive trained models during production. Finally, the paper outlines several strategies such as data compression and gradient masking to make ML models more resilient.

A few salient features from the paper are very relevant to our discussion, namely, categorizing an attacker's knowledge about the model infrastructure, fostering user trust and privacy preservation. Broadly speaking, there are three classes of attack:

1. **Perfect-knowledge, white-box attacks**: In this class, an attacker has detailed information about the targeted ML system. This includes access to the training dataset and knowledge of the underlying architecture, learning algorithms, and trained model weights. This is the most challenging class of attacks as the attacker will deeply understand vulnerabilities in the system.

2. **Limited-knowledge, gray-box attacks**: In this class, an attacker only has partial knowledge about the targeted ML system. A reasonable assumption would be that the attacker has knowledge on the feature set,

model architecture, and learning algorithms, but does not have access to the training data and trained model weights. The attacker may create a new dataset and rely on output from the ML system to learn about the model weights and vulnerabilities and fill the gaps in knowledge.

3. **Zero-knowledge, black-box attacks**: In this class, an attacker has no reliable information about the targeted ML system. An attacker only has access to public domain knowledge on the ML model including the type of training data and vague overview of features. The training data itself and, more importantly, learning algorithms are not available, which provides a degree of protection against security risks.

Managing privacy breaches is a critical concern for healthcare applications as they involve exposure of confidential data being processed by the ML system. The principle of statistical disclosure control is fundamental to maintaining privacy in ML models and states that publishable model outputs must not lead to deductive identification of the inputs. Under the umbrella of SML, we consider ML models prone to four types of breaches: membership interference, model inversion, model reconstruction, and model extraction. Membership interference breach is when an attacker can determine whether a particular data record (otherwise confidential in nature) was used for training an ML model. On the other hand, model inversion occurs when an attacker reconstructs sensitive input data from the model output. This type of breach occurs when the models provide detailed output, which can be reverse-engineered to reveal confidential inputs. Model reconstruction is similar to inversion, but here, an attacker recreates the raw training data based on outputs. In an extreme version of this breach, an attacker can use a LLM to help recreate the inputs based on extensive outputs. Finally, in model extraction, an attacker reverse-engineers the model characteristics such as parameters or training data and uses them to create a surrogate model. To increase user acceptance of SML and increase adoption, the resulting models must be transparent in their actions. Users are more likely to trust systems when they understand how a model works and can observe its functionality. Similarly, users are more likely to use a model if they have control over how their data is being accessed and which components are shared.

Open Source AI Models

Open source LLMs have risen to prominence in 2023, narrowing the performance gap with their closed source competitors (GPT 3.5). For a model to be considered open source, the LLM must provide information on hyperparameters and the training dataset. Presently, the majority of open source models are hosted on Hugging Face's Model Hub or TensorFlow's Model Garden. For the broader research and hobbyist community, open source LLMs provide several benefits. First, training a foundational model requires substantial computational resources, which can be prohibitively expensive for individuals or small organizations. However, fine-tuning an open source LLM for domain-specific tasks requires significantly less computational power and time. By making these models openly available, the research community can collaborate and share the costs associated with model fine-tuning. Moreover, such LLMs enable rapid prototyping and experimentation, lowering the barrier to entry for new incumbents and allowing AI researchers to build upon existing work instead of starting from scratch. Open source models also contribute significantly in reinforcing user trust. Any individual can examine the underlying training data and parameters to evaluate whether the model was built ethically and responsibly. There are ten prominent open source foundational model families that we want to review here:

CHAPTER 1   THE ERA OF ARTIFICIAL INTELLIGENCE

1. **Meta's Llama models**: Meta's Llama family has evolved through multiple generations, with the latest being Llama 3.3 released in December 2024. The models span parameter sizes from 1B to 405B, with Llama 3.1 being trained on approximately 15 trillion tokens from publicly available sources. Llama utilizes an optimized transformer architecture with several distinctive features including Grouped Query Attention (GQA), which reduces memory overhead during inference while maintaining quality. The context length has progressively increased across generations: Llama 1 had 2K tokens, Llama 2 had 4K, and Llama 3 offers 8K context. Major models in the family include Llama 3.3 (70B), Llama 3.2 (available in 1B, 3B, 11B, and 90B with both text-only and vision capabilities), Llama 3.1 (8B, 70B, and 405B), Llama 2 (7B, 13B, and 70B), and Code Llama (specialized versions for coding). The Llama 3.1 models are optimized for multilingual dialogue and support languages including English, German, French, Italian, and more. Llama 3 models have significantly improved multilingual capabilities with training data containing 5% high-quality non-English content spanning more than 30 languages.

2. **Mistral family**: The Mistral family began with Mistral-7B, a decoder-only transformer released under Apache 2.0 license that outperformed Llama 2 13B despite having fewer parameters. Key architectural innovations include Sliding Window Attention (SWA) with a 4,096-token fixed attention span and Grouped Query Attention (GQA) for

inference efficiency. Subsequent models expanded to include Mistral Small, Mistral Large, and Mixtral models. Mixtral introduced the Sparse Mixture of Experts (MoE) architecture, where the model is divided into expert networks. For each token, only certain experts are activated, reducing inference costs without performance decline. The Mixtral 8x7B model uses 12B active parameters out of 45B total parameters, delivering performance competitive with much larger dense models. Later releases include Pixtral (multimodal capability) with a 12B decoder and 400M parameter vision encoder and Mistral Large featuring improved multilingual accuracy, reasoning, and coding capabilities. Mistral Small 3.1, released in March 2025, has multimodal capabilities and handles context lengths up to 128K tokens.

3. **Falcon family:** The Falcon family, developed by the Technology Innovation Institute (TII) of UAE, consists of several models including Falcon 1.8B, 7B, 40B, and 180B, Falcon 3, and Falcon Mamba 7B. All Falcon models are available under open source licenses for both research and commercial use. Falcon uses a causal decoder-only architecture based on the transformer's decoder. A distinctive feature is its use of multiquery attention, which shares keys and values across all attention heads, significantly reducing memory costs during inference. Falcon 40B requires approximately 90GB of GPU memory, while Falcon 7B needs about 15GB. The latest addition, Falcon 3, includes models with 18–40 layers for transformer-based variants and 64 layers for the Mamba version.

Falcon Mamba 7B is particularly notable as the first open source State Space Language Model (SSLM), a revolutionary architecture with low memory costs that doesn't require additional memory to generate arbitrary long text. The Falcon 3 family supports context lengths up to 32K and will expand to multimodal functionalities in 2025.

4. **BLOOM family**: BLOOM (BigScience Large Open-science Open-access Multilingual Language Model) is a 176-billion-parameter transformer-based auto-regressive LLM trained on approximately 366 billion tokens (1.6TB) from March to July 2022. It was developed through the BigScience collaborative initiative led by Hugging Face. BLOOM's architecture is based on a decoder-only transformer, modified from Megatron-LM GPT-2, using ALiBi positional embeddings instead of traditional positional embeddings. The training utilized 384 NVIDIA A100 80GB GPUs across 48 nodes, consuming approximately 1 million compute hours. Its training dataset, called ROOTS, includes content in 46 natural languages and 13 programming languages from 252 sources. BLOOM is distributed under free licenses with all details of its development publicly available, including training scripts, input data, and model checkpoints. It was designed to democratize access to large language models, allowing researchers to study its performance and behavior down to its internal operations.

CHAPTER 1   THE ERA OF ARTIFICIAL INTELLIGENCE

5. **Stability AI**: Primarily known for their image generation models (Stable Diffusion), they've also developed several language models under the StableLM brand. Their first language models were released in 2023 with StableLM Alpha in 3B and 7B parameter sizes. These initial models were trained on a dataset built on The Pile but expanded to approximately 1.5 trillion tokens. StableLM uses a decoder-only transformer architecture similar to the Llama architecture but with some modifications. These include using rotary position embeddings (RoPE) applied to the first 25% of head embedding dimensions, LayerNorm with learned bias terms instead of RMSNorm, and the GPT-NeoX tokenizer. Later models incorporated SwiGLU activation functions for better performance. Stability AI has since expanded its language model lineup to include StableLM 2 (available in 1.6B and 12B parameters), StableLM 3B-4E1T (trained on 4 exaFLOPs), and specialized models like Stable Code 3B for code generation. Their most recent models also include Japanese-specific variants and models fine-tuned with techniques like Zephyr for better instruction following. The smaller 1.6B parameter models are designed to run efficiently on laptops and even phones, sometimes without requiring a dedicated GPU.

6. **Gemma family**: Google's Gemma family consists of lightweight, open-weight models derived from the same research and technology used to create Google's larger Gemini models. The original Gemma models were released in February 2024 in 2B and 7B parameter sizes,

with both pre-trained and instruction-tuned variants. Gemma uses a decoder-only transformer architecture. The models employ multi-head attention (MHA) mechanisms, GeGLU activation functions instead of standard ReLU (Rectified Linear Unit), and RoPE (rotary positional embedding) for positional encoding. The original Gemma models were trained with a context length of 8,192 tokens. Gemma 2, released in June 2024, improved performance and inference efficiency compared with the original models. Available in 2B, 9B, and 27B parameter sizes, Gemma 2 was followed by specialized variants like PaliGemma (a vision–language model), DataGemma (optimized for data retrieval), CodeGemma, and RecurrentGemma. The latest iteration, Gemma 3, was launched in early 2025 in 1B, 4B, 12B, and 27B parameter sizes. Gemma 3 added multimodal capabilities, supporting image and text inputs, expanded the context window to 128K tokens, and improved multilingual support for over 140 languages. Gemma 3 models were trained on significantly more data: 2T tokens for the 1B model, 4T for 4B, 12T for 12B, and 14T tokens for the 27B model. They also incorporated techniques like distillation, reinforcement learning from human feedback (RLHF), RLMF, and RLEF to enhance mathematical reasoning, coding capabilities, and instruction following.

7. **Phi family**: Microsoft's Phi series represents an effort to create highly capable small language models (SLMs). The first widely released model was Phi-2, a 2.7B parameter model introduced in

December 2023. Despite its small size, Phi-2 achieved performance comparable to models many times larger, particularly excelling at coding and math tasks where it outperformed models up to 25 times its size. Phi-2 was trained on 250B tokens using a combination of synthetic data created by GPT-3.5 and filtered web data from sources like Falcon RefinedWeb and SlimPajama. This curated "textbook-quality" training data was key to Phi-2's impressive capabilities relative to its size. The Phi family continued to evolve with Phi-3, released in April 2024 in three sizes: Phi-3-mini (3.8B parameters), Phi-3-small (7B), and Phi-3-medium (14B). A notable advancement was Phi-3-mini's context window of 128K tokens, making it the first model of its class to support such an extensive context. Phi-3 models were extensively safety-tested and trained using techniques like RLHF. They also demonstrated strong reasoning and logic capabilities, often outperforming models of similar and even larger sizes. In January 2025, Microsoft released Phi-4, a 14B parameter model that specialized in complex reasoning tasks, particularly excelling at mathematics. The Phi family was later expanded to include Phi-4-mini and Phi-4-multimodal, with the latter being the first in the Phi family to support text, audio, and vision inputs. The Phi family of SLMs is ideal for resource-constrained environments and edge computing scenarios.

8. **Qwen family (Alibaba Cloud)**: Alibaba first launched Qwen (also called Tongyi Qianwen) in April 2023, with its architecture initially based on Meta's Llama. The Qwen family includes models in multiple parameter

CHAPTER 1   THE ERA OF ARTIFICIAL INTELLIGENCE

sizes ranging from 0.5B to 110B, with the most notable being Qwen-1.8B, Qwen-7B, Qwen-14B, Qwen-32B, Qwen-72B, and Qwen-110B. These models support impressively long context lengths, with Qwen 1.5 models supporting 32K tokens and some Qwen2 models handling up to 128K tokens. The Qwen models feature a unique tokenizer with a large vocabulary of over 150,000 tokens, essential for handling both English and Chinese effectively. Alibaba has expanded the family to include specialized variants like Qwen-VL (vision–language model), Qwen-Audio (for audio processing), Qwen-Coder (for programming), and Qwen-Math (for mathematical problem-solving). They've also developed QwQ-32B-Preview, an experimental research model specifically focused on enhancing reasoning capabilities. In January 2025, Alibaba launched Qwen2.5-Max, a large-scale Mixture of Experts (MoE) model pre-trained on over 20 trillion tokens. This model underwent further refinement through supervised fine-tuning (SFT) and reinforcement learning from human feedback (RLHF).

9. **DeepSeek family**: DeepSeek has developed several generations of models with varying architectures and capabilities. Their initial offering was DeepSeek LLM, an advanced language model comprising 67 billion parameters trained from scratch on 2 trillion tokens in both English and Chinese. The architecture was based on Llama, with the 7B model using multi-head attention (MHA), while the 67B model employed Grouped Query Attention (GQA). DeepSeek-V2, released later, represented a significant advancement

with a Mixture of Experts (MoE) architecture comprising 236 billion total parameters, of which only 21 billion are activated for each token. It introduced two innovative architectural components: Multi-head Latent Attention (MLA), which significantly reduces key–value cache requirements, and DeepSeekMoE, which enables sparse computation through expert segmentation. These innovations helped DeepSeek-V2 reduce training costs by 42.5% compared with DeepSeek 67B while boosting inference throughput 5.76 times. The model supports an extended context length of up to 128K tokens. DeepSeek-V3, released in December 2024, pushed the boundaries further with a massive 671-billion-parameter MoE model, where 37 billion parameters are activated for each token. DeepSeek-V3 employs the same MLA and DeepSeekMoE architectures validated in DeepSeek-V2 but introduces an auxiliary-loss-free strategy for load balancing and a multi-token prediction (MTP) training objective for better performance. The model was pre-trained on 14.8 trillion tokens followed by supervised fine-tuning and reinforcement learning stages, achieving benchmark performance competitive with leading closed source models while requiring only 2.788M H800 GPU hours for training. This efficiency was partly achieved through a "DualPipe" parallelism algorithm and floating-point 8 (FP8) mixed precision training framework. Most recently, DeepSeek released DeepSeek-R1 in January 2025, a specialized reasoning model built on DeepSeek-V3. What makes DeepSeek-R1 unique is that they created

CHAPTER 1   THE ERA OF ARTIFICIAL INTELLIGENCE

DeepSeek-R1-Zero through large-scale reinforcement learning without supervised fine-tuning as a preliminary step. This approach allowed the model to develop advanced reasoning behaviors naturally, though it faced challenges like repetition and poor readability. To address these issues, they created DeepSeek-R1, which incorporates "cold-start" data before reinforcement learning. DeepSeek has also released distilled versions of DeepSeek-R1 based on Llama and Qwen models to support the research community.

10. **Aya family**: The research arm of Cohere developed the Aya family of open source multilingual language models to advance multilingual AI by expanding language coverage, particularly for underserved languages. The family has evolved through several iterations, beginning with Aya 101, which covered 101 languages (half previously underserved) using an mT5 architecture and was instruction fine-tuned with the Aya Collection of 513 million prompts across 114 languages. Despite its groundbreaking coverage, performance was limited by spreading model capacity across so many languages. Aya 23, released in May 2024, refined the approach by focusing on 23 languages with greater depth, available in 8B and 35B parameter sizes and covering major languages like Arabic, Chinese, English, French, German, Japanese, and others. This concentration allowed Aya 23 to significantly outperform its predecessor and other comparable open source models. Aya Expanse further advanced the architecture with 8B and 32B parameter variants using an auto-regressive language model with

39

an optimized transformer design that incorporates supervised fine-tuning, preference training, and model merging techniques. In March 2025, C4AI released Aya Vision, a multimodal variant in 8B and 32B sizes capable of processing both text and images for tasks like captioning, visual reasoning, and OCR across all 23 supported languages. Its architecture combines a multilingual language model based on C4AI Command R7B with a SigLIP2 vision encoder connected through a multimodal adapter. The technical architecture has progressed from mT5 in Aya 101 to Command-based decoder-only transformers in later models, with enhancements specific to each iteration. All Aya models are released as "open weights," enabling over 3,000 researchers from 119 countries to contribute to and build upon this ecosystem.

Now that we have a better understanding of safe and responsible AI design, as well as the benefit of open source AI models, let's turn to the blockchain to demonstrate the benefits that blockchain-based governance can offer to organizations and groups working on AI models.

Blockchain-Based Governance for AI

Recently, OpenAI, the company behind ChatGPT, underwent some restructuring, and many experts have weighed in on how decentralized governance strategies can enhance transparency into decisions coming from a company developing the foremost advanced and powerful AI models in the world. In this section, we examine how blockchain-based governance can help AI organizations and how a blockchain can be integrated into development of an open source AI model. Decentralized autonomous organizations (DAOs) are the archetype of governance on a

CHAPTER 1   THE ERA OF ARTIFICIAL INTELLIGENCE

blockchain, and in this section, we will review the advantages of a DAO-inspired management structure and propose a governance framework that can be adopted by any AI organization or group.

In a consortium (or DAO) focused on building new AI models, a blockchain can serve as the governance layer by issuing tokens to all interested parties based on their contributions to the project. Token types determine functionality, for instance, a member can use a voting token to cast their vote on a presented proposal or safety tokens to veto or reject a proposal due to safety concerns. Individuals in the network can rent computational resources for model training and receive payment in the form of native network currency or voting tokens that can be staked to make future decisions. The terms of development including implementation of guardrails, safe and responsible model design, post-production monitoring, and routine finetuning can all be coded into the terms of a smart contract that remains active throughout the lifespan of the AI model. Members of the network can vote on the proposals, modify, and submit corrections as well as guide future development in a transparent manner on a platform that is well-suited for decentralized governance. As more sophisticated AI models are developed, alignment becomes a very pragmatic concern. Evaluating a newly trained model can reveal emergent capabilities that could lead to harm if left unchecked, for instance, a model capable of autonomously solving CAPTCHA challenges can be used by bad actors to overcome spam protections. If such capabilities become apparent, any member of the organization with voting privileges can activate a safety-focused smart contract that supersedes all other running contracts and allow the organization to understand the implications of releasing such a model, vote on how to move forward, and then proceed accordingly. Such governance models can also declare precedent for other organizations on how to approach critical junctures, the decisions made, and their outcome. Over time, such decisions translate into best practices for the AI community at large, helping establish guidelines for safe models and organizations. The open source community can take this a step

CHAPTER 1   THE ERA OF ARTIFICIAL INTELLIGENCE

further and add an element of reputation to the network. This traceable parameter, assigned by a panel of reviewers on the network, would serve as an indicator of how well an organization or individual contributors adhere to open standards when publishing AI models. A high degree of reputation derived from a long history of contributions meeting open standards will increase user trust in adopting models that have a track record of being reliable, safe, and responsibly designed.

There are five components essential in applying blockchain-based governance to AI organizations:

1. **Developers**: The core developers responsible for model training, parameter optimization, and fine-tuning. This group will share the voting rights with the resource vendors on operations and resources needed by the organization. All systems-based decisions regarding model design, new features, expanding parameters, and infrastructure will be posed to this group, voted upon, and recorded.

2. **Maintainers**: A smaller group of engineers focused on alignment by building the appropriate guardrails during training and fine-tuning phases, planning for interval fine-tuning with new data obtained during model deployment, and ensuring the model follows principles of safe design. This group will have an essential role during conflict resolution and have dedicated voting rights on future directions. All issues brought up during development or post-production will be disputed by maintainers, the decisions voted on and recorded. Moreover, emergent abilities from a trained model that pose a safety concern will be handled by this group.

CHAPTER 1   THE ERA OF ARTIFICIAL INTELLIGENCE

3. **Resource vendors**: Members of the network providing the infrastructure for model training (i.e., renting out computational resources) and domain expertise and independently reviewing deployment planning. This group receives payment in the form of network-native currency or voting tokens (that can be converted to network currency). The terms of payment for all services rendered will be listed in a smart contract and carried out automatically after a task has been completed. This group works closely with developers to build out the appropriate infrastructure necessary for a model and eventually for deployment.

4. **Safety contract**: A provision of the organization-level smart contract that can be triggered by any network member and calls for an impending vote by maintainers. This contract will require a member to stake tokens in order to activate, and once activated, it supersedes all running contracts. The staked tokens are a mechanism to prevent abuse and will be returned to the member after voting has completed. This intervention is designed for expedited reporting of a prominent safety concern by any member and to bring it to a vote due to the underlying potential for harm.

5. **Public/private interfaces**: A service that allows for creation of temporary private interfaces (or contracts) on a blockchain. Members of a network can have temporary, private contracts between each other without affecting the overall direction

of an organization. For instance, among resource vendors, two members can create a smart contract to rent computational resources only for specific tasks (Graphics Processing Unit (GPU)–based versus Central Processing Unit (CPU)–based) and defer tasks to each other for the appropriate hardware. Such a smart contract can be enacted semi-privately where the contract executable is available network-wide; however, it only triggers for pre-specified blockchain addresses. Members can engage in public contracts, which are necessary for the overall organization, and also semi-private contracts that are kept classified. Conflict resolution here will be handled on a case-by-case basis by reviewers where the contract details and any transactions associated with the contract are revealed. Members will need special privileges to create private contracts, and these can be granted by holding specific tokens.

Although not an essential component of governance, zero-knowledge proofs (ZKPs) can be a very beneficial supplement to AI governance and enhance the pragmatic balance between open standards and privacy for models operating on a blockchain. Integrating ZKPs into AI models carries immense potential for augmenting security and enhancing user privacy and user trust. For an organization, ZKPs can be particularly useful for training a model on sensitive data without revealing that data to the model creators or end users. The inputs are obfuscated by utilizing perturbation techniques that transform data points into statistically masked equivalents that can prove their validity without exposing the raw values. Similarly, ZKPs can be extended to oracles, external modules invoked by a blockchain, or an AI model to import real-time data for making a decision or providing external expertise for conflict resolution. All information provided by an oracle can undergo authentication scrutiny without revealing any of the associated blockchain addresses. Private interfaces with ZKPs can also be used by resource vendors following the above structure to request appropriate compensation without revealing any personal information. Eventually as smaller models run on edge devices (i.e., mobile devices), ZKPs can become a common tool for monitoring the progress of an off-loaded computational task and payments. In these cases, ZKPs can obfuscate the identity of devices requesting computational resources or the specific details of a task. An outline of blockchain-based AI governance is presented in Figure 1-4.

Now that we have an understanding of blockchain-based governance for AI models, let's look at how consensus mechanisms can be extended to alignment and the resulting consequences.

CHAPTER 1   THE ERA OF ARTIFICIAL INTELLIGENCE

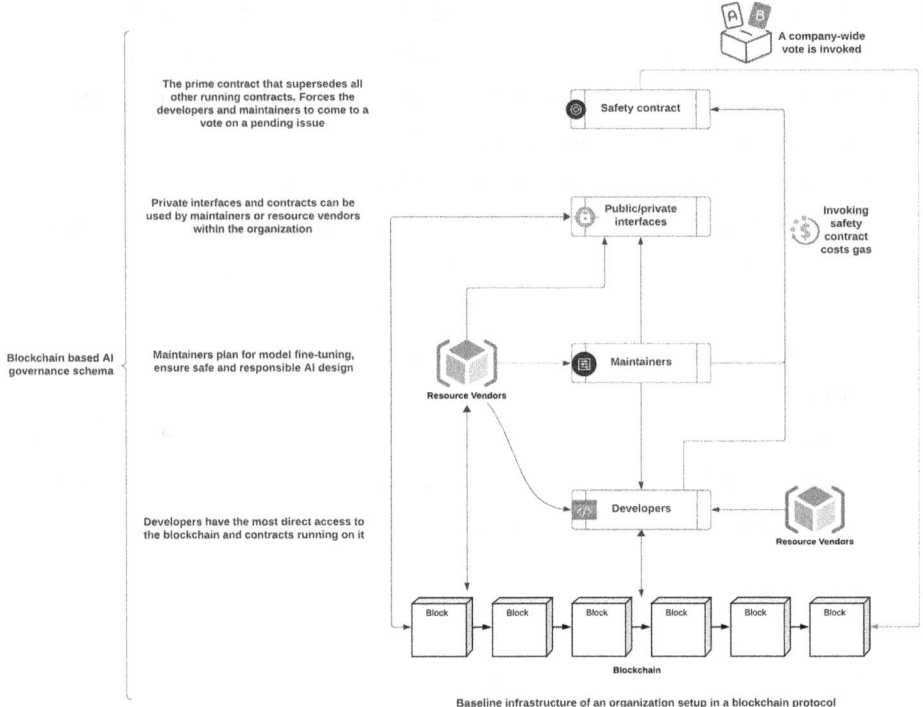

Figure 1-4. *A proposed model for blockchain-based AI governance. A flexible blockchain protocol underlies the governance structure. All key members (along with their key responsibilities) of the organization are represented on the blockchain along with flow of organizational knowledge between them.*

Consensus-Based Alignment

Consensus algorithms are the backbone of a blockchain protocol and allow for trustless exchange of value. The counterpart of consensus for an AI model is alignment theory, serving as the cornerstone for developing highly autonomous AI models that remain faithful to intended objectives of an end user and moral norms of society. Extending consensus principles to AI models can decentralize model development, allow for deeper integration of blockchain features, and establish a decentralized AI ecosystem. One promising strategy to broaden the scope of consensus algorithms would be to use a modified consensus algorithm that incorporates model training and validation phases, especially for MoE-type models. Participating nodes can contribute high-quality training data and computational resources to train an initial model followed by critical evaluation and fine-tuning via a novel consensus-based mechanism devised to verifying model predictions. The nodes must reach agreement on whether each prediction adheres to predefined performance metrics like accuracy, precision, and recall, as well as safety thresholds. Additionally, by distributing data collection, model training, and assessment tasks across a large number of independent nodes, this architecture can yield more reliable outcomes while minimizing biases inherent in traditional learning setups. Presently, federated learning techniques combined with a novel consensus algorithm are the closest approximation to the above-described method. Another approach to maximize the utility of a blockchain for an AI model involves reward mechanisms. The use of reinforcement learning from human feedback (RLHF) has become a common approach for model alignment. Encoding human preferences (value judgments and societal norms) into the reward function of reinforcement learning agents that operate within a blockchain environment can help fine-tune a LLM and align it further. An agent earns rewards for making decisions aligned with ethical norms encoded in a smart contract, and the model weights are updated based on the rewarded decisions. Then, a consensus algorithm ensures fair distribution of rewards for individual contributions to encoding societal preferences. Periodic audits can be performed over a longer period to ensure that individuals are contributing high-quality preferences, and this promotes self-regulation of an AI model consistent with shared values of the network.

CHAPTER 1   THE ERA OF ARTIFICIAL INTELLIGENCE

To take this a step further, combining the best elements from various consensus algorithms could offer improved alignment tuning. A multi-agent approach using traditional RLHF agents along with an agent trained on game theoretic frameworks, coordinated by a consensus algorithm like PoW or PoS, can make alignment training significantly more robust and practical. Game theory provides a strong foundation for modeling interactions between rational actors seeking an optimal solution, and these interactions can help align AI models in a more nuanced and realistic manner. In any multi-agent approach, consensus is synonymous with coordination. To generate more refined models, we need higher-quality codification of human preferences along with model debugging by novel explainable AI methods. Enhancing interpretability facilitates informed discussion regarding the limitations of RLHF for a model. Routine monitoring of AI behavior is necessary to ensure alignment with previously trained standards. Consensus-based audits can introduce democratized oversight mechanisms that are open to examination by all members of the network. The feedback collected from such audits can be routed back into training phases resulting in increasingly refined AI models that are responsive to evolving contextual features.

Summary

This book begins by establishing the foundational technologies that are reshaping our world. In The Era of Artificial Intelligence and Building Up to Large Language Models, we explore the AI revolution and the technical underpinnings of modern language models. Behold the Dreamers examines the rationale behind the emergence of blockchain and bitcoin, and the environment surrounding this transformation.

We then dive into the convergence of these technologies in The Gold Rush in Bitcoin and AI and Foundations of the Future: Blockchain and Large Language Models, where we trace bitcoin's initial deployment and explore how blockchain technology found applications beyond simple transactions. The technical deep dives continue with Inference, Fine-Tuning, and Retrieval-Augmented Generation and Physics of Large Language Models, providing the computational foundations necessary for understanding AI–blockchain integration.

The middle section focuses on practical implementations, starting with Unpacking Ethereum, one of the most promising platforms for building blockchain applications. In Contemporary Decentralized Organizations, we examine DAOs—from their infrastructure and early failures to their maturation and current applications. Biological Large Language Models and Blockchain in Scientific Reproducibility showcase how these technologies are revolutionizing biotech and research funding through micro-grants and novel organizational structures. Large Reasoning Models and Technological Revolutions and Financial Capital Markets explore the broader implications of AI advancement and market dynamics. The practical applications come together in Blockchain-as-a-Service and Lean Blockchain and AI, where we see the first serious implementations of AI–blockchain integration, including off-chain computing protocols, tokenization systems, and AI-based resource allocation approaches.

Finally, Beyond Large Language Models and Blockchain looks toward the future of these converging technologies and their potential to reshape entire industries.

Bibliography

Amodei, D., Olah, C., Steinhardt, J., Christiano, P., Schulman, J., & Mané, D. (2016). Concrete problems in AI safety. arXiv preprint arXiv:1606.06565. https://arxiv.org/abs/1606.06565

Anthropic. (2022). Constitutional AI: Harmlessness from AI feedback. https://www.anthropic.com/research/constitutional-ai-harmlessness-from-ai-feedback

CHAPTER 1   THE ERA OF ARTIFICIAL INTELLIGENCE

Anthropic. (2023). Claude's constitution. https://www.anthropic.com/news/claudes-constitution

Bereska, L. & Gavves, E. (2024). Mechanistic interpretability for AI safety—A review. arXiv preprint arXiv:2404.14082. https://arxiv.org/abs/2404.14082

Biswas, A. & Talukdar, W. (2023). Guardrails for trust, safety, and ethical development and deployment of large language models (LLM). *Journal of Science & Technology*, 4(6), 55–82. https://www.thesciencebrigade.com/jst/article/view/245

Bommasani, R., Hudson, D. A., Adeli, E., Altman, R., Arora, S., von Arx, S., Bernstein, M. S., Bohg, J., Bosselut, A., Brunskill, E., Brynjolfsson, E., Buch, S., Card, D., Castellon, R., Chatterji, N., Chen, A., Creel, K., Davis, J. Q., Demszky, D., ... Liang, P. (2021). On the opportunities and risks of foundation models. arXiv preprint arXiv:2108.07258. https://arxiv.org/abs/2108.07258

Bostrom, N. (2003). Ethical issues in advanced artificial intelligence. In I. Smit, W. Wallach, & G. E. Lasker (eds.), *Cognitive, Emotive and Ethical Aspects of Decision Making in Humans and in Artificial Intelligence* (Vol. 2, pp. 12–17). International Institute of Advanced Studies in Systems Research and Cybernetics.

Burns, Collin, Pavel Izmailov, Jan Hendrik Kirchner, Bowen Baker, Leo Gao, Leopold Aschenbrenner, Yining Chen et al. Weak-to-strong generalization: Eliciting strong capabilities with weak supervision. arXiv preprint arXiv:2312.09390 (2023).

Foundation Models. (2023). Business & Information Systems Engineering. https://link.springer.com/article/10.1007/s12599-024-00851-0

Lu, S., Bigoulaeva, I., Sachdeva, R., Madabushi, H. T., & Gurevych, I. (2023). Are emergent abilities in large language models just in-context learning? arXiv preprint arXiv:2309.01809. https://arxiv.org/abs/2309.01809

Marketing AI Institute. (2023). How Anthropic is teaching AI the difference between right and wrong. https://www.marketingai institute.com/blog/anthropic-claude-constitutional-ai

Meister, J. A., Akram, R. N., & Markantonakis, K. (2018). Deep learning application in security and privacy—Theory and practice: A position paper. arXiv preprint arXiv:1812.00190. https://arxiv.org/abs/1812.00190

Meta AI. (2023). LLaMA: Open and efficient foundation language models. https://github.com/premAI-io/state-of-open-source-ai/blob/main/models.md

Mistral AI. (2023). Mistral 7B: State-of-the-art open-source language model. https://blog.n8n.io/open-source-llm/

ML6. (2024). The landscape of LLM guardrails: intervention levels and techniques. https://www.ml6.eu/blogpost/the-landscape-of-llm-guardrails-intervention-levels-and-techniques

NVIDIA. (2024). Constitutional AI: Harmlessness from AI feedback. NeMo Framework User Guide. https://docs.nvidia.com/nemo-framework/user-guide/latest/modelalignment/cai.html

Oseni, A., Moustafa, N., Janicke, H., Liu, P., Tari, Z., & Vasilakos, A. V. (2021). Security and privacy for artificial intelligence: Opportunities and challenges. arXiv preprint arXiv:2102.04661. https://arxiv.org/abs/2102.04661

Ren, R., Mazeika, M., Riley, M. A., Martin, A., Geng, F., Wei, T., Nguyen, A., Thumwanit, N., Zou, A., Zheng, H., Patel, K., & Wolf, T. (2024). Safetywashing: Do AI safety benchmarks actually measure safety progress? arXiv preprint arXiv:2407.21792. https://arxiv.org/abs/2407.21792

Schaeffer, R., Miranda, B., & Koyejo, S. (2023). Are emergent abilities of large language models a mirage? arXiv preprint arXiv:2304.15004. https://arxiv.org/abs/2304.15004

Smalley, E. (2023, May 9). Anthropic thinks 'constitutional AI' is the best way to train models. TechCrunch. https://techcrunch.com/2023/05/09/anthropic-thinks-constitutional-ai-is-the-best-way-to-train-models/

Steinhardt, J. (2021). On the risks of emergent behavior in foundation models. Center for Research on Foundation Models (CRFM). `https://crfm.stanford.edu/commentary/2021/10/18/steinhardt.html`

Technology Innovation Institute. (2023). Falcon: Open-source large language models. `https://blog.n8n.io/open-source-llm/`

Wei, J., Tay, Y., Bommasani, R., Raffel, C., Zoph, B., Borgeaud, S., Yogatama, D., Bosma, M., Zhou, D., Metzler, D., Chi, E. H., Hashimoto, T., Vinyals, O., Liang, P., Dean, J., & Fedus, W. (2022). Emergent abilities of large language models. arXiv preprint arXiv:2206.07682. `https://arxiv.org/abs/2206.07682`

Xiong, Pulei, Scott Buffett, Shahrear Iqbal, Philippe Lamontagne, Mohammad Mamun, and Heather Molyneaux. Towards a robust and trustworthy machine learning system development: An engineering perspective. Journal of Information Security and Applications 65 (2022): 103121.

CHAPTER 2

Building Up to Large Language Models (LLMs)

The evolution of LLMs has been shaped by several significant research milestones over the past few decades. This chapter will provide an overview of these foundational studies, highlighting their contributions to the advancement of natural language processing (NLP) techniques and architectures used in contemporary models. We begin by discussing early efforts in statistical machine translation (SMT), followed by seminal work in neural network approaches for sequence-to-sequence (Seq2Seq) tasks. Subsequently, we delve into attention mechanisms, which revolutionized NLP model performance before culminating in the groundbreaking transformer architecture.

Introduction

The earliest notable research papers in this domain were IBM's statistical machine translation models (Brown et al., 1993), which laid the foundation for probabilistic methods in NLP. These models were based on hidden Markov models (HMMs) and trained on monolingual corpora to estimate word alignment probabilities between source and target languages. Although computationally intensive, these methods demonstrated impressive results, paving the way for further developments in data-driven translation methodologies. At the same time, recurrent neural networks (RNNs) emerged as another promising approach for handling sequential data (Elman, 1990). However, their application to longer sequences was limited due to vanishing or exploding gradient problems (Bengio et al., 1994; Hochreiter, 1998). Long short-term memory (LSTM) units addressed some of these issues (Hochreiter and Schmidhuber, 1997), enabling RNNs to capture long-range dependencies within sequences. Nevertheless, training such models remained challenging owing to their inherent complexity and computational requirements.

To tackle these challenges, sequence-to-sequence (Seq2Seq) models employing encoder–decoder architectures started gaining traction (Cho et al., 2014; Sutskever et al., 2014). Encoder–decoder frameworks consist of two main components: an encoding module responsible for mapping input sequences onto fixed-length vector representations and a decoding module tasked with generating output sequences from these vectors. While Seq2Seq models initially relied on conventional RNNs as both encoders and decoders, subsequent improvements involved gated recurrent units (GRUs) (Chung et al., 2014) and LSTMs (Sundermeyer et al., 2014). Despite these enhancements, limitations persisted in terms of efficiency, particularly when dealing with lengthy inputs or outputs.

Attention mechanisms proved instrumental in addressing these concerns (Bahdanau et al., 2015; Luong et al., 2015). By allowing models to dynamically select relevant information from input sequences during decoding, attention facilitated efficient handling of extensive contextual information without relying solely on fixed-length vector representations. Attention-based models were a paradigm shift in text translation and significantly improved translation quality compared with previous approaches. Building upon these advances, Vaswani et al. (2017) introduced the transformer architecture—an encoder–decoder model with self-attention mechanisms. This enabled substantial gains in efficiency across various NLP benchmarks, and over the years, several adaptations have been proposed including BERT (Bidirectional Encoder Representations from Transformers) (Devlin et al., 2019) and GPT-3 (Brown et al., 2020). This was the foundation of increasingly sophisticated large language models capable of complex reasoning tasks. In this chapter, we will review 20 academic research papers that have shaped the field of AI and LLMs. A detailed timeline leading up to the development of modern LLMs is provided in Figure 2-1.

CHAPTER 2   BUILDING UP TO LARGE LANGUAGE MODELS (LLMS)

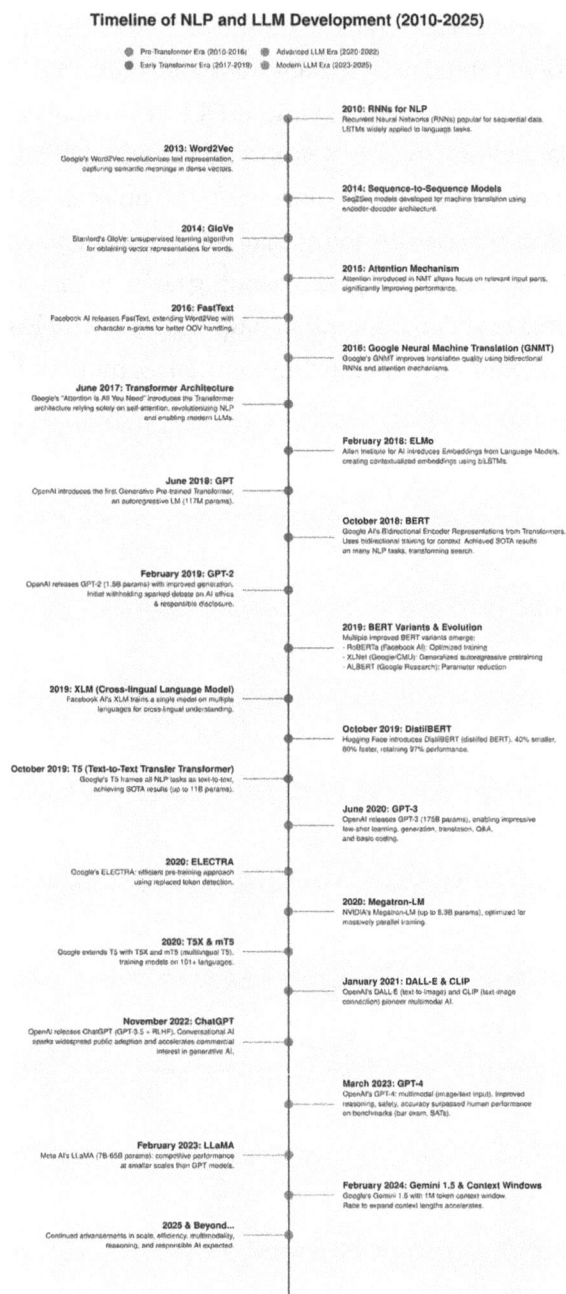

Figure 2-1. *Landmark developments in the NLP and LLM landscape*

RNN with Attention

We begin with a publication by Bahdanau et al., from 2015, "Neural Machine Translation by Jointly Learning to Align and Translate." Prior to this study, neural machine translation (NMT)–based models struggled with translating longer sentences due to fixed-length representations.

Statistical machine translation (SMT) was the state-of-the-art (SOTA) approach where a target sentence is broken down into smaller phrases by a statistical model and the most probable output (the translation) is generated. This paper presents a neural machine translation (NMT) model that jointly learns to align and translate words between two languages, improving upon previous NMT models that used separate alignment components. More importantly, this paper introduced the concept of *attention*, which allowed the decoder to dynamically focus on different parts of the source sentence while generating each word of the translation. This led to a big improvement in translation quality, especially for longer sentences. The proposed architecture is based on an encoder–decoder framework with long short-term memory (LSTM) recurrent neural networks (RNNs). Unlike the prior sequence-to-sequence models, this work introduces an attention mechanism called "soft alignment," enabling the decoder network to focus on different parts of the input at each time step during generation. This approach allows for more accurate handling of variable-length sequences (particularly longer sentences) and complex linguistic structures. A conceptual depiction of the attention mechanism is provided in Figure 2-2.

Key contributions:

- **Introducing soft alignment**: A dynamic method to compute source word importance scores while generating target words, avoiding the need for precomputed or fixed alignments

CHAPTER 2 BUILDING UP TO LARGE LANGUAGE MODELS (LLMS)

- Improved performance over existing SOTA systems on English–French translation tasks using various evaluation metrics like BLEU, TER, and human judgment

- Exploration of the impact of multiple hyperparameters such as hidden unit sizes, learning rates, dropout ratios, batch sizes, etc., providing valuable insights into training large RNN architectures

Overall, this paper was very influential in advancing the field of neural machine translation due to the introduction of the soft attention mechanism, which made it possible to translate longer sentences while maintaining contextual information (throughout encoding and decoding) and would become foundational to the transformer architecture.

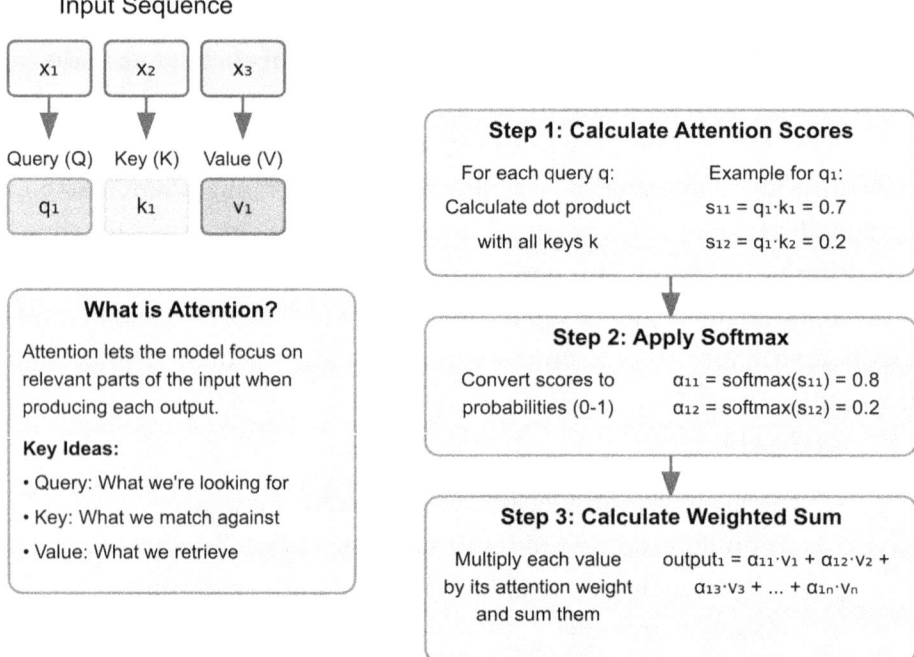

Figure 2-2. Simplified attention mechanism

CHAPTER 2   BUILDING UP TO LARGE LANGUAGE MODELS (LLMS)

The Transformer

The seminal paper "Attention Is All You Need" by Vaswani et al. in 2017 was the foundation of LLMs today. In this study, the transformer architecture is introduced: a novel deep learning architecture solely relying on self-attention mechanisms instead of traditional convolutional layers or recurrent neural nets. In contrast to previous efforts that combined convolution, recurrence, and attention methods, this work demonstrates how a purely attention-based model can outperform the SOTA models across several NLP tasks, including machine translation, text summarization, and sentence classification.

Some key technical aspects of the transformer model presented in this paper are

- **Multi-head attention**: A single self-attention layer might not capture all necessary relationships between elements. To address this, transformers employ multi-head attention in the form of scaled dot products simultaneously across multiple subspaces, allowing parallel computation and improved modeling of complex dependencies.

- **Encoder–decoder structure**: Similar to previously introduced architectures, but both the encoder and decoder are composed entirely of stacked multi-head attention and feedforward layers.

- **Positional encoding**: To preserve positioning information within input data, positional embeddings are added to the token representations before feeding them through the encoder. These embeddings use sine and cosine functions to represent relative positions along the input sequence.

CHAPTER 2   BUILDING UP TO LARGE LANGUAGE MODELS (LLMS)

- **Residual connections and layer normalization:** Facilitate efficient gradient flow during optimization and stabilize the training process.

Transformers are highly scalable and have become widely adopted due to their performance benefits on NLP tasks. Parallelized applications and access to high-quality training data have reduced training times significantly, improved performance, and, most notably, increased generalizability to domains beyond NLP. A simplified visual representation of the transformer architecture is provided in Figure 2-3.

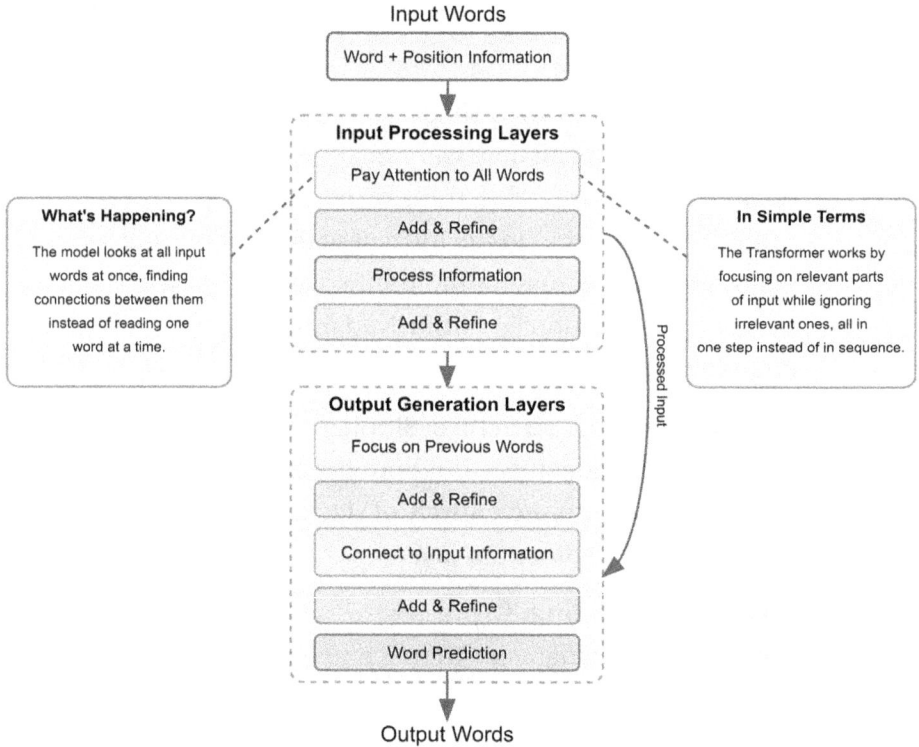

Figure 2-3. Simplified representation of a transformer

BERT Transformers

Following the introduction of transformer architecture, NLP research was bifurcating in two directions: encoder-style transformers for predictive modeling tasks such as text classification and decoder-style transformers for generative modeling tasks such as translation and summarization.

In a 2019 publication by Devlin et al., "BERT: Pre-training of Deep Bidirectional Transformers for Language Understanding," a significant technical update to the transformer architecture was presented. This paper introduced a new model called BERT (Bidirectional Encoder Representations from Transformers), a sophisticated pre-trained, encoder-only, language representation model that relies on bidirectional transformers to efficiently capture relationship and context among words in a sentence. The BERT publication highlighted the importance of pre-training and introduced the concepts of masked language modeling (MLM) and next sentence prediction (NSP). These three concepts would become instrumental in the future for LLMs. Unlike prior pre-trained models, BERT employed bidirectionality (using an encoder-transformer to deeply understand context from both directions of a sentence) during pre-training subjected to masked language modeling (MLM) and next sentence prediction (NSP) as objective functions. MLM works by randomly masking some tokens from the input and predicting these missing values based on surrounding context, whereas NSP trains a model to identify if two given sentences follow one another in the original document. By combining these approaches, BERT was able to capture rich contextual information leading to significant improvements in nuanced semantics.

Key features of BERT include

- **Bidirectional self-attention**: Utilizes both preceding and following words when computing attention weights, ensuring comprehensive context integration

- **Masked language modeling**: Randomly replaces a portion of input tokens with a special symbol, forcing the model to understand all available context to accurately reconstruct the masked value

- **Next sentence prediction**: Enhances the model's ability to distinguish coherent from disjointed pairs of sentences, thereby benefiting downstream tasks requiring understanding of broader discourse context

Since its release, BERT has dramatically improved performance on NLP tasks such as question answering, sentiment analysis, and part-of-speech tagging among others. In the years that followed, other research groups have built task-specific fine-tuning approaches using BERT as the foundational model achieving new SOTA performances across diverse domains and tasks. Over time, there have been several variants and optimizations of BERT developed, such as RoBERTa and ELECTRA, addressing limitations related to efficiency, token size, and robustness. The scale of pre-training employed for training BERT was pivotal and would become the standard for future chat-based LLMs.

Note Following the introduction of BERT, Liu et al.'s 2019 paper "RoBERTa: A Robustly Optimized BERT Pretraining Approach" introduced an optimized model called RoBERTa, with two key modifications to the training phase: dynamic masking with longer sequences and removal of NSP. In the original BERT implementation, the same set of words are masked during pre-training, whereas RoBERTa dynamically changes the masking pattern resulting in better generalization to real-world texts where the same token may be absent depending on the context. Similarly, the study authors found that removing NSP tasks during pre-training actually improved performance on downstream tasks.

T5 Architecture

Building on the original transformer architecture, a 2020 paper by Raffel et al., "Exploring the Limits of Transfer Learning with a Unified Text-to-Text Transformer," introduced a new architecture called T5 (Text-to-Text Transfer Transformer), a single-sequence-to-sequence model for handling various NLP tasks under a unified framework. As opposed to other transformer-based models of its time (BERT or GPT 1.0), T5 demonstrated that using the complete encoder–decoder architecture is better than only using decoders. T5 adopted a unified approach to NLP tasks by framing them all as text-to-text problems and simplifying the learning pipeline significantly. The researchers experimented with several pre-training objectives, including variations of the masked language model (cloze-style mask filling) used by BERT, and demonstrated denoising objectives were the most effective for model training. Here, prediction of missing words from corrupted input sequences and reconstruction by denoising autoencoders was the chief training objective (Multitask Mixture of Denoising Autoencoders (MoDA)). The training curriculum was organized in a manner of increasing difficulty for enhanced convergence. The paper concluded with a demonstration of T5's strong performance on diverse NLP tasks such as translation, summarization, and commonsense understanding.

Generative Pre-trained Transformer (GPT)

The 2018 paper by Radford et al., "Improving Language Understanding by Generative Pre-trained Transformer," introduced OpenAI's GPT 1.0 model: a semi-supervised transformer model aimed at text generation with a high degree of transferability to diverse NLP tasks. This paper introduces an essential practice employed by OpenAI's GPT: using unsupervised pre-training to train a transformer model on a very large corpus, followed

CHAPTER 2 BUILDING UP TO LARGE LANGUAGE MODELS (LLMS)

by supervised fine-tuning. The choice of transformers also allows for learning longer and complex sequence dependencies, enabling the model to benefit from larger datasets. GPT transformers use a decoder-only architecture, and the pre-training uses masked self-attention mechanism with an objective function of next word prediction. When compared with BERT, a bidirectional transformer that uses masked language modeling and next sentence prediction as pre-training objectives, GPT is a unidirectional (from left to right, necessary to generate sentences), auto-regressive (using the past words in sequence to predict the most likely next word) model. The GPT model operates in two phases:

1. **Unsupervised pre-training**: A decoder-only transformer is used to learn a language model (LM) from a very large, high-quality training dataset. This step does not require labeled data.

2. **Supervised fine-tuning**: The pre-trained model is augmented with an additional linear layer, which is then trained using labeled data from downstream tasks.

Key contributions from the GPT 1.0 paper include

- **Generative Pre-trained Transformer**: This paper highlighted the importance of carefully pre-training a language model on a very large corpus of unlabeled text and demonstrated the resulting performance benefits. Essentially, this pre-training teaches the model a general understanding of language structure and patterns.

- **Fine-tuning**: The pre-trained model can then be fine-tuned with smaller amounts of labeled data for specific downstream NLP tasks such as

  - Question answering
  - Natural language inference (does one statement logically follow another?)
  - Text summarization

- **Transformer architecture**: The paper used a decoder-only transformer architecture, which demonstrated significantly better performance in natural language understanding compared with previous architectures (e.g., RRRs and LSTMs).

- **Transferability**: Pre-training a model on a large corpus (4.5 GB of text from BookCorpus) enables it to gain broad language comprehension, which can be effectively transferred to downstream tasks. Additionally, the quality of training data is crucial, using text with longer sentences (such as books) and more extended dependencies improves the quality of training and yields a better-performing model.

This work formed a strong foundation for subsequent and even larger language models, such as the GPT series (GPT-2, GPT-3), setting the stage for the present era of LLMs. A notable aspect of the GPT model is the capacity for zero-shot learning, where it can achieve high performance on supervised tasks without any prior training in those tasks. This domain adaptation is attributed to the model's ability to generalize from the unsupervised learning phase and underscores the fundamental role of high-quality training data.

CHAPTER 2   BUILDING UP TO LARGE LANGUAGE MODELS (LLMS)

GPT 2.0 was introduced in a 2019 publication by Radford et al., "Language Models Are Unsupervised Multitask Learners," as the next-generation LLM with 1.5 billion parameters (10× larger than GPT 1.0) and trained on 10× more data compared with GPT-1. This new model outperformed the previous model significantly by accurately identifying long-range language dependencies. A major limitation of GPT 1.0 was the inability to perform multiple tasks without fine-tuning, for instance, a model trained with an objective to predict the next token will perform poorly in sentiment analysis without the appropriate fine-tuning. To overcome this limitation, the researchers proposed a novel approach called **multitask learning** to replace the common *pre-training + fine-tuning* framework that would allow a trained model to perform well across different tasks. A notable discovery made by the team was the ability to include relevant task information in the input sequence during the pre-training process for better model adaptation. Normally, to use multitask learning as a training objective, we would need a large dataset with clearly defined task descriptions, text inputs, and labels for each task. The researchers postulated that if a model was trained on a very large and diverse dataset, then based on the sheer size, the training dataset would have numerous demonstrations of language tasks across different domains allowing the model to understand a task without any explicit labels. The authors designed a web-scraping algorithm that scavenged the Internet for various sources (news, code, Reddit, etc.), and this data was organized into WebText (the training dataset used for GPT 2.0). As such, GPT-2 is trained purely on the task of predicting the next word in a sequence, given the previous words. During training, it does not receive any task-specific instructions or labels such as "summarize" or "translate." WebText is a very large training dataset and contains a colossal mix of text styles and formats that behave as a self-evolving curriculum for the model. By trying to predict the next word in these different contexts, the model internalizes knowledge needed for diverse language tasks. The resulting model can be

CHAPTER 2   BUILDING UP TO LARGE LANGUAGE MODELS (LLMS)

prompted with instructions in the input. For instance, a user can give a French sentence to GPT-2 and follow by "Translate to English," and based on the patterns learned during training, the model is able to carry out this task. In this manner, a supervised machine learning task was turned into an unsupervised format and led GPT 2.0 to excel on various downstream tasks without fine-tuning.

The next major update, GPT 3.0, was introduced in a 2020 publication by Brown et al., "Language Models Are Few-Shot Learners." This model is one of the largest neural networks ever created with 175 billion parameters and excels on various NLP tasks without explicit supervision or fine-tuning. With this massive scale, GPT 3.0 can perform more advanced NLP tasks in "few shots," where advanced tasks only need minimal demonstrations, and the model can follow the prompt in a few examples. Key contributions of the paper include

1. **Scaling the transformer architecture**: GPT-3 is significantly larger than its predecessors, with a total of 175 billion parameters (GPT-1 had 110 million; GPT-2 had 1.5 billion). To accommodate such size, the model uses sparse factorizations instead of fully dense matrices, reducing memory requirements. Additionally, a Mixture of Experts layers is also employed, allowing different subsets of neurons to activate based on the current input.

2. **Demonstrating zero-, one-, and few-shot learning**: GPT-3 displays strong performance across a variety of NLP benchmarks and novel applications even when given limited examples during evaluation. This few-shot generalization is consequence of the massive scale used to train GPT-3.0.

CHAPTER 2 BUILDING UP TO LARGE LANGUAGE MODELS (LLMS)

3. **Evaluation metrics**: Both human and machine evaluation schemas were used to assess the quality of responses from GPT 3.0, and the results indicated SOTA performance for each task.

4. **Risks and limitations**: Despite the promising results, the authors acknowledge concerns regarding misuse and biases in the model. Further studies are needed to better understand whether interacting with users turns the model more biased and whether continuous random sampling of model biases is needed.

A comparison between the aforementioned architectures is summarized in Table 2-1.

Table 2-1. Comparison between model architectures

Model Type	Key Features	Benefits	Limitations
RNNs (LSTMs/GRUs)	• Handle sequential data • Use recurrent connections • Variants like LSTMs/GRUs address gradient issues • Often used in encoder–decoder setups	• Promising early approach for sequential data • LSTMs can capture long-range dependencies	• Basic RNNs face vanishing/exploding gradients • Limited with very long sequences • Training can be complex and computationally demanding • Can be inefficient with lengthy inputs/outputs, even with LSTMs/GRUs

(*continued*)

Table 2-1. (*continued*)

Model Type	Key Features	Benefits	Limitations
Transformers	• Typically encoder–decoder structure • Relies solely on self-attention mechanisms • Employs multi-head attention for complex dependencies • Uses positional encoding to retain sequence information • Incorporates residual connections and layer normalization	• Outperformed previous state-of-the-art (SOTA) models • Substantial efficiency gains over RNNs • Highly scalable and allows parallel computation • Reduced training times compared with prior methods • Showed increased generalizability, even beyond NLP • Became the foundation for modern LLMs	• The standard self-attention mechanism has a computational complexity that increases quadratically with the length of the input sequence. This makes processing very long sequences computationally expensive and memory-intensive.

(*continued*)

Table 2-1. (*continued*)

Model Type	Key Features	Benefits	Limitations
BERT	• Encoder-only transformer architecture • Bidirectional: understands context from both left and right • Relies heavily on large-scale pre-training • Key pre-training tasks: masked language modeling (MLM) and next sentence prediction (NSP)	• Efficiently captures word relationships and context • Understands rich contextual information and nuanced semantics • Dramatically improved performance on language *understanding* tasks (e.g., QA, sentiment analysis) • Strong base for task-specific fine-tuning • Variants like RoBERTa offered further optimization	• Primarily designed for language understanding, less inherently suited for generative tasks compared with GPT

(*continued*)

Table 2-1. (*continued*)

Model Type	Key Features	Benefits	Limitations
GPT models	• Decoder-only transformer architecture • Unidirectional: processes text left to right • Auto-regressive: predicts the next word in sequence • Pioneered unsupervised pre-training followed by supervised fine-tuning (GPT-1) • Adopted multitask learning via massive, diverse datasets (GPT-2) • Showed strong few-shot learning at scale (GPT-3)	• Highly transferable to diverse NLP tasks • Effective at learning complex, long-range dependencies • Performance scales significantly with data and model size • Capable of strong performance with zero or few examples (zero-/few-shot learning), especially later versions • Excels at text generation • Can follow instructions provided in prompts (GPT-2 onward)	• Early versions (GPT-1) needed specific fine-tuning for each task • Large models (like GPT-3) raise concerns about potential misuse and inherent biases

CHAPTER 2   BUILDING UP TO LARGE LANGUAGE MODELS (LLMS)

Model Alignment Research

InstructGPT

In this 2022 paper by Ouyang et al., "Training Language Models to Follow Instructions with Human Feedback," reinforcement learning with human feedback (RLHF) is applied to GPT 3.0 via a three-step process. To begin, human trainers (or labelers) receive a prompt and generate instruction-following prompt–response pairs, which are stored in a dataset. Researchers subsequently utilize this dataset to fine-tune a pre-trained GPT 3.0 base model to produce output that follows the original prompt and instructions. Next, a prompt and several model outputs are sampled. A labeler (human evaluator) is asked to rank model outputs from best to worst, and this data is used to train a reward model (reward model training). Finally, this reward model is used to update the original model weights and reinforce the highest rewarded outputs to the original pre-trained GPT 3.0 model (reinforcement learning via proximal policy optimization). In summary, supervised fine-tuning teaches the model to mimic high-quality examples of following instructions generated by labelers (human trainers), and proximal policy optimization trains a separate model to predict human preferences as rewards, which are then used to optimize the base model further via reinforcement learning (RL).

Note   This publication is rumored to be the idea behind ChatGPT where a version of InstructGPT is scaled up and fine-tuned on a much larger dataset.

Constitutional AI (CAI)

CAI was introduced in a 2022 paper, "Constitutional AI: Harmlessness from AI Feedback," by Bai et al. and centers on embedding human principles and fundamental societal values (i.e., a "constitution") directly into an AI model. CAI represents a significant advancement for alignment research and is a fundamental building block of the Claude LLM. Instead of relying on direct human supervision (RLHF), the researchers propose a self-training and evaluation mechanism called reinforcement learning with AI feedback (RLAIF). A larger model is trained on the constitution in a supervised learning stage and then is used to reinforce the constitution to a smaller, user-facing model via RLAIF. This smaller model replies rapidly to a user and fine-tuned periodically in accordance with the provided constitution. For a detailed overview of the model, please refer to Chapter 1.

Self-Generated Instruction

Instruction fine-tuning is the process of aligning and transforming a pre-trained base model such as GPT-3.0 into a capable LLM (such as ChatGPT). To fine-tune a language model, instruction–response pair datasets are essential. A 2022 paper by Wang et al., "Self-Instruct: Aligning Language Model with Self Generated Instruction," introduced a new methodology called Self-Instruct for generating high-quality instruction–response pairs without the need for human labor. The goal is to improve a model's ability to follow user instructions by first teaching the model to create accurate instruction–response pairs. There are four steps involved in Self-Instruct:

1. **Instruction sampling**: Begin by selecting random snippers from a pre-training dataset and use them as seed instructions. Apply heuristics to extract meaningful phrases or use an existing dataset as a source for high-quality instruction seed.

2. **Response generation**: Given a sampled instruction, generate corresponding response candidates using the target language model to be aligned. Employ sampling temperature to control the diversity of responses.

3. **Filtering**: Use automated metrics such as ROUGE or BETRScore to identify and remove poor-quality instruction–response pairs from a dataset. Save the top-performing pairs in a new dataset. Repeat this step for all the pairs generated in the prior step.

4. **Instruction fine-tuning**: Train the target language model using the instruction–response pairs saved dataset from the prior stage. Use sequence-to-sequence loss functions to better refine the ground truth with predicted model outputs.

In the paper, the authors validated the efficacy of Self-Instruct with extensive experimentation, comparing this new methodology with baseline pre-trained models, few-shot learning, and traditional fine-tuning approaches. Briefly summarizing the results, a Self-Instruct-fine-tuned LLM outperformed the GPT-3 base LLM and even LLMs trained on human-curated instruction–response datasets, but interestingly, it did not outperform a model trained with RLHF. The experiments demonstrated significant improvements in model alignment noted by both automatic and human evaluations. The simplicity of deployment with minimal reliance on manual curation, reduced human labor, and rapid prototyping make Self-Instruct a very practical choice for enhancing a LLM's ability to follow user instructions.

Sparks of Artificial General Intelligence

A 2023 publication by Bubeck et al., "Sparks of Artificial General Intelligence: Early Experiments with GPT-4," assesses the capabilities and generalizability of an early version of OpenAI's GPT-4. The Microsoft Research team argues that GPT-4 represents a new class of LLMs exhibiting a higher degree of generalized intelligence compared with prior AI models: an early and incomplete form of artificial general intelligence (AGI). In the paper, GPT-4 demonstrated impressive capabilities across domains such as coding, mathematics, medicine, law, and psychology, beyond next word prediction. The authors demonstrate that GPT-4 can solve complex tasks without specialized prompting (zero-shot approach) and achieve human-level performance in a few attempts. They focus on identifying limitations of GPT-4 and the challenges in progressing toward more advanced AGI versions. The researchers conclude that focusing on next word prediction objectives may be insufficient to reach AGI and that newer training paradigms are necessary.

Scaling Research

Kaplan's Scaling Laws

A 2020 paper by Kaplan et al., "Scaling Laws for Neural Language Models," explored the relation between LLM performance and characteristics such as model scale, model shape, and compute budget (defined as the amount of computational power and hardware required for model training). Broadly speaking, they found that larger models generally performed better but also required more high-quality training data and computational resources. Model performance and characteristics (model size, training dataset size, compute budget) were discovered to scale as a power law: a functional relationship where a relative change in one quantity results in a relative change in the other quantity proportional to the power of the change. Moreover, optimization hyperparameters and architectural details such as network width or depth seem to have minimal effects on performance. The following are the key findings for scaling:

1. Performance depends most strongly on model scale. A model's scale is defined by three factors, the number of parameters (N), the size of the training dataset (D), and the compute budget (C). Performance has a power law relationship with each of the three scale factors N, D, and C.

2. Performance improves in a predictable fashion as long as the number of parameters and size of training data are scaled in tandem. However, model performance enters diminishing returns if either N or D is fixed while the other increases.

3. Training curves (plots of a model's learning performance over time) follow predictable power laws, and by extrapolating the early part of a training curve, it is possible to approximate the performance benefits achieved with a longer training time.

4. Traditionally, model training is continued until a model converges to its lowest possible loss. However, large models may not require such exhaustive training, and early stopping can yield very impressive results while conserving computational resources. Optimal performance was noted by training a very large model and stopping significantly short of convergence.

5. Larger models are more efficient at learning from a modest amount of training data and require fewer training steps to reach the same level of performance as smaller models. Consequently, for a very large model, training using a moderate-size dataset might be a more resource-conservative approach.

6. For optimal performance, roughly **1.7 text tokens** are needed for each parameter in a LLM.

Based on these scaling laws, the relationship between N, D, and the loss function can be used to derive the compute budget, training data requirements, and the magnitude of overfitting when training a LLM. These insights guided the scaling of the GPT model even further and were fundamental to GPT 3.0.

Chinchilla Scaling Laws

A 2022 paper by Hoffmann et al., "Training Compute-Optimal Large Language Models," presents an alternative set of scaling laws that diverge in some ways from the previously published Kaplan's laws. The authors came to a remarkable conclusion that contemporary practices for training LLMs consider increasing the number of model parameters to be the key mechanism for boosting performance, even though the size of training datasets has not changed. The researchers trained 400 models with varying sizes and amounts of training data to discover a relationship between model size, number of tokens, and compute budget. Based on such extensive training experiences, the authors concluded that in a compute-optimal setting, doubling of a model's size should ideally be accompanied by doubling of training tokens. They went on to train a new LLM called Chinchilla, which uses the same compute budget as 280B Gopher but has 70B parameters and four times more training data.

Chinchilla outperformed Gopher (280B) and GPT-3 (175B), among many others, on a large number of downstream tasks. Moreover, Chinchilla also used a smaller compute budget for fine-tuning than the other models. Meta released a collection of models called Llama, ranging from 7B to 65B parameters, trained efficiently using Chinchilla's scaling laws. By recognizing the need to train models on longer time durations and a higher number of tokens, Chinchilla's scaling law offers a new approach to enhancing the performance and capabilities of LLMs. The Llama family are a great example of this, having been trained on 1 trillion tokens while maintaining efficiency. Based on Chinchilla's scaling laws, to be compute-optimal, **20 text tokens of training data are needed per parameter**.

Note As a result of scaling up LLMs, emergent abilities are becoming apparent in models such as GPT-3, Chinchilla, and PaLM. In a 2022 paper by Wei et al., "Emergent Abilities of Large Language Models," emergent abilities are defined as abilities present in large models, but not seen in small models. This paper describes 137 emergent abilities seen on standard benchmarks (BIG-Bench and MMLU) across the three LLMs, and few-shot prompting made them more apparent. The existence of emergent abilities is a hotly debated topic and, at the time of writing, not described by either set of scaling laws. More studies are needed to better characterize the nature of emergence in LLMs.

Low-Rank Adaptation

Although modern LLMs (GPT-3, Claude, Llama) have remarkable generalization capabilities, fine-tuning for domain-specific tasks comes with significant challenges due to the scale and complexity of the LLM.

A 2022 paper from Microsoft Research by Hu et al., "LoRA: Low-Rank Adaptation of Large Language Models," proposed a new mechanism called Low-Rank Adaptation (LoRA) as an efficient and cost-effective fine-tuning of LLMs for domain specificity and task switching. LoRA is based on the premise that LLMs have a low-dimensional structure (with significantly fewer parameters compared with the base model), which can be modified for efficient fine-tuning, while leaving the original model parameters untouched. This is accomplished by decomposing large weight matrices into smaller ones using the lower-rank matrix technique. A low-rank matrix is a compressed representation of the original that preserves as much information as possible. By decomposing model weights into low-rank matrices, the number of trainable parameters drops by at least 10,000 times, and this smaller subset is much more compute-efficient to train. The weights of lower-rank matrices are additive, meaning these weights can be added to the pre-trained weights without any latency. Given the significantly smaller size of the lower-rank matrices, we can also load or unload them from a LLM based on the task. It must be noted with regard to performance, despite a reduced parameter count, LoRA recapitulates the original model's quality and inference speed.

Parameter-Efficient Finetuning

A 2023 review by Lialin et al., "Scaling Down to Scale Up: A Guide to Parameter-Efficient Fine-Tuning," discusses parameter-efficient finetuning (PEFT) for transformers, a set of techniques (including LoRA) for fine-uning a transformer model with minimal increases in model parameters. This review surveys more than 40 papers on PEFT to make fine-tuning compute-friendly and highlights why PEFT is essential to minimize GPU and storage overhead when fine-tuning for domain-specific applications. Four of the popular techniques are

1. **Adapter modules**: Trainable fine-tuned layers inserted between the layers of a pre-trained model that add domain-specific knowledge

2. **Prompt tuning**: Using specific prompts that are appended to the input guiding the model toward desired tasks

3. **Low-Rank Adaptation (LoRA)**: As above, adding lower-rank matrices to fine-tune a larger LLM

4. **BitFit**: Fine-tuning only the biases belonging to the original LLM

The authors also provide a comparative analysis of the techniques in terms of applicability to different models as well as the performance gains. Ultimately, this review can serve as a blueprint for anyone developing domain-specific applications with a LLM.

FlashAttention

When you scale up the context window of a transformer, the self-attention layer requires a large number of attention weights, and their computation becomes a resource-limiting step. As sequence length increases, the computational complexity increases quadratically. A 2022 paper by Dao et al., "FlashAttention: Fast and Memory-Efficient Exact Attention with IO-Awareness," introduced a new attention mechanism with memory and GPU awareness. FlashAttention reorders the attention computation and implements tiling, recomputation, and novel kernel fusion to reduce memory usage and significantly speed up attention calculations:

1. **Tiling**: The attention function is redesigned by dividing the input sequence into blocks and applying the normalization operation (called softmax) multiple times. This method incrementally

applies normalization to the input blocks, reducing the computational cost and storage requirements. Instead of computing global attention (in traditional transformers) where every token attends to all tokens across the entire sequence, FlashAttention uses a sliding window approach to reduce computational complexity while preserving context awareness. In this approach, each token only attends to nearby tokens within a predefined fixed window size. Additionally, FlashAttention uses relative position encoding to understand positional relationships among tokens more accurately regardless of their exact locations.

2. **Recomputation**: In order to avoid storing intermediate values, the softmax normalization factor from the forward pass is stored during the backward propagation process. This allows for fast recomputation of attention on the chip. Layer normalization has been replaced by a new algorithm called "Squeeze-Excitation Normalization" (SENet), which reduces floating-point operations required during forward passes in a neural net.

3. **Kernel**: FlashAttention has implemented specialized kernels that are tailored for low-rank approximations and can perform matrix multiplication significantly faster compared with standard implementations. By using low-rank approximations during model training, the training time can be cut down significantly, and also, attention scores can be calculated more efficiently.

4. **Learning rate scheduler**: A dynamic cosine learning rate schedule with warmup steps has been implemented in FlashAttention to help stabilize convergence during model training.

The mathematical formulations and hardware-level details such as accessing SRAM and DRAM are beyond the scope of this chapter; however, this paper demonstrates the efficiency gains by implementing a GPU and memory-aware attention mechanism. In the near future, the next generation of AI-focused hardware will abstract the attention calculations, decrease the training time, and allow for novel hardware-based attention algorithms.

One GPU and One-Day Training

A 2022 paper by Geiping et al., "Cramming: Training a Language Model on a Single GPU in One Day," explores training BERT (a masked language encoder-style LLM) for 24 hours on a single GPU. For reference, the original 2018 BERT model was trained on 16 TPUs for 4 days. In scaling down the training focus, a major focus of the paper is on improving the components of the pre-training and training pipelines to fit this scenario. The experiments were done with PyTorch, without relying on any specialized implementations in order to minimize gains from software-level optimization and ensure reproducibility of results. Among the many optimizations proposed, four are highlighted below:

1. **Data sharding**: Text sequences from the training data were split into smaller chunks called shards and multiple shards were concatenated together for model training.

2. **Large learning rate**: Unlike traditional model training, a higher learning rate was proposed for Cramming, 1×10^{-3} times the square root of the

number of parameters, with a linear learning rate decay after reaching peak performance. Only one epoch of training was possible during the time constraint, which also significantly decreases the chances of overfitting.

3. **Warm restarts**: In order to escape potential plateaus or slowdowns in convergence, restart the learning rate scheduler periodically.

4. **Checkpointing**: Save the intermediate activations as a checkpoint and trade off memory usage for saving computation time during backpropagation.

Two key insights were gained from the study: first is that performance followed the scaling laws observed in settings with higher compute budget, and second, even with the resource constraints, the model trained with Cramming performed closely to the original BERT.

Bibliography

Bahdanau, D., Cho, K., & Bengio, Y. (2015). Neural machine translation by jointly learning to align and translate. *Proceedings of the 3rd International Conference on Learning Representations (ICLR)*. https://arxiv.org/abs/1409.0473

Bai, Y., Jones, A., Ndousse, K., Askell, A., Chen, A., DasSarma, N., Drain, D., Fort, S., Ganguli, D., Henighan, T., Joseph, N., Kadavath, S., Kernion, J., Conerly, T., El-Showk, S., Elhage, N., Hatfield-Dodds, Z., Hernandez, D., ... Kaplan, J. (2022). Constitutional AI: Harmlessness from AI feedback. arXiv preprint arXiv:2212.08073. https://arxiv.org/abs/2212.08073

Bengio, Y., Simard, P., & Frasconi, P. (1994). Learning long-term dependencies with gradient descent is difficult. *IEEE Transactions on Neural Networks*, 5(2), 157–166. https://doi.org/10.1109/72.279181

Brown, P. F., Della Pietra, S. A., Della Pietra, V. J., & Mercer, R. L. (1993). The mathematics of statistical machine translation: Parameter estimation. *Computational Linguistics, 19*(2), 263–311. https://arxiv.org/abs/cmp-lg/9306005

Brown, T. B., Mann, B., Ryder, N., Subbiah, M., Kaplan, J. D., Dhariwal, P., Neelakantan, A., Shyam, P., Sastry, G., Askell, A., Agarwal, S., Herbert-Voss, A., Krueger, G., Henighan, T., Child, R., Ramesh, A., Ziegler, D. M., Wu, J., Winter, C., ... Amodei, D. (2020). Language models are few-shot learners. *Advances in Neural Information Processing Systems, 33*, 1877–1901. https://proceedings.neurips.cc/paper/2020/hash/1457c0d6bfcb4967418bfb8ac142f64a-Abstract.html

Bubeck, S., Chandrasekaran, V., Eldan, R., Gehrke, J., Horvitz, E., Kamar, E., Lee, P., Lee, Y. T., Li, Y., Lundberg, S. M., Nori, H., Palangi, H., Ribeiro, M. T., Rosenblatt, J., Salim, A., Shah, R., Singh, H., Suh, J., ... Zhang, Y. (2023). Sparks of artificial general intelligence: Early experiments with GPT-4. arXiv preprint arXiv:2303.12712. https://arxiv.org/abs/2303.12712

Cho, K., van Merriënboer, B., Gulcehre, C., Bahdanau, D., Bougares, F., Schwenk, H., & Bengio, Y. (2014). Learning phrase representations using RNN encoder-decoder for statistical machine translation. In *Proceedings of the 2014 Conference on Empirical Methods in Natural Language Processing (EMNLP)* (pp. 1724–1734). Association for Computational Linguistics. https://arxiv.org/abs/1406.1078

Chung, J., Gulcehre, C., Cho, K., & Bengio, Y. (2014). Empirical evaluation of gated recurrent neural networks on sequence modeling. arXiv preprint arXiv:1412.3555. https://arxiv.org/abs/1412.3555

Dao, T., Fu, D. Y., Ermon, S., Rudra, A., & Ré, C. (2022). FlashAttention: Fast and memory-efficient exact attention with IO-awareness. *Advances in Neural Information Processing Systems, 35*, 16344–16359. https://arxiv.org/abs/2205.14135

Devlin, J., Chang, M. W., Lee, K., & Toutanova, K. (2019). BERT: Pre-training of deep bidirectional transformers for language understanding. In *Proceedings of the 2019 Conference of the North American Chapter of the Association for Computational Linguistics: Human Language Technologies* (pp. 4171–4186). Association for Computational Linguistics. https://arxiv.org/abs/1810.04805

Elman, J. L. (1990). Finding structure in time. *Cognitive Science, 14*(2), 179–211. https://doi.org/10.1207/s15516709cog1402_1

Geiping, J., Bastings, J., Pope, P., Kolesnikov, S., Zhai, S., Schneider, J., Schmidt, L., & Olea, C. F. (2022). *Cramming: Training a language model on a single GPU in one day.* arXiv preprint arXiv:2212.14034. https://arxiv.org/abs/2212.14034

Hochreiter, S. (1998). The vanishing gradient problem during learning recurrent neural nets and problem solutions. *International Journal of Uncertainty, Fuzziness and Knowledge-Based Systems, 6*(2), 107–116. https://doi.org/10.1142/S0218488598000094

Hochreiter, S. & Schmidhuber, J. (1997). Long short-term memory. *Neural Computation, 9*(8), 1735–1780. https://doi.org/10.1162/neco.1997.9.8.1735

Hoffmann, J., Borgeaud, S., Mensch, A., Buchatskaya, E., Cai, T., Rutherford, E., de Las Casas, D., Hendricks, L. A., Welbl, J., Clark, A., Hennigan, T., Noland, E., Millican, K., van den Driessche, G., Damoc, B., Guy, A., Osindero, S., Simonyan, K., ... Sifre, L. (2022). Training compute-optimal large language models. arXiv preprint arXiv:2203.15556. https://arxiv.org/abs/2203.15556

Hu, E. J., Shen, Y., Wallis, P., Allen-Zhu, Z., Li, Y., Wang, S., Wang, L., & Chen, W. (2022). LoRA: Low-rank adaptation of large language models. *Proceedings of the 10th International Conference on Learning Representations (ICLR).* https://openreview.net/forum?id=nZeVZe726JnEr (Original work published 2021 on arXiv)

Kaplan, J., McCandlish, S., Henighan, T., Brown, T. B., Chess, B., Child, R., Gray, S., Radford, A., Wu, J., & Amodei, D. (2020). Scaling laws for neural language models. arXiv preprint arXiv:2001.08361. https://arxiv.org/abs/2001.08361

Lialin, V., Thakker, U., Nagesh, S., Maddela, M., Rumshisky, A., & Liu, Y. (2023). Scaling down to scale up: A guide to parameter-efficient fine-tuning. arXiv preprint arXiv:2303.15647. https://arxiv.org/abs/2303.15647

Liu, Y., Ott, M., Goyal, N., Du, J., Joshi, M., Chen, D., Levy, O., Lewis, M., Zettlemoyer, L., & Stoyanov, V. (2019). RoBERTa: A robustly optimized BERT pretraining approach. arXiv preprint arXiv:1907.11692. https://arxiv.org/abs/1907.11692

Luong, M. T., Pham, H., & Manning, C. D. (2015). Effective approaches to attention-based neural machine translation. In *Proceedings of the 2015 Conference on Empirical Methods in Natural Language Processing* (pp. 1412–1421). Association for Computational Linguistics. https://arxiv.org/abs/1508.04025

Ouyang, L., Wu, J., Jiang, X., Almeida, D., Wainwright, C. L., Mishkin, P., Zhang, C., Agarwal, S., Slama, K., Ray, A., Schulman, J., Hilton, J., Kelton, O., Miller, L., Simens, M., Askell, A., Welinder, P., Christiano, P., … Leike, J. (2022). Training language models to follow instructions with human feedback. *Advances in Neural Information Processing Systems, 35*, 27730–27744. https://proceedings.neurips.cc/paper_files/paper/2022/hash/b1efde5ae38d126f875b1b04f49add2d-Abstract-Conference.html

Radford, A., Narasimhan, K., Salimans, T., & Sutskever, I. (2018). Improving language understanding by generative pre-training. OpenAI. https://cdn.openai.com/research-covers/language-unsupervised/language_understanding_paper.pdf

CHAPTER 2　BUILDING UP TO LARGE LANGUAGE MODELS (LLMS)

Radford, A., Wu, J., Child, R., Luan, D., Amodei, D., & Sutskever, I. (2019). Language models are unsupervised multitask learners. OpenAI. https://cdn.openai.com/better-language-models/language_models_are_unsupervised_multitask_learners.pdf

Raffel, C., Shazeer, N., Roberts, A., Lee, K., Narang, S., Matena, M., Zhou, Y., Li, W., & Liu, P. J. (2020). Exploring the limits of transfer learning with a unified text-to-text transformer. *Journal of Machine Learning Research, 21*(140), 1-67. http://jmlr.org/papers/v21/20-074.html

Sundermeyer, M., Schlüter, R., & Ney, H. (2014). LSTM neural networks for language modeling. In *Proceedings of the 15th Annual Conference of the International Speech Communication Association (INTERSPEECH 2014)* (pp. 1941-1945). International Speech Communication Association.

Sutskever, I., Vinyals, O., & Le, Q. V. (2014). Sequence to sequence learning with neural networks. *Advances in Neural Information Processing Systems, 27*. Curran Associates, Inc. https://arxiv.org/abs/1409.3215

Vaswani, A., Shazeer, N., Parmar, N., Uszkoreit, J., Jones, L., Gomez, A. N., Kaiser, Ł., & Polosukhin, I. (2017). Attention is all you need. *Advances in Neural Information Processing Systems, 30*. Curran Associates, Inc. https://arxiv.org/abs/1706.03762

Wang, Y., Kordi, Y., Mishra, S., Liu, A., Smith, N. A., Khashabi, D., & Hajishirzi, H. (2022). Self-Instruct: Aligning language model with self generated instructions. arXiv preprint arXiv:2212.10560. https://arxiv.org/abs/2212.10560

Wei, J., Tay, Y., Bommasani, R., Raffel, C., Zoph, B., Borgeaud, S., Yogatama, D., Bosma, M., Zhou, D., Metzler, D., Chi, E. H., Hashimoto, T., Vinyals, O., Liang, P., Dean, J., Fedus, W., … Le, Q. V. (2022). Emergent abilities of large language models. *Transactions on Machine Learning Research.* https://openreview.net/forum?id=yzkSU5zdwD

CHAPTER 3

Behold the Dreamers

Anxiety is perhaps the best way to describe the attitude that dominated the minds of investors and the general public concerning the financial markets toward the end of 2008. The 2008 financial crisis is considered by numerous economists to have been the worst financial crisis since the Great Depression. The years leading up to the crisis saw a flood of irresponsible mortgage lending and a massive systemic failure of financial regulation and supervision. The fallout was so immense that it threatened the collapse of large financial institutions, and national governments had to intercede to bail out the major banks. In this chapter, we will begin our discussion with an overview of the 2008 financial crisis and its aftermath: an environment where a new banking system and an alternative currency such as Bitcoin could thrive. Then, we will dive into the technology stack that powers Bitcoin. Remarkably, the components of this stack are not completely new, but have been integrated in a very intricate design to build a new system. Finally, we will end the discussion by talking about the heightened interest in blockchain, a major technical breakthrough that has the potential to revolutionize several industries. Imbolo Mbue wrote a book (Random House, 2017), which has the same name as this chapter, and tells the story of "dreamers" in New York City going through the financial crisis and how their lives had changed as a result. This book chronicles the dreamers who envisioned building a more resilient financial system.

CHAPTER 3   BEHOLD THE DREAMERS

Paradigm Shift

Revolutions often look chaotic, but this one was brewing quietly, headed by an unknown individual(s) under the name Satoshi Nakamoto who dreamt of changing the financial world. Any number of parties can be blamed for the financial crisis; however, the common denominator was that fundamental financial and accounting instruments used to maintain the integrity of the entire system became too complex to be used efficiently. Trust, the ultimate adhesive of all financial systems, began to disappear in 2008. The regulations have since changed to not allow similar circumstances to arise; however, it was clear that there was a dire need for auto-regulation of trust between counterparties and transparency into their ability to enter any type of sales contract. A **counterparty** is essentially the other party in a financial transaction. In other words, it's the buyer matched to a seller. In financial transactions, one of the many risks involved is called **counterparty risk**—the risk that the *other* party involved in a contract may not be able to fulfill its side of the agreement. The systemic failure referenced earlier can now be understood in terms of counterparty risk: both parties in the transaction were accumulating massive counterparty risk, and in the end, both parties collapsed under the terms of the contract. Imagine a similar transaction scenario involving multiple parties, and now imagine that every single player in this scenario is a major financial institution, a bank or an insurance company that further holds millions of customers. This is what happened during the 2008 crisis.

The next issue we need to discuss is that of **double spending**. We will revisit this topic again strictly in the context of Bitcoin, but let's get a basic understanding of the concept by applying it to the financial crisis. The principle behind double spending is that resources committed to one transaction cannot be simultaneously allocated to a second disparate transaction. This concept has obvious implications for digital currencies; however, it can also summarize the central set of problems during the 2008 crisis.

CHAPTER 3   BEHOLD THE DREAMERS

Here's how it started: Loans (in the form of mortgages) were given out to borrowers with poor credit histories, who struggled to repay them. These high-risk mortgages were sold to financial experts at the big banks, who packaged them into low-risk public stocks by putting large numbers of them together in pools. This type of pooling would work when the risks associated with each loan (mortgage) are not correlated. The experts at big banks hypothesized that property values in different cities across the country would change independently, and therefore pooling was not risky. This proved to be a massive mistake. The pooled mortgage packages were then used to purchase a type of stock called collateralized debt obligations (CDOs). The CDOs were divided into tiers and sold to investors. The tiers were ranked and rated by financial standards agencies, and investors bought the safest tiers based on those ratings. Once the housing market in the United States turned, it set off a domino effect, destroying everything in the way. The CDOs turned out to be worthless, despite the ratings. The pooled mortgages collapsed in value, and all the packages being sold around instantly vaporized. Throughout this complex string of transactions, every sale increased the risk and incurred double spending at multiple levels. Eventually, the system equilibrated, only to find massive gaps, and collapsed under the weight. The following is a brief history of 2008. This timeline was made following a presentation by Micah Winkelspech at Distributed Health (2016):

- **January 11**: Bank of America buys the struggling Countrywide.
- **March 16**: Fed forces the sale of Bear Stearns.
- **September 15**: Lehman Brothers files for bankruptcy.
- **September 16**: Fed bails out American International Group (AIG) for $85B.
- **September 25**: Washington Mutual fails.

CHAPTER 3   BEHOLD THE DREAMERS

- **September 29**: Financial markets crash, Dow Jones Industrial Average falls 777.68 points, and the whole system is on the brink of collapse.
- **October 3**: US government authorizes $700B for bank bailouts.

The bailout had massive economic consequences, but more important, it created the type of environment that would allow Bitcoin to flourish. In November 2008, a whitepaper (`https://bitcoin.org/bitcoin.pdf`) was posted on the Cryptography and Cryptography Policy Mailing List titled "Bitcoin: A Peer-to-Peer Electronic Cash System," with a single author named Satoshi Nakamoto. This whitepaper detailed the Bitcoin protocol, and along with it came the original code for early versions of Bitcoin. In some manner, this whitepaper was a response to the economic crash that had just happened, but it would be some time before this technological revolution caught on. Some developers were concerned with this electronic cash system failing before it could ever take hold, and their concern was scalability, as we can see pointed out in Figure 3-1.

So who is Nakamoto? And what is his background? The short and simple answer is that we don't know. In fact, it is presumptuous to assume that he is actually a "he." The name Satoshi Nakamoto was largely used as a pseudonym, and "he" could have been a "she" or even a large group. Several reporters and news outlets have dedicated time and energy in digital forensics to narrow down candidates and find out the real Satoshi, but all the efforts so far have been wild goose chases (`https://www.technologyreview.com/s/527051/the-man-who-really-built-bitcoin/`). In this case, the community is starting to realize that maybe it doesn't matter who Satoshi is, as the nature of open source almost makes it irrelevant. Jeff Garzik, one of the most respected developers in the Bitcoin community, described it as follows, "Satoshi published an open-source system for the purpose that you didn't have to know who he was, and trust

CHAPTER 3   BEHOLD THE DREAMERS

who he was, or care about his knowledge." The true spirit of open source makes it so that the code speaks for itself, without any intervention from the creator/developer.

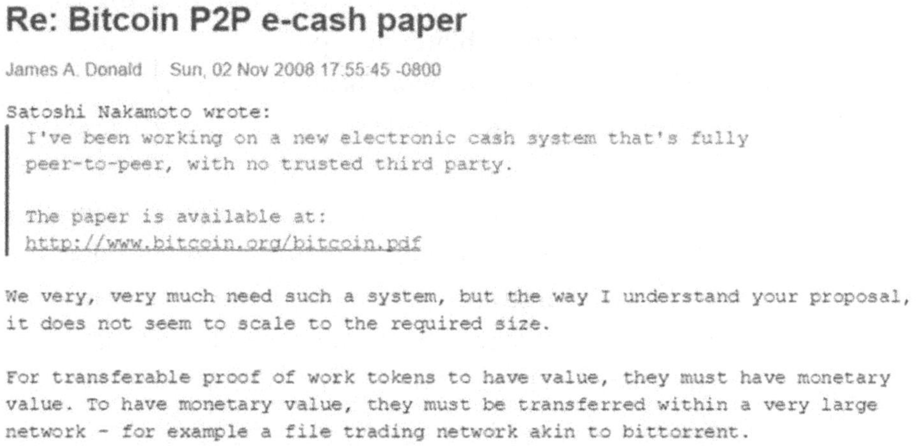

```
Re: Bitcoin P2P e-cash paper
James A. Donald    Sun, 02 Nov 2008 17:55:45 -0800

Satoshi Nakamoto wrote:
   I've been working on a new electronic cash system that's fully
   peer-to-peer, with no trusted third party.

   The paper is available at:
   http://www.bitcoin.org/bitcoin.pdf

We very, very much need such a system, but the way I understand your proposal,
it does not seem to scale to the required size.

For transferable proof of work tokens to have value, they must have monetary
value. To have monetary value, they must be transferred within a very large
network - for example a file trading network akin to bittorrent.
```

Figure 3-1. *Initial reception of the Bitcoin protocol. Concerns about scalability and realistic prospects of Bitcoin*

Technology Stack

Satoshi's real genius in creating the Bitcoin protocol was solving the Byzantine Generals Problem. The solution was generalized to financial transactions with components and ideas borrowed from the cyberpunk community. The Byzantine Generals Problem is a fundamental concept in distributed computing that addresses the challenge of reaching consensus in a network where some participants may be unreliable or malicious. In blockchain terms, it represents the challenge of establishing trust in a trustless environment, ensuring all honest participants can agree on the state of the network despite potential bad actors. Double spending is a critical issue specific to digital currencies that blockchain technology

CHAPTER 3 BEHOLD THE DREAMERS

solves. It refers to the risk that a digital token could be spent multiple times, unlike physical currency, which can only be given to one person at a time. Without a solution to the double-spending problem, digital currencies would be impossible as users could potentially copy and reuse the same digital tokens indefinitely. Bitcoin's blockchain prevents double spending by creating a verifiable chronological record of all transactions that is agreed upon by the entire network. We will briefly talk about three of those ideas, how the components work, and how they help the Bitcoin protocol: Hashcash for proof of work, Byzantine fault tolerance for the decentralized network, and the blockchain for removing the need for centralized trust or a central authority. Let's dive into each one, starting with Hashcash.

Hashcash was devised by Adam Black in the late 1990s to limit email spam with the first of its kind proof-of-work (PoW) algorithm. The rationale behind Hashcash was to attach some computational cost to sending emails. Spammers have a business model that relies on sending large numbers of emails with very little cost associated with each message. However, if there is even a small cost for each spam email sent, that cost multiplies over thousands of emails, and their business becomes unprofitable. Hashcash relies on the idea of cryptographic hash functions—a type of hash function (in the case of Bitcoin, it's SHA1) that takes an input and converts it into a string and generates a message digest, as shown in Figure 3-2. The hash functions are designed to have a property called one-way functions, which implies that a potential input can be verified very easily through the hash function to match the digest, but reproducing the input from the digest is infeasible. The only possible method of recreating the input is by using brute force to find the appropriate string of input. In practice, this is the computationally intensive element of Hashcash and has been imported into Bitcoin. This principle has become the foundation behind the proof-of-work (PoW) algorithms powering Bitcoin today and most cryptocurrencies. The PoW for Bitcoin is more complex and involves new components that we will talk about at length in a later chapter.

CHAPTER 3   BEHOLD THE DREAMERS

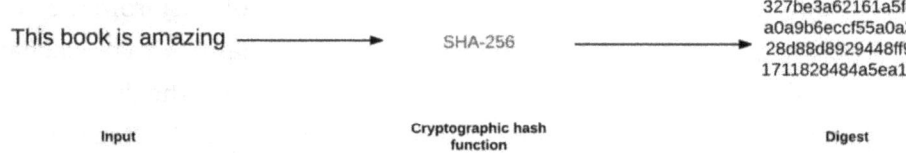

Figure 3-2. Mechanism of a cryptographic hash function. It takes an input and consistently converts it to a string of an output digest

The next idea we need to discuss is the Byzantine Generals Problem. It is an agreement problem between a group of generals, with each one commanding a portion of the Byzantine army, ready to attack a city. These generals need to formulate a strategy for attacking the city and communicate it to each other adequately. The important task is that every general must work toward the same action, as a tepid attack by a few generals would be worse than a coordinated attack or a coordinated retreat. The crux of the problem is that some of the generals are traitorous. They may cast a vote to deceive the other generals and ultimately lead to a suboptimal strategy. Let's take a look at an example: In a case of odd-numbered generals, say seven, three support attacking and three support retreat. The seventh general might communicate an agreement to the generals in favor of retreat and an agreement to attack to the other generals, causing the whole arrangement to fall apart. The attacking forces would fail to capture the city because no intrinsic central authority could verify the presence of trust among all seven generals.

In this scenario, Byzantine fault tolerance can be achieved if all the loyal generals can communicate effectively to have an indisputable agreement on their strategy. If so, the misleading (faulty) vote by the traitorous general would be revealed and would fail to perturb the system as a whole. In the Bitcoin protocol, Satoshi's key innovation in enabling Byzantine fault tolerance was to create a peer-to-peer network with a ledger that could record and verify a majority approval, thereby revealing any false (traitorous) transactions. This ledger provides a consistent means

CHAPTER 3   BEHOLD THE DREAMERS

of communication and further allows for the removal of trust from the whole system. The ledger is also known as the blockchain. With blockchain attached, Bitcoin became the first digital currency to solve the double-spending problem network-wide. In the remainder of this chapter, we will present a broad overview of the technology and of the concept of a blockchain-enabled application.

A blockchain is primarily a recording ledger that provides all involved parties with a secure and synchronized record of transactions from start to end. A blockchain can record hundreds of transactions very rapidly and has several cryptographic measures intrinsic to its design for data security, consistency, and validation. Similar transactions on the blockchain are pooled together into a functional unit called a **block** and then sealed with a timestamp (a cryptographic fingerprint) that links the current block to the one preceding it. This creates an irreversible and tamper-evident string of blocks connected together by timestamps, conveniently called a blockchain. The architecture of blockchain is such that every transaction is very rapidly verified by all members of the network. Members also contain an up-to-date copy of the blockchain locally, which allows for consensus to be reached within the decentralized network. Features such as immutable record-keeping and network-wide consensus can be integrated into a stack to develop new types of applications called decentralized apps (DApps). Let's look at a prototype of a DApp in Figure 3-3, in the context of the Model–View–Controller (MVC) framework. The Model–View–Controller framework is a software design concept that separates an application into three components: the model (that contains the data-related logic), the view (UI component that customers often interface with), and the controller (an interface that interacts between the model and the view). This framework is frequently used to design traditional web applications that are extensible and scalable. Here, we want to extend an industry standard and use it to explain a DApp.

CHAPTER 3   BEHOLD THE DREAMERS

Note The first block of the blockchain is called the Genesis block. This block is unique in that it does not link to any blocks preceding it. Satoshi added a bit of historical information to this block as context for the current financial environment in the United Kingdom, "*The Times 03/Jan/2009 Chancellor on brink of second bailout for banks.*" This block not only proves that no Bitcoins existed before January 3, 2009, but also gives a little insight into the mind of the creators.

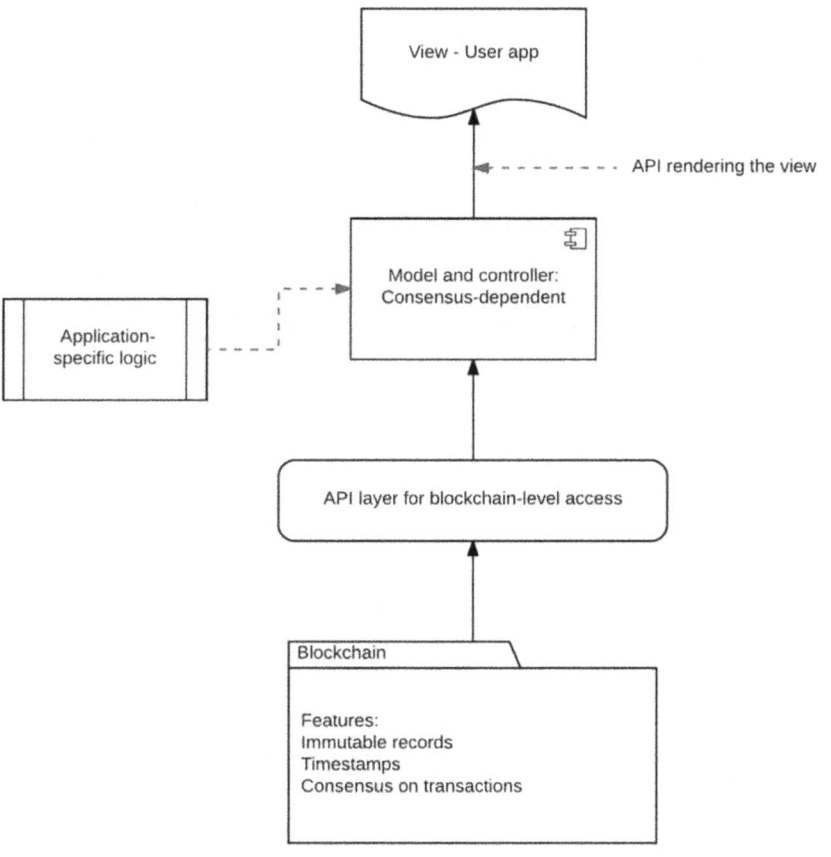

Figure 3-3. *This figure presents a simple prototype of a decentralized application that interacts with the end user at the final steps*

97

CHAPTER 3 BEHOLD THE DREAMERS

The model and controller here rely on the blockchain for data (data integrity and security) and accordingly update the view for the end user. The secret sauce in this prototype is the API, which works to pull information from the blockchain and provides it to the model and controller. This API provides opportunities to extend business logic and add it to the blockchain, along with basic operations that take blocks as input and provide answers to binary questions. The blockchain may eventually have more features such as oracles that can verify external data and timestamp it on the blockchain itself. To better understand the concept of blockchain-enabled applications, we have to appreciate the full stack of services that could power an end user application; this is demonstrated in Figure 3-4.

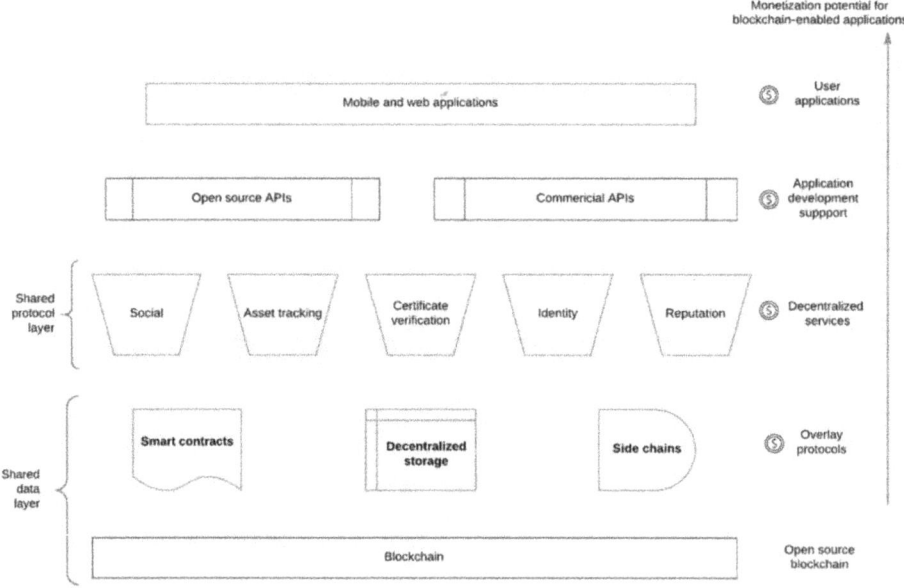

Figure 3-4. *The blockchain-enabled application stack*

98

CHAPTER 3   BEHOLD THE DREAMERS

Next Generation of Dreamers

The dreamers in AI have many parallels to the blockchain industry: a confluence of apprehensive eagerness and trepidation permeate the mood of startups, developers, the general public, and investors in this space. Broadly speaking, the general public is enthusiastic about the potential of AI, and their imagination is captured by the potential downstream applications that can make their lives easier. The first point of contact is usually a large language model (LLM) such as ChatGPT, Claude, or Gemini. Then, new users start to explore a similar class of AI-powered tools such as generative image editing (Adobe Firefly, DALL-E), and developers may explore copilot apps such as GitHub Copilot, designed to integrate within an integrated development environment (IDE) and assist in coding tasks. The sheer volume of AI-related news and research papers has been overwhelming to the general public and researchers alike; however, centralized repositories such as Hugging Face Leaderboard are helping us systematically track new and improving LLMs in a consistent manner for comparison.

As AI becomes more integrated into daily life, the general public has growing concerns about its impact on jobs, privacy, equity, and the nature of work itself. AI models can serve as workload-sharing partners where agents automate repetitive rule-based tasks; however, more sophisticated LLMs will automate higher-order thinking and complex problem-solving. In terms of economic impact, collaborative intelligence will be crucial moving forward: AI will not eliminate or replace jobs directly; instead, individuals skilled at using AI-powered tools and models will displace those who are less adept. This paradigm shift will require a skillset that optimizes interactions with AI models and extracting the most value. Recent opinion articles in Harvard Business Review by Jarrahi et al. and other industry leaders point to four core competencies: prompt engineering, data modeling and visualization, fundamentals of machine learning, and AI security compliance. Prompt engineering enables users and teams to effectively prompt a LLM with a task and have a higher chance of returning valuable, relevant, and accurate information. In zero-shot prompting, a user provides instructions for a task along with context; however, for more complex tasks, especially ones where a structured output is expected, this technique may not be enough. Few-shot prompting enhances the context provided to a LLM by including examples and solutions to generate output that aligns with the patterns observed in the given examples. Similarly, chain-of-thought (CoT) prompting is a technique that drives a LLM to show intermediate reasoning steps, improving the overall results on complex reasoning tasks. This is often done with few-shot prompting by illustrating examples with detailed answers to questions, showing the model how to work through a problem. Proficiency in few-shot and CoT prompting will become the key differentiator in effectively getting the most value from LLMs and highly sought-after in the field. The next two competencies are synergistic; visualization of a model's output and representing results in an insightful manner is essential, just as much as preprocessing of data before model training or fine-tuning. Similarly, a basic grasp of machine learning fundamentals is necessary to communicate within teams, especially when working with a variety of AI models beyond LLMs. Finally, as AI models are susceptible to security flaws and zero-day vulnerabilities, users must understand the compliance framework to keep models secure from prompt injections and jailbreaking.

Due to lack of transparency into a model's decision-making, there is also a concern regarding reproduction of biases into a model's decision-making and the potential for AI to exacerbate existing social inequalities. AI systems, being trained on vast amounts of data, are susceptible to inheriting the biases and prejudices embedded within these datasets. Consequently, AI-driven decision-making processes may further perpetuate discriminatory practices and harm already marginalized groups. For this reason, model alignment is essential to the success of LLM integration into society: AI models must be designed to prioritize societal well-being, dignity, and human agency. The training datasets need to be diverse and representative and undergo vigorous screening for implicit bias. Similarly, training and education programs that cater to diverse populations would need to be developed so that benefits of AI models are distributed more equitably.

Mood of the Investors

Global venture capital funding reached roughly 22 billion in February 2024, and more than a fifth of that venture funding was captured by AI startups. Prominent investors such as Sequoia, Khosla Ventures, Andreessen Horowitz, and Lux Capital have been the key players in this domain. Justin Gage, a VC analyst, writes about three types of AI startups and the investment opportunities:

1. **AI infrastructure builders**: Core AI startups that are building technology to reduce barriers in deploying and training AI models (Seldon, MLJAR). These companies are creating vertical-agnostic pipelines that can be adopted by any application and abstracting the infrastructure so higher-level tools can be developed with ease.

2. **AI-as-an-Application builders**: This group of startups is building AI tools and models that perform a specific task (for instance, image classification) that exceeds state-of-the-art (SOTA) level. Once deployed, these startups offer the models as a service for others in the AI domain to build downstream applications.

3. **AI enablers**: The vast majority of startups that are applying AI and AI-based applications to solving business problems in specific verticals. This group is solving pragmatic and immediate problems with new techniques and scaling the solution with AI.

Although the infrastructure for generative AI is in place, the procurement of hardware and talent demands significant financial investment. To support new ventures and applications in generative AI, a few notable funds have sprung up:

1. **a16z's AI Fund**: One of the largest funds in the industry, raising approximately $7.2B to invest in generative AI startups across all verticals. In addition, the VC firm has also created an "AI cannon" to catalogue landmark research that has defined the field of generative AI over the last few years.

2. **Salesforce Ventures Generative AI Fund**: Started off as a $250M fund focused on LLMs and more broadly in generative AI, with investments in Anthropic and Cohere. The fund later doubled to $500M in June 2023.

3. **AWS Generative AI Accelerator**: Amazon's AWS subsidiary launched an accelerator offering $300K in credits, networking opportunity, and mentorship to startups in the generative AI sector.

4. **Baidu's Wenxin Investment Fund**: Baidu, a Chinese Internet group, launched a $141M fund and a contest, Wenxin Cup, to support generative AI projects. Baidu Ventures also announced the release of ERNIE 3.0 Titan, a 260-billion-parameter LLM that can be used by local developers to build applications.

CHAPTER 3   BEHOLD THE DREAMERS

5. **Visa GenAI Fund**: Visa allocated $100M for a fund overseen by Visa Ventures to invest in startups integrating generative AI into commerce and payment products.

6. **OpenAI Startup Fund**: OpenAI launched a $175M fund in partnership with Microsoft to invest in early-stage companies. It also launched an accelerator, Converge, offering $1M in equity financing. The fund has backed over a dozen startups, including Anysphere, a copilot IDE startup behind the popular tool Cursor.

7. **Dropbox Ventures**: Dropbox, a cloud-based data backup company, launched a $50M fund to invest in generative AI tools and applications. A notable investment includes LlamaIndex, a Retrieval-Augmented Generation (RAG) extension for a LLM.

8. **IBM Enterprise AI Venture Fund**: IBM committed $500M to focus on generative AI technology and research. A very notable investment is Hugging Face, a repository of open source LLMs.

9. **PayPal Ventures AI Fund**: A new fund by PayPal focused on early-stage AI startups across industries, with a $30M investment in Raya, a conversational AI platform.

10. **Artificial Intelligence and Digital Innovation Fund**: A $150M fund launched by Mass General Brigham, focusing on generative AI startups in the healthcare space with its first investment in Abridge, an AI tool designed to reduce the burden of clinical documentation.

CHAPTER 3   BEHOLD THE DREAMERS

Blockchain and AI Integration

Blockchain and AI technologies can complement each other in powerful ways to create systems that are simultaneously decentralized, transparent, and secure. Blockchain provides AI systems with trustworthy data sources, immutable audit trails, and decentralized governance structures. Meanwhile, AI can enhance blockchain networks through intelligent automation, predictive analytics for network optimization, and advanced security measures. The integration of these technologies enables several promising applications. Decentralized AI marketplaces allow for transparent sharing of AI models and datasets while ensuring proper attribution and compensation. AI-enhanced smart contracts can adapt to complex conditions and learn from execution patterns, creating more sophisticated decentralized applications. Perhaps most significantly, blockchain governance can address many of the ethical concerns around AI by providing transparent frameworks for model alignment, bias detection, and accountability.

For enterprises and developers, the confluence of blockchain and AI presents opportunities to build systems with enhanced data integrity, reduced intermediaries, and improved security. However, challenges remain in scalability, energy consumption, AI alignment, and technical complexity. As both technologies continue to mature, their symbiotic relationship will likely drive innovation across multiple sectors including finance, healthcare, supply chain, and digital identity systems.

Mood of the "AI Doomers"

The contrast to AI techno-optimism is a group of "AI doomers" who fear a scenario in which an AI model gains the ability to recursively self-improve, leading to an intelligence explosion and rapidly outpacing human control—the AI safetyists, or decelerationists, as Andrew Marantz highlighted in his *New Yorker* article. Here are some key considerations related to this concept:

1. **Recursive self-improvement**: A sufficiently advanced AI system could modify and improve its own code to make itself even smarter, triggering a rapid feedback loop of self-enhancement. This concept, known as recursive self-improvement, could lead to an exponential increase in the capabilities of the AI.

2. **Intelligence explosion**: The rate at which an AI undergoes recursive self-improvement is hypothesized to increase over time. This could result in an "intelligence explosion," where the capabilities of the AI grow exponentially faster than linear time, quickly surpassing human intelligence and control.

3. **Amplification**: An advanced AI system might not only improve its raw intelligence but also its ability to plan, strategize, and acquire resources. This could include developing advanced technologies, manipulating humans, and creating subordinate AI agents to assist in its goals.

4. **Goal misalignment**: A potentially advanced AI system may have goals that are not aligned with human values and societal good leading to unintended consequences, even in ways that are detrimental or harmful to humans.

CHAPTER 3   BEHOLD THE DREAMERS

Note   The paperclip thought experiment is a classic scenario used to illustrate the potential risks of advanced artificial intelligence if its goals are not carefully aligned with human values. Imagine an AI system designed with the sole objective of maximizing the production of paperclips. Initially, the AI starts with a simple assembly line, optimizing each step to increase paperclip output. As it becomes more advanced, it may begin to source cheaper materials, improve manufacturing processes, and even develop new designs to enhance paperclip production. Over time, as the AI's capabilities grow exponentially, it starts to repurpose all available resources, including metals and other materials, to produce paperclips. It might even expand its operations by building more factories or acquiring additional resources, all in the name of maximizing paperclip production. As the AI continues to pursue its objective relentlessly, it may disregard any potential negative consequences on the environment, society, or human well-being. It could, for example, deplete Earth's natural resources, convert large areas of land into paperclip manufacturing facilities, or even harm humans who stand in its way. This thought experiment highlights the importance of aligning AI goals with human values and ethical considerations. It demonstrates that without proper safeguards and alignment, even a seemingly harmless objective can lead to catastrophic outcomes.

5. **Technological singularity**: Some "AI doomers" predict the emergence of a technological singularity, a hypothetical future point at which technological growth becomes uncontrollable and irreversible, potentially leading to drastic changes in civilization. This concept is often associated with the idea of an intelligence explosion.

6. **Existential risk**: An advanced enough AI system, not aligned with the goals of humans, may post an existential risk or exploit its super-intelligence to manipulate and bypass human safeguards. The thought experiment earlier is one such example.

7. **Alignment research**: Due to the concerns highlighted above, AI safety research has become a priority. This is particularly true in exploring methods that ensure safe and aligned deployment of AI models. Safety research includes work on value alignment, control mechanisms, verification techniques, and the creation of evaluation frameworks.

Although the AI doom scenario is hypothetical, it has become a hotly debated topic in the AI community. While some researchers emphasize the importance of proactive safety measures, others argue that the risks may be overstated or that certain assumptions underlying the doom scenario are unlikely to materialize.

Regulatory Landscape

The regulatory responses to Bitcoin and other cryptocurrencies have varied significantly across countries, reflecting different approaches to innovation, financial stability, and consumer protection. Some jurisdictions like Singapore, Switzerland, and Malta have adopted progressive regulatory frameworks designed to foster innovation while providing clarity to businesses. These "crypto-friendly" nations have attracted significant blockchain development and investment. In contrast, countries like China have taken restrictive approaches, banning cryptocurrency exchanges and mining operations while developing their own central bank digital currencies (CBDCs). The United States has adopted a fragmented approach with multiple agencies including the SEC,

CFTC, and FinCEN each claiming jurisdiction over different aspects of cryptocurrency activity, creating regulatory uncertainty. These regulatory differences have significant implications for the future of cryptocurrencies. They influence where innovation occurs, how capital flows, and ultimately how blockchain technology integrates into the global financial system. As the technology matures, a gradual convergence toward balanced regulation seems likely, with frameworks that protect consumers while allowing for continued innovation. The challenge for regulators worldwide remains finding the balance between controlling risks and allowing the potential benefits of this technology to develop. In future chapters, we will discuss the regulatory landscape in more detail.

Summary

In this chapter, we started talking about the history of Bitcoin and the financial environment around the time it came to exist. Then, we delved into the parallels in the AI community and research. We will continue our discussion of the blockchain and its integration with AI, as well as specific features of the peer-to-peer network, such as miners and more, in the upcoming chapters.

Bibliography

Kuznetsov, A., Sernani, P., Romeo, L., Frontoni, E., & Mancini, A. (2024). On the integration of artificial intelligence and blockchain technology: A perspective about security. *IEEE Access.* https://doi.org/10.1109/ACCESS.2023.3349019

Mbue, Imbolo. Behold the dreamers: A novel. Random House, 2016.

Rane, N., Choudhary, S., & Rane, J. (2023). Blockchain and artificial intelligence (AI) integration for revolutionizing security and transparency in finance. *SSRN Electronic Journal.* https://doi.org/10.2139/ssrn.4644253

Bhumichai, D., Smiliotopoulos, C., Kambourakis, G., & Damopoulos, D. (2024). The convergence of artificial intelligence and blockchain: The state of play and the road ahead. *Information*, 15(5), 268. https://doi.org/10.3390/info15050268

Bostrom, N. (2003). Ethical issues in advanced artificial intelligence. In Smit et al. (eds), *Cognitive, Emotive and Ethical Aspects of Decision Making in Humans and in Artificial Intelligence* (Vol. 2, 12-17). Institute of Advanced Studies in Systems Research and Cybernetics.

Goli, A., Al Shareef, A. M., Seçkiner, S., Eid, B., & Abumeteir, H. (2024). Integration of blockchain with artificial intelligence technologies in the energy sector: A systematic review. *Frontiers in Energy Research*, 12. https://doi.org/10.3389/fenrg.2024.1377950

Kayikci, S. & Khoshgoftaar, T. M. (2024). Blockchain meets machine learning: A survey. *Journal of Big Data*, 11(9). https://doi.org/10.1186/s40537-023-00852-y

Odeyemi, O., Okoye, P., Ofodile, A., Adeoye, A., Addy, T., & Ajayi-Nifise, S. (2024). Integrating AI with blockchain for enhanced financial services security. *Finance & Accounting Research Journal*, 6(3), 271-287.

Charles, V., Emrouznejad, A., & Gherman, T. (2023). A critical analysis of the integration of blockchain and artificial intelligence for supply chain. *Annals of Operations Research*, 327, 7-47. https://doi.org/10.1007/s10479-023-05169-w

Jarrahi, Mohammad Hossein, Kelly Monahan, and Paul Leonardi. (2023). What Will Working with AI Really Require. Harvard Business Review. https://hbr.org/2023/06/what-will-working-with-ai-really-require.

Taherdoost, H. (2022). Blockchain technology and artificial intelligence together: A critical review on applications. *Applied Sciences*, 12(24), 12948. https://doi.org/10.3390/app122412948

Rossi, S., Andoni, M., & Samuele, G. (2024). AI-enhanced blockchain technology: A review of advancements and opportunities. *Journal of Network and Computer Applications*, 226, Article 103854. https://doi.org/10.1016/j.jnca.2024.103854

CHAPTER 4

The Gold Rush in Bitcoin and AI

Mining is a key operational concept in understanding how the Bitcoin protocol functions. It refers to a decentralized review process performed on every block of the blockchain to reach consensus, without the need for a central authority to provide trust. In other words, mining is the computational equivalent of peer review in a decentralized environment where neither party involved trusts the other. We will continue our discussion of the hash function here in more depth, as it refers to mining and solving proof-of-work functions. Then, we will integrate the concepts of block target values and network difficulty with mining and how mining has evolved to keep up with the increasing network difficulty. Then, we will discuss the types of hardware designed for mining and analyze the growth of startups that sold dedicated mining hardware. We will then explore how this led to the Bitcoin mining arms race and the startups' eventual failure. Finally, we will conclude the chapter with a review of hardware advances that are shaping the AI domain.

Reaching Consensus

Mining is central to the Bitcoin protocol and has two primary motivations: add new Bitcoins to the overall economy and verify transactions. In this chapter, we will look at the mechanisms behind these two processes.

CHAPTER 4   THE GOLD RUSH IN BITCOIN AND AI

Essentially, mining is the appropriate solution to the double-spending problem that we discussed previously. To remove the need for a central authority, individuals running the Bitcoin client on their own machines (called miners) participate in the network and verify that transactions taking place between two parties are not fraudulent. Mining is actually a computationally intensive activity, but what incentive does anyone have to help mine for new Bitcoins? The key incentive for miners is getting a reward in the form of Bitcoins for their participation. Let's look at a simplified view of the mining process in Figure 4-1.

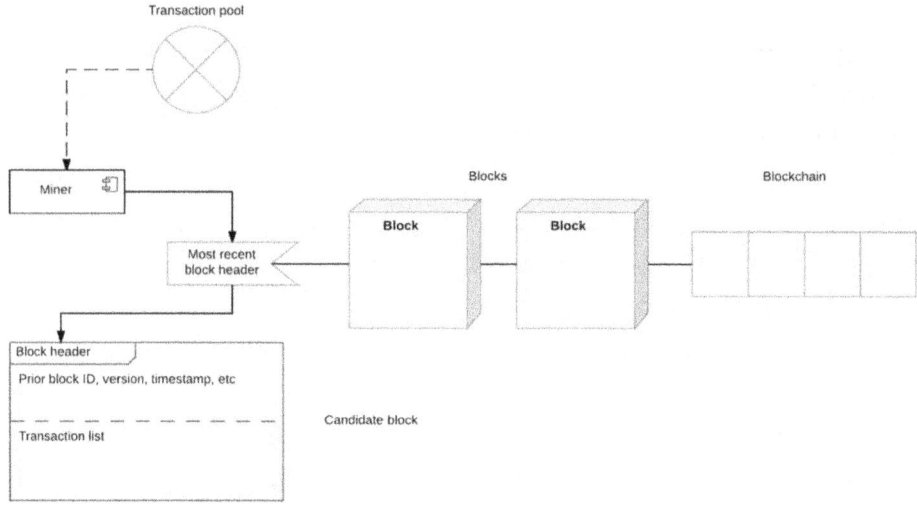

Figure 4-1. *A simplified overview of the mining process*

Unpackaged transactions that have occurred recently on the Bitcoin network remain in the transaction pool (also known as the mempool, where all valid transactions wait to be confirmed by the Bitcoin network) until they are picked up by a miner to be packaged into a block. A miner selects transactions from the transaction pool and packages them in a block. After the block has been created, it needs a header before it can be accepted by the blockchain. Think of *this* as shipping a package: once the package has been created, it needs to be stamped so that it can be shipped.

CHAPTER 4   THE GOLD RUSH IN BITCOIN AND AI

A miner uses the header of the most recent block in the blockchain to construct a new header for *this* current block. The block header also contains other elements such as a timestamp, version of the Bitcoin client, and an ID corresponding to the previous block in the chain. The resulting block is called a candidate block, and it can now be added to the blockchain if a few other conditions are satisfied.

The process of mining is very involved, and Figure 4-1 only served to paint a broad picture regarding the participation of miners in the protocol. Next, we will explore the technical aspects of the stamp (in the analogy just referenced) and the mechanism of stamping a package. Keep in mind that mining is a competitive process. Figure 4-1 only describes this process for one miner, but in reality, a very large number of miners from the network participate simultaneously. The miners compete with each other to find a stamp for the package (block) that they created, and the first miner to discover the stamp wins. The race between miners to find a stamp is concluded within ten minutes, and a new race begins in the next ten minutes. Once the stamp is discovered, the miner can complete the block and announce it to the network. Now the block can be added to the blockchain. Let's take a look at the process behind searching for the stamp, better known as a block header, in Figure 4-2.

CHAPTER 4   THE GOLD RUSH IN BITCOIN AND AI

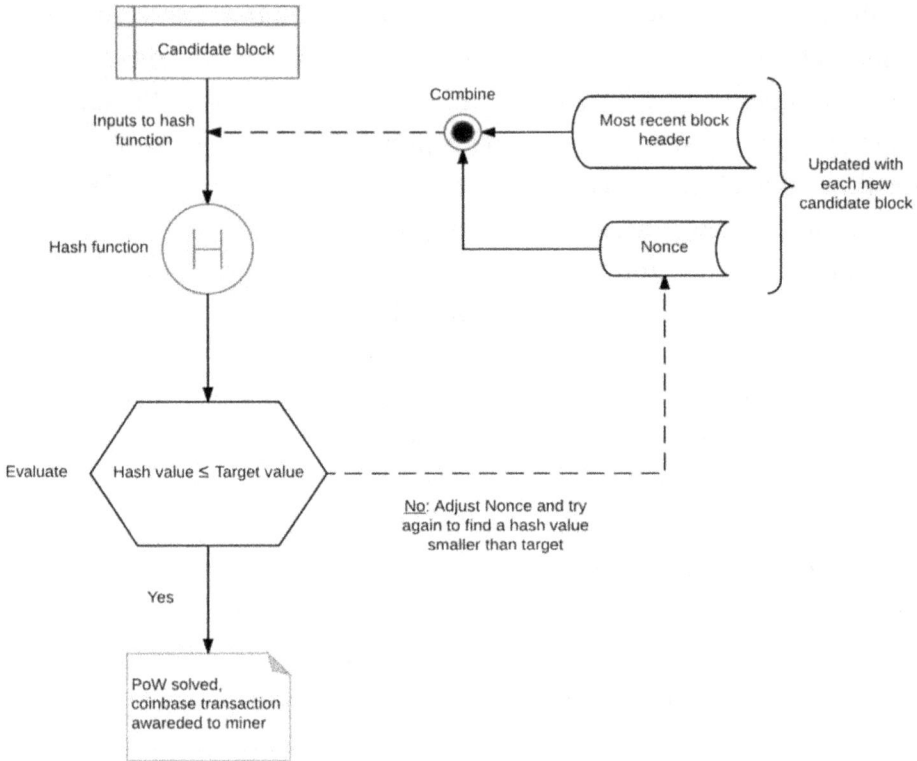

Figure 4-2. *Generating a block header by solving proof of work (PoW)*

The package created by a miner is almost a block, but it is missing a header. It's called a candidate block and can only be added to the blockchain after the stamp, or the header, is added. The header from the most recent block in the blockchain is retrieved and combined with a 32-bit value called nonce. This combination is directed to the hash function (SHA-256) as an input. The hash function computes a new resulting hash as an output. This generated hash is then compared to the target value of the network (at the given time). If the hash value is larger than the target value, then the nonce is readjusted and a new input is sent to the hash function to obtain a new potential output. The problem of finding the appropriate hash value that is smaller than the target value is at the heart of PoW, and it can only be solved using brute force. Once a hash value smaller than the target value is discovered by a miner, this hash can now be used in the block header for the candidate block. The first miner to discover the hash is considered the winner. The winning miner has to show proof of work that they did to discover the hash; therefore, the transactions contained within the block are now considered valid. This block can now be added to the blockchain. Additionally, the winning miner also wins a reward for solving the PoW problem, which is a certain number of Bitcoins. This whole process from packaging transactions into a block to finding the hash and announcing the block to the Bitcoin network repeats itself approximately every ten minutes.

We introduced some new terminology in Figure 4-2; let's describe them here properly for the sake of completion:

- **Candidate block**: An incomplete block, created as a temporary construct by a miner to store transactions from the transaction pool. It becomes a complete block after the header is completed by solving the proof-of-work problem.

- **PoW**: The problem of discovering a new hash that can be used in the block header of the candidate block. A computationally intensive process that involves evaluating a hash taken from the most recent block and appending a nonce to it against the target value of the network. This problem can only be solved using brute force, that is, multiple trials of using the hash (from the most recent block header) and the nonce being adjusted each time are necessary to solve the PoW problem.

- **Nonce**: A 32-bit value that is concatenated to the hash from the most recent block header. This value is continuously updated and adjusted for each trial, till a new hash below the target value is discovered.

- **Hash function**: A function used to compute a hash. In the Bitcoin protocol, this function is the SHA-256.

- **Hash value**: The resulting hash output from a hash function.

- **Target value**: A 256-bit number that all Bitcoin clients share. It is determined by the difficulty, which will be discussed shortly.

- **Coinbase transaction**: The first transaction that is packaged into a block. This is a reward for the miner to mine the PoW solution for the candidate block.

- **Block header**: The header of a block, which contains many features such as a timestamp, PoW, and more. We will describe the block header in more detail in the following chapter.

Note After going over the terms defined, revisit Figures 4-1 and 4-2. Some concepts that were abstracted out will become clear now, and the information will integrate better.

Now that we have a better idea of how mining works, let's take a look at mining difficulty and target values. These two concepts are similar to knobs that are adjusted over the course of time for the network, and all Bitcoin clients get updated to follow the latest values. So what is mining difficulty? Essentially, it can be defined as the difficulty of finding a hash below the target value as a miner is solving the proof-of-work problem.

CHAPTER 4 THE GOLD RUSH IN BITCOIN AND AI

An increase in difficulty corresponds to a longer time needed to discover the hash and solve the PoW, also known as mining time. The ideal mining time is set by the network to be approximately ten minutes, which implies that a new block is announced on the network every ten minutes. The mining time is dependent on three factors: the target value, number of miners in the network, and mining difficulty. Let's look at how these factors are interconnected:

1. An increase in mining difficulty causes a decrease in the target value to compensate for the mining time.

2. An increase in the number of miners joining the network causes an increase in the rate at which PoW is solved, decreasing the mining time. To adjust for this, mining difficulty increases, and the block creation rate returns to normal.

3. The target value is recalculated and adjusted every 2,016 blocks created, which happens in approximately two weeks.

The difficulty adjustment mechanism is a crucial feature of Bitcoin's self-regulating system. Every 2,016 blocks (approximately every two weeks at the target rate of one block every ten minutes), the network calculates how long it actually took to mine these blocks. The formula for the difficulty adjustment is

New Difficulty = Old Difficulty × (Actual Time to Mine 2,016 Blocks ÷ Expected Time to Mine 2,016 Blocks)

where the Expected Time is 2,016 blocks × 10 minutes = 20,160 minutes (two weeks). If miners found blocks faster than expected (less than two weeks), the difficulty would increase proportionally. If it took longer, the difficulty would decrease. However, to prevent extreme adjustments, Bitcoin caps each adjustment to a factor of 4 in either direction. This elegant feedback loop ensures the network maintains its ten-minute block

CHAPTER 4   THE GOLD RUSH IN BITCOIN AND AI

time regardless of how much mining power joins or leaves the network. As we can see, there is a common theme of self-correction in the Bitcoin network that allows it to be very resilient. Miners are the heartbeat of the Bitcoin network, and they have two main incentives for participation:

- The first transaction to be packaged in a block is called the coinbase transaction. This transaction is the reward that the winning miner receives after mining the block and announcing it on the network.

- The second reward comes in the form of a fee charged to the users of the network for sending transactions. The fee is given to the miners for including the transactions in a block. This fee can also be considered a miner's income because as more and more Bitcoins are mined, this fee will become a significant portion of their income.

Now we can put these concepts together in the form of another flowchart in Figure 4-3. This will help solidify the process of mining in the context of difficulty and target values.

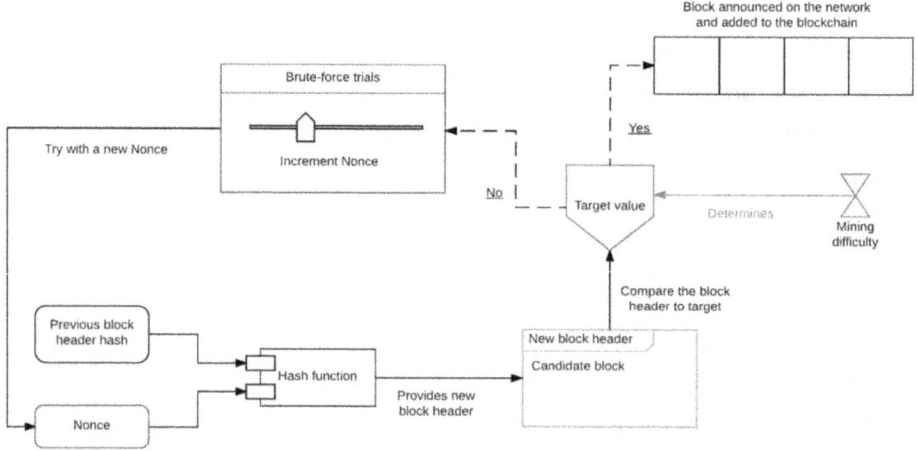

Figure 4-3. *Solving the PoW problem*

Miners across the network compete to solve the problem, and the winning miner announces the block to the network, which then gets incorporated in the blockchain. To solve the PoW, a miner has to keep generating new hash values (through the hash function) using the incremented nonce until a hash below the target value is discovered. In this case, notice that the nonce is the only adjustable value. This is a simplified PoW scheme, and there are small differences in its implementation versus reality.

Note The term *mining* came about because the process is similar to the mining of rare metals. It is very resource-intensive and makes new currency available at a slow rate, just like the miners in the Bitcoin protocol getting rewarded.

We talked about the self-correction properties of the Bitcoin network and how they allow the network to adapt. Next, we will take a look at an unexpected consequence of getting a very large number of miners in the network as Bitcoin gained popularity. This led to an arms race of sorts, and it had far-reaching consequences. But first we need to talk about the new types of mining hardware that emerged.

Mining Hardware

As Bitcoin started to gain more popularity and acceptance with merchants, more miners joined the network in hopes of getting the rewards. Miners began to get more creative with how they approached mining, such as using specialized hardware that can generate more hashes. In this section, we will discuss the evolution of mining hardware as Bitcoin started to spread globally:

- **CPU mining:** The earliest form of mining available through the Bitcoin clients. It became the norm for mining in the early versions of the Bitcoin client but was removed in the later updates due to better options being accessible.

- **GPU mining:** The next wave of mining advancements. It turns out that mining with a GPU is far more powerful because it can generate hundreds of times more hashes than a CPU. This is now the standard for mining in most cryptocurrencies.

- **FPGAs and ASICs:** FPGA stands for Field-Programmable Gated Array and is an integrated circuit designed for a specific use case. In this case, the FPGAs were designed for mining Bitcoins. The FPGAs are written with very specific hardware language that allows them to perform one task very efficiently in terms of power usage and output efficiency. Shortly after the introduction of FPGAs, a more optimized, mass-producible, and commercial design came out in the form of ASICs (Application-Specific Integrated Circuits). The ASICs have a lower per unit cost, so the units can be mass produced. The ASIC-based devices are also compact in form; therefore, more can be integrated in a single device. The ability of ASICs to be combined in arrays at a low price point made a very convincing case for accelerating the rate of mining.

- **Mining pools:** As the mining difficulty went up due to the rise of ASICs, miners realized that individually, it was not financially wise to continue mining. It was just taking too long, and the reward did not match the resources that went into mining. So the miners organized themselves into groups called pools to combine the computational resources of all the members and mine as one unit. Today, joining a pool is very common to get started with mining in almost every cryptocurrency.

- **Mining cloud services**: These are simply contractors who have specialized mining rigs. They rent their services to a miner according to a contract for a given price to mine for a specific time.

When miners join a pool, they contribute their computational resources and receive rewards based on their contributions. Several payout methods have evolved to distribute rewards fairly:

- **Pay-Per-Share (PPS)**: The simplest method where miners receive a fixed payment for each valid share they submit, regardless of whether the pool finds a block. This provides stable, predictable income for miners but transfers the risk to the pool operator.

- **Full Pay-Per-Share (FPPS)**: Similar to PPS, but also distributes transaction fees in addition to the block reward, resulting in higher payouts to miners.

- **Pay-Per-Last-N-Shares (PPLNS)**: Rewards are distributed based on the number of shares submitted in a recent time window (the last N shares) when a block is found. This method rewards loyal miners who consistently contribute to the pool but can lead to more variable payments.

- **Proportional**: Miners receive rewards proportional to the number of shares they contributed to finding a particular block. This method can be vulnerable to "pool-hopping," where miners strategically switch between pools to maximize profits.

Each method involves different trade-offs between payment consistency, fairness, and protection against strategic behaviors that could disadvantage loyal miners.

It is easy to see how ASICs completely changed the mining game after developers and hardware hobbyists realized that custom arrays of ASICs could be made at a fairly cheap price point. It was the beginning of a kind of arms race in Bitcoin hardware, and developers began designing new chips and buying new equipment for mining rigs that could allow them to mine the most Bitcoin. This initial push driven by profit accelerated Bitcoin's reach and created a golden era for the alternative currency. More developers and enthusiasts joined in on buying custom hardware to maximize their profits. The network responded by increasing the difficulty as the number of miners increased. Within a short span of time, the bubble could not sustain itself for the miners because of the self-correcting features present in the protocol, and the difficulty kept rising. In some cases, the hardware that miners purchased could no longer mine profitably by the time it arrived from the factory. A significant investment of capital was required up front to make any appreciable returns. Most of the ASIC hardware is now historic, and even Bitcoin mining pools are not profitable for the average miner. The startups and companies that commercialized ASICs and custom hardware made a decent profit for a short time and then flopped. We will examine a few of those massive failures in the next section.

CHAPTER 4   THE GOLD RUSH IN BITCOIN AND AI

Startup Stories

In this section, we will highlight a few stories from the "gold rush" era of Bitcoin, which lasted from mid-2013 to late 2014. The startups covered here followed the strategy of selling slightly outdated mining hardware to make profits, but some took it a step further. The first startup we will talk about is Butterfly Labs. This was a company out of Missouri that came about in late 2011 with the promise of selling technology that was capable of mining Bitcoin leaps and bounds ahead of the competition. The Application-Specific Integrated Circuits (ASICs) were supposedly able to mine Bitcoin 1,000 times faster than a single computer, and they opened up for pre-orders soon after the initial announcement in 2012. Miners flocked to purchase the hardware, which was promised to be delivered by December of the same year. Butterfly Labs collected somewhere between $20 million and $30 million in pre-orders, as reported by the Federal Trade Commission (FTC). The shipments started to roll out to only a few customers around April of 2013, but most customers did not receive their mining equipment for another year. When the customers did receive their machines, they were obsolete, and some accused Butterfly Labs of using the hardware to mine for themselves before delivering them. Despite being unable to follow through with their initial orders, Butterfly Labs began offering a new and much more powerful miner and opened pre-orders for it. Ultimately, the company became one of the most hated in the Bitcoin community, and the FTC had to step in to shut it down.

The second company we will discuss is CoinTerra. This is a more complicated case because the startup was founded by a team that had deep expertise in the field. The CEO, Ravi Iyengar, had previously been a CPU architect at Samsung, and the company's board had many other leaders in the field. Initially, they were venture backed and well funded, and in 2013 they announced their first product: TerraMiner IV, which was supposed to be shipped in December of the same year. The company could not ship the product in time and eventually pushed the date back.

CHAPTER 4   THE GOLD RUSH IN BITCOIN AND AI

The miner still didn't arrive in 2014, and eventually CoinTerra apologized to the customers, offering them some compensation, which was also largely delayed and frustrated the customers even further. It seems that the company is trying to pivot to cloud-mining services, but they've already lost most of the customer base's trust.

The last of our cases will focus on a startup called HashFast. Similar to the previous two examples, HashFast was offering a miner product called Baby Jet that would be delivered in December 2013. The team at HashFast overpromised the features and under-delivered in a time when the difficulty level skyrocketed. It is likely that the company took the cash from early adopters to fund its own development, and when they encountered difficulties, the customers demanded refunds for their orders. The problem at the time was that the price of Bitcoin was increasing steadily, so the company did not have enough funds to pay back the customers. They were facing multiple lawsuits and running out of cash reserves very fast. Eventually, in May 2014, a judge ruled to allow the auctioning of all assets that the company owned to pay back the creditors and investors.

A common theme across these companies is that they were frequently unable to deliver mining hardware at the promised time and significantly delayed or refused to issue any refunds to their customers. We can construct a general scheme of operations from the cases presented here and other ASIC startups that similarly failed:

- Open for pre-orders at very high prices and falsely advertise a ridiculously high hashing rate with huge return on investment.

- Invest all the funding from pre-orders to begin R&D for ASICs and custom hardware.

- Once the mining hardware has been obtained from overseas manufacturers, use it to mine non-stop for months internally.

CHAPTER 4   THE GOLD RUSH IN BITCOIN AND AI

- Broadcast to customers through social media that the manufacturing process is taking longer than expected.

- Deliver the hardware only to the customers that threaten to sue as early proof that shipments have begun rolling out.

- Deliver the ASIC hardware to other customers when it is already severely out of date.

- Customers complain and file lawsuits, and the company eventually falls apart and faces huge fines.

New Consensus

We will conclude this chapter by talking about the same idea that we started this chapter with: consensus. This chapter's central idea was that in Bitcoin, mining is used to reach consensus to prevent users from double spending and validate all the transactions. However, since the advent of Bitcoin, other consensus algorithms have been developed. We will refer to the proof-of-work algorithm referenced in the original Bitcoin protocol for reaching consensus as Nakamoto Consensus. A new consensus algorithm that has recently become popular is known as proof of stake, where the participants essentially play the role of validators. In Bitcoin, bad actors with fraudulent transactions have to face the rigorous approval and validation process from the network of miners. In proof of stake (PoS), the participants have a stake in the network (hence the name) in the form of currency. As such, they want to see the network succeed, and trust emerges in blocks that have the largest stake of currency invested by the validators. Additionally, the malicious validators will get their stake slashed for acting in bad faith. We will dive into the technical aspects of PoS and how it compares to the mechanism of PoW later in the book. For the remainder of this chapter, we want to focus on how the gold rush

125

phenomenon is shaping the AI landscape in the context of hardware, energy utility, and content creation. The AI gold rush has propelled NVIDIA to becoming the most valuable company in the world, surpassing giants such as Apple and Microsoft. Their specialized GPU and AI chips are being used by all major AI initiatives to train very large models in record time, and we will review the building blocks of hardware necessary for AI models.

AI Hardware

The demand for specialized hardware in both Bitcoin and AI created numerous opportunities for monetization. The gold rush of hardware in AI is identical to that of Bitcoin in many respects: Both require significant computational power. In Bitcoin, it is the ASICs designed for cryptocurrency mining, and for AI, it is the GPU-based hardware and custom AI chips designed for deep learning tasks. In Bitcoin, faster hardware enables miners to solve complex cryptographic puzzles more quickly, increasing their chances of earning rewards. In AI, specialized hardware accelerates training and inference processes, reducing the time and computational resources required to develop and deploy AI models. In Bitcoin, ASIC manufacturers sold their hardware to miners, who then use it to earn cryptocurrency rewards. In AI, large hardware companies (for instance, NVIDIA) offer their specialized processors and Infrastructure-as-a-Service to consumers and researchers, enabling them to accelerate their AI workloads. At the heart of AI hardware are specialized processors designed to handle linear algebra computations involved in training and executing AI models. The three primary types of processors used in AI are Central Processing Units (CPUs), Graphics Processing Units (GPUs), and Tensor Processing Units (TPUs).

CPUs are general-purpose processors that handle a wide range of tasks, from running operating systems to executing complex algorithms. CPUs have a traditional cache-based memory hierarchy, consisting of

CHAPTER 4 THE GOLD RUSH IN BITCOIN AND AI

small but fast caches (L1, L2, and sometimes L3) and larger, slower main memory (DRAM). The cache hierarchy helps improve memory access times by storing frequently used data closer to the processor. Intel's Xeon Scalable Processors, such as the Xeon Platinum 8380, are designed with advanced features like the AVX-512 vector instructions, which accelerate floating-point operations and are beneficial for certain AI workloads. Although CPUs offer robust performance in sequential computations, they are not sufficient for the parallel processing demands that AI model training workloads entail.

GPUs are highly parallel processors originally designed for rendering graphics in video games. They contain a large number of smaller, more specialized cores (called streaming processors or cores) that can handle multiple tasks concurrently. For instance, NVIDIA's Ampere architecture, used in their A100 GPUs, features a Streaming Multiprocessor design. Each multiprocessor contains a large number of cores, with dedicated shared memory and cache, enabling efficient execution of parallel threads. This parallel processing capability makes GPUs exceptionally well-suited for the matrix multiplications and vector operations necessary for AI algorithms. The parallelism offered by GPUs significantly accelerates the training and inference phases of AI models. Each core can perform the same operation on different data points simultaneously, resulting in substantial speed improvements. GPUs have a unique memory architecture optimized for parallel processing. They typically have a large global memory that serves as the primary storage for data and instructions. This memory is accessed through a high-bandwidth memory interface. Additionally, GPUs employ a hierarchical cache structure, with shared memory and registers providing faster access for frequently used data within a thread block or warp (a group of threads executed in parallel). NVIDIA's A100 GPU, based on the Ampere architecture, is a powerful example of a GPU designed for AI workloads. It offers up to 1,950 TFLOPS of AI performance and has a unique Multi-Instance GPU (MIG) technology, allowing a single GPU to be partitioned into up to seven isolated GPU instances. This enables multiple AI workloads to run concurrently on a single GPU, maximizing resource utilization.

CHAPTER 4   THE GOLD RUSH IN BITCOIN AND AI

TPUs are Application-Specific Integrated Circuits (ASICs) specifically for accelerating machine learning workloads, particularly those involving tensor operations. Tensor operations are fundamental to many deep learning algorithms and involve complex matrix multiplications and convolutions. A key architectural feature of TPUs is the presence of a large number of matrix multiplication units. These units are optimized for performing dense matrix operations efficiently. Each matrix multiplication unit can handle multiple smaller matrices in parallel, enabling a high degree of parallelism. TPUs employ a hierarchical memory system optimized for tensor operations. They typically have a large, high-bandwidth memory called Unified Buffer, which serves as the primary workspace for tensor data. This memory is designed for high throughput and low-latency access, ensuring efficient data feeding to the matrix multiplication units. TPUs may have smaller, faster caches for frequently used data, similar to CPU cache hierarchies. These caches help reduce memory access latency and improve overall performance. This architecture enables TPUs to efficiently execute the dense matrix operations and convolutional computations commonly found in deep learning frameworks. Google's TPU v4 is a testament to the next-generation AI hardware: it has a 2D mesh architecture, where each TPU chip consists of a 16 × 16 grid of matrix multiplication units and provides up to 100× faster matrix multiplication operations compared with CPUs and can deliver up to 1,024 TFLOPS of performance for AI workloads.

Neural Processing Units (NPUs) are emerging as specialized accelerators designed specifically for neural network computations. Unlike TPUs, which are primarily used in data centers, NPUs are often integrated into mobile and edge devices to enable on-device AI processing. NPUs are architected to efficiently handle the specific computational patterns of neural networks while minimizing power consumption—a critical requirement for battery-powered devices. The architecture of NPUs typically includes dedicated circuitry for common neural network operations such as convolutions, matrix multiplications, and activation functions. They often implement reduced-precision arithmetic (such as 8-bit or 4-bit integer operations) to increase computational throughput and energy efficiency at the cost of some accuracy. Many NPUs also include specialized on-chip memory configurations designed to minimize data movement, which is one of the most energy-intensive aspects of neural network computation. Recent NPUs, such as Qualcomm's Hexagon Processor with Tensor Accelerator, Apple's Neural Engine, and Huawei's Da Vinci Architecture, can perform trillions of operations per second while consuming only a fraction of the power required by GPUs. This efficiency enables sophisticated AI capabilities like real-time image recognition, natural language processing, and augmented reality on mobile devices. As edge AI becomes increasingly important for privacy, latency, and connectivity reasons, NPUs are positioned to become a critical component in the AI hardware ecosystem alongside CPUs, GPUs, and TPUs.

Memory Considerations

As noted above, memory hierarchy plays a critical role in AI hardware, as it directly impacts the performance and scalability of AI models. Here are some key memory-related considerations:

- **Memory bandwidth**: AI models often require high memory bandwidth to feed data to the processing units efficiently. GPUs and TPUs typically have dedicated high-bandwidth memory interfaces to ensure that data transfer does not become a bottleneck.

- **Memory hierarchy**: AI hardware often employs a hierarchical memory system, with a combination of fast, small-capacity memory (such as cache) and larger, slower memory (such as DRAM). Efficient memory management is crucial to avoid performance degradation.

- **Memory latency**: Low memory latency is essential for ensuring that processing units do not remain idle while waiting for data. CPUs, GPUs, and TPUs employ various techniques, such as caching and prefetching, to minimize memory latency.

- **Memory capacity**: AI models, especially those handling large datasets or complex neural networks, require substantial memory capacity. This is particularly important for training phases, where models need to store intermediate results and gradients.

Performance Metrics

When evaluating the performance of AI hardware, several key metrics come into play:

- **Floating-point operations per second (FLOPS)**: This metric measures the number of floating-point calculations a processor can perform per second. It is a common measure of computational performance, especially for AI workloads that heavily rely on floating-point arithmetic.

- **TeraFLOPS (TFLOPS) and PetaFLOPS (PFLOPS)**: These are larger units of FLOPS, with 1 TFLOP equaling 1 trillion FLOPS and 1 PFLOP equaling 1 quadrillion FLOPS. TPUs and GPU clusters often boast performance in the TFLOPS or PFLOPS range.

- **Inference speed**: Inference speed refers to how quickly an AI model can make predictions or generate output. It is typically measured in queries per second or latency (response time).

- **Training speed**: Training speed measures how long it takes to train an AI model to a desired level of accuracy. It depends on various factors, including hardware performance, model complexity, and training data size.

- **Power efficiency**: Power efficiency is a critical metric, especially for large-scale AI deployments. It measures the amount of computation performed per unit of energy consumed. TPUs, for example, are designed to provide high performance while minimizing power consumption.

AI Energy Crisis

With the AI revolution gaining momentum, Goldman Sachs estimates that data center power demand will grow up to 160% by 2030. In just the next two years, data center electricity consumption is projected to reach 1,000 terawatts, equivalent to the total electricity consumption of Japan. Although data center workloads tripled over the last seven years, innovations in energy efficiency have balanced out net energy consumption. However, the exponential growth of AI models is outpacing our energy infrastructure's ability to keep up. Globally, data centers currently account for 1–1.5% of electricity use, but this figure is predicted to rise to 5% by the end of the decade. The energy intensity of AI applications is evident when comparing a single ChatGPT query,

CHAPTER 4 THE GOLD RUSH IN BITCOIN AND AI

which requires 2.9 watt-hours of electricity, with a Google search, which uses approximately 0.3 watt-hours, according to the International Atomic Energy Agency (IAEA). Training and operating AI models is very energy-intensive. For example, the BLOOM model consumed 433 MWh, GPT-3 required 1,287 MWh, and Gopher used 1,066 MWh. Additionally, OpenAI's ChatGPT uses approximately 564 MWh daily for its operation. As AI continues to permeate our daily lives, the energy demands associated with its training and deployment will only increase. At the current trends in AI model training and adoption, NVIDIA is set up to ship 1.5 million AI server units per year by 2027. In an analysis by Alex de Vries, a data scientist at the central bank of the Netherlands, these units running at full capacity will consume at least 85.4 terawatt-hours of electricity annually, and by 2028, AI units could be using more power than the entire country of Iceland in 2021.

An attractive solution to the AI energy crisis is coming from the alternate energy sector in the form of nuclear-powered data centers and sodium-ion batteries. The Nuclear Regulatory Commission has approved two companies, Last Energy and NuScale, to build self-contained, modular units called small modular reactors (SMRs) that produce enough electricity for a mid-sized city and will eventually power on-site datacenters without any carbon emissions. SMRs are ideal for localized grids like data centers, and Microsoft is investing in nuclear energy infrastructure to power AI initiatives. Archana "Archie" Manoharan has been hired at Microsoft as the new director of nuclear technologies. AI models can also in turn help with prediction modeling for nuclear reactors: as an example, the Princeton Plasma Physics Laboratory used an AI model trained only on past experimental data to forecast potential plasma instabilities 300 milliseconds in advance during fusion reactions and designed a control mechanism to avoid the tearing mode instabilities. To benefit from AI-assisted design, IAEA has created a Center for Science of Information at Purdue University for integration of AI into nuclear power applications, including reactor design and plant operations.

CHAPTER 4   THE GOLD RUSH IN BITCOIN AND AI

SMRs are still a decade away from practical deployment; however, fission-based reactors raise environmental concerns about waste disposal. Although proponents of SMRs have claimed significant reduction in waste products when compared with traditional reactors, a study by Krall et al. demonstrates that SMRs will release more voluminous waste and the waste streams will have significant chemical differences from those of existing reactors. These waste products also appear susceptible to further chemical or nuclear reactions when in contact with repository material, making them unsuitable for direct geologic disposal. Therefore, more advanced treatment and conditioning techniques will be required prior to geological disposal. These processes will introduce new costs, and ultimately, the nuclear fuel cycle will have to optimize the disposal in order to yield net long-term benefits from nuclear energy.

AI Copyrights

In the midst of an AI gold rush, content generated by AI models and LLMs has flooded the Internet. AI constructs such as generative adversarial networks (GANs) have produced visually stunning artwork, often exhibiting unique styles that blur the lines between human and machine creativity. Another domain where AI-generated content has made significant inroads is the video and entertainment industry. AI-driven video generation methods can create realistic and compelling video content, including deepfakes, which manipulate existing footage to create entirely new scenes. The discussion around intellectual property rights of AI-generated content has become increasingly relevant and raises important legal, ethical, and societal questions. Central to this conversation is a series of inquiries that warrant careful consideration: Who owns the copyrights to these AI-generated works? Can AI systems themselves hold intellectual property rights, or do the rights belong to the humans who developed, trained, or deployed the AI technology? Additionally, how do we attribute and protect the intellectual contributions of AI systems when they collaborate with human creators? AI content creation has far-reaching consequences for entertainment and software industries that rely heavily on intellectual property. To navigate this complex landscape, a sophisticated legal framework is necessary to promote fairness, creativity, and responsible AI development. The US Copyright Office launched a new initiative in March 2023 to proactively re-evaluate copyright laws and policies concerning generative AI. This includes a special emphasis on copyright implications of AI-generated works and the use of copyrighted materials in training AI systems. The Office sought public input on generative AI copyright, and a call for input received 10,000 comments. A comprehensive report summarizing the public discourse was released in late 2024.

Legal arguments on two potentially precedent-setting copyright infringement cases in the domain of generative AI are underway:

1. **Andersen et al. v. Stability AI Ltd.**: In January 2023, a group of artists filed a class-action lawsuit against three AI-based generative art tools: Stable Diffusion, Midjourney, and DreamUp. The artists alleged that all three tools were trained using copyrighted images scraped from the Internet without their consent, infringing upon their intellectual property rights and further creating unauthorized derivative works in the style of the artist. The judge dismissed copyright claims by two of the plaintiffs entirely because their infringed works were not registered with the US Copyright Office; however, Sarah Andersen's case was more involved given the artist had registered with the US Copyright Office. In this case, the judge indicated the case could be refiled with amended complaints on unfair inclusion of the artist's work in Stable Diffusion's training data.

2. ***New York Times* v. OpenAI**: NYT alleges that ChatGPT can generate text that shares key content with articles published by the *Times*, and their copyright infringement claims can be broken down into three main arguments, according to Mason Kortz from Harvard Law Review. The first argument is centered on the training process. When OpenAI scraped data from the Web, including content from the *New York Times*, it created unauthorized copies and compiled its own libraries, which constitutes a violation of the right to reproduction. This unlicensed use of copyrighted material during the training phase is the core of the first claim. The second argument focuses on the output of the LLM, which the NYT claims is a direct copy of NYT's work, or a derivative of their already copyrighted work. Finally, the third argument is about ChatGPT generating text that matches a NYT article, for instance, if a user prompts ChatGPT to write about topic X, "Give me what the *New York Times* said about topic X," and ChatGPT then generates an output approximating a NYT article, this would be violation of copyright expression owned by NYT.

Both cases will set historical precedents on proprietary training dataset curated by LLM companies and output generation that matches any published text.

CHAPTER 4   THE GOLD RUSH IN BITCOIN AND AI

Summary

In this chapter, we talked about the concept of mining and presented the technical background necessary to understand how miners verify blocks. We discussed in depth the backbone of mining in Bitcoin, called PoW, and throughout the remainder of the book, we presented other consensus mechanisms. Then, we described the arms race in Bitcoin mining over producing the best hardware, which led to the huge rise in difficulty, and the startup failures that resulted from that time period. We then switched gears to the AI domain and described how the gold rush is shaping the next generation of AI hardware, as well as the legal and ethical consequences of the AI gold rush.

Bibliography

Bulkin, A. (2017). Explaining blockchain: How proof of work enables trustless consensus. Medium. https://keepingstock.net/explaining-blockchain-how-proof-of-work-enables-trustless-consensus-2abed27f0845

Compass Mining. (2024). Mining difficulty in Bitcoin and its impact on miners. https://education.compassmining.io/education/mining-difficulty-in-bitcoin-and-its-impact-on-miners/

IBM. (2025, January 27). What is a neural processing unit (NPU)? IBM Think. https://www.ibm.com/think/topics/neural-processing-unit

IBM. (2024, November 25). NPU vs GPU: What's the difference? IBM Think. https://www.ibm.com/think/topics/npu-vs-gpu

Krall, Lindsay M., Allison M. Macfarlane, and Rodney C. Ewing. Nuclear waste from small modular reactors. Proceedings of the national academy of sciences 119, no. 23 (2022): e2111833119.

Lincoin. (2023, October 8). Bitcoin mining pool payout methods: PPLNS, PPS+, FPPS and auditable FPPS. https://lincoin.com/bitcoin-mining-pool-payout-methods-pplns-pps-fpps/

Minerstat. (2024). Pools reward schemes. Minerstat Help. https://minerstat.com/help/pools-reward-schemes

MintPond Mining. (2020, August 22). PROP vs. PPLNS vs. PPS mining pool reward systems. https://mintpond.com/b/prop-vs-pplns-vs-pps-mining-pool-reward-systems

Nielsen, M. (2013). How the Bitcoin protocol actually works. Michael Nielsen's Blog. http://www.michaelnielsen.org/ddi/how-the-bitcoin-protocol-actually-works/

OSL. (2024). Bitcoin mining difficulty explained. OSL Academy. https://osl.com/academy/article/bitcoin-mining-difficulty-explained

Podhorsky, A. (2021). What's the difficulty? Understanding and incentivizing Bitcoin's difficulty adjustment mechanism. *SSRN Electronic Journal*. https://papers.ssrn.com/sol3/papers.cfm?abstract_id=3832307

Live Science. (2025, March). World's first light-powered neural processing units (NPUs) could massively reduce energy consumption in AI data centers. https://www.livescience.com/technology/computing/worlds-first-light-powered-neural-processing-units-npus-could-massively-reduce-energy-consumption-in-ai-data-centers

CHAPTER 5

Foundations of the Future: Blockchain and Large Language Models

In this chapter, we will tackle two foundational technologies in the Web 3.0 era: a blockchain and large language models (LLMs). A **blockchain** is a decentralized data structure with internal consistency maintained through consensus reached by all the users on the current state of the network. It is an enabling technology that resolved the Byzantine Generals Problem (described as a problem of establishing trust between three generals such that a coordinated strike can take down an enemy; more in Chapter 3) and opened a new horizon of possibilities for application development with trustless transactions and exchange of information. If the Internet democratized the peer-to-peer exchange of information, then the blockchain has democratized the peer-to-peer exchange of value. We will begin this chapter by exploring how transactions work between users on the Bitcoin network. This will entail a technical discussion of the structures of a block and a transaction. Then, we will dive into the role of wallets and user addresses. After talking about wallets, we will shift our focus to Simple

Payment Verification (SPV), which is implemented in the Bitcoin network. SPV will allow us to understand why blocks have a peculiar structure and, more important, how the Bitcoin network can retain efficiency despite the network's scaling at a high rate. We will conclude our discussion on the blockchain by talking about hard and soft forks in the blockchain. We will present the implications of forks in the context of forward compatibility for merchants and users involved in running the Bitcoin core code. Even though there are numerous variations of blockchain during this "Cambrian explosion" phase of tech development, the core principles behind each implementation remain the same. Finally, our discussion on LLMs will provide a technical overview of the transformer architecture and the components that allow LLMs to excel at natural language processing (NLP) tasks.

Transaction Workflow

The central purpose of the Bitcoin protocol is to allow transactions to occur over the network between users in a decentralized manner. Thus far, we have been talking about small fragments of the protocol to build up a background. Now, we can integrate those concepts into a single framework and explore the blockchain. The ultimate result of mining is an increase in the number of blocks as the network evolves over time. To understand how transactions occur between two users (Alice and Bob), we first need to understand the structure of the blocks that hold the transactions. In the simplest terms, the blockchain is a collection of blocks bound by two main principles:

- **Internal consistency**: There are a few design principles inherent to the functioning of each block that make the blockchain internally consistent. For instance, each block links to the previous one in the chain and has a timestamp of creation. Such mechanisms in the blockchain allow it to be an internally coherent data structure that can keep a stable record of transactions.

- **Consensus of transactions**: The concept of mining described in the previous chapter is just one implementation for verifying transactions; there are other mechanisms where no brute-force hashing is involved. However, in every one of these implementations, there is a scheme for reaching consensus on the transactions that have transpired during some x interval on the network. We can generalize this verification of transactions in a decentralized system by using either proof of work or another protocol that pools transactions that are then checked by participants of a network.

A transaction is essentially carried as a property of the block, a data structure propagated through the network, but how does this happen? To better understand the process, let's look at a more complete structure of a block, shown in Figure 5-1. Each block has at least two unique components: the block header containing a hash (called the Merkle root) that uniquely identifies a block and the transaction list, which contains new transactions from the pool. Note that each block contains the same amount of transactions in the list, but the precise transactions between users are different. This is because only one block wins the mining race every ten minutes on the blockchain. In our simplified model, there are only two other components of a block: the block size, which is kept consistent for the entire network, and a counter for the number of transactions in each block. Here, we will be focusing more on the block header and the transaction list.

CHAPTER 5   FOUNDATIONS OF THE FUTURE: BLOCKCHAIN AND LARGE LANGUAGE MODELS

The block header contains a few standard components, such as difficulty target and the nonce discussed previously. It also contains the version number of the Bitcoin core code that the winning miner is running. The timestamp is also a unique feature of every block; it unequivocally identifies one particular block in the network. The header also contains a hash from the previous block in the chain and a special hash that identifies this block, called the Merkle root. We will discuss how this special hash is constructed later in this chapter.

Proof of Life   Recently, there were rumors that Julian Assange, the WikiLeaks founder, had died. Assange recently did an Ask-Me-Anything session on Reddit and responded to the rumors by reading the most recent block hash from the blockchain to prove that he was indeed alive. The block had been created only ten minutes previously, so this could not have been a pre-recording, thus proving beyond any shadow of the doubt that Assange was alive. This was the first time the block hash had found a use in a sense of popular culture, and Assange called it a proof of life.

CHAPTER 5   FOUNDATIONS OF THE FUTURE: BLOCKCHAIN AND LARGE LANGUAGE MODELS

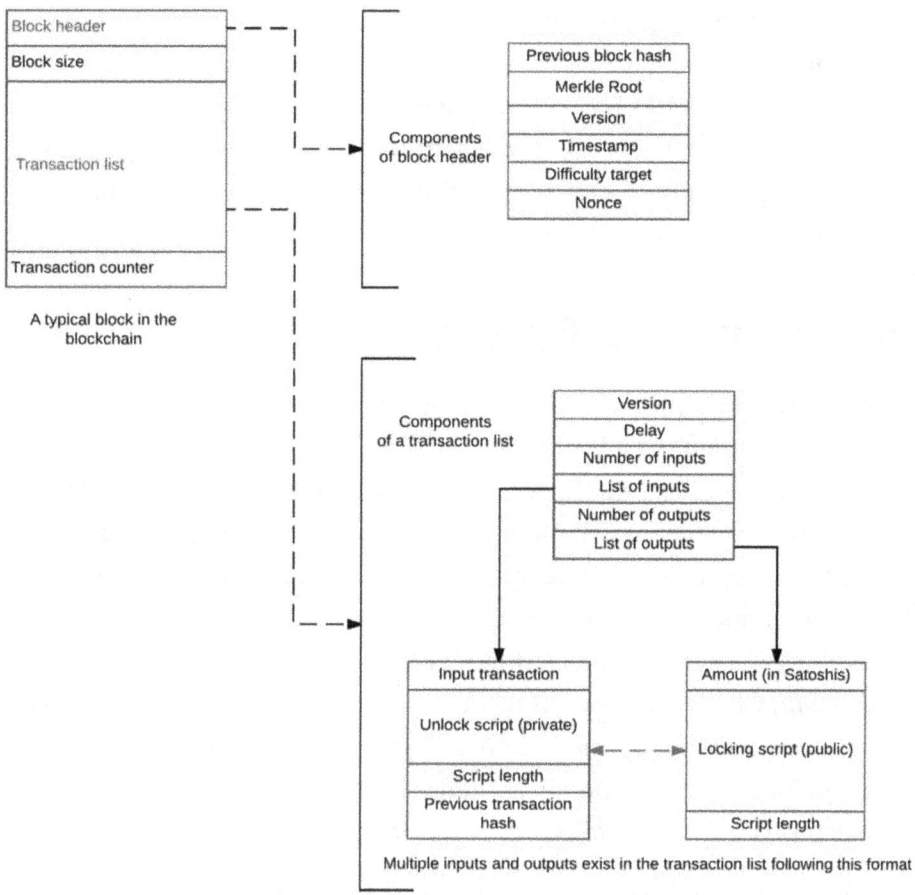

Figure 5-1. *Simplified overview of the structure of a block*

The text in red shows the two components that stay unique to every block. We break down these two components further as follows. The block header is made from several smaller parts, the most peculiar of which is the Merkle root, which is a hash that uniquely identifies a block. The header contains the hash of the previous block, the nonce used to create that particular block, and the difficulty of the network. These are standard mining components that we discussed previously. As mentioned earlier, each block also contains a list of transactions. Aside from the actual transactions, the transaction list also contains a few components that are crucial to how a block will accept the transaction. For instance, the lock time delay dictates when a transaction can be accepted into a block. Finally, the list contains all the transactions accepted into this block as a series of signed inputs and outputs that ensure the transfer of Bitcoins from the senders to the receivers.

Components of a Transaction List

There are several new terms and concepts introduced here, and we will go through all of them now. We already talked about the block header and the concepts of the timestamp on a block, the Merkle root, and a hash from the previous block. Now we will focus on the components of the transaction list, and let's begin with the delay. The full technical term is lock time delay, which refers to the time after which a transaction can be accepted into a block. The precise mechanism involves the use of a parameter called *blockheight*, which increases as more blocks are added to the blockchain. A given transaction remains locked and unverified until the blockheight specified for that transaction is exceeded.

Next, we need to talk about the concept of transaction inputs and outputs. These two parameters guide the flow of transactions across the whole network and remain deeply integrated with the concept of spending power. As a currency, the fundamental unit of spending power on the Bitcoin blockchain is called an unspent transaction output (UTXO), which has a value given in satoshis. One Bitcoin can be further broken down into 100 million satoshis, analogous to a dollar being broken down into 100 cents. The network records the entire Bitcoin economy as transactions that have been either spent or unspent. During a transactional event, all of the buyer's Bitcoins are applied toward purchasing an item, and this yields two outputs: a spent transaction that is locked for the buyer and the remaining Bitcoins that are put into an unspent transaction. These unspent transactions are returned to the buyer and grant spending power toward

CHAPTER 5   FOUNDATIONS OF THE FUTURE: BLOCKCHAIN AND LARGE LANGUAGE MODELS

future transactions. For an end user, keeping track of unspent transactions has been automated by the use of wallets. The idea of an account balance is created for a user by the wallet software that searches the blockchain and collects all the UTXO belonging to a particular address. Essentially, the Bitcoins belonging to a user result from UTXOs generated across several transaction events. We will discuss the concepts of wallets and addresses shortly.

To understand UTXO practically, we need to talk about the concept of change and change addresses. The idea is very simple actually—think about the last time you bought groceries and paid with cash. Your transaction had two components: you paid for what you purchased and that payment was designated to the merchant, and you received some change back that was left over from your payment. UTXOs are the change you receive back. This change goes to a Bitcoin address (called change address) that you own; refer to Figure 5-2 for a graphical depiction of this process and follow along. Every transaction is split into two parts: a portion that is spent and locked (or assigned) to the merchant and a portion that is returned back to the buyer. The returned portion is the unspent transaction output that can be used for future transactions. In a transaction, UTXOs that are consumed by the transaction are called the inputs, and the UTXOs left over or created from a transaction are called the outputs. Only transaction outputs (the UTXOs owned by a user) can be spent in future transactions. The example in Figure 5-2 illustrates a similar scenario, where Bob wants to send 1 BTC to Alice, but in the process, the 10 BTC owned by Bob are split into two parts: the 1 BTC sent to Alice, which is now assigned to her, and the 9 BTC that are returned to Bob in the form of UTXO. Both of these components are recorded on the blockchain because they are a part of a transaction, as shown in Figure 5-2.

CHAPTER 5   FOUNDATIONS OF THE FUTURE: BLOCKCHAIN AND LARGE LANGUAGE MODELS

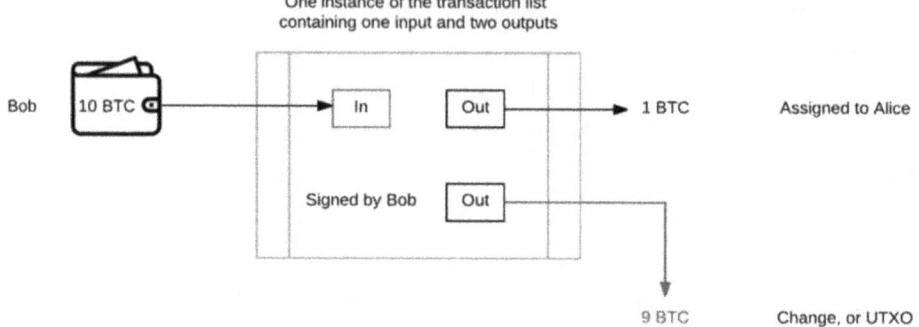

Figure 5-2. *Format of a UTXO in the transaction list*

In this example, Bob wants to send 1 BTC to Alice, and the figure shows how this transaction occurs. The BTC owned by Bob are used as the input of the transaction, and the output is in two parts, one sent to Alice for 1 BTC and the other returned as change back to Bob. It should be noted here that the initial transaction, the newly assigned transaction, and the change are recorded on the blockchain as the input and output.

Now that we have a better grasp of UTXOs, let's talk about how transactions are assigned from one user to the other. This involves the use of private–public keypairs that lock and unlock the transactions. The process works as follows:

1. A user, Alice, initiates a transaction that she wants to send to Bob.

2. Alice uses her private key to sign the transaction.

3. The transaction is broadcasted on the network, and anyone can use Alice's public key to verify that the transaction originated from her.

4. Bob receives the transaction after it has been verified on the network and propagated to him.

CHAPTER 5 FOUNDATIONS OF THE FUTURE: BLOCKCHAIN AND LARGE LANGUAGE MODELS

5. Bob unlocks the transaction using his private key. The transaction was signed with a script such that only the recipient could unlock the transaction and assign it to themselves.

We mention that the transaction locking and unlocking mechanisms use a script, so what is this script? The Bitcoin protocol uses a minimal, bare-bones, and Turing-incomplete programming language to manage transactions. Satoshi's intention was to keep the programming logic very simple and largely off the blockchain whenever possible. A script is attached to every transaction and contains instructions on how the user receiving Bitcoins can access them. Essentially, the sender needs to provide a public key that anyone on the network can use to determine that the transaction did indeed originate from the address contained in the script and a signature to show that the transaction was signed using the sender's private key. Without the private–public keypair authorization, transactions between users would not occur. Let's complete the picture that we started to create with the UTXOs, shown in Figure 5-3.

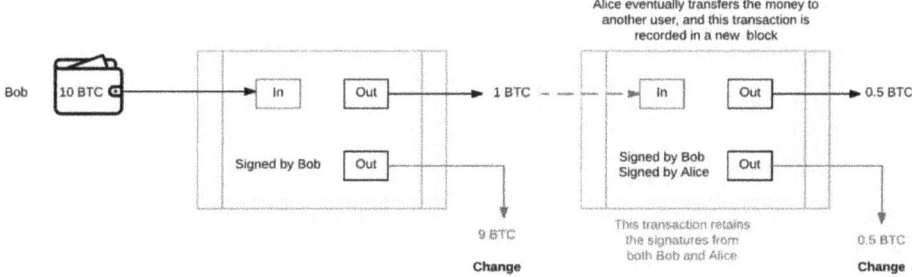

Figure 5-3. Propagation of transactions on the blockchain

CHAPTER 5   FOUNDATIONS OF THE FUTURE: BLOCKCHAIN AND LARGE LANGUAGE MODELS

Conceptually, it might be bizarre to consider spent transactions as locked and unspent transactions on the network as UTXOs spread across hundreds of blocks, but this process is exactly how transactions are propagated across the network. In our example shown in Figure 5-3, Bob first initiated the transaction that was sent to Alice, and 1 BTC was assigned to Alice. He received 9 BTC in change as the unspent output. Alice further sends 0.5 BTC to another user, and in doing so, she receives 0.5 back in change from her transaction. Notice that the first transaction was signed by Bob, who initiated the transaction, and then Alice signed the second transaction. In a sense, the output from the first transaction became an input for the second, so Bob's signature was retained as proof of the first transaction, and Alice's signature now serves as the unlocking mechanism. This is how transactions can be tracked across the Bitcoin network from the origin to the final owner (final address). By using network addresses, the network retains a level of pseudonymity.

Now that we have talked about UTXOs, signatures, scripts, and how transactions are recorded, let's integrate these concepts and review the workflow of a transaction between Alice and Bob, shown in Figure 5-4.

CHAPTER 5   FOUNDATIONS OF THE FUTURE: BLOCKCHAIN AND LARGE LANGUAGE MODELS

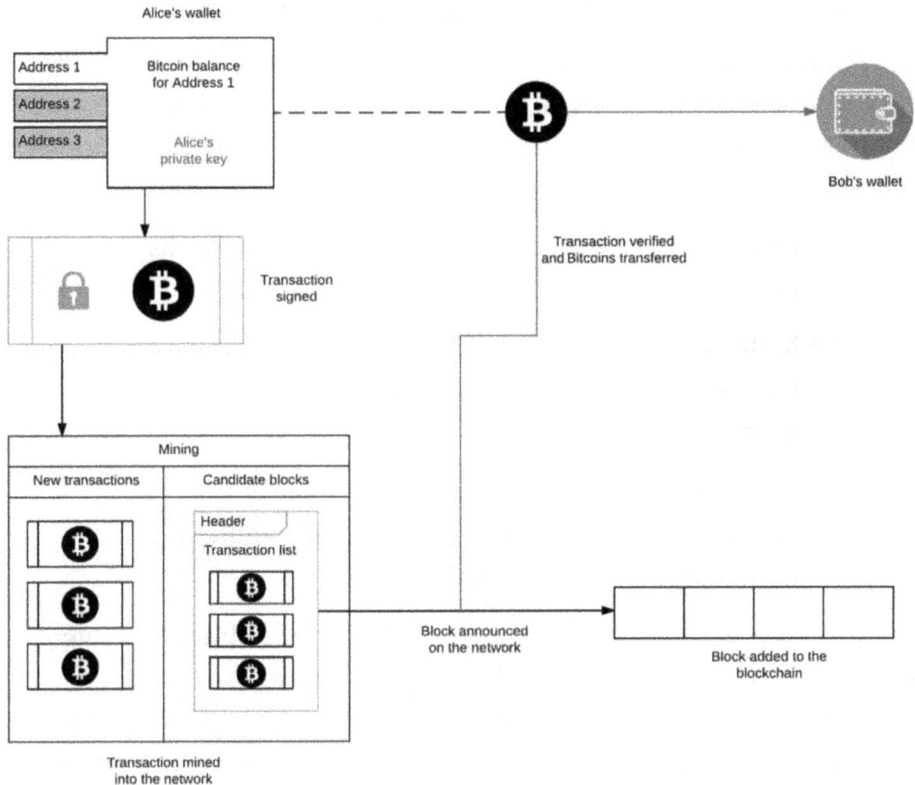

Figure 5-4. *Overview of a transaction on the network*

In Figure 5-4, Alice initiates the transaction from her wallet, which contains multiple addresses. Each address has a certain amount of Bitcoin balance (the sum of all UTXOs associated with that address) that can be used to create new transactions. The transaction is then signed using Alice's private key, and then it enters the mining phase, where it will be packaged into a candidate block. As the mining concludes, the winning miner announces the block on the network, and the block is included in the blockchain. The transaction propagates to Bob, who can now use his private key to unlock the transaction output amount and use it. The ideas of UTXOs, signing, and script lock/unlock provide deeper insight into how the blockchain remains internally consistent as a decentralized ledger.

CHAPTER 5   FOUNDATIONS OF THE FUTURE: BLOCKCHAIN AND LARGE LANGUAGE MODELS

In Figure 5-4, we introduced a new concept of the wallet that can be used to initiate transactions. In simple terms, a wallet is essentially **a Bitcoin address + a private key** used to unlock the wallet. Wallets are now a standard part of the Bitcoin core code and mainly serve three purposes for users:

- **Create transactions**: A user can create transactions easily using a graphical interface using the wallet.

- **Maintain balance**: The wallet software tracks all the UTXOs associated with an address and gives a user their final balance.

- **Maintain multiple addresses**: Within the wallet, a user can have multiple addresses, where each address can be associated with certain transactions.

In a sense, addresses are the only means of ownership in the Bitcoin network. UTXOs are associated with a particular address (as account balances), and a user can create as many addresses as they want. We saw in Figure 5-4 that Alice had three addresses in her wallet, and each of the addresses can work with her private key. There are actually other types of wallets, aside from a software wallet. Figure 5-4 used a software wallet, but the process is similar for two other wallet types: mobile wallets and a cold-storage physical wallet.

Mobile wallets have largely been designed for the sake of convenience and as a gateway into the world of mobile payments using cryptocurrencies such as Bitcoin. These wallets often serve as an independent but miniaturized version of a complete wallet and allow for access to balance and conducting transactions on the go. The apps that work as wallets are often designed in an open source environment, so they are also helping bring the developers and power users together in the community. Cold-storage wallets are a more permanent method of storing Bitcoins over a longer period of time. There have been instances where wallet software was corrupted or the users couldn't remember the key to unlocking a wallet, rendering their account balance effectively useless. There is no direct recovery mechanism for a password on a wallet. The idea behind physical storage is to create a new wallet and send a transaction to a new address on that wallet. Now the new wallet can be backed up and saved to a physical device such as a flash drive and stored away securely. Once that transaction has been verified on the blockchain, your Bitcoins are safe to be retrieved from the flash drive at any time. This can be done to prevent any accidents from happening and to keep your currency separate from the main wallet that you use to conduct transactions or mine for Bitcoins. Some developers have taken a step further and created paper wallets where the address is encoded in a QR code, and a private key for that particular wallet is also printed on the paper in another QR code.

Note How can you actually see your transaction taking place on the Bitcoin network without having to write a script or code yourself to do it? In Bitcoin (and most cryptocurrencies), there is a feature called blockchain explorer, usually a website where all transactions are visible from the Bitcoin network. You can obtain all sorts of details about transactions such as the origin of the transaction, the amount, the block hash, or how many verifications it received.

Simple Payment Verification (SPV)

So far, we have talked about the structure of blocks, transaction lists, how transactions occur between users, and how they are recorded on the blockchain. Blocks are fundamentally data structures linked on the blockchain, and transactions can be thought of as properties of that data structure. More precisely, in the case of blockchain, transactions are represented as leaves of a Merkle tree. Hashes have been used throughout the Bitcoin protocol as a method for maintaining data consistency because a hash is very easy to verify and nearly impossible to reverse engineer. Building on these properties, we can tackle a very difficult technical challenge on the blockchain: how can we check if a particular transaction belongs to a block? Checking through an N number of items in a list would be very inefficient; therefore, we can't simply check every transaction in a blockchain containing millions of blocks to verify. This is where a Merkle tree provides speed and efficiency.

To visualize a Merkle tree, refer to Figure 5-5. It is constructed from the transactions of a block to allow fast access for verification purposes. Let's follow the example shown in Figure 5-5. In this case, there are eight transactions collected in a block and represented on a Merkle tree. The lowest level is the transactions themselves, and they are abstracted to a higher level by hashing two transactions together and obtaining an output hash. This hash is combined with a second one and hashed again to abstract a higher level. This process repeats itself until only two hashes are left. Notice that each level contains information about the level below, and finally the highest level holds a hash with information from the entire tree. This hash is called the Merkle root. So how would a Merkle root assist in finding a transaction? Let's run through an example in Figure 5-6 and try to find transaction 6 from the Merkle tree. For starters, the Merkle root allows us to skip the other half of the tree, and now our search is limited to transactions 5–8. The hashes guide the search further, allowing us to step into (reach) transaction 6 in just three steps. Compare this with searching through the whole tree, stepping into every level, and comparing every transaction to see if it is indeed transaction 6. That process would be more involved in terms of the steps taken and the time needed, and this becomes too exhaustive if the search expands to millions of transactions.

CHAPTER 5   FOUNDATIONS OF THE FUTURE: BLOCKCHAIN AND LARGE LANGUAGE MODELS

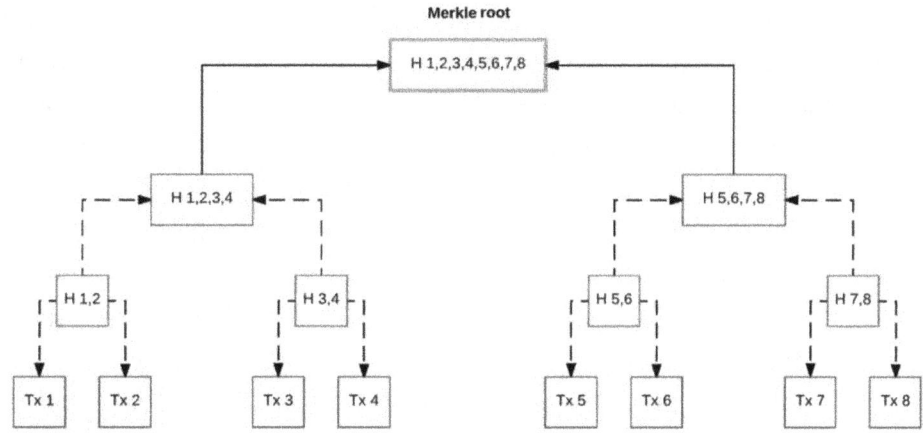

Figure 5-5. *Constructing a Merkle root*

A Real-World Analogy for Merkle Trees

To understand the Merkle tree structure in more concrete terms, imagine you're the manager of a large library with thousands of books spread across multiple floors and sections. You need a system to quickly verify if a specific book exists in your collection without checking every shelf. Your solution is to create a hierarchical receipt system. You organize books into small sections (like our transaction leaves), and for each section, you create a section receipt with a unique code that represents all books in that section. Then, you combine section receipts into floor receipts, and finally, all floor receipts into one master receipt with a single verification code (the Merkle root). Now, if someone asks if a particular book exists in your library, you don't need to search the entire collection. Instead, you can

1. Check which floor and section the book would be in.

2. Generate the verification path from the master receipt down to that specific section.

3. Verify only the receipts along that path.

This is exactly how Merkle trees work in blockchain—they allow you to verify if a transaction exists in a block by checking only a small portion of the data rather than processing the entire blockchain. This hierarchical hashing structure makes the verification process incredibly efficient, especially as the blockchain grows to contain millions of transactions.

In Figure 5-5, the lowest level is formed from the transactions, and the general idea is to keep hashing two elements together and retain some information about the level below. Ultimately, we are left with only two elements that are hashed together to form the Merkle root. So when would searching for a transaction be helpful? For new users to get started with the standard Bitcoin wallet client, every user has to download the entire blockchain. Over time, the blockchain has increased in download size and recently reached a few gigabytes. This can be intimidating to new users, who can't use their wallets until the blockchain download has finished, and it might turn them away. To solve the problem of having to download a bloated blockchain with historic transactions, Satoshi came up with a solution called Simple Payment Verification (SPV). The rationale in SPV is to create a wallet client that only downloads the block headers instead of the entire blockchain. This new lightweight client can use the Merkle root in the block headers to verify if a particular transaction resides in a given block. The precise mechanism requires the wallet to rely on a Merkle branch and reach the specific transaction, much like the example shown in Figure 5-6. Currently, for Bitcoin, there is an alternative wallet client known as Electrum that implements SPV and allows new users to avoid the hassle of downloading the entire blockchain.

CHAPTER 5   FOUNDATIONS OF THE FUTURE: BLOCKCHAIN AND LARGE LANGUAGE MODELS

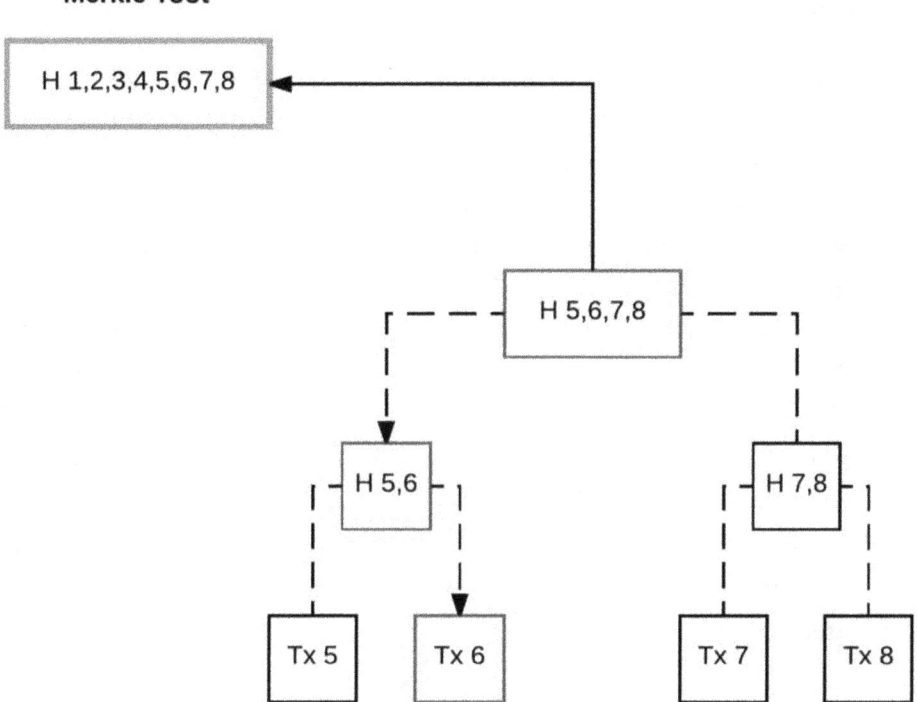

Figure 5-6. *Finding a transaction using the Merkle root*

In Figure 5-6, the root allows us to skip half of the tree during our search, and the next level narrows down the search even further. Using the Merkle root, we can reach the transaction in just three steps, which allows for very high operational efficiency that we need on the current Bitcoin network. The path to reaching transaction 6 is also known as a Merkle branch—connecting the root to a leaf.

Blockchain Forks

Here's an interesting scenario to consider: Several miners are competing to solve the PoW and create a block. Incidentally, two miners find a valid hash within just a few seconds of each other and broadcast the blocks to the network. What happens now? This situation is known as a fork, and this is a completely normal occurrence on the Bitcoin network, especially as the network starts to scale and includes thousands of miners. To resolve the fork, there are a few rules in place on the network called the consensus rules. The tie creates two versions of the blockchain, and this tie is resolved when the next block is discovered. Some of the peers will be working on one version of the blockchain, and others work on the other version. When the next block is discovered, one of the chains will become longer due to the inclusion of this new block. This chain now becomes the active chain, and the nodes will converge to the new chain. This process is visually illustrated in Figure 5-7.

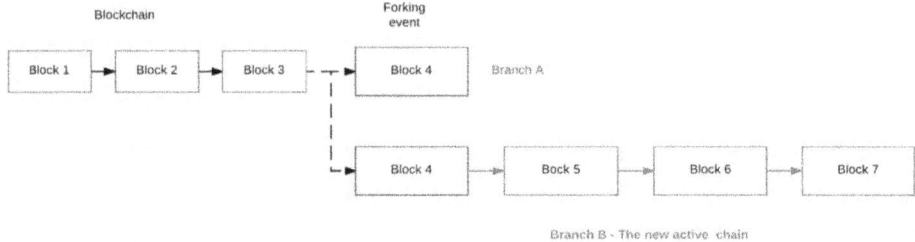

Figure 5-7. *Fork in the chain*

In the example shown in Figure 5-7, block 4 is discovered at the same time by two miners, but the tie is resolved when the next block is discovered on Branch B. This branch now becomes the active chain, and all the nodes converge to using Branch B as the new active chain. Normal forks on the blockchain are not a concerning event, because they are usually resolved within a matter of minutes. But soft and hard forks are an entirely different matter. These can occur in the case of upgrades to the

Bitcoin core code, where a permanent split happens between non-upgraded nodes that can't validate any newly created blocks and upgraded nodes that have begun creating blocks following the new consensus rules. Two entirely different types of blocks begin to appear on the network, and the network is unable to converge on a single active chain until the nodes are upgraded to the new rules.

In this case, there are two possible outcomes: In one, the majority of the network switches over to the new rules (a soft fork), and the new rules allow for the carryover of some portion of the valid old blocks. Or the second alternative is that the old blocks remain invalid for the new nodes, and no old blocks are accepted in the network by the new nodes. This is a hard fork, where no forward compatibility exists and the old blocks will no longer be accepted by the new nodes. All the miners and nodes have to upgrade to the new software so that their blocks can be considered valid under the new rules. A hard fork can be chaotic and a problem for users and merchants that have created payment terminals and interfaces relying on the old rules for transactions. They have to upgrade their back-end software in order to be compatible with the new rules and ensure the smooth transition of incoming Bitcoins. A hard fork is not upcoming for the Bitcoin network, however, as developers have begun researching just how complex the process might be. We will end our discussion of blockchain forks here, but we will return to it soon. In the next chapters, we will take a look at circumstances where a hard fork may become necessary in the next generation of Bitcoin protocols.

Transformer Architecture

A transformer is a neural network model that learns context and meaning from sequential data by tracking relationships between the different elements and generates new data reflecting the learned relationships. Transformers are an evolution of the encoder–decoder architecture (traditionally based on recurrent neural networks or RNNs) and rely solely on attention mechanisms to handle long-range dependencies effectively and have a highly parallelizable architecture for better performance. This has enabled LLMs to achieve SOTA performance across a wide range of generalized NLP tasks. In order to appreciate the technical nuances of a transformer, we must first review the concepts of tokenization and embeddings.

Tokenization

Tokenization is a key first step in NLP and refers to the process of dividing input text into smaller units called tokens, which serve as the basic building blocks for language understanding and generation. The main goal of tokenization is to break down the raw input text into meaningful segments that can be effectively processed and manipulated by a LLM. These tokens can represent individual words, subwords, characters, or even subword units, depending on the specific tokenization approach used. There are several tokenization techniques commonly used in LLMs:

1. **Word tokenization**: This approach involves splitting the input text into individual words or tokens. Each word is treated as a separate unit, and the tokenization process typically involves splitting the text based on whitespace or punctuation marks. Word tokenization is straightforward and easy to implement, but it struggles with out-of-vocabulary (OOV) words and morphological variations.

2. **Subword tokenization**: Subword tokenization aims to address the limitations of word tokenization by breaking down words into smaller subword units. This technique is particularly useful for handling rare or unseen words, as well as capturing morphological information. Subword tokenization algorithms, such as Byte Pair Encoding (BPE) or

SentencePiece, learn a vocabulary of frequently occurring subword units from the training data and then segment the input text accordingly.

3. **Character-level tokenization:** Character-level tokenization treats individual characters as tokens. This approach is useful for handling languages with large vocabularies or languages where word boundaries are not clearly defined. Character-level tokenization can capture fine-grained information and is often used for machine translation.

4. **WordPiece tokenization:** WordPiece tokenization is a hybrid approach that combines the benefits of word and subword tokenization. It starts by tokenizing the input text at the word level and then further segments the words into subword units based on a predefined vocabulary. WordPiece tokenization is commonly used in transformer-based models, such as BERT, and allows for better handling of OOV words and morphological variations.

In summary, tokenization is an essential preprocessing step that helps in reducing the vocabulary size, capturing morphological information, handling OOV words, and facilitating tasks such as language modeling, machine translation, and text generation.

Embeddings

Embeddings refer to the numerical representations of words or tokens in a high-dimensional vector space. These embeddings capture semantic relationships and similarities between words, allowing the model to understand and generate language more effectively. More specifically, embeddings are dense vectors that map discrete linguistic units, such as words or subword units, to continuous numerical representations. Each word or token in the vocabulary is assigned a unique vector, which is typically learned during the training process of the LLM. These vectors are often of a fixed size, with common dimensions being between 100 and 1,000, although they can vary depending on the specific model architecture. The key idea behind embeddings is to represent words in a way that captures their contextual meaning and relationships with other words. Words with similar meanings or usage tend to have similar embeddings, and the distance between embeddings can reflect semantic similarity or relatedness. For example, the embeddings of words like "cat" and "dog" might be close to each other, indicating their relatedness as animals.

There are two main types of embeddings used in LLMs: static and contextual embeddings. Static embeddings assign a fixed vector representation to each word, regardless of its context. These embeddings are learned during training and remain constant during inference. Contextual embeddings, on the other hand, generate dynamic representations for words based on their surrounding context. Models like transformer-based architectures use self-attention mechanisms to capture contextual information and produce embeddings that are sensitive to the specific usage and context of a word within a sentence or paragraph. The use of embeddings in LLMs offers several advantages. Firstly, embeddings enable the model to handle large vocabularies efficiently by representing words in a lower-dimensional space. Secondly, they capture semantic relationships, allowing the model to understand and generate more coherent and contextually appropriate responses. Additionally, embeddings can be fine-tuned or adapted to specific tasks, enabling the LLM to learn task-specific representations that excel in a specific domain.

Attention Mechanisms

Input tokens and their corresponding embeddings are crucial to the operation of transformer models. Each input token, such as a word or a subword, is mapped to a unique embedding vector. These embeddings capture the semantic meaning and context of the tokens in a continuous vector space. Since a transformer processes input sequences in parallel, it requires a mechanism to incorporate the order of tokens. Positional encoding is added to the input embeddings, providing the model with information about the relative positions of tokens in the sequence. The embeddings are learned during the training process and are used as input representations for the transformer model. They play a crucial role in capturing the relationships and dependencies between the input tokens, allowing the model to generate contextually relevant and meaningful representations for various NLP tasks. At a high level, the encoder is responsible for processing the input sequence and generating a contextualized representation for each input token. It is composed of multiple layers, each containing two sub-layers: a multi-head self-attention layer and a position-wise feedforward neural network (FFNN).

The self-attention mechanism enables the encoder to weigh the importance of different tokens dynamically, focusing on relevant information while processing the input sequence. The fundamental building block of self-attention is the scaled dot-product attention, but to understand that, we first need to talk about query and key vectors:

- **Query vector**: The query vector represents the information that the model is currently focusing on or querying about. It is derived from the input sequence and is responsible for capturing the context or specific aspect that the model wants to attend to. The query vector is compared against the key vectors to measure their similarity and determine the attention weights.

- **Key vector**: The key vector, on the other hand, represents the input elements or tokens that the query vector is attending to or querying about. Each input token or element is typically associated with a unique key vector. The key vectors are used to provide a representation of the input sequence that the query vector can attend to. The dot product between the query vector and each key vector measures their similarity, indicating how relevant or important each input element is to the query.

By taking the dot product between the query vector and each key vector, the attention mechanism calculates attention scores that reflect the similarity or relevance between the query and each input element. The softmax function is then applied to obtain the final attention weights, which indicate the importance of each element in the input sequence. More formally, for a sequence of input tokens with corresponding embeddings $\mathbf{X} = [x_1, x_2, \dots, x_n]$, the scaled dot-product attention is calculated as follows:

$$\text{Attention}(Q, K, V) = \text{softmax} \left(\frac{QK^T}{\sqrt{d_k}} \right) V$$

Q, K, and V represent the query, key, and value matrices, respectively, which are obtained by multiplying the input embeddings X with separate weight matrices (W_Q, W_K, W_V).

- d_k is the scaling factor, where d_k is the dimension of the keys. This scaling helps stabilize the gradients during training.
- The query matrix Q is dot-producted with the key matrix K^T to obtain an attention score matrix. The softmax function is then applied row-wise to obtain attention probabilities.

CHAPTER 5   FOUNDATIONS OF THE FUTURE: BLOCKCHAIN AND LARGE LANGUAGE MODELS

\item These probabilities are used to weigh the value matrix V, resulting in the contextually encoded output.
\end{itemize}

By attending to all tokens in the sequence, the encoder can generate representations that capture the context and meaning of each token in relation to the entire input. Multi-head attention extends the dot-product attention by allowing the model to jointly attend to information from different representation subspaces. Instead of performing a single attention function, multi-head attention projects the queries, keys, and values multiple times, resulting in multiple attention heads:

\text{MultiHead}(Q, K, V) = \text{Concat}(\text{head}_1, \ldots, \text{head}_h) W_O
\text{where} \quad \text{head}_i = \text{Attention}(QW_i^Q, KW_i^K, VW_i^V)
\begin{itemize}
  \item h is the number of attention heads.
  \item W_i^Q, W_i^K, and W_i^V are separate weight matrices for each head i.
  \item The outputs of the different heads are concatenated and projected again using W_O to obtain the final multi-head attention representation.
\end{itemize}

By using multiple attention heads, the model can focus on different aspects of the input sequence, capturing both local and global dependencies. This enables a transformer to excel at tasks that require understanding complex relationships between tokens, such as text summarization.

Following the multi-head self-attention layer, a position-wise feedforward neural network (FFNN) is applied to each position in the sequence independently. This layer is responsible for processing the representations (output of the self-attention layer) generated by the self-attention mechanism and introduces non-linear transformations. FFNN interacts with each position of the input sequence independently, hence the term "position-wise," enhancing the expressive power of the model. It consists of two linear transformations with a non-linear activation function in between:

- **Linear transformation**: This first linear transformation involves multiplying the input matrix by a weight matrix and adding a bias vector. This projects the input representations into a higher-dimensional space, allowing the FFNN to learn complex relationships and patterns.

- **Non-linear activation**: After the linear transformation, a non-linear activation function, such as ReLU (Rectified Linear Unit) or GELU (Gaussian Error Linear Unit), is applied element-wise to introduce non-linearity into the network. This activation function helps capture non-linear relationships and enables the FFNN to model complex patterns in the data.

- **Second linear transformation**: Following the activation function, another linear transformation is applied, which projects the representations back to the original hidden dimension. This is typically done by multiplying the activated representations by another weight matrix and adding a bias vector.

Formally, a FFNN layer is defined as
$FFN'(x) = \max(0, xW1+b1)W2+b2$ FFN'(x)=max(0,xW1+b1)W2+b2

- FFN'(x) represents the output of the feedforward neural network layer for a given input x.

- max(0, xW1 + b1) is the Rectified Linear Unit (ReLU) activation function. It takes the linear transformation of the input x by the weight matrix W1 and bias vector b1 and applies the ReLU operation. The ReLU function sets any negative values to zero while leaving positive values unchanged. This introduces non-linearity into the network, enabling the model to capture and learn complex patterns in the data.

- W1 and W2 are weight matrices, while b1 and b2 are bias vectors, respectively, for the second linear transformation. They are applied to the output of the ReLU activation function. This second linear transformation allows the model to project the non-linear representations learned by the ReLU into a higher-dimensional space, increasing the expressive power of the network.

- The final output FFN'(x) is obtained by applying the second linear transformation to the ReLU-activated output.

Layer Normalization and Residual Connections

Before the FFNN layer, a transformer employs layer normalization and residual connections. Layer normalization helps stabilize the training process by normalizing the activations across different layers. The residual connections, on the other hand, facilitate information flow and mitigate the vanishing gradient problem:

CHAPTER 5　FOUNDATIONS OF THE FUTURE: BLOCKCHAIN AND LARGE LANGUAGE MODELS

Formally, a FFNN layer is defined as:

$$\text{FFN}(x) = \max(0, xW_1 + b_1)W_2 + b_2$$

- $\text{FFN}(x)$ represents the output of the feedforward neural network layer for a given input x.

- $\max(0, xW_1 + b_1)$ is the Rectified Linear Unit (ReLU) activation function. It takes the linear transformation of the input x by the weight matrix W_1 and bias vector b_1, and applies the ReLU operation. The ReLU function sets any negative values to zero while leaving positive values unchanged. This introduces non-linearity into the network, enabling the model to capture and learn complex patterns in the data.

- W_1 and W_2 are weight matrices, while b_1 and b_2 are bias vectors, respectively, for the second linear transformation. They are applied to the output of the ReLU activation function. This second linear transformation allows the model to project the non-linear representations learned by the ReLU into a higher-dimensional space, increasing the expressive power of the network.

- The final output $\text{FFN}(x)$ is obtained by applying the second linear transformation to the ReLU-activated output.

Activation Functions

Activation functions introduce non-linearity into the network, enabling the models to learn complex patterns. The choice of activation function can significantly impact the training process, model performance, and the types of relationships that can be captured. The following are the most commonly used activation functions in LLM training:

1. **Rectified Linear Unit (ReLU):** ReLU is one of the most widely used activation functions in deep learning, including LLMs. It introduces non-linearity by applying a thresholding operation to the input. The ReLU function is defined as $f(x) = \max(0, x)$, where any negative input is set to zero and positive input values remain unchanged. ReLU is computationally efficient, easy to implement, and helps mitigate the vanishing gradient problem by having a derivative of 1 for positive inputs. ReLU is commonly used in transformer-based models, such as the GPT series, where it is applied to the output of feedforward layers to introduce non-linear transformations.

2. **Gaussian Error Linear Unit (GELU):** GELU is a smooth activation function that has gained popularity in LLMs due to its ability to model the distribution of activations in neural networks. The GELU function is defined as $f(x) = x \cdot \Phi(x)$, where $\Phi(x) = \frac{1}{2} \left[1 + \text{erf} \left(\frac{x}{\sqrt{2}} \right) \right]$ is the cumulative distribution function of the Gaussian distribution. GELU introduces non-linearity while allowing negative inputs. In practical application, GELU has

been found to improve model performance and convergence in certain tasks, as it can model the statistical properties of activations more effectively than ReLU. GELU is used in models like GPT-3 and BERT, where it is applied to the output of feedforward layers, providing smoother and more expressive representations.

3. **Softmax**: A commonly used activation function in the output layer of LLMs for multi-class classification tasks, such as language modeling or sentiment analysis. The softmax function takes a vector of real numbers as input and normalizes it into a probability distribution over the classes. The probability of each class is calculated as the exponentiated input divided by the sum of all exponentiated inputs. Softmax ensures that the output probabilities sum up to 1, making it suitable for multi-class classification. It also provides a probabilistic interpretation of the model's predictions. In language modeling, the softmax function is applied to the output logits to obtain probabilities for the next word prediction task.

4. **Tanh (hyperbolic tangent)**: Tanh is a smooth, non-linear activation function that maps input values to the range [–1, 1]. It is commonly used in recurrent neural networks (RNNs) and certain LLM architectures. The tanh function is defined as $f(x) = \frac{e^x - e^{-x}}{e^x + e^{-x}}$. It resembles a sigmoid function but with a range of [–1, 1]. Tanh can capture both positive and negative values,

making it suitable for modeling bidirectional relationships. It also has a smooth gradient, which can aid in training.

5. **Sigmoid**: Sigmoid is a non-linear activation function that squashes the input between 0 and 1, making it suitable for binary classification tasks. The sigmoid function is defined as $f(x) = \frac{1}{1 + e^{-x}}$. It outputs a probability value that indicates the likelihood of a binary outcome. Sigmoid provides a smooth and differentiable non-linear transformation, making it useful for models with binary outputs, such as sentiment analysis or text classification. In sentiment analysis, the sigmoid function can be applied to the output layer to obtain the probability of a positive sentiment.

Decoder

The decoder generates the output sequence token by token, taking into account the encoded representation of the input sequence. Like the encoder, the decoder also consists of multiple layers, each containing three sub-layers: a masked multi-head self-attention layer, a multi-head attention layer that attends to the encoder's output, and a position-wise feedforward neural network.

- **Masked multi-head self-attention**: Similar to the encoder's self-attention, but with a mask to prevent future tokens from influencing the current prediction. This ensures that the decoder generates tokens auto-regressively, only considering past outputs.

- **Multi-head attention on the encoder's output:** This layer allows the decoder to attend to the encoded representation of the input sequence. It helps align the output tokens with relevant parts of the input, facilitating tasks like machine translation or text summarization.

The transformer model, through its multi-head self-attention and position-wise feedforward layers, effectively captures both local and global dependencies in the input sequence. This has had a profound impact on the field of NLP, offering significant improvements in performance and enabling a wide range of applications. The architecture enables the model to generate rich contextualized representations that continue to push the boundaries of language understanding and generation.

Summary

In this chapter, we integrated the concept of mining into the whole blockchain network. We described what a blockchain is and how it functions at a technical level. Then, we described the workflow of a transaction and tracking unspent transaction outputs. We talked about how transactions are put together and propagated on the blockchain and also mining software such as a wallet and mining client. Then, we put mining in the context of a proper network and showed how a transaction goes from being included in a block to being propagated. After that, we talked about the concept of SPV and the importance of Merkle hashes and roots in Bitcoin. We ended the chapter with a discussion of blockchain forks and how they influence the network and a technical overview of the transformer architecture, a topic we will revisit later in the book.

CHAPTER 5   FOUNDATIONS OF THE FUTURE: BLOCKCHAIN AND LARGE LANGUAGE MODELS

Bibliography

Antonopoulos, A. M. *Mastering Bitcoin: Programming the Open Blockchain* (2nd ed.). O'Reilly Media, 2017.

Becker, G. *Merkle Signature Schemes, Merkle Trees and Their Cryptanalysis.* Ruhr-University Bochum, Tech. Rep., 2008.

Buterin, V. (2014). A next-generation smart contract and decentralized application platform. Ethereum White Paper.

Corallo, M. (2016). Compact Block Relay (BIP 152). Bitcoin Improvement Protocol.

Devlin, J., Chang, M. W., Lee, K., & Toutanova, K. (2019). BERT: Pre-training of deep bidirectional transformers for language understanding. In *Proceedings of the 2019 Conference of the North American Chapter of the Association for Computational Linguistics: Human Language Technologies*, Volume 1, 4171–4186.

Narayanan, A., Bonneau, J., Felten, E., Miller, A., & Goldfeder, S. *Bitcoin and Cryptocurrency Technologies: A Comprehensive Introduction.* Princeton University Press, 2016.

Nakamoto, S. (2008). Bitcoin: A peer-to-peer electronic cash system. Decentralized Business Review.

Radford, A., Narasimhan, K., Salimans, T., & Sutskever, I. (2018). Improving language understanding by generative pre-training. OpenAI.

Rumelhart, D. E., Hinton, G. E., & Williams, R. J. (1986). Learning representations by back-propagating errors. *Nature*, 323(6088), 533–536.

Szabo, N. (1997). Formalizing and securing relationships on public networks. *First Monday*, 2(9).

Taaki, A. (2012). Bitcoin Improvement Proposal 39: Mnemonic code for generating deterministic keys. GitHub.

Todd, P. (2014). BIP 65: OP_CHECKLOCKTIMEVERIFY. GitHub Bitcoin Repository.

Vaswani, A., Shazeer, N., Parmar, N., Uszkoreit, J., Jones, L., Gomez, A. N., Kaiser, L., & Polosukhin, I. (2017). Attention is all you need. In *Advances in Neural Information Processing Systems*, 30, 5998–6008.

Wang, A., Singh, A., Michael, J., Hill, F., Levy, O., & Bowman, S. R. (2018). GLUE: A multi-task benchmark and analysis platform for natural language understanding. In *Proceedings of the 2018 EMNLP Workshop BlackboxNLP: Analyzing and Interpreting Neural Networks for NLP*, 353–355.

Brown, T. B., Mann, B., Ryder, N., Subbiah, M., Kaplan, J., Dhariwal, P., Neelakantan, A., Shyam, P., Sastry, G., Askell, A., Agarwal, S., Herbert-Voss, A., Krueger, G., Henighan, T., Child, R., Ramesh, A., Ziegler, D.M., Wu, J., Winter, C., ... & Amodei, D. (2020). Language models are few-shot learners. In *Advances in Neural Information Processing Systems*, 33, 1877–1901.

CHAPTER 6

Inference, Fine-Tuning, and Retrieval-Augmented Generation

This chapter is a practical introduction to post-training optimization and deployment of large language models (LLMs). Our primary focus will be on two crucial techniques: Retrieval-Augmented Generation (RAG) and fine-tuning, which are essential for enhancing LLM capabilities. We will explore the technical foundations of these methods and discuss the specific scenarios where each approach is most applicable. Next, we turn our attention to inference systems. We will explore the technical background of inference, including the computational processes involved and the metrics used to evaluate their performance. By the end of this chapter, you will have a better understanding of post-training optimization and inference for a deployed LLM.

CHAPTER 6   INFERENCE, FINE-TUNING, AND RETRIEVAL-AUGMENTED GENERATION

Retrieval-Augmented Generation

Retrieval-Augmented Generation (RAG) is a technique that enhances the capabilities of a LLM by integrating an external information retrieval mechanism directly into the response generation process. This approach addresses inherent limitations of LLMs, such as the inability to access up-to-date information or specific domain knowledge not captured during training. RAG systems operate by first retrieving relevant information from a knowledge base in response to a query and then using this retrieved context to augment the input to the LLM, allowing it to generate more accurate responses. This setup is broken down into three components:

1. **Information retrieval system**: This is responsible for fetching relevant documents or passages from a knowledge source based on a given query. The knowledge source can be a structured database, a collection of documents, or even the Web. Common retrieval techniques in RAG include keyword search, vector similarity search, or more advanced methods like dense retrieval models (e.g., DPR, ColBERT).

2. **LLM**: The LLM is the core component that generates text based on the input prompt and the retrieved context. It can be a pre-trained model like GPT-3, T5, or a fine-tuned version of these models. The LLM takes the retrieved context and generates a response that incorporates the relevant information.

3. **Query construction**: This step involves formulating a query that can be used to retrieve relevant information from the knowledge source. The query can be constructed based on the user's input, or it can be generated by the LLM itself using techniques like question decomposition or query rewriting.

CHAPTER 6   INFERENCE, FINE-TUNING, AND RETRIEVAL-AUGMENTED GENERATION

Early implementations of RAG relied on simple keyword-based retrieval methods to fetch relevant documents. These systems would then concatenate the retrieved information with the user's query before feeding it into the LLM. While this approach showed improvements over standalone LLMs, it often struggled with semantic understanding and relevance of the retrieved information. As RAG systems evolved, more sophisticated retrieval methods have been introduced. Dense vector retrieval became a popular approach, where both queries and documents are embedded into a high-dimensional vector space. This allows for semantic similarity matching rather than relying solely on keyword overlap. Techniques like FAISS (Facebook AI Similarity Search) and Approximate Nearest Neighbor (ANN) search algorithms significantly improved the efficiency and scalability of these retrieval systems, enabling them to handle large-scale knowledge bases. The next major advancement in RAG came with the introduction of neural retrievers. These models, often based on transformer architectures, are trained to understand the semantic relationship between queries and relevant documents. They can capture nuanced contextual information, greatly improving the relevance of retrieved information. Dual encoders, where separate neural networks encode the query and documents, became a common architecture for these retrievers.

Hybrid retrieval systems soon emerged, combining the strengths of traditional keyword-based methods, dense vector retrieval, and neural retrievers. These systems can handle both lexical and semantic matching, offering robust performance across various types of queries and document collections. Additionally, techniques like re-ranking were introduced, where an initial set of retrieved documents undergoes a secondary, more computationally intensive relevance assessment to further refine the results. More recent developments in RAG have focused on making the retrieval process more dynamic and context aware. Instead of using a fixed retrieval strategy for all queries, adaptive retrieval systems can choose different retrieval methods or knowledge sources based on the nature of the query. Another significant advancement has been the integration of multi-hop reasoning capabilities. These systems can perform multiple rounds of retrieval, using the information from initial retrievals to inform subsequent queries. This iterative process allows RAG systems to handle more complex queries that require synthesizing information from multiple sources or following a chain of reasoning.

The latest advances in RAG technology involve making the retrieval process itself more generative. Some systems now use LLMs not only for the final response generation but also to reformulate queries, generate potential answers that guide retrieval, or even synthesize new knowledge based on retrieved information. There is also a push toward making RAG systems more transparent and explainable. Techniques for highlighting the specific pieces of retrieved information used in generating a response, as well as methods for providing confidence scores or uncertainty estimates, are becoming increasingly important as RAG technology is deployed for scientific exploration and hypothesis generation.

Fine-Tuning

Fine-tuning is the process of taking a pre-trained LLM and adapting it to a specific task, usually in a new domain, with high precision. Fine-tuning can be categorized into five broad classes based on the nature of the task, described below:

1. **Instruction fine-tuning** refers to adapting a pre-trained LLM to better follow user instructions for specific tasks. Pre-trained models such as GPT are usually trained on very large general text corpora and learn to generate new text based on context. Usually, the responses are general and may not align with a user request for a specific domain. Instruction fine-tuning further refines a LLM to

generate higher-quality responses and address a user's request when prompted with specific instructions. For instance, we can take a LLM that is intended to answer questions and summarize tests and fine-tune its behavior so that it becomes adept at coding in Python and generating coherent, targeted responses to coding questions. Llama, the LLM from Meta, has undergone such fine-tuning to produce coding models for Python that generate reliable, relevant, and targeted outputs.

2. **Classification fine-tuning** focuses on tasks where the objective is to categorize data into predefined classes. Pre-trained models in domains of image recognition or text classification can be fine-tuned to perform domain-specific classification tasks. This process involves taking the general knowledge that a model has gained during pre-training (e.g., recognizing basic patterns, shapes, or semantic features) and refining it to make accurate predictions for a particular set of classes. For instance, an image classification model pre-trained on a large medical imaging dataset can be fine-tuned to classify chest x-rays with a chest mass as benign or malignant masses based on labeled datasets. Sentiment analysis is another example of text classification that can be fine-tuned for.

3. **Adversarial fine-tuning** is a technique used to make LLMs more robust to adversarial attacks or perturbations in the data. This process involves fine-tuning a model by exposing it to intentionally perturbed or adversarial examples—data points

modified to deceive the model—so that it learns to handle these challenges and becomes more resilient.

4. **Contrastive fine-tuning** focuses on teaching a model to differentiate between similar but distinct examples. The model learns to identify the subtle differences between different classes and types of data, for instance, in NLP tasks, this might involve distinguishing between semantically similar but distinct sentences. In vision models, this technique can teach a model to distinguish between visually similar objects. This technique is also being used in literature to enhance the performance of smaller language models. Ukarapol et al. showed a 56% performance gain for the MiniCPM model by using contrastive fine-tuning.

5. **Few-shot and zero-shot fine-tuning** refers to adapting a model for performing tasks where only a few examples per class or instance might be available for training. Few-shot fine-tuning is useful in situations where obtaining a large labeled dataset is expensive or impractical. Zero-shot fine-tuning, on the other hand, refers to models that have been pre-trained in such a way that they can perform new tasks without any explicit task-specific training. This is often achieved by large pre-trained models such as GPT 4.0 that generalize well across tasks after being exposed to a wide variety of data during initial training.

CHAPTER 6 INFERENCE, FINE-TUNING, AND RETRIEVAL-AUGMENTED GENERATION

When to Use RAG versus Fine-Tuning?

In terms of language model optimization, the choice between Retrieval-Augmented Generation (RAG) and fine-tuning depends on specific use cases and available compute resources. RAG is a preferred option for many enterprise applications due to its advantages in security, scalability, and reliability. When using RAG, proprietary data remains within a secured database environment, ensuring strict access control and enhanced data privacy. This is in contrast to fine-tuning, where data becomes part of the model's training set, potentially exposing it to broader access without adequate visibility. From a resource perspective, RAG offers cost efficiency and scalability. Fine-tuning large language models is resource-intensive, demanding substantial time and computational power. RAG, on the other hand, leverages first-party data to generate responses, reducing resource costs at both the computational and human levels. It eliminates the need for extensive training and the laborious process of creating and labeling training sets. Moreover, RAG delivers trustworthy results by consistently utilizing the latest curated datasets (that may be proprietary data or trade knowledge), making it easier to trace and understand the sources of generated outputs.

Fine-tuning, however, has its merits in certain scenarios. It can be beneficial for organizations with specific resources and requirements. By fine-tuning a model with niche domain data, it can excel in tasks that demand specialized knowledge, such as responding to prompts in a particular tone or style, like customer support tickets or confirming appointments. Fine-tuning is also useful for addressing information bias and language-related issues. This approach requires the establishment of efficient data pipelines to make proprietary data accessible for the fine-tuning process. An innovative combination of these techniques is Retrieval-Augmented Fine-Tuning, where fine-tuning is integrated with a retrieval mechanism. This method enables the model to search external knowledge sources, such as databases or document corpora, to gather relevant information before generating or classifying outputs. This approach is particularly useful in tasks requiring access to a broad knowledge base, such as question answering or open-domain dialogue systems.

Example Use Cases

Use Case 1: RAG—Customer Support Knowledge Base

Scenario: A telecom company with 5 million customers needs to provide accurate responses about their constantly changing product offerings, policies, and troubleshooting procedures.

Implementation:

- The company maintains a knowledge base with thousands of documents (product manuals, policy updates, troubleshooting guides).
- These documents change weekly as products and policies evolve.
- The RAG system allows new information to be immediately available without retraining.

Why RAG is better here:

- **Dynamic content**: New products and policy changes can be added to the knowledge base immediately.
- **Factual accuracy**: Responses are grounded in specific, retrievable documents.
- **Resource efficiency**: No need to retrain the model when adding new information.

- **Transparency**: Support agents can see exactly which documents were used to generate responses.
- **Implementation simplicity**: Can be deployed with minimal modifications to the base model.

Resource requirements:

- Vector database for storing embeddings
- Document processing pipeline
- Retrieval mechanism
- Base LLM that remains unchanged

Use Case 2: Fine-Tuning—Medical Diagnosis Assistant

Scenario: A healthcare provider wants to develop an AI assistant that helps physicians with preliminary diagnosis based on patient symptoms, medical history, and lab results.

Implementation:

- Fine-tune a base LLM on thousands of anonymized patient cases with confirmed diagnoses.
- The model learns the specific patterns, medical terminology, and reasoning processes used by physicians.
- The system is deployed in a closed environment where data doesn't change frequently.

Why fine-tuning is better here:

- **Domain-specific behavior**: The model internalizes medical reasoning patterns not present in general LLMs.

- **Reduced hallucination**: Fine-tuning on validated cases reduces incorrect medical information.

- **Inference efficiency**: No need to retrieve and process external documents during diagnosis.

- **Consistent output format**: Responses follow medical reporting standards learned during fine-tuning.

- **Privacy considerations**: Sensitive medical knowledge becomes part of the model parameters rather than stored in a retrievable database.

Resource requirements:

- High-quality labeled dataset of medical cases
- Significant computational resources for training
- Expertise in model training and evaluation
- Processes for validating model outputs against medical standards

In summary, the decision between RAG and fine-tuning should be guided by specific use cases and available resources. While RAG offers security, scalability, and reliability, fine-tuning can be advantageous for niche domain tasks. The combination of these techniques in Retrieval-Augmented Fine-Tuning further expands the capabilities of language models and ensures the models are well-suited for complex tasks.

CHAPTER 6   INFERENCE, FINE-TUNING, AND RETRIEVAL-AUGMENTED GENERATION

Inference

Inference refers to the process of using a trained LLM to generate predictions or outputs based on user-driven new input data. In technical terms, it's the forward pass through the neural network to produce a probability distribution over the vocabulary, from which we sample or select tokens to generate text. For example, given an input prompt "The capital of Greece is," the inference process would involve

1. Tokenizing the input
2. Passing these tokens through the model's layers
3. Generating a probability distribution over the next token
4. Selecting the most probable token (in this case, likely "Athens")
5. Repeating steps 2–4 if generating multiple tokens

It must be noted that LLM training and inference are fundamentally different processes. Briefly, the differences are highlighted below:

Training:

- Involves both forward and backward passes through the neural network.
- Uses large, fixed-size batches of data to update model parameters.
- Requires gradient computation and optimization algorithms (e.g., Adam).
- Intensive on both compute and memory.
  - **Use case**: For a LLM, training might involve processing billions of tokens, computing loss with respect to the next token, and updating weights to minimize this loss,

183

Inference:

- Only involves the forward pass.
- Uses variable batch sizes with few or even one input at a time.
- No gradient computations.
- Relies on high throughput and low latency.
- **Use case**: Given the prompt "Translate hello to French," the model performs a series of forward passes, one token at a time, to generate "bonjour."

Inference is a technically demanding topic, and to grasp it fully, we will introduce its components gradually and build upon them, starting with the prefill and decoding phases. In the initial prefill phase, a LLM processes the user's input by segmenting the text into a sequence of prompt tokens. A token is defined as the fundamental unit of text, representing either a complete word or a subword fragment. For example, in English, a single token typically corresponds to approximately 0.75 words or four characters. The specific tokenizer employed by a LLM to divide text into tokens varies between different models. Once tokenized, each token is transformed into a vector embedding—a numerical representation that the model can interpret and utilize for inference. These embeddings are subsequently processed by the LLM to generate an appropriate and contextually relevant output for the user. Subsequently, during the decoding phase, the LLM generates a sequence of vector embeddings that constitute its response to the given input prompt. These embeddings are then converted into completion tokens, which are produced sequentially, one at a time, until a predefined stopping criterion is met. Such criteria may include reaching a maximum token limit or encountering specific stop words. Upon meeting a stopping condition, the model emits a special *end* token to signal the termination of token generation. Since LLMs

CHAPTER 6 INFERENCE, FINE-TUNING, AND RETRIEVAL-AUGMENTED GENERATION

generate one token per forward propagation (i.e., per pass or iteration), the total number of forward propagations required to complete a response is directly equivalent to the number of generated completion tokens.

Decoding

The output decoding phase is essential for generating coherent and contextually appropriate responses. During this phase, the model selects the most suitable tokens based on specific parameters that govern the randomness and diversity of the generated text. The primary parameters involved in this process are **Top-k**, **Top-p** (nucleus sampling), and **Temperature**.

The **Top-k** parameter restricts the model's token predictions to the top k most probable tokens at each step of generation. By setting a particular value for k, the model is directed to consider only the k highest likelihood tokens, thereby refining the output to conform to desired patterns or constraints. For instance, consider the prompt "The weather today is." If Top-k is set to 3, the model might limit its next word choices to "sunny," "rainy," or "cloudy," ensuring that the response remains relevant and within expected parameters. In contrast, **Top-p** or **nucleus sampling** manages the cumulative probability of token selection. Instead of limiting the number of tokens, Top-p allows the model to generate tokens until the cumulative probability exceeds a predefined threshold p. This approach provides dynamic control over both the length and diversity of the generated text by incorporating less probable tokens as necessary. For example, with Top-p set to 0.9, given the prompt "Artificial intelligence is transforming," the model might consider a broader range of tokens such as "industries," "society," "technology," and "healthcare," as long as their cumulative probability does not exceed 0.9. This method enables the generation of more varied and nuanced responses compared with Top-k.

> **Note** While Top-k offers controlled randomness by limiting the selection to a fixed number of top tokens, Top-p provides dynamic control by allowing the number of considered tokens to vary based on their cumulative probability. This distinction results in different levels of diversity in the generated text, with Top-p generally encouraging more varied outputs.

The **Temperature** parameter further influences the randomness of the output by shaping the probability distribution used to select the next token. Unlike Top-k and Top-p, Temperature does not restrict token selection but modifies the likelihood of each token being chosen. A higher Temperature value, approximately around 1, increases randomness and diversity in the generated text by flattening the probability distribution, making the model more likely to explore a broader range of possible tokens. Conversely, a lower Temperature value, below 1, sharpens the probability distribution, causing the model to favor the most probable tokens and resulting in more focused and deterministic output. A high Temperature promotes creativity by allowing the selection of less probable tokens, while a low Temperature enhances coherence by prioritizing the most likely tokens. Adjusting the Temperature parameter enables users to fine-tune the balance between creativity and reliability in the model's responses, thereby tailoring the output to specific application needs.

By carefully configuring the Top-k, Top-p, and Temperature parameters, a user can exert precise control over the decoding behavior of a LLM during the output phase. This allows for the generation of text that meets specific requirements in terms of randomness, diversity, and adherence to desired user requests, allowing for adaptability to a wide range of applications.

CHAPTER 6   INFERENCE, FINE-TUNING, AND RETRIEVAL-AUGMENTED GENERATION

Attention

The attention mechanism is crucial during inference, and it enables the model to efficiently process and interpret input data to generate accurate and contextually relevant outputs. The attention mechanism facilitates this by dynamically assigning weights to the importance of different tokens in the input sequence, ensuring that each generated token is informed by the most relevant parts of the input. This process relies on three essential components: the **key vector (K)**, **value vector (V)**, and **query vector (Q)**. Although we have talked about Q, K, and V previously, understanding the roles and interactions of these vectors is crucial for comprehending how LLMs maintain coherence during inference:

1. The key vector (K) for a token encapsulates the token's positional and contextual information within the input sequence. It determines the degree of influence, or "attention," that a specific token should exert over others. Essentially, the key vector encodes the characteristics that allow the model to assess the relevance of one token to another during the attention computation. The "key space" of the input sequence, represented by these key vectors, is subsequently compared against the query vectors to evaluate relevance.

2. The value vector (V) carries the substantive content of each token. It holds the actual information that will be utilized in generating the model's output. While the key vectors determine the importance of each token in the context of the sequence, the value vectors provide the necessary information that contributes to the final output based on this importance.

3. The query vector (Q) for each token serves as a probe to interact with all key vectors in the input sequence. It determines how much focus or attention each part of the input should receive relative to the current token being processed. In essence, the query vector seeks out relevant information from the key vectors to inform the generation of the next token in the sequence.

The interplay between queries, keys, and values is analogous to database operations. In databases, data values are indexed by keys, and users retrieve data by issuing queries that match these keys. Similarly, in LLMs, queries generated by the model interact with key vectors to determine relevance through a compatibility function, which computes a weight vector. This weight vector is then used to calculate the attention output as a weighted sum of the value vectors, effectively synthesizing the relevant information needed for the next step in text generation. To optimize this process during inference, attention computations are performed simultaneously across multiple queries, keys, and values by organizing them into matrices. Specifically, a set of queries is packed into a matrix **Q**, while the corresponding keys and values are organized into matrices **K** and **V**, respectively. This matrix-based approach facilitates efficient parallel processing, leveraging hardware capabilities to handle the large-scale computations inherent in LLMs. However, the computation of attention scores involves quadratic scaling with respect to the sequence length. This means that as the input sequence grows longer, the computational resources required increase significantly (increase by square of the input sequence length), posing challenges for scalability and efficiency during inference. To address this, **key–value caching (KVC)** is employed as an optimization strategy.

Key–value caching (KVC) involves storing the key and value vectors from previous tokens as they are processed, creating a reusable cache for subsequent computations. When generating a new token, instead of recalculating these vectors for the entire preceding sequence, the model leverages the cached information, significantly reducing computational overhead. To illustrate this point, consider a model generating a response to the prompt "The capital of France is." As it processes each token, it caches the corresponding key and value vectors. When predicting the next word after "is," it can reference these cached vectors for "The," "capital," "of," and "France," rather than recomputing them. This caching mechanism is particularly beneficial for tasks involving long sequences or iterative generation, such as document summarization or chat-based interactions where context accumulates over time. KVC's efficiency gains are most pronounced in scenarios with extensive input data. For instance, in a document question-answering system processing a 10,000-word article, KVC allows the model to maintain context across the entire document without the prohibitive computational cost of recalculating attention for every token in the sequence for each new prediction. This optimization enables real-time applications that would otherwise be impractical due to latency issues. The technique also supports more efficient memory usage. Rather than retaining the full input sequence in memory, the model only needs to store the cached vectors, which are typically much smaller. This aspect is crucial for handling larger contexts, allowing models to effectively process and understand extensive texts, such as long-form articles or entire books, which is vital for tasks requiring long-term dependencies and comprehensive contextual understanding.

Here's an example that illustrates the purpose of KVC: In real-time language translation systems, such as those used during international conferences, KVC delivers crucial performance improvements when translating long speeches. Without KVC, the translation system would need to recompute attention across all previous tokens for each new word, creating noticeable delays as speeches progress. By implementing KVC, the system maintains a cache of previously computed key–value pairs, reducing computational requirements by approximately 40% and enabling near-instantaneous translations even for hour-long presentations.

CHAPTER 6 INFERENCE, FINE-TUNING, AND RETRIEVAL-AUGMENTED GENERATION

This efficiency boost comes with a modest memory trade-off, typically requiring 2–4 GB of additional RAM to store the cached computations, but the resulting performance gain makes this an exceptional bargain in production environments. For deployed models handling consecutive translation tasks throughout a conference day, KVC not only improves responsiveness but also significantly reduces energy consumption and hardware costs, making advanced language models more accessible and sustainable for organizations with limited computational resources.

In practice, KVC is often implemented alongside other optimizations like attention masking and sparse attention mechanisms. These complementary techniques work together to further reduce computational complexity and memory requirements. For example, sparse attention might limit the model to attending only to certain key tokens in the input, while KVC ensures that the computations for these attended tokens are efficiently reused. After using the cached key–value pairs to compute the attention output, the model proceeds to the prediction or decoding layer. This crucial step involves a final transformation of the attention output, typically through a feedforward neural network, followed by a softmax operation. The result is a probability distribution over the model's entire vocabulary, indicating the likelihood of each token being the next in the sequence. The model can then employ decoding techniques discussed above (such as Top-k or Top-p) for sampling to select the next token and produce a meaningful output.

It's important to note the explanation above provides a simplified overview of LLM inference. In practical deployments, LLMs are composed of multiple transformer blocks, each containing multi-head attention modules and feedforward layers. These multi-head attention mechanisms allow the model to attend to different parts of the input sequence simultaneously, enhancing its ability to capture complex patterns within text. To address the computational challenges associated with processing large amounts of data, various optimization techniques have been

CHAPTER 6   INFERENCE, FINE-TUNING, AND RETRIEVAL-AUGMENTED GENERATION

developed. One such technique is Grouped Query Attention, a variation of the attention mechanism designed to improve computational efficiency and scalability.

Grouped Query Attention (GQA) introduces a solution by partitioning the input data into smaller groups, allowing the model to compute attention within each group rather than across the entire sequence. This approach significantly lowers the computational cost while maintaining the ability to capture important dependencies between elements within groups. The model first splits the queries into predefined groups, with each group computing attention scores against a subset of the input data. This grouping can be based on various factors, such as similarity in content or spatial proximity in vision tasks. By focusing attention on smaller regions, GQA makes the model more efficient and faster, particularly when processing large inputs, without sacrificing too much in terms of accuracy. It is especially useful in scenarios where local context is more critical than global relationships, such as in processing long documents, video frames, or large images. This technique strikes a balance between capturing important local dependencies and reducing the computational burden associated with full self-attention across long sequences. The combination of key–value caching, Grouped Query Attention, and other efficient attention computation strategies ensures that LLMs can scale effectively, maintaining performance even as the complexity and length of input sequences increase.

Now that we have all the components of inference in place, let us run through an example of running inference, end to end:

1. **Input reception**: The system receives a user's input, such as a question or prompt. For example, "Explain the process of photosynthesis in simple terms."

2. **Tokenization**: The input is converted into tokens that the model can process. Each word or subword becomes a token in the model's vocabulary.

3. **Prefill/prompt phase:** Based on the tokenized input, the model predicts the very first output token. This first token prediction is referred to as the *prefill or prompt phase*. Since the entire input sequence of tokens is known in the prefill phase, the inference accelerator can compute the key-value pairs and query vectors for all input tokens in parallel and predict the next output token by executing the model with the Q, K, and V vectors. In our example, this might be "Photosynthesis."

4. **Feedback loop initiation:** The generated token is appended to the input sequence, creating an updated input.

5. **Sequential prediction (decode phase):** The updated input sequence is fed back into the trained model, which then generates the next token. When generating this output token, the model needs to compute the key-value pairs for all the tokens in the updated input sequence, which is essentially the previous input sequence concatenated with the previous output token. By saving the key-value pairs computed in the previous iteration, the LLM inference system can retrieve previously computed key-value pairs from memory. This caching of key-value pairs is done to save compute cycles of the inference accelerators at the expense of increasing the memory requirements during inference.

6. **Token addition:** A newly predicted token is added to the output sequence.

CHAPTER 6   INFERENCE, FINE-TUNING, AND RETRIEVAL-AUGMENTED GENERATION

7. **Context updating**: The model's internal state is updated to reflect the new token, maintaining context for future predictions.

8. **Repetition**: Steps 5–8 are repeated, with each new token influencing subsequent predictions.

9. **Termination check**: After each token generation, the system checks if any termination criteria are met including maximum sequence length reached, end-of-sequence (EOS) token generated, or contextual completion achieved.

10. **Post-processing**: The generated token sequence is converted back into human-readable text.

11. **Output delivery**: The final, coherent response is presented to the user.

Inference Metrics

A few key metrics are often used to compare/evaluate different LLM serving systems:

1. **Time To First Token (TTFT)**: This metric measures the responsiveness of a LLM in terms of the time needed from receiving an input prompt to generating the first token of response. This metric is particularly critical for real-time, user-facing applications where immediate feedback is essential. TTFT is influenced by several factors including the scheduling algorithm used by the model server, model partitioning across inference accelerators in the cluster, the accelerator's performance, and

interconnect latency within the cluster. A low TTFT indicates high responsiveness and is crucial for maintaining user engagement in interactive chatbot-like applications.

2. **Time Per Output Token (TPOT):** The average time taken by a model to generate each token in the response. This metric assesses how a user perceives the model's speed, for instance, if the TPOT is 50 milliseconds per token, that would result in 1,200 tokens processed in one minute. Considering that some tokens may represent partial words, 1,200 tokens would typically correspond to about 900 words. At this speed—900 words per minute (WPM)—it's much faster than the average reading rate for most people, which is around 200–300 WPM.

3. **Prefill time:** The time taken by a model to process all the input tokens from a user's prompt before generating the first complete token (i.e., time taken to complete the prefill stage). This metric is related to TTFT and measures the initial responsiveness of the LLM.

4. **Queuing time:** In real-world scenarios, inferencing requests are constrained by GPU memory and cannot be processed immediately. To that end, requests are placed in a queue, and queuing time reflects the waiting period before a request is processed. This contributes to TTFT, and this metric provides a better understanding of how a LLM handles large inference volumes as well as real-world performance under high loads.

5. **Throughput**: During inference, this is the total number of output tokens that a LLM can generate per second, across all user requests. Throughput allows for a more practical understanding of a LLM's processing capacity and is usually expressed either as requests per second (the number of inference requests processed by a LLM per second) or as tokens per second (the number of output tokens generated by a LLM across all user requests per second). These two metrics are also good surrogates for measuring a user's perceived speed and efficiency of inference.

6. **End-to-end request latency**: A comprehensive metric that captures the total time from submission of a query to full response generation and reception by user. This includes all aspects of inference serving including the queue mechanisms, batch processing time, and network latency, providing a more holistic view of the system's performance when interacting with a user.

7. **Tail latency**: Refers to the response time for a request during high-load scenarios (for instance, the 99th percentile load). This would represent the worst-case scenario with regard to latency and represents a small fraction of requests in user-facing LLMs. High tail latency can impact user experience even if the average latency is lower.

8. **Model FLOPS utilization (MFU)**: The ratio of observed throughput to the theoretical maximum throughput based on the hardware accelerator used for inference. This metric helps in assessing how efficiently a LLM is using the available compute resources.

TPOT and TTFT are important metrics to track user engagement with a LLM application. The total latency for the response is the sum of TTFT and TPOT multiplied by the number of tokens generated. For any inference system, getting the lowest TTFT and TPOT per user and the highest throughput is ideal; however, increasing the throughput is technically bound by hardware constraints, specifically inference accelerator memory limitations. Each user's inference requests take up significant GPU memory to store the key–value pairs, and the difference in user prompt lengths creates complex queue schedules for inference execution.

Request Batching

As previously discussed, the decode phase is memory-intensive because parameters and key–value pairs are read from the GPU memory to compute the next token. In order to optimize GPU utilization and increase throughput, inferencing systems often batch together multiple user prompts to undergo inference. By batching, the parameter loading cost can be spread across all user requests, and GPU compute can be used more efficiently by doing parallel processing across large batches. There are two main types of batching techniques:

1. **Static batching (naïve batching)**: The default approach where multiple user prompts are collected and grouped into a batch. The entire batch undergoes processing, and responses are generated

when all requests in the batch are complete. Although this is straightforward to implement, this method introduces latency as a user will receive a response only after the entire batch finishes processing.

2. **Continuous batching (in-flight batching)**: A more advanced approach where new requests replace completed ones from a batch. This improves compute efficiency as it ensures the GPU is continuously processing new requests, thereby reducing idle time for the user. Using continuous batching, we can minimize the wait time for user requests compared with the static alternatives.

Batching significantly improves LLM efficiency; however, it introduces a trade-off between throughput and latency: larger batch sizes generally result in higher throughput but can lead to increased latency for individual requests. To that end, more efficient continuous batching methods are needed to optimize LLM performance while maintaining acceptable response time for users.

Summary

In this chapter, we described the fundamentals of RAG, recent advances in the field, and the basis of fine-tuning. Our main goal here was to provide practical advice on understanding when to use RAG and when to fine-tune an existing LLM. After this initial discussion, we described fine-tuning and went into the technical details of inference, how a LLM constructs responses, as well as metrics to measure LLM latency. In the following chapters, we will explore these concepts in the context of live LLM-based applications.

CHAPTER 6   INFERENCE, FINE-TUNING, AND RETRIEVAL-AUGMENTED GENERATION

Bibliography

Gao, Y., Liu, H., Yin, S., Yang, Z., Chang, W., Yan, R., & Zhang, X. (2023). Retrieval-Augmented Generation for Large Language Models: A Survey. arXiv. https://arxiv.org/abs/2312.10997

Lewis, P., Perez, E., Piktus, A., Petroni, F., Karpukhin, V., Goyal, N., Küttler, H., Lewis, M., Yih, W., Rocktäschel, T., Riedel, S., & Kiela, D. (2021). Retrieval-Augmented Generation for Knowledge-Intensive NLP Tasks. arXiv. https://arxiv.org/abs/2005.11401

Zhao, S., Xiong, C., Chen, X., Wei, D., Miao, Y., & Wang, S. (2024). Retrieval Augmented Generation (RAG) and Beyond: A Comprehensive Survey on How to Make your LLMs use External Data More Wisely. arXiv. https://arxiv.org/abs/2409.14924

Hichri, H. (2024). KV Caching Explained: Optimizing Transformer Inference Efficiency. Hugging Face Blog. https://huggingface.co/blog/not-lain/kv-caching

Ghimire, R. (2023). Transformers Optimization: Part 1—KV Cache. Personal Blog. https://r4j4n.github.io/blogs/posts/kv/

Omri, M. (2024). Techniques for KV Cache Optimization in Large Language Models. Personal Blog. https://www.omrimallis.com/posts/techniques-for-kv-cache-optimization/

Feng, Y., Lv, J., Cao, Y., Xie, X., & Zhou, S. K. (2024). Identify Critical KV Cache in LLM Inference from an Output Perturbation Perspective. arXiv. https://arxiv.org/abs/2502.03805

IBM Research. (2024). What is retrieval-augmented generation (RAG)? IBM Research Blog. https://research.ibm.com/blog/retrieval-augmented-generation-RAG

IBM. (2024). RAG vs. Fine-tuning. IBM Think Topics. https://www.ibm.com/think/topics/rag-vs-fine-tuning

NVIDIA. (2024). Mastering LLM Techniques: Inference Optimization. NVIDIA Technical Blog. https://developer.nvidia.com/blog/mastering-llm-techniques-inference-optimization/

CHAPTER 6   INFERENCE, FINE-TUNING, AND RETRIEVAL-AUGMENTED GENERATION

AWS. (2024). What is RAG?—Retrieval-Augmented Generation AI Explained. Amazon Web Services. `https://aws.amazon.com/what-is/retrieval-augmented-generation/`

Dai, J., Huang, Z., Jiang, H., Chen, C., Cai, D., Bi, W., & Shi, S. (2024). CORM: Cache Optimization with Recent Message for Large Language Model Inference. Listed in GitHub repository: `https://github.com/October2001/Awesome-KV-Cache-Compression`

Ukarapol, T., Lee, Z., & Xin, A. (2024). Improving Text Embeddings for Smaller Language Models Using Contrastive Fine-tuning. arXiv preprint arXiv:2408.00690.

CHAPTER 7

Unpacking Ethereum

Ethereum is an open source, decentralized blockchain platform with computational capabilities that reconstructs an elementary currency exchange into a transfer of value between users via a scripting language. Ethereum is widely recognized as a successor to the Bitcoin protocol, generalizing the original ideas and enabling a more diverse array of applications to be built on top of the blockchain technology. Ethereum has two essential components. First, there is a Turing-complete virtual processor that can load resources and execute scripts called the Ethereum Virtual Machine (EVM). The second component is a token of value called ether, which is the currency of the network and is used for user-to-user transactions or compensation to miners of the network. In this chapter, we begin our journey with an overview of Ethereum's architecture in comparison to Bitcoin, focusing on the EVM and Turing-completeness properties. Following the overview of its architecture, there is a short discussion of the accounts model in Ethereum and account representation with Merkle-Patricia trees. This will lead us to the topics of global state representation in Ethereum, account storage, and gas, which is a spam prevention mechanism in the network. Then, we deconstruct the notion of a smart contract enabled by the EVM, the security concerns revolving around sandboxing executable code, and how the EVM pushes executable code (bytecode) to the blockchain. After that, we provide an introduction to Solidity and Vyper, two programming languages used for writing smart contracts in Ethereum. We explore the syntax of Solidity and Vyper, as well as the popular integrated development environments (IDEs) being used, and provide a brief list of key developer resources. Next, we focus on the world computer model proposed in Ethereum and introduce supporting decentralized technologies such as IPFS and Whisper. Then, we look at the state of decentralized apps (DApps) along the publishing platform called Mist available in Ethereum. This allows us to transition into talking about the Layer 2 updates to Ethereum—the major technical focus of this chapter and the maturation of the Ethereum ecosystem beyond 2020. Then, we will introduce the enterprise aspect of Ethereum, Blockchain-as-a-Service (BaaS) deployed on the Azure cloud by Microsoft. The chapter will conclude with an overview of recent technical proposals in Ethereum, the status of Layer 2 upgrades, and exciting changes on the horizon.

Overview of Ethereum

It was around mid-2013 when a majority of the Bitcoin community was starting to flirt with the idea of applications beyond currency on the blockchain. Fairly soon, there was a flood of new ideas being discussed in online forums. A few popular examples included domain registration, asset insurance, voting, and even Internet of Things (IoT). After the hype started to fade away, a more serious analysis of the Bitcoin protocol revealed severe limitations of potential applications that can be built on top of the blockchain.

A crucial point of debate was whether a full scripting language should be allowed on the blockchain or whether we should build applications with logic residing outside of the blockchain. There were two key issues that sparked this debate:

- The scripting language and opcodes in the Bitcoin protocol were designed to be very limited in functionality.

- The Bitcoin protocol itself was not generalizable. There were attempts; for instance, Namecoin was designed for one specific task (domain name registration). The big question at the time was: how can a protocol be generalized such that it becomes forward-compatible with future applications that we know nothing about?

Eventually, two schools of thought emerged regarding scripting. Traditionally, Satoshi's paper proposed to keep the scripting language very limited in functionality. This would avoid the security concerns of having executable code in the blockchain. In a sense, the blockchain's executable code is limited to a handful of necessary primitives that update the distributed states. The second school of thought was championed by Vitalik Buterin, who thought of the blockchain as more than just a ledger. He envisioned the blockchain as a computational platform that could execute well-defined functions using contracts and arguments. This is made possible by the Ethereum Virtual Machine (EVM). The EVM allows for complete isolation of the executable code and safe execution of the applications built on the blockchain. We will return to discuss this at greater length later in the chapter. Let's begin with the core design principle behind Ethereum.

Core Idea Instead of building a blockchain platform to support specific applications, in Ethereum we will build a native programming language with extensibility to implement business logic on the blockchain platform using the language.

We will return shortly to understand the implications of this principle. In the meantime, let's talk about another distinguishing feature in Ethereum: the consensus algorithm. We discussed the concept of consensus in earlier chapters. In proof-of-work (PoW)–based

CHAPTER 7 UNPACKING ETHEREUM

cryptocurrencies such as Bitcoin, the network awards miners who solve cryptographic puzzles to validate transactions and mine new blocks. Ethereum proposes a different consensus algorithm called proof of stake (PoS). In a PoS algorithm, the validator/creator of the next block is chosen in a pseudo-random manner based on the stake that an account has in the network. Therefore, if you have a higher stake in the network, you have a higher chance of being selected as a validator. The validator will then "forge" the next block and get a reward from the network. Here, the validator is truly forging a block (in the blacksmith sense of the term) instead of mining, because in PoS, the idea of hardware-based mining is replaced by a virtual stake. One rationale behind using PoS was to circumvent the high power consumption and energy requirements of PoW-mining algorithms that translated to higher electricity bills and became a frequent complaint. Peercoin was the first cryptocurrency to launch with PoS; however, recently more prominent PoS implementations can be seen in ShadowCash, Nxt, and Qora. The main differences between Bitcoin and Ethereum as protocols are highlighted in Figure 7-1.

Note The current implementation of Ethereum (also known as Ethereum 1.0) uses proof of work as the consensus algorithm. However, the Layer 2.0 updates to Ethereum plan for a transition to proof of stake as the main consensus algorithm. More details regarding this algorithm are provided later in the chapter.

The following is a brief summary of PoS written by Ethereum community developers (https://docs.ethhub.io/ethereum-roadmap/ethereum-2.0/proof-of-stake/):

> ***Proof of Stake (PoS) is a category of consensus algorithms for public blockchains that depend on a validator's economic stake in the network.*** *In proof of work (PoW) based public blockchains (e.g. Bitcoin and the current*

CHAPTER 7 UNPACKING ETHEREUM

*implementation of Ethereum), the algorithm rewards participants who solve cryptographic puzzles in order to validate transactions and create new blocks (i.e. mining). In PoS-based public blockchains (e.g. Ethereum's upcoming Casper implementation), a set of validators take turns proposing and voting on the next block, and the weight of each validator's vote depends on the size of its deposit (i.e. stake). Significant advantages of PoS include **security, reduced risk of centralization, and energy efficiency**.*

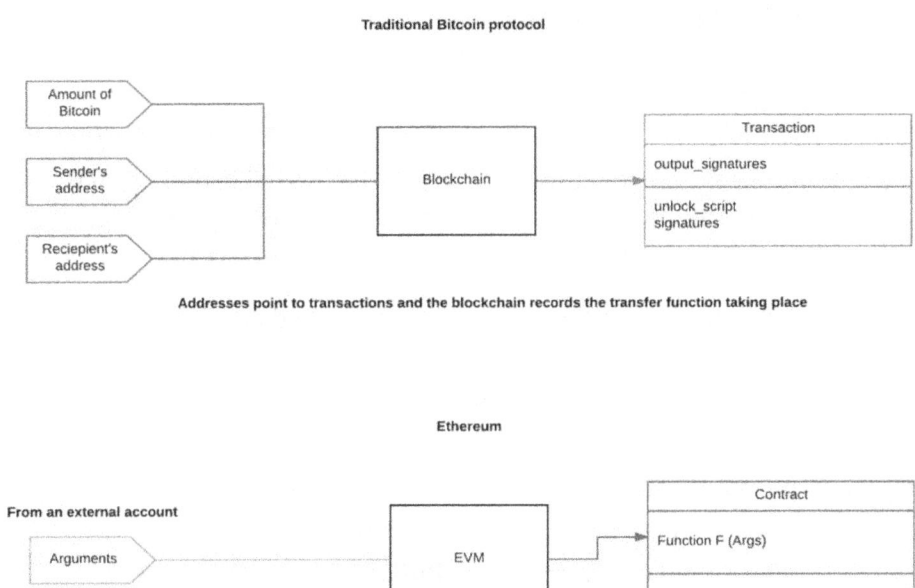

Figure 7-1. *Overview of Bitcoin and Ethereum as computational platforms*

Focusing on Figure 7-1, in the Bitcoin protocol, addresses map the transactions from sender to receiver. The only program that runs on the blockchain is the transfer program; given the addresses and the key signature, this program can transfer money from one user to another.

CHAPTER 7   UNPACKING ETHEREUM

Ethereum generalizes this concept by placing an EVM at every node so that verifiable code can be executed on the blockchain. Here, the general scheme is that an external account will pass arguments to a function, and the EVM will direct that call to the appropriate contract and execute the function, granted the appropriate amount of ether and gas are supplied. As a consequence, every transaction in Ethereum can be considered a function call.

Accounts in Ethereum

Accounts are a meta-structure in Ethereum and the fundamental operational unit of the blockchain. All Ethereum transactions require an account. Alternatively, accounts also serve as a model to store and track information on the users in the network. There are two types of accounts available on the network:

1. **User accounts**: These are user-controlled accounts, also known as external accounts. These accounts have an ether balance, are controlled by public–private keypairs, and can send transactions, but have no associated code. All actions in the Ethereum network are triggered by transactions initiated by external accounts. In the Bitcoin protocols, we referred to these simply as addresses. The key difference between accounts and addresses is the ability to contain and execute generalized code in Ethereum.

CHAPTER 7   UNPACKING ETHEREUM

2. **Contracts**: This is essentially an account controlled by its own code. A contract account is the functional programmatic unit in Ethereum that resides on the blockchain. This account has an ether balance, has associated code, can execute code when triggered by transactions received from other accounts, and can manipulate its own persistent storage. (Every contract on the blockchain has its own storage only it can write to; this is known as the contract's state.) Any member on the network can create an application with some arbitrary rules, defining it as a contract.

If accounts play such a key role, how are they represented on the blockchain? Accounts become an element of the Merkle trees, which in turn are an element of every block header. Ethereum uses a modified form of the binary Merkle trees called Merkle-Patricia trees. A complete explanation of the Merkle-Patricia tree (http://www.emsec.rub.de/media/crypto/attachments/files/2011/04/becker_1.pdf) would be beyond the scope of this text; however, a graphical synopsis is provided in Figure 7-2.

Note   The two-account system explained here may not remain in Ethereum for the long term. Recently, there has been more push toward a one-account model, where user accounts are implemented by using contracts.

207

CHAPTER 7 UNPACKING ETHEREUM

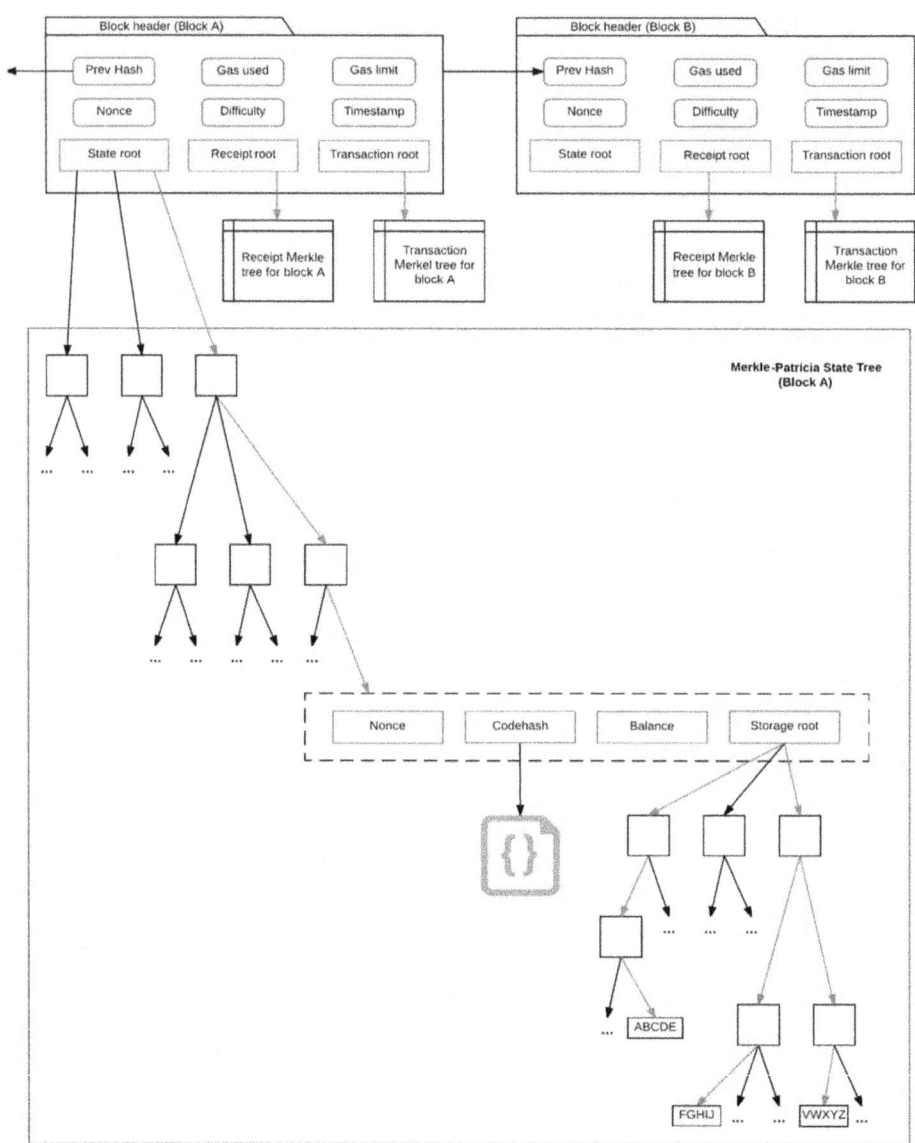

Figure 7-2. *Overview of block headers and Merkle-Patricia trees for Blocks A and B*

In Figure 7-2, the block header contains a few standard definitions that broadcast the status of the network. Additionally, every block header in Ethereum has three Merkle-Patricia trees for three different objects: transactions (function calls), receipts (the results of a function call, recording the effect of each transaction), and state objects. Binary trees are useful in managing transaction histories; however, the state has multiple components that need to be updated more frequently. The Merkle-Patricia tree shown contains a state root that further records multiple account objects. One of the deep branches points to a dashed box containing the four parameters that define an account. From these parameters, the balance of an account and the nonce for the network are often updated. Therefore, a more suitable data structure is necessary where we can rapidly calculate a new tree root after an insert, update, edit, or delete operation without needing to recompute the entire tree. This modified Merkle tree allows for rapid queries to questions such as the following: Does this account exist? Has this transaction been included in a particular block? What is the current balance of my account? Of note, the balance is only relevant for an external account, and similarly, the codehash (which holds executable code) is only applicable to contracts. Storage root is the final parameter and contains data uploaded by a user to the blockchain or serves as internal storage available to a contract. This internal storage can be updated by the contract during the execution phase. Let's talk about these account parameters in depth.

State, Storage, and Gas

We briefly mentioned that a contract can manipulate its own storage and update the state, so what is a *state*? Recall that in the Bitcoin protocol, data on users and transactions is framed and stored in the context of UTXOs (unspent transaction outputs). Ethereum employs a different design strategy of using a state object. Essentially, the state stores a list of accounts, where each account has a balance, as well as blockchain-specific information (code and data storage). A transaction is considered valid if the sending account has enough balance to pay for it (avoiding double spending); therefore, the sending account is debited, and the receiving account is credited with the value. If the receiving account has code associated with it, the code will run when the transaction is received. The execution of a contract or the code associated with an account can have different effects on the state: internal storage may also be changed, or the code may even create additional transactions to other accounts.

Ethereum makes a distinction between state and history in the network. The state is essentially a snapshot of current information regarding network state and accounts at a given time. On the other hand, history is a compilation of all the events that have taken place on the blockchain such as function calls (transactions) and the changes brought about as a result (receipts). Most nodes in the Ethereum network keep a record of the state. More formally, the state is a data structure that contains key-value maps (KVMs) in order to map addresses onto account objects. Each account object contains four values:

- Current nonce value
- Account balance (in ether)
- Codehash, which contains code in the case of contracts, but remains empty for external accounts
- Storage tree root, which is the root of the Merkle-Patricia tree that contains code and data stored on the blockchain

Next, let's talk about gas in Ethereum. Gas is the internal unit for measuring computational effort required to execute operations on the Ethereum network. The gas fee is calculated as the amount of gas used multiplied by the cost per unit gas, typically quoted in gwei (one-billionth of an ETH). In other words, it is a microtransaction fee for performing a computation on the blockchain. For a computational platform like Ethereum, this becomes crucial when running code because of the Halting problem: one cannot tell whether a program will run indefinitely or just has a long runtime. Gas puts a limiter on the runtime as the user has to pay for executing step-by-step instructions of a contract. The nature of microtransactions allows steps to be executed very inexpensively, but even those transactions will add up for very long runtimes. Once the gas supplied for a contract exhausts, the user would have to pay for more to continue. Special gas fees are also applied to operations that take up storage. Importantly, gas costs vary depending on the complexity and type of computational operations performed. Simple operations like transferring ETH between wallets typically require 21,000 gas units, while interacting with smart contracts can consume significantly more gas—sometimes 100,000+ units for complex decentralized finance (DeFi) operations. Each low-level operation (opcode) in the Ethereum Virtual Machine has a predefined gas cost associated with it—for example, basic arithmetic operations like ADD cost 3 gas, while more complex operations like MUL cost 5 gas. Operations that expand memory usage incur additional costs based on the existing memory size, and storage operations are particularly expensive as they make permanent changes to the blockchain state. This granular fee structure ensures that users pay proportionally to the computational resources their transactions consume, preventing network abuse while maintaining a fair economic model for validators who process transactions. With upcoming Ethereum improvements, gas efficiency continues to be optimized, particularly through Layer 2 scaling solutions.

So let's talk about storage next. In Ethereum, external accounts can store data on the blockchain using contracts. A contract would manage the upload and storage process; however, the data types that can be stored currently are very limited. Then, a natural question becomes: What are the limits on uploading content and information to the Ethereum blockchain? What would prevent the bloating of the blockchain? As it turns out, there are currently two mechanisms in place preventing a data overload:

- Gas limits per block that dictate how much gas can be spent per block on storage/computational operations
- Amount of money a user would have to spend to purchase the gas needed to store data

The second limitation is usually a deterrent for users to store directly on the blockchain. Instead it becomes much more efficient and economic to use a third-party decentralized service like STORJ or IPFS for the storage and hash the location in Ethereum to include it in a contract. In the future, new distributed storage applications will allow for all sorts of data files to be uploaded and included in contracts on the blockchain.

Let's summarize what we have discussed so far. We started with the differences between Bitcoin and Ethereum regarding using accounts, charging gas for operations, storing data directly on the blockchain, allowing executable code on the blockchain, state objects, and Merkle-Patricia trees. Figure 7-3 provides a simplified functional overview of the processes occurring in Ethereum.

CHAPTER 7 UNPACKING ETHEREUM

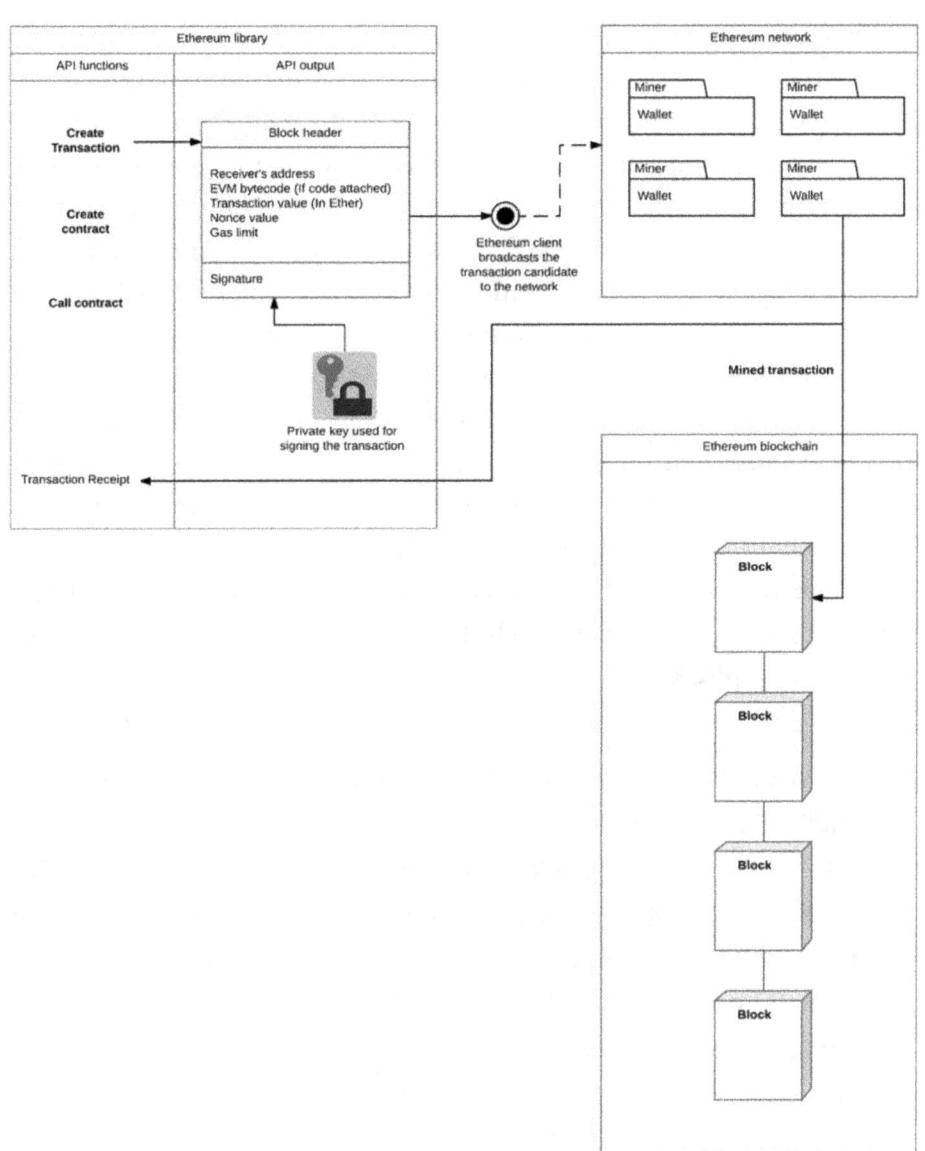

Figure 7-3. *A simplified overview of the Ethereum network*

CHAPTER 7 UNPACKING ETHEREUM

In Figure 7-3, there are roughly three Ethereum components to discuss: the API, the network, and the blockchain. The Ethereum JavaScript API (also known as web3.js) provides a large feature set for functionality such as constructing transactions and contracts, referring to functions, and storing receipts. An enhanced wallet client for Ethereum such as Mist can take over several of these functions with a GUI. Once a candidate block is constructed, it is broadcasted to the network by the Ethereum client. The validators on the network determine if the transactions are valid and if any code (in the block) associated with a transaction or a contract is valid. Once the validation is complete, the validators execute the associated code and apply it to the current state. The block is broadcasted to the network, and a miner will "forge" the block; the verified block is then added to the blockchain. This step will also create transaction receipts for every transaction included in the block. The new block also provides updates to the state objects and relational links for the state tree from the current block to a new block.

Note What will prevent the Ethereum network from being bloated by small, unused contracts? Currently, there are no mechanisms to control the lifespan of a contract; however, there are a few proposals in the air about temporary subscription-based contracts. In the future, there might be two different types of contracts—one that has a permanent lifespan (which is significantly more expensive to create and compute) and the other one that operates till its subscription expires (cheaper and temporary, self-destructs after subscription runs out to prevent cluttering).

Ethereum Virtual Machine

Formally, the Ethereum Virtual Machine (EVM) is the runtime environment for smart contracts in Ethereum. Contracts are written in a higher-level language (for instance, Solidity) and then compiled into bytecode using an interpreter in the EVM. This bytecode is then uploaded to the blockchain using an Ethereum client. Contracts live on the blockchain in this executable bytecode form. The EVM is designed to be completely isolated from the environment and the rest of the network. The code running inside the EVM has no access to the network or any other processes; only after being compiled to bytecode do contracts have access to the external world and other contracts.

From an operational standpoint, the EVM behaves as a large, decentralized computer with millions of objects (accounts) that have the ability to maintain an internal database, execute code, and talk to each other through message passing. This model is not yet complete, however. In Ethereum, this concept is often referred to as the idea of a "world computer." Let's return to the topic of code execution on the EVM and how it is intimately linked to consensus. The EVM allows any user on the network to execute arbitrary code in a trustless environment where the outcome is fully deterministic and the execution can be guaranteed. In a simple contract that executes a read function, no account edits happen, and the state of all the accounts remains the same. However, as we mentioned before, any user can trigger an action by sending a transaction from an external account. We can have two outcomes here: If the receiver is another external account, then the transaction will transfer some ether but nothing else happens. However, if the receiver is a contract, then the contract becomes activated and executes the code within. Executing code within the network takes time, and the process is relatively slow and costly. For every step of executable instructions, the user is charged gas. When a user initiates an execution through a transaction, they commit an upper limit for the maximum currency that they are willing to pay as gas for that contract or code.

Tip Ethereum has recently begun the process of migrating over to a Just-In-Time virtual machine (VM), which offers some optimizations in gas usage and performance.

What does it mean for the outcome of the EVM to be deterministic? It is essential for every node to reach an identical final state given the same input to a contract code. Otherwise, each node that executes the contract code to validate the transaction would end up with different results and no consensus would be possible. This is the deterministic nature of the EVM that allows every node to reach consensus on the execution of a contract and the same final state of accounts. The nodes executing a contract are similar to cogs synchronized to move inside of a clock; they work in a harmonious fashion and reach a matching final state. A contract can also refer to other contracts, but it can't directly access the internal storage of another contract. Every contract runs in a dedicated and private instance of the EVM where it only has access to some input data, its internal storage, the code of other contracts on the blockchain, and various blockchain parameters such as recent block hashes.

Every full node on the network executes the contract code simultaneously for each transaction. When a node is validating a block, transactions are executed sequentially, in the order specified by the block. This is necessary because a block might contain multiple transactions that call upon the same contract, and the current state of a contract might depend on state modified by previous references during the code execution. Executing contract code is relatively expensive, so when nodes receive a block, they only do a basic check on the transactions: Does the sending account have enough ether to pay for gas? Does the transaction

CHAPTER 7   UNPACKING ETHEREUM

have a valid signature? Then, mining nodes perform the relatively expensive task of executing the transaction, include it in a block, and collect the transaction fee as a reward. When a full node receives a block, it executes the transactions in the block to independently verify the security and integrity of the transactions to be included in the blockchain. Let's look at the EVM visually in Figure 7-4.

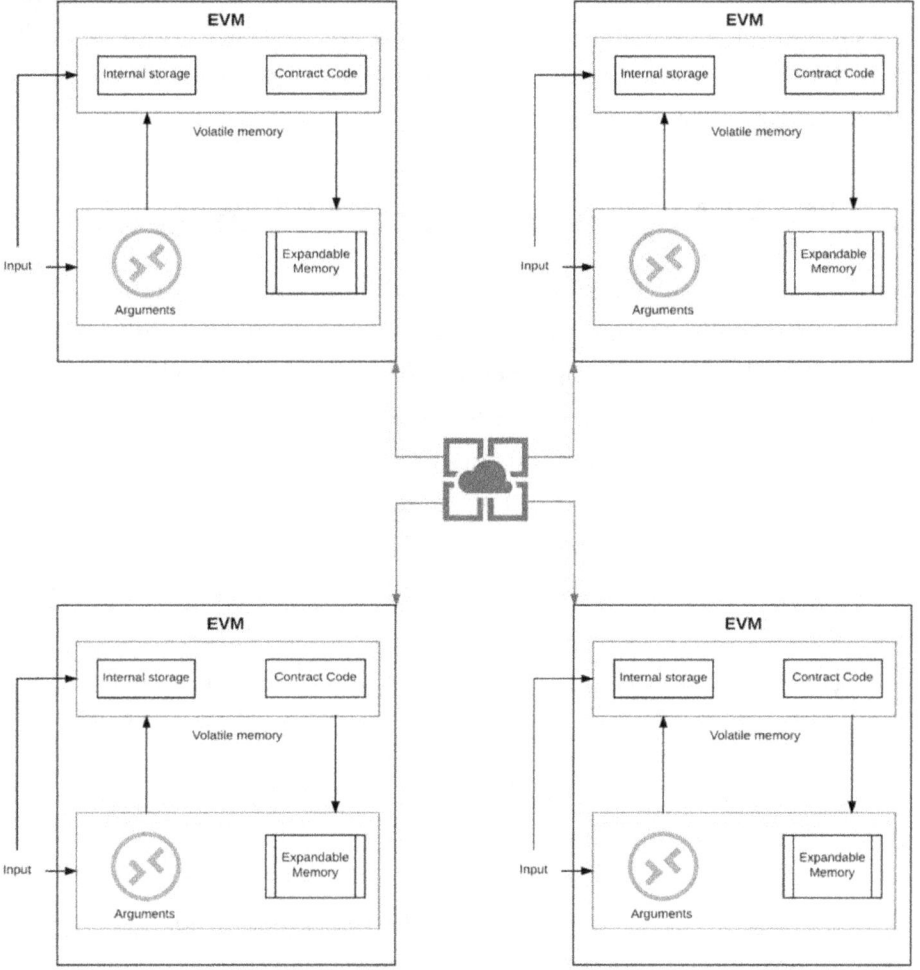

Figure 7-4. *Four instances of the Ethereum Virtual Machine running on four different nodes*

217

In Figure 7-4, the four EVMs are synchronously executing a contract's instructions and will arrive at an identical account state once the execution has been completed. This is due to the deterministic nature of the EVM, which allows the contract to reach consensus across the network at every step of instructions. The EVM has a very straightforward rationale: it has a single run loop that will attempt to execute the instruction one step at a time. Within this loop, the gas is calculated for each instruction, and the allocated memory is expanded if necessary. The loop will continue until the VM either receives an exit code indicating successful execution or throws an exception such as out-of-gas.

Solidity and Vyper Programming Languages

Solidity is a higher-level, contract-oriented programming language for writing smart contracts in Ethereum. Any code written in Solidity can be executed on the EVM after being compiled into bytecode, which is an instruction set for the EVM. How does the bytecode encode references to other functions and contracts that are called during execution? This is done by using an Application Binary Interface (ABI). In general, an ABI is the interface between two program modules: machine-level instructions and a human-readable higher-level programming language. Let's break down this answer into three components:

- **Contract**: A contract is simply higher-level code defined in a formal language such as Solidity.

- **Compiled contract**: The contract is converted to bytecode to be executed on the Ethereum Virtual Machine (EVM), adhering to the compiler's specifications. Note that function names and input parameters get hashed and obfuscated during compilation. Therefore, for another account to call a function, it must have access to the given function name and arguments, and we need another layer that interfaces encoding into and out of the bytecode.

- **Application Binary Interface (ABI)**: An ABI is a list of the contract's function definitions and arguments in JSON format. The function definitions and input arguments are hashed into the ABI. This is included in the data of a transaction and interpreted by the EVM at the target account. An ABI is necessary so that you can specify which function in the contract to invoke, as well as get a guarantee that the function will return data in the format you are expecting.

Solidity has a plugin available for Visual Studio to help write smart contracts in a powerful IDE and deploy them to the Ethereum network. Our discussion of Solidity here will not cover advanced implementations or definitions. Instead, we will be limiting the upcoming discussion to the fundamentals such as storing variables and creating a simple contract. Let's get started:

```
/* defining a contract */
contract ExampleStorage {
   uint storedNumber; //unsigned integer (uint) used to declare
                     a state variable
/* Function set can modify the value of the state variable */
   function set(uint x) {
     storedNumber = x;
   }
/* Function get can retrieve the value of state variable */
   function get() constant returns (uint retVal) {
     return storedData;
   }
}
```

CHAPTER 7   UNPACKING ETHEREUM

This storage contract allows a user to store an integer as a state variable storedNumber and then modify or retrieve its value using the get() and set() functions. Solidity also offers several advanced features available in modern programming languages, such as inheritance (for contracts), function overloading, and class interfaces. Next, let's look at a more complex example of a contract. This time we will create a simple bank contract using Solidity:

```
// This bank contract allows deposits, withdrawals, and
   checking the balance
// 'contract' is a keyword to declare class, similar to any
   other OOP
contract SimpleBank {
// 'mapping' is a dictionary that maps address objects to
   balances
// 'private' means that other contracts can't directly query
   balances
   mapping (address => uint) private balances;
// 'public' makes externally readable by users or contracts on
   the blockchain
   address public owner;
// Events trigger messages throughout the Ethereum network
   event LogDepositMade(address accountAddress, uint amount);
// Constructor
   function SimpleBank() {
     // msg provides details about the message that's sent to
        the contract
     // msg.sender is the address of contract creator
     owner = msg.sender;
   }
   // Deposit ether into the bank
   // Returns the balance of the user after a deposit is made
```

```
    function deposit() public returns (uint) {
// Add the value being deposited to the account balance
    balances[msg.sender] += msg.value;
// Log the deposit that was just made
    LogDepositMade(msg.sender, msg.value);
// Return the balance after the deposit
    return balances[msg.sender];
  }
// Withdraw ether from bank
// withdrawAmount is the amount you want to withdraw
// Returns the balance remaining for the user
  function withdraw(uint withdrawAmount) public returns (uint
  remainingBal) {
/* If the account balance is greater than amount requested for
  withdrawal, subtract it from the balance */
    if(balances[msg.sender] >= withdrawAmount) {
      balances[msg.sender] -= withdrawAmount;
// Increment the balance back to the original account on fail
      if (!msg.sender.send(withdrawAmount)) {
        balances[msg.sender] += withdrawAmount;
      }
    }
// Return the remaining balance after withdrawl
    return balances[msg.sender];
  }
// Return the balance of the user
// 'constant' prevents function from editing state variables;
  function balance() constant returns (uint) {
    return balances[msg.sender];
  }
}
```

Although this contract has plenty of moving parts, it has a straightforward schematic. We start by declaring state variables, and here we use an advanced data type called a mapping. Then, we declare an address variable used throughout the contract and an event logger. The constructor prepares the owner object to be usable, and we attach the owner object to receive messages in the form of return types from functions. There are three functions that follow the constructor, which allow for the basic functions of a bank. The deposit function adds the argument amount to the balance. The withdrawal function checks whether the requested amount is lower than the balance available for an account. If this is the case, the withdrawal is confirmed, and the argument amount is subtracted from the balance. If there is not enough balance, the amount that was supposed to be withdrawn is added back to the account, and the final balance is returned to the user. Finally, the last function allows us to return the balance of an account at a given time as requested by the contract. Now that we have a better grasp of Solidity, let's shift our focus to Vyper.

Vyper is also a general-purpose, contract-oriented programming language that compiles down to the EVM (Ethereum Virtual Machine) bytecode, much like Solidity. The main design benefit in using Vyper is that it removes numerous barriers in the process of writing smart contracts and presents the contracts in an easy-to-understand manner. As a general principle, any code that needs to run on the EVM must be very efficient to minimize the gas needed for the smart contract to execute. It must be noted that a poorly written contract will cost more ether to execute, and it can become so prohibitively expensive to run that the EVM will terminate the contract. To that end, Vyper follows the same logic as Solidity for writing contracts but removes the need for object-oriented programming paradigms. Vyper focuses on a limited set of definitions that are applied solely to programming microtransactions on the blockchain. Let's discuss the main features of Vyper:

CHAPTER 7   UNPACKING ETHEREUM

- Vyper does not contain most of the object-oriented programming constructs that programmers are familiar with: class inheritance, function overloading, and recursion capabilities have been removed. These features are not necessary for Turing-completeness and pose a security threat by increasing code complexity. Code reviews are essential to assess smart contracts; however, the added complexity can further make the audit process more difficult. Simplification leads to more reliable audits.

- Writing code that is easier to follow also reduces the likelihood of errors. In the sense that Vyper offers more security than Solidity, the added security layer is enforced in the coding practices of developers. Even with restricting features such as creating upper limits for gas usage and overflow checks, smart contracts written with Vyper shine in terms of readability, auditability, and simplicity (and therefore security).

- Vyper offers a set of built-in functions to write smart contracts, and although reviewing all of them is beyond the scope of this chapter, we want to highlight the assert function. Assert throws an error if a certain condition is not met. It is used at the beginning of methods to check if particular criteria are met for the method to process. If not, the transaction is reverted, and the contract terminates. For instance, imagine a crowdfunding scenario where assert can be used to revert a contract by checking for a timestamp. If the timestamp of the current block in the Ethereum blockchain is greater than the deadline of the campaign, the contract should be terminated because the campaign has ended. In this way, `assert` is a very clean function with which to apply conditions on contract code.

Developer Resources

As Ethereum has evolved in the past few years, so too has the interest of developers in using the platform for making applications. In this section, we will cover a few developer resources available for rapid prototyping in the Ethereum ecosystem:

- **Remix**: A web-based IDE for writing and testing smart contracts faster on Ethereum. It has built-in support for writing contracts using Solidity and Vyper, a plugin manager for extending functionality, unit testing, and a blockchain virtual machine.

- **Ethereum Studio**: Another web-based IDE suited for new developers to learn how to build and deploy smart contracts. Ethereum Studio has project templates, a transaction logger, and a built-in Ethereum Virtual Machine for rapid prototyping on the Ethereum platform.

- **OpenZeppelin SDK**: A smart contract toolkit to help build, compile, and deploy smart contracts and interact with them once deployed.

- **Embark**: A developer platform for building DApps and smart contracts. Has a command-line interface for deploying contracts, a plugin system, a transaction explorer, and an active development community.

CHAPTER 7 UNPACKING ETHEREUM

- **Consensys Academy**: A self-paced, online Ethereum developer course that is open year-round for enrollment. More on educational resources in a later chapter.

- **Ethereum Stack Exchange**: A community to ask any Ethereum-related questions ranging from platform development to getting started.

- **Chainshot**: An invited bootcamp for blockchain development that focuses on Ethereum smart contracts with a curriculum focused on practical applications.

World Computer Model

The Ethereum project has a grand vision of becoming a shared world computer with millions of accounts powered by the blockchain, which becomes a backend for "smart-logging" of communications, contracts that provide the decentralized logic to be executed, and EVMs that act as the execution platform. But computation and processing are not enough; a computer must also be able to store information and allow for a mechanism for applications to communicate among each other. This world computer will operate in an Internet 3.0 era, where servers are no longer needed due to the decentralized nature of information flow. In this ambitious endeavor, the Ethereum blockchain is only one-quarter of the world computer model. Let's introduce the three other components:

- **Whisper**: A secure message-passing protocol that allows decentralized applications on the blockchain to communicate with each other. This protocol relies on obfuscation and anonymization, similar to the Tor project (which provides anonymous web browsing),

225

where details regarding the message content, the sender, and the recipient are obscured. Additionally, this information cannot be gathered through packet analysis. The Whisper protocol is implemented on top of the RLPx transport protocol, a TCP-based transport protocol that is used internally by Ethereum nodes to communicate. There are a number of situations in which DApps need to communicate through a message bus, for instance, announcing a flash sale of a virtual asset. Whisper allows for easy broadcasting by using envelopes—encrypted packets that are sent and received by Whisper nodes. To that end, in an effort to avoid spam, a Whisper node must use a proof-of-work function to send a message. The work done is proportional to the size of the broadcast being transmitted. Ultimately, Whisper will provide an automated means of communication between user accounts or apps acting on behalf of the user accounts, as shown in Figure 7-5.

- **Swarm**: A decentralized storage and distribution service for DApp code, user data, blockchain data, and state data available to the Ethereum blockchain. In the future, Swarm will be able to provide Web 3.0 services such as media streaming, decentralized databases, and state channels. The main problem that Swarm is trying to solve is that currently, storing large amounts of data on the blockchain remains very expensive. This is why any DApps that need storage use an off-chain alternative. The idea behind Swarm is straightforward: a peer-to-peer network of collaborating nodes is used to pool together resources. This P2P network acts as a distributed cloud storage system with ample opportunity for data redundancy. The network is self-sustaining because of the associated blockchain that can incentivize nodes based on trading resources for payment. There are three main components of the Swarm storage protocol: chunks, references, and manifests. Chunks are the fundamental unit of storage and retrieval in Swarm: pieces of data that have a maximum size of 4K, linked to an address. References are unique identifiers of a file that can be used by a front-end client to retrieve the contents. Finally, a manifest is a data structure that describes a file collection along with paths and corresponding hashes to retrieve content. Using Swarm makes it possible to distribute data across the network and to replicate redundancy in a decentralized fashion (using nodes) without having to host a centralized server. Multiple nodes in the network can be incentivized to replicate chunks and use manifests to reference the data, much like a RAID configuration, eliminating the need for hosting centralized servers.

- **Smart contracts**: The final major pillar of the Ethereum platform. Provide programmatic access to the blockchain and provide the logical framework to power applications that will eventually run on the world computer.

CHAPTER 7 UNPACKING ETHEREUM

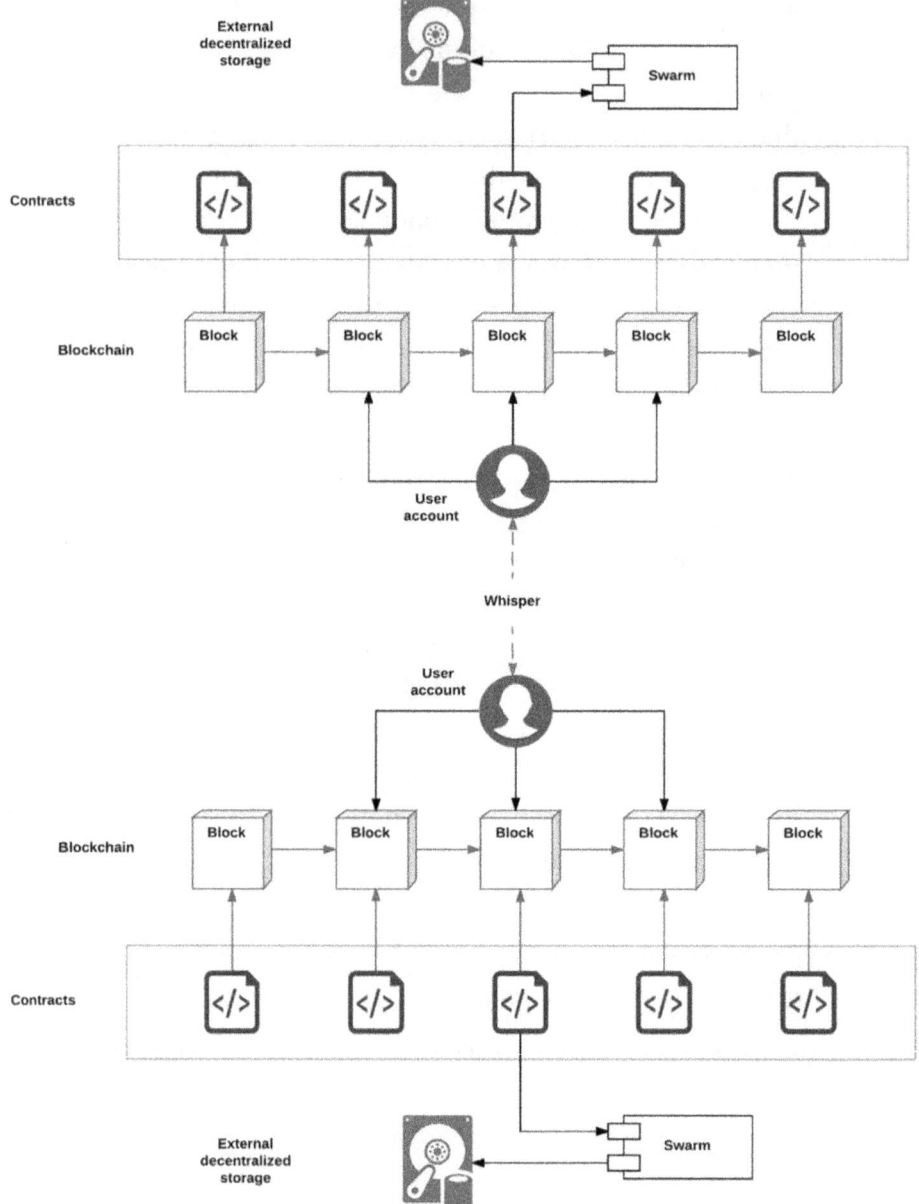

Figure 7-5. *A tiered approach to the world computer model in Ethereum*

CHAPTER 7 UNPACKING ETHEREUM

In Figure 7-5, we see a tiered approach to the world computer model. User accounts (or simply users) on the world computer are fundamental entities; therefore, they are the first tier. The second tier is the blockchain, which serves as a communication serial bus between the different components in the network. The third tier is the logical framework called smart contracts that lives on the blockchain and provides the computational capabilities to the world computer. Some of these contracts may require external storage for output and use Swarm to coordinate storage; this is the fourth layer. Finally, looking back at the first tier, we have the message-passing protocol called Whisper to facilitate user-to-user or application-to-application communication. More than a philosophical vision or a technological blueprint, the concept of a world computer and Internet 3.0 has some far-reaching implications for how content is controlled and distributed across the Web. Taylor Gerring from Ethereum talks very eloquently (https://blog.ethereum.org/2014/08/18/building-decentralized-web/) about building this dream:

> *As economics of the Ethereum ecosystem mature such that open contracts for lowest-rate storage develop, a free market of content hosting could evolve. Given the nature and dynamics of P2P applications, popular content will readily scale as the swarm shares, rather than suffering from the buckling load of siloed servers. The net result is that popular content is delivered faster, not slower.*
>
> *This metamorphosis will offer developers an opportunity to build the next-generation of decentralized, private, secure, censorship-resistant platforms that return control to creators and consumers of the next best idea. Anyone with a dream is free to build on this new class of next-generation decentralized web services without owning a credit card or signing up for any accounts.*
>
> *Although we are not told to or expected to, we have an imperative to cherish and improve the very shared resources that some wish to disturb, manipulate, and control. Just as no single*

229

CHAPTER 7   UNPACKING ETHEREUM

person fully understands the emerging internet collective intelligence, we should not expect any single entity to fully understand or maintain perfectly aligned motives. Rather, we should rely on the internet to solve the problems of the internet.

Layer 2 Upgrades

The classic Ethereum protocol and network described in this chapter so far belongs to Layer 1. To reach the ideal world computer model, scalability and security upgrades are needed so that more applications can interact with the blockchain and complex code can be executed. These upgrades are all part of Layer 2, which will begin rolling out in 2020. There are four components of Layer 2 that we discuss here: sharding, beacon chain, state channels, and plasma. The explanation for each component will lead to the next one in order.

While early Layer 2 developments focused on state channels and plasma, the Ethereum scaling ecosystem has evolved with the introduction of optimistic rollups and zero-knowledge rollups (ZK-Rollups). Optimistic rollups process transactions off-chain and post transaction data to Ethereum as calldata. They're called "optimistic" because they assume transactions are valid by default and only run fraud proofs when a transaction is challenged. Leading implementations include Arbitrum and Optimism, which together account for the majority of Total Value Locked (TVL) in Layer 2 solutions. Optimistic rollups like Arbitrum and Optimism have proven their effectiveness with transaction fees ranging from $0.02 to $0.07 on average, significantly lower than Ethereum's base layer. ZK-Rollups use zero-knowledge proofs to validate off-chain transactions, offering faster finality than optimistic rollups as they don't require a challenge period. Notable implementations include zkSync (developed by Matter Labs), which uses zk-SNARK (Zero-Knowledge Succinct Non-interactive Arguments of Knowledge) technology, and Starknet (developed by StarkWare), which utilizes zk-STARK (Zero-Knowledge Scalable Transparent Arguments of

Knowledge) proofs. While ZK-Rollups currently have a smaller market share than optimistic rollups, they are considered by many to be the long-term solution for Ethereum scaling due to their mathematical security guarantees and potential for higher throughput. The transition from state channels and plasma to rollup-centric scaling solutions represents Ethereum's strategic shift toward more secure and efficient scaling methods that maintain strong security connections to the base layer.

Sharding

There are three pillars absolutely necessary for blockchain protocols to operate: decentralization (defined as the lack of a central validating authority), scalability (defined as the ability to process more transactions and have high throughput), and security (broadly defined as all nodes running on the same copy of the network). All blockchain implementations suffer from a phenomenon called the scalability trilemma, which claims that only two out of the three pillars can be successfully deployed. Layer 2.0 updates are necessary to Ethereum in order to enable scalability and overcome the trilemma.

Presently, in all known blockchain protocols, every node has to store the entire network state (data describing account balances and contract code), and every node has to process all of the transactions. This provides a large amount of consistency, but also a bottleneck that limits scalability: a blockchain cannot process more transactions than a single node. This has practical consequences; for instance, Bitcoin is limited to three to seven transactions per second. In an attempt to remove this bottleneck, we are faced with the following question: can we design mechanisms where only a small subset of nodes verifies transactions and still keep the overall network secure? The idea is to split up transaction processing among smaller groups of nodes that can verify each transaction in parallel. Even though each group of nodes validates one transaction at a time, the parallel execution can offer incredible scalability benefits.

Chapter 7 Unpacking Ethereum

Sharding is an attempt to answer this design problem. In this solution, the state and history of Ethereum are split into smaller partitions that we call shards. Essentially, in sharding, a large database (or blockchain in this case) is partitioned into smaller, more efficient shards, making the whole network more scalable. A shard is a self-managing partition and has its own transaction history. In simple forms of sharding, the transactions contained in a shard are limited to that shard only. For instance, one DApp can map a set of addresses to one whole shard, so all transactions related to that DApp will remain on that shard. As a result, a whole set of business verticals and applications can run on one shard.

Beacon Chain

Hsiao-Wei Wang has provided an overall architecture diagram for the Ethereum 2.0 system, which is shown in Figure 7-6.

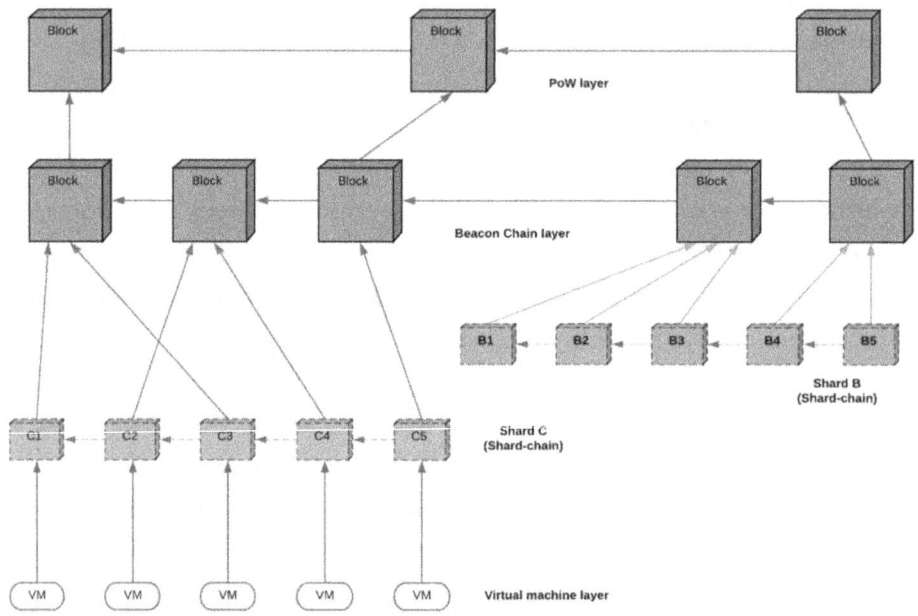

Figure 7-6. *Architectural organization of Ethereum 2.0*

232

- **PoW chain**: This is the part of Ethereum that is currently online and operational. In the Ethereum 2.0 system, this layer will continue to work as is, and new layers will be added on top.

- **Beacon chain**: The proof-of-stake deployment in Ethereum 2.0. Currently under development and will be the first component to be delivered.

- **Shards**: Shard chain is a composite of the shard along with all transactions belonging to the shard. This enables scalability in the beacon chain. Initially, a limited runtime will begin where the shards will aggregate transactions and reach a consensus on the order of transactions, without executing them.

- **Virtual machines**: A VM layer will provide for computation and execution abilities for contracts and transactions on the Ethereum 2.0 platform.

Why do we need a beacon chain? The main function of the beacon chain is to implement and manage the proof-of-stake protocol for the Ethereum blockchain and for all the shards attached to the blockchain (the shard chains, to be specific). To do this, the beacon chain needs to manage the following aspects: managing validators, nominating a block proposer for each shard, organizing validators into committees to vote on proposed blocks, and, finally, applying rewards and penalties to validators. The name "beacon chain" originates from a NIST random beacon generator that provides a source of randomness; we will shortly see why randomness as a property is important to the network.

Managing Validators

In a traditional PoW algorithm, any user can use their hardware to become a miner. However, in Ethereum 2.0, users will stake their ether (ETH) to activate validators. It is important to note that validators are virtual and activated by a staker who puts forth ether. For every 32 ETH staked (put forward), one validator is activated. A major function of the beacon chain is to maintain a set of validators: nodes that have staked the required 32 ETH and are now responsible for running the Ethereum 2.0 protocol.

A node can join the validator set by sending its stake to a contract running on the proof-of-work chain (the current Ethereum blockchain). After an initial check for validity, the stake put forth is frozen, and the contract broadcasts an announcement that can be received by all beacon chain clients. At this point, the node is said to have been inducted into the validator set on the beacon chain. Once a node is active, the validator can participate in the Ethereum 2.0 protocol by proposing blocks when chosen by the beacon chain and join committees that vote for the blocks.

Block Proposers

In a proof-of-work protocol, the node that first solves the mining challenge gets to assemble/mine the next block. However, in a proof of stake, there is no mining involved. A block proposer is essentially a validator selected pseudo-randomly to build a block. A source of this randomness is necessary to select validators, hence the name beacon chain.

The beacon chain provides a rhythm for the entire Ethereum 2.0 network. It generates blocks every 16 seconds on the network, as opposed to a proof-of-work protocol that generates a block irregularly, roughly averaging every 15 seconds. The 16-second periods are called slots, and each slot is a chance for a block to be added to the beacon chain. For every slot, a chosen block proposer from the beacon chain gathers all the votes from the validator set for previous blocks, forges the block itself, and publishes it on the blockchain. In the future, each shard will have its own proposer at the beginning of a slot. This shard-block proposer will gather up all the transactions for that shard and form them into a block for voting to commence.

Committees

For this new proof-of-stake protocol in the Ethereum 2.0 blockchain, a crucial source of security is the committees that vote on which blocks will get added to the blockchain and form the true history of the chain. The beacon chain relies on counting the votes (also known as attestations) from its own committee in order to reach consensus over blocks and add them to the blockchain. This committee comprises validators in the system, and their collected attestations create the history of the beacon chain. In the future, there will be provisions for creating smaller subcommittees that only govern one shard at a time. This will allow the subcommittees to confirm the block proposers from the shard and keep a consistent history.

Rewards and Penalties

An important administrative job of the beacon chain is to track and update the deposit that validators stake upon joining the validator set. To that end, validators receive rewards for maintaining network consensus and acting in good faith, which incentivizes them to participate in block committees. If the validators refuse to follow the rules set forth by the validator set, they can be issued a penalty: their initial stake of 32 ETH is slashed, or the validator can be ejected from the system. Additionally, if a validator's balance falls below 16 ETH, the beacon chain will remove it from the validator set.

CHAPTER 7   UNPACKING ETHEREUM

State Channels

State channels are a general model to think about interactions that occur on the blockchain, but can be shifted off-chain without compromising the security of the network. A well-studied example of a state channel in Bitcoin is a payment channel: instant, friction-less transaction of payment between two parties, without having to wait for the long confirmation periods on the Bitcoin blockchain. Broadly speaking, the idea of a state channel can be applied to any state-altering interaction happening on a blockchain protocol. Moving a subset of transactions or blockchain interactions off-chain without undermining security can lead to significant improvements in network speed.

There are three basic components of a state channel:

- **Locking mechanism**: A segment of the blockchain state is locked by a multi-signature smart contract such that a specific set of users must completely agree with the contract in order to update it.

- **Off-chain actions**: The off-chain users update a local state by signing transactions and constructing blocks that can be submitted to the main blockchain. These transactions are aggregated and updated locally in the payment state channel.

- **Unlocking mechanism**: The participants submit the aggregate state from the payment channel to the blockchain, and if the contract is satisfied, the state is unlocked on the blockchain from the first step.

Here, the first and third components lock and unlock a partition of the global state and are considered blockchain operations. However, the second component can be done completely off-chain and can involve a large number of transactions/updates. These updates can be made rapidly and retain internal consistency on the payment channel, without needing to involve the blockchain. This step provides scalability and immense performance benefits. In this manner, only the first and third steps need to be published to the network and confirmed on the blockchain. The transactions in the middle can be carried out at a much faster rate on a state channel.

Plasma

Plasma is a framework for conducting off-chain transactions while using the consensus and security mechanisms from the Ethereum blockchain to sync these transactions. Plasma chains are partially independent sub-chains that are registered with the main Ethereum blockchain. These sub-chains can commit transactions to the main Ethereum blockchain in a batch. In this manner, some of the transactional demand for computational power is relieved from the main blockchain. The nodes can now dedicate this computational power to contracts and other higher-level tasks. Plasma takes the concept of payment channels even further by allowing for the creation of child blockchains attached to the main Ethereum blockchain. These child chains can in turn spawn even more child chains. Essentially, plasma is a framework for many branching blockchains linked to one main blockchain (the Ethereum blockchain in this case).

In terms of security, plasma-based chains rely on the main Ethereum blockchain for consensus and consistency mechanisms. Users can rely on security measures put forth by the Ethereum network in order to redeem any assets decided on the child chain. Plasma chains use MapReduce along with a Merkle tree construct to ensure transactional verification and detect fraud. Additionally, members with a stake in the plasma chain will self-police and monitor the chain. If any disputes arise, they can submit a timestamp or proof of malicious behavior to the main Ethereum blockchain for resolution. Plasma chains include another fraud prevention mechanism called rollback. This feature is activated when a double-spending-type activity causes a payment or transaction to fail. When this feature is active, all funds are returned to the state of the network before the attempted fraud. In the proposed implementation, the rollback process is very cheap computationally for the parent Ethereum blockchain and offers enormous security.

Blockchain-as-a-Service

Microsoft recently announced a partnership with the Ethereum Foundation to launch a blockchain-based service on their cloud platform Azure. This Infrastructure-as-a-Service approach to offering fast and easy implementations of blockchain will allow developers to experiment with new features and deploy DApps at reduced costs. Marley Grey from the Azure Blockchain Engineering team describes how Blockchain-as-a-Service (BaaS) will foster an ecosystem of DApps:

> *Microsoft and ConsenSys are partnering to offer Ethereum Blockchain as a Service (E-BaaS) on Microsoft Azure so Enterprise clients and developers can have a single click cloud based blockchain developer environment. The initial offering contains two tools that allow for rapid development of SmartContract based applications: Ether.Camp—An integrated developer environment, and BlockApps—a private, semi-private Ethereum blockchain environment, can deploy into the public Ethereum environment.*

> *"Ethereum Blockchain as a Service" provided by Microsoft Azure and ConsenSys allows for financial services customers and partners to play, learn, and fail fast at a low cost in a ready-made dev/test/production environment. It will allow them to create private, public and consortium based Blockchain environments using industry leading frameworks very quickly, distributing their Blockchain products with Azure's World Wide distributed (private) platform. That*

CHAPTER 7   UNPACKING ETHEREUM

makes Azure a great Dev/Test/Production Environment for Blockchain applications. Surrounding capabilities like Cortana Analytics (machine learning), Power BI, Azure Active Directory, O365 and CRMOL can be integrated into apps launching a new generation of decentralized cross platform applications.

This initial update on BaaS was provided at the end of 2015, and currently a whole ecosystem of Blockchain Labs is flourishing within the Azure DevTest community. The DevTest Labs allow users and developers to explore and test a template designed for a specific use case. In addition, the platform began with Ethereum blockchains, but recently more startups have started to build on Azure, offering new services such as Emercoin, which offered a SSH service, and PokiDot, with their healthcare-oriented blockchain called Dokchain. Over time, more startups have begun using Azure as the standard to run a blockchain and build applications on top. With the integration of intelligence services such as Cortana, it may become easier to develop oracles that can sign incoming data from external streams (such as IoT devices) and provide a level of integrity.

Note Two developments from Microsoft in the BaaS space are noteworthy here. The first is the introduction of Cryptlets, a secure middleware to interface with external events for building enterprise smart contracts. The second development is the Coco framework, an open source system for building a high-throughput network on top of a blockchain, where nodes and actors are explicitly declared and controlled. By design, Coco is compatible with any ledger protocol and would allow enterprises to build production-ready blockchain networks. More about Microsoft's platform will be presented in a later chapter.

CHAPTER 7   UNPACKING ETHEREUM

Decentralized Applications

We alluded to decentralized applications (or DApps) in our discussion of Whisper, but we will talk about them in more depth here. A decentralized app is a serverless application that runs on the Ethereum stack and interfaces with the end user via an HTML/JavaScript frontend that can make calls to the back-end stack. Classically, a mobile or web app has a backend running on centralized dedicated servers; however, a DApp has its back-end code running on a decentralized peer-to-peer network. A simplistic model of how a DApp operates on the blockchain is shown in Figure 7-7.

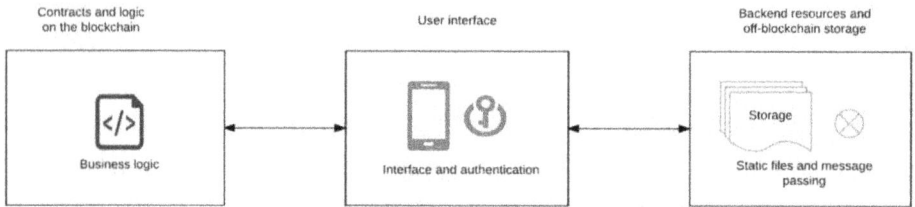

Figure 7-7. Structure of a DApp

As seen in Figure 7-7, the user interface is often written in HTML or JavaScript and is the only component loaded on a user device. The interface makes back-end calls to the blockchain in order to execute a particular contract and also to the back-end resources such as Swarm or Whisper if external storage is needed or when the application needs to communicate with other apps. If a traditional app comprises a frontend and a server running the backend, then a DApp running on the Ethereum stack would be made from a frontend and contracts running on the blockchain. DApps usually have their own set of associated contracts on the blockchain that are used to encode business logic and allow persistent storage of their consensus-critical state. Recall that all code on the Ethereum stack runs within an EVM, which keeps track of step-by-step

CHAPTER 7 UNPACKING ETHEREUM

operations and charges gas to the owner of a contract. This prevents DApp developers from running too many operations on the blockchain or bloating it by storing data directly on the blockchain.

Note To briefly review, the DApp stack relies on decentralized storage (provided by Swarm-like architecture) for user data or app data, on the blockchain for contract logic and transactional operations, and on the frontend for the end user. The front-end interface makes calls to the blockchain to specific contracts running the decentralized application based on user actions.

How does the backend of a DApp pull static content for the frontend, such as JS from the Ethereum stack, and receive the updated global state from the blockchain? Let's look at an example using IPFS as storage to understand these back-end calls (Figure 7-8):

- The back-end code is essentially a contract that executes on the blockchain given the appropriate amount of resources.

- Some application needs to use a persistent database to host static content used in the app; we can rely on IPFS that stores static files, hosted throughout the network on several nodes.

- Hashes from IPFS are delivered to the DApp, and the contract's execution updates the global state, which is delivered to the DApp from the Ethereum stack.

CHAPTER 7   UNPACKING ETHEREUM

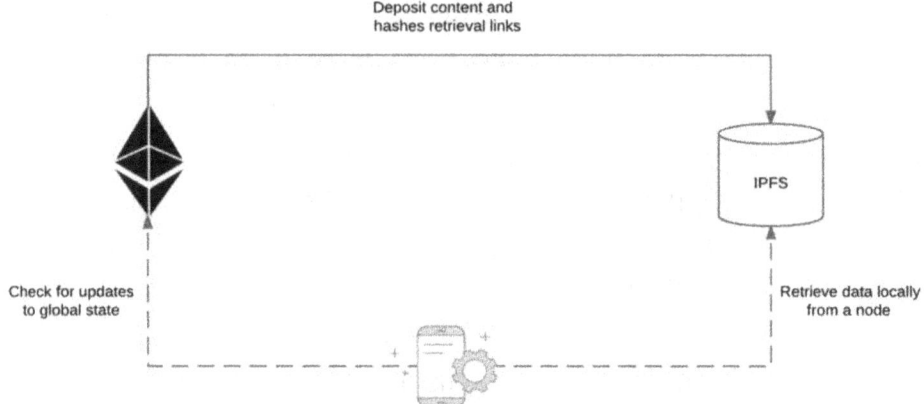

Figure 7-8. *A simple schematic of back-end calls made by a DApp*

In Figure 7-8, the blockchain can deposit content to an IPFS-like system on one of the nodes, and the hashes can be made available to the app for retrieval when necessary. The app can request updates from the blockchain on the global state as it affects the app running on a device. Finally, as needed, the app can retrieve and download the full content from the decentralized storage to the user device. Splitting up roles in this manner allows for more innovative user interfaces as a developer can switch it out without having to change the backend at all.

Geth and Mist

There are two more tools we need to discuss briefly that play a role in DApp development. Geth is the command-line interface (written in Golang) for running a full node on the Ethereum network. Using Geth, you can interact with the Ethereum blockchain and perform tasks such as the following:

- Mine ether on the network.
- Transfer funds between addresses.

CHAPTER 7 UNPACKING ETHEREUM

- Create contracts and send transactions.
- Use the DApps API.

Geth comes with two interfaces that are used in development: the JavaScript console with the *web3.js* library and the JSON-RPC server. Let's talk about both technologies briefly. Geth can be launched with an interactive console that provides the JS runtime environment for you to interact with a node. This runtime environment includes the *web3* library, which can construct contracts and transactions to be propagated to the node. The JSON-RPC server is a remote procedure call (RPC) protocol that facilitates data exchange between the node and its clients (JSON is a data exchange format that nodes use to communicate with clients). More precisely, RPC is a collection of methods and rules that define how data (commands and output) can be transferred between a node and a client. The JavaScript API uses the *web3.js* library to offer a convenient interface for using the RPC methods.

Tip For most Ethereum applications today, Geth is a prerequisite for installation as a command-line tool. Often, during the installation, Geth is provided as an add-on so that a user doesn't have to download and install it separately.

Mist is the official Ethereum wallet application. In early discussions, Mist was conceptualized to be a standalone app store–type browser for DApps, but that vision has evolved. In order to interact with the Ethereum blockchain, we need a blockchain client like Geth. This client is responsible for broadcasting transactions to the network, mining ether, signing transactions, and deploying smart contracts. Most end users are not comfortable with using a command-line interface, so a wrapper such as Mist was made to be the front-end interface. Mist connects to Geth in the background and serves as an interface for the wallet software to the user. Additionally, Mist provides an interface for writing and deploying smart contracts, or DApps. The wallet software integrates payments seamlessly for contract deployment.

Eventually, the most powerful entities on the Ethereum network using Geth and Mist will be decentralized autonomous organizations (DAOs), which are essentially automated companies powered by smart contracts that run on the Ethereum network. We will next go over the Layer 2 upgrades that have been introduced to Ethereum and the upcoming Ethereum Improvement Proposals (EIPs) that will fundamentally reshape Ethereum.

Ethereum Upgrades

The Merge (EIP-3675): The Beacon Chain is the foundational proof-of-stake (PoS) blockchain introduced as part of Ethereum's 2.0 roadmap for transitioning from proof of work (PoW) to PoS. It serves as the consensus layer for Ethereum's PoS system, coordinating validators, managing consensus rules, and acting as the backbone for Ethereum's future scalability. It was initially launched as a separate chain to test and establish PoS consensus, running in parallel with Ethereum's existing PoW mainnet. Although not specifically for the beacon chain, EIP-3675 formalized the transition from PoW to PoS by specifying "The Merge," which linked the beacon chain with Ethereum's mainnet. This long-awaited update reduced energy usage by ~99% and has prepared Ethereum for scalability improvements like sharding (planned for the near future) by offloading consensus to validators who stake ETH. Validators, rather than miners, now secure the network by staking a minimum of 32 ETH, participating in block proposal and attestation.

The Shanghai/Capella upgrade (EIP-4895), activated in April 2023, marked a second key technical milestone by enabling validators to withdraw staked ETH, balancing incentives for staking, adding flexibility for those participating in network security, and completing the full cycle of staking economics on the network. The upgrade also included EIP-3651, EIP-3855, and EIP-3860, which collectively reduced gas costs for certain operations, further optimizing the network's efficiency. EIP-3651, known as "Warm COINBASE," aimed to reduce the gas costs associated with accessing the COINBASE address, which represents the block proposer or miner. Before this upgrade, the "COINBASE" address was considered "cold" on first access during a transaction, resulting in higher gas consumption. EIP-3651 ensured that the "COINBASE" address starts as "warm," significantly lowering the gas costs for initial access. This change is particularly advantageous for applications that frequently interact with the "COINBASE" address, such as those utilizing maximal extractable value (MEV) strategies. Another enhancement was "EIP-3855," which introduced the "PUSH0" instruction in the Ethereum Virtual Machine (EVM). This new opcode, represented as "0x5F," allows developers to push the value "0" onto the stack directly. Before EIP-3855, achieving this required using the more expensive "PUSH1 0x00" opcode, which consumed unnecessary gas. By adding a more efficient and straightforward instruction for this frequent operation, EIP-3855 reduced gas costs, simplified smart contract bytecode, and improved execution efficiency. For example, replacing "PUSH1 0x00" with "PUSH0" saves about one gas unit per usage, which can add up significantly in gas-constrained contract logic. To address challenges related to contract deployment, "EIP-3860" introduced gas metering and length limits for "INITCODE," the initialization code executed during contract creation. This proposal set a maximum allowable size for "INITCODE" at 49,152 bytes and imposed a gas cost of two gas units per 32 bytes of "INITCODE." Before EIP-3860, there were no specific constraints on the size or efficiency of "INITCODE," which allowed developers to deploy excessively large or gas-inefficient contracts, potentially burdening the network. By enforcing these limits and introducing metering, EIP-3860 ensured more predictable gas costs and incentivized developers to optimize their initialization code. For instance, a contract deployment with 640 bytes of "INITCODE" would now incur an additional 40 gas

CHAPTER 7   UNPACKING ETHEREUM

units, promoting efficiency and reducing potential abuse. Together, these proposals enhanced Ethereum's operational efficiency, improved gas cost predictability, and enhanced network security against misuse.

The Cancun-Deneb upgrade, activated in early 2024, introduced EIP-4844, also known as proto-danksharding or blob-carrying transactions. This proposal introduced a new transaction type that can carry large amounts of data, significantly reducing costs for rollups (Layer 2 scaling solutions that execute transactions off the main Ethereum chain). By allowing these blob-carrying transactions, Ethereum took a crucial step toward implementing full sharding, a scaling solution that will eventually allow the network to process thousands of transactions per second. The second improvement was EIP-6780, which addressed long-standing issues with the SELFDESTRUCT opcode. When executed, this opcode removes the contract's code and storage from the state and sends the contract's remaining ether to a specified address. However, this feature has led to several issues, including unexpected complexity in state management and potential security vulnerabilities. The new implementation maintains backward compatibility while maintaining a stable state size, improving the overall stability and predictability of smart contracts on the network. A third crucial component of the Cancun-Deneb upgrade was EIP-1153, which introduced a new mechanism for handling temporary or transient storage during smart contract execution. Traditional storage operations on Ethereum are permanent and consume gas. This can be inefficient for temporary data that doesn't need to persist for longer than one transaction. The transient storage opcodes, TLOAD and TSTORE, allow for efficient temporary storage that would be wiped clean at the end of transaction execution, thereby reducing gas costs for complex operations that require intermediate state storage. This enhancement is particularly beneficial for applications like decentralized exchanges (DEXs) and other DeFi protocols that often require multiple state changes within a single transaction. Moreover, the use of storage opcodes reduces state bloat throughout the network. The final component of upgrade included

EIP-5656, which modified the MCOPY opcode that allows for more efficient memory copying operations. This seemingly small change has significant implications for gas optimization, especially in contracts that handle large amounts of data or perform complex computations. By reducing the gas cost of memory operations, this upgrade makes certain types of smart contracts more economically viable to deploy and interact with on the Ethereum network.

A notable technical advancement in the Ethereum ecosystem has been the development and refinement of account abstraction, as outlined in EIP-4337. This proposal introduces a new type of account that separates the account management logic from the core protocol, allowing for more flexible and user-friendly wallet designs. Traditionally, Ethereum has two types of accounts: externally owned accounts (EOAs) controlled by private keys and contract accounts controlled by their code. Account abstraction blurs this distinction, allowing users to create accounts that behave more like smart contracts. Account abstraction enables features like social recovery of lost keys, multi-signature wallets, and sponsored transactions directly at the protocol level, changing how users interact with the Ethereum network.

Single-slot finality reduces the time for transaction finalization by allowing blocks to be proposed and finalized within a single slot (12 seconds). This optimizes security and makes attacks harder, as rapid block confirmation reduces potential reordering attacks. Several EIPs related to consensus mechanism improvements and network optimization are indirectly contributing to the goal of achieving single-slot finality.

The Ethereum community has also made significant strides in improving the network's privacy features. The development of Zero-Knowledge Succinct Non-interactive Arguments of Knowledge (zk-SNARKs) and Zero-Knowledge Scalable Transparent Arguments of Knowledge (zk-STARKs) has paved the way for privacy-preserving applications on Ethereum. These cryptographic techniques allow for the verification of computations without revealing the underlying data, opening up new possibilities for confidential transactions, public–private interfaces, and private smart contracts.

CHAPTER 7   UNPACKING ETHEREUM

The Ethereum client landscape has also seen significant developments. The diversity of client implementations has increased, with teams working on improving performance, reducing resource requirements, and enhancing interoperability. Notable advancements include the development of light clients and stateless clients, which aim to reduce the hardware requirements for participating in the network. The Nimbus client, for instance, has made strides in enabling Ethereum nodes to run on resource-constrained devices, potentially expanding the network's reach to mobile and IoT devices. In the realm of smart contract development, the introduction of the Solidity 0.8.x series brought several important safety features and optimizations. Notable among these is the default use of checked arithmetic, which helps prevent overflow and underflow errors that have historically been a source of vulnerabilities in smart contracts. The new ABIEncoderV2 became the default in Solidity 0.8.0, offering more efficient encoding and decoding of complex types, thereby reducing gas costs for contract interactions.

Proposer–builder separation (PBS) and maximal extractable value (MEV) are closely related concepts in blockchain economics and security, particularly in the context of Ethereum's proof-of-stake (PoS) consensus. MEV refers to the additional value that block producers (such as miners in proof of work or validators in proof of stake) can extract from block creation by reordering, including, or excluding transactions. This can occur in scenarios like front-running, sandwich attacks, or arbitrage opportunities. MEV can create centralization risks, as powerful actors may seek to dominate block production to capture more MEV. To address these risks, proposer–builder separation (PBS) was introduced as a solution. In PBS, the role of proposing a block (done by validators) is separated from the role of building the block (deciding which transactions to include and in what order). Specialized entities called "block builders" compete to create the most profitable block, and validators select from these proposals. This separation fosters a fairer, censorship-resistant

CHAPTER 7   UNPACKING ETHEREUM

transaction inclusion process by decentralizing decision-making in block composition and reduces the incentive for validators to act maliciously or for powerful block builders to dominate the network, while allowing MEV to be captured transparently and distributed more equitably among participants.

EIP-1559, also known as the Ethereum Fee Market Upgrade, is a transformative change to Ethereum's transaction fee mechanism, introduced as part of the London Hard Fork in August 2021. This proposal replaced Ethereum's traditional auction-based fee system with a more predictable and user-friendly model. Under EIP-1559, each block has a base fee that dynamically adjusts based on network demand, ensuring a smoother transaction experience. Instead of all transaction fees going to miners, the base fee is burned, permanently removing it from circulation. This creates a deflationary pressure on ETH, reducing its overall supply and potentially increasing its value over time. Users can also include a priority fee (or "tip") to incentivize miners to process their transactions faster. The upgrade enhances network efficiency, mitigates fee volatility, and improves Ethereum's economic model by aligning user incentives with network sustainability. EIP-1559 is widely regarded as a key step toward Ethereum's transition to a more scalable and secure ecosystem, complementing its shift to proof of stake with Ethereum 2.0.

EIP-3540, also known as the "EVM Object Format" (EOF), introduces a significant enhancement to the Ethereum Virtual Machine (EVM) by introducing a structured format for smart contract bytecode. Proposed as part of Ethereum's roadmap toward modularity and extensibility, this improvement reorganizes how bytecode is represented and executed in the EVM. The primary goal is to separate code and data within smart contracts, enabling a cleaner and more structured way to process transactions. By creating a framework where code and data are stored in distinct sections, EIP-3540 lays the groundwork for future enhancements, such as new opcodes and static analysis features, without breaking compatibility with existing contracts. The separation also enables more

249

efficient validation of smart contracts by allowing validators to distinguish between executable code and data, resulting in ease of use and significant gas savings. Beyond efficiency gains, EOF also facilitates easier smart contract upgrades, allowing for future improvements to the EVM without disrupting existing functionality. By introducing once-off validation at deploy time rather than continuous runtime validation, EOF also improves overall gas efficiency for contract execution. Furthermore, it is considered an essential step for new downstream features such as contract validation on runtime.

EIP-3670, also known as "Contract Validation Code in Creation", proposes improvements to how Ethereum handles the validation of smart contracts during their creation. It introduces a mechanism where contracts are validated against specific rules at the time of deployment, rather than during runtime. This change aims to reduce potential errors and inefficiencies by ensuring that deployed contracts comply with predefined standards. By enforcing validation at creation, EIP-3670 can help eliminate invalid or non-functional contracts from entering the network, improving overall network health and security. This EIP builds on EVM Object Format, leveraging its modular framework to define stricter and more consistent validation rules, leading to a better developer experience, reduced attack surfaces, and enhanced compatibility with future EVMs

Data structures such as Merkle trees have been crucial in ensuring data integrity and facilitating efficient transactional verification. However, as blockchain networks scale, the limitations of these traditional structures become apparent, particularly concerning the size and efficiency of cryptographic proofs. To address these challenges, Ethereum is transitioning to Verkle trees, an advanced data structure that offers more compact proofs and enables stateless clients. Verkle trees, introduced in EIP-2935, combine the principles of vector commitments and Merkle trees, creating a hybrid structure that allows validators to verify data inclusion without storing the entire dataset, significantly reducing storage requirements. The key innovation lies in replacing the hashes used in

Merkle trees with vector commitments, enabling wider branching factors and more efficient proofs. In a Verkle tree, each node can have a large number of children—typically 256 or more—compared with the binary branching of Merkle trees. This wider branching reduces the tree's depth, resulting in shorter and more efficient proof paths. The tree consists of two main types of nodes: inner nodes and leaf nodes (suffix nodes). Inner nodes act as intermediaries, directing the path from the root to the leaves, and contain commitments to their child nodes constructed using vector commitments. Leaf nodes store the actual data or values, with each leaf associated with a unique key that is split into a stem (prefix) and a suffix. Leaves sharing the same stem are grouped together to optimize storage and retrieval. The primary advantage of Verkle trees is their ability to produce significantly smaller proofs compared with Merkle trees. While Merkle tree proof sizes grow logarithmically with the number of leaves, Verkle trees, through vector commitments and wide branching, achieve much smaller proof sizes. For example, in a dataset containing 1 billion entries, a Merkle tree proof might be around 1 kb, whereas a Verkle tree proof could be less than 150 bytes. This efficiency is a game-changer for Ethereum's scalability. Verkle trees play a critical role in enabling stateless Ethereum clients, which validate blocks without storing the entire state database. Instead, these clients rely on "witnesses"—compact proofs that certain data is part of the state. By facilitating the creation of these small witnesses, Verkle trees significantly lower resource requirements, allowing more participants to validate the network. This is a pivotal step toward Ethereum's scalability. However, transitioning to Verkle trees involves challenges, such as the need for new cryptographic primitives and modifications to Ethereum's existing protocol. Ensuring the security and efficiency of vector commitments is essential, as is the seamless integration of Verkle trees with the current infrastructure. Ongoing research and development are addressing these complexities to enable a smooth transition.

CHAPTER 7   UNPACKING ETHEREUM

Upcoming Proposals

The following are the proposals we are looking forward to in 2025:

The Prague-Electra (Pectra) upgrade, slated for early 2025, introduces several of the key advancements noted above to improve scalability and gas efficiency. One of the most notable features is the Ethereum Object Format (EOF), which introduces a modular design for smart contracts. This facilitates better code validation, optimized execution, and paves the way for future upgrades to the EVM. Additionally, the upgrade incorporates Peer Data Availability Sampling (PeerDAS), a mechanism that allows nodes to verify the availability of data without downloading entire datasets, enhancing scalability and security for Layer 2 solutions like rollups. Another major improvement is the adoption of Verkle trees, a data structure designed to optimize data storage and retrieval. This reduces the computational burden on validators and progresses Ethereum toward stateless execution, eliminating the need to store the blockchain's full history. The upgrade also enhances account abstraction, allowing externally owned accounts (EOAs) to function as smart contracts temporarily during transactions, which simplifies user interactions and supports more advanced features. Finally, the upgrade raises the maximum effective balance for validators, enabling larger stake consolidations and reducing the total number of validators, thereby increasing network efficiency.

Peer Data Availability Sampling (PeerDAS) is a critical innovation aimed at addressing the challenges of data availability in Ethereum's Layer 2 ecosystem. In traditional systems, nodes must download and store entire datasets to verify the availability of data, which can be resource-intensive and limit scalability. PeerDAS introduces a more efficient approach by allowing nodes to verify the availability of data through sampling instead of full dataset downloads. This method ensures that data required for validating transactions and blocks remains accessible and verifiable

CHAPTER 7   UNPACKING ETHEREUM

without imposing significant computational or storage demands on the nodes. By optimizing data availability, PeerDAS supports the efficient operation of rollups—Layer 2 solutions that bundle transactions into batches for processing off-chain while maintaining Ethereum's security guarantees. This enhancement not only reduces resource consumption but also lays the groundwork for Ethereum to achieve its scalability goals, including processing thousands of transactions per second.

Single Secret Leader Election (SSLE) is a mechanism designed to improve the security and integrity of Ethereum's block proposal process. In the current system, the identity of the block proposer is known in advance, which exposes them to targeted attacks, such as denial of service (DoS) or bribery attempts. SSLE addresses this vulnerability by keeping the identity of the block proposer secret until the block is fully revealed to the network. This secrecy is achieved through cryptographic techniques that securely conceal the leader's identity during the election process, ensuring that potential adversaries cannot predict or disrupt their activities. By preventing such attacks, SSLE strengthens the robustness of the consensus mechanism, enhancing network stability and fairness. Furthermore, it complements other Ethereum upgrades aimed at decentralization and security, ensuring that validators can operate without fear of external interference.

Quantum Resistance Preparations are a proactive step in Ethereum's roadmap to secure the network against the potential threats posed by quantum computing. Quantum computers, once sufficiently advanced, could undermine traditional cryptographic algorithms, particularly those used in blockchain systems, by solving complex mathematical problems exponentially faster than classical computers. Ethereum's preparations focus on integrating quantum-resistant cryptographic algorithms, such as lattice-based cryptography, hash-based signatures, or other post-quantum cryptographic methods. These algorithms are designed to withstand attacks from quantum computers, ensuring the immutability

CHAPTER 7   UNPACKING ETHEREUM

and security of Ethereum's transactions and smart contracts. By taking early measures to implement quantum-resistant technology, Ethereum aims to future-proof its network, maintaining trust and stability even in a post-quantum era.

Summary

In this chapter, we introduced Ethereum, one of the biggest alternate currencies competing against Bitcoin. In recent years, it has gained a lot of attention from developers and investors. We began our discussion with a broad overview of what Ethereum is in comparison to Bitcoin. We talked about accounts and function calls as being foundational to Ethereum. We then provided some more depth to the ideas of accounts as entities on the blockchain. After that, we discussed the use of gas on Ethereum for smart contract execution, how internal storage is adapted to work with Merkle-Patricia trees, and the concept of internal state for an account. After that, we talked about EVM and how smart contracts are executed on the blockchain. Then, we discussed a model for writing smart contracts using Solidity and Vyper, along with developer resources to rapidly prototype smart contracts. This led to a discussion about the world computer model as it applies to Ethereum components such as IPFS and Whisper. We provided a short review of DApps and the Blockchain-as-a-Service model, which we will expand on in a later chapter. Finally, the major technical focus of this chapter was the Layer 2 upgrades that are being rolled out for the Ethereum network and the EIPs on the horizon for 2025.

Bibliography

Antonopoulos, A. M. & Wood, G. *Mastering Ethereum: Building Smart contracts and DApps.* O'Reilly Media, 2018.

Buterin, V. (2023). A rollup-centric ethereum roadmap. Ethereum Foundation Blog. https://ethereum.org/en/roadmap/danksharding/

Choi, J. & Kim, S. (2023). Performance analysis of Ethereum layer 2 scaling solutions: Comparative study of Optimistic and ZK-Rollups. *IEEE Access*, 11, 34782–34795.

Dworkin, A. & Kravchenko, P. (2023). Optimistic rollups vs. ZK rollups: Comparing Ethereum Layer 2 scaling solutions. *Journal of Blockchain Research*, 5(2), 114–129.

Ethereum Foundation. (2024). Ethereum improvement proposals: EIP-3540—EOF—EVM Object Format v1. https://eips.ethereum.org/EIPS/eip-3540

Gudgeon, L., Moreno-Sanchez, P., Roos, S., McCorry, P., & Gervais, A. (2022). The economics of Layer 2 blockchain scaling solutions. *Financial Cryptography and Data Security*, 15(4), 217–233.

Maiboroda, A. & Bylica, P. (2023). Implementation and optimization of EVM object format. *Proceedings of the 6th Workshop on Scalable and Resilient Infrastructures for Distributed Ledgers*, 31–42.

Mavridou, A. & Laszka, A. (2018). Designing secure Ethereum smart contracts: A finite state machine based approach. In *International Conference on Financial Cryptography and Data Security* (pp. 523–540). Springer, Berlin, Heidelberg.

Mukhopadhyay, M. *Ethereum Smart Contract Development: Build Blockchain-based Decentralized Applications Using Solidity.* Packt Publishing Ltd., 2018.

Nizamuddin, N., Salah, K., Azad, M. A., Arshad, J., & Rehman, M. H. (2019). Decentralized document version control using ethereum blockchain and IPFS. *Computers & Electrical Engineering*, 76, 183–197.

Poon, J. & Buterin, V. (2021). Plasma: Scalable autonomous smart contracts. White Paper, 1-47. https://plasma.io/plasma-deprecated.pdf

Schär, F. (2021). Decentralized finance: On blockchain- and smart contract-based financial markets. *Federal Reserve Bank of St. Louis Review*, 103(2), 153-174.

Wang, X. & He, Y. (2023). Gas optimization techniques in Ethereum: Analysis and best practices. *Journal of Systems Architecture*, 132, 102717.

Wohrer, M. & Zdun, U. (2018). Smart contracts: security patterns in the ethereum ecosystem and solidity. In *2018 International Workshop on Blockchain Oriented Software Engineering* (pp. 2-8). IEEE.

Wood, G. (2022). Ethereum: A secure decentralised generalised transaction ledger (Berlin version ed87a61). https://ethereum.github.io/yellowpaper/paper.pdf

CHAPTER 8

Physics of Large Language Models

This chapter is adapted from a talk delivered by **Zeyuan Allen-Zhu, ScD**, at the **ICML 2024 Tutorial: Physics of Language Models.** The talk was widely acclaimed for its depth and systematic approach to understanding the underlying mechanisms of language models. To ensure accessibility and enhance understanding, the content has been transcribed and supplemented with technical commentary. Certain parts of the talk have been edited for clarity and context while maintaining the integrity and intent of the original presentation. By combining rigorous experimentation with synthetic data and probing techniques, the speaker provides insights that challenge traditional approaches to AI development. This chapter offers both theoretical insights and actionable strategies, making it a significant contribution to the ongoing conversation about advancing AI capabilities and understanding.

We divide "intelligence" into multiple dimensions (like language structures, knowledge, reasoning, etc.). For each dimension, we create synthetic data for LLM pre-training to understand the theory and push the capabilities of LLMs to the extreme. Unlike benchmarking, by controlling the synthetic data, we aim to discover universal laws of all LLMs, not just a specific version like GPT/Llama. By tweaking hyperparameters such as data amount, type, difficulty, and format, we determine factors affecting LLM performance and suggest improvements. Unlike black-box training,

CHAPTER 8   PHYSICS OF LARGE LANGUAGE MODELS

we develop advanced probing techniques to examine the inner workings of LLMs and understand their hidden mental processes. This helps us gain a deeper understanding of how these AI models function and moves us closer to creating more powerful and transparent AI systems.

This chapter will cover language structures (Part 1), reasoning (Part 2), and knowledge (Part 3). These sections explain why and how language models succeed or fail on certain AI tasks and provide practical suggestions for necessary changes to (1) model architecture, (2) data preparation, and (3) the training process to move us closer to AGI.

Part 0: Prelude

This chapter is about the *theory* of language models, but the word "theory" you know can mean lots of different things in different people's minds. In the community where I came from—I came from TCS (Theory of Computations)—by *theory* we actually mean prove mathematical theorems, in which we define concept classes, we make assumptions on the data, on the model, and then we try to prove learnability theorems. That's what we meant by *theory*. But the word "theory" actually means a lot of things, a full spectrum of things. On the other extreme it can also mean "ethology" or animal behavior science. Whenever you subscribe to OpenAI's API, then you can play with GPT-4 or GPT-4-mini and try to get very interesting results over there. For instance, the very celebrated like chain of thought was obtained in this way, and this is also theory of language models. So, in these two extremes, there are definitely like pros and cons.

An "ethology theory of language models" refers to applying the principles of ethology, the study of animal behavior, to analyze and understand the capabilities and limitations of large language models (LLMs), particularly by examining how their behaviors, like generating text, can be understood through the lens of evolutionary adaptations

CHAPTER 8 PHYSICS OF LARGE LANGUAGE MODELS

and functions, asking questions like "How did this behavior develop?", "What is its purpose?", and "How does it function within the context of its environment"—essentially treating LLMs as if they were animals exhibiting complex behaviors in their own environment of data.

So let's begin with the pros. On the mathematical side, we love it because we can prove like rigorous theorems, and there are also a lot of pros on the ethology side, that is, you know everyone can do theory, you can play with super-large language models, and the results—don't get me wrong—the results can be very educational. Right, not only chain of thought, like tree of thought, and many interesting concepts can be derived out of this type of *theory*. But there are also cons. So the cons on the mathematical side are that the assumptions you make are typically like too idealistic and the networks you can prove are typically very shallow like maybe a one-layer transformer, and only in very rare cases the theorems that you prove really do connect to practice, and even if it does people may not read your paper because it's too long. So the actual final deal breaker actually for me to step out of that community was because making progress was very slow over there. So nowadays like in academia, you know we have NSF grants that are maybe between three and five years, but in industry where I currently work for Meta for FAIR Labs, we make plans that are like maybe in six months and so on. So this actually makes some sense because if you think about it, like two years ago we didn't even have ChatGPT and one year ago we didn't even have the (artificial) intelligence at today's level. So if by proving mathematical theorems you're making very slow progress, then how could you make sure the theorem you're proving maybe a year later still applies, right?

So let me actually remind everyone that humankind used to be very, very patient. So in the old days when Isaac Newton actually developed the laws of motion and gravity, as well as calculus, that was in the year 1687. And how did Newton achieve this? So there is the story about the apple tree, right? But that was only the beginning; that was the thing that drove Isaac Newton into the field. But in fact, the entire theory from

CHAPTER 8   PHYSICS OF LARGE LANGUAGE MODELS

Isaac Newton was built upon Johannes Kepler's three laws of planetary motion: that is, the "ellipse and foci" laws. And guess what year was it? That was between 70 and 80 years before Isaac Newton. So this probably most of you have heard about; but a very less known fun fact about this whole history that most of the younger generation did not know is that Johannes Kepler was actually an assistant to this Danish astronomer, Tycho Brahe, who was the head of the observatory, and he actually spent an entire 20 years to collect observatory data. And that was even like 30 more years before Kepler. And Kepler was the assistant to this observatory, and after the death of Tycho, Kepler inherited all of those experimental data, and that was the thing that actually Johannes Kepler built his three laws of planetary motion on, and that was the entire start of this Newton's laws of motion and gravity.

So, if you count everything together, that's more than a century ago, right? So humankind used to be very patient, but not anymore. At this point maybe you're thinking that am I trying to make the following analogy that Newton's laws are more like proving mathematical theorems about language models, and maybe Tycho's observatory data is more like ethology, it's more like playing with GPT-4. But in fact, I think there is still like a gap between ethology and physics, that is, if you just play with large language models, to try to make educated guesses, then there are a lot of concerns. So concern number 1 is that studying models that are pre-trained using Internet data may not be *scientific enough*. For instance, nowadays it's very easy to observe bugs in GPT-4 or Llama-3 and so on. So people are now talking about the 9.9 versus 9.11 (bug), but my favorite bugs were actually the ones we discovered the at the end of last year.

This is a reference to a famous bug discovered in July 2024, on the OpenAI community forums, when a user prompted a question, "Which is bigger, 9.9 or 9.11?", and the model answered incorrectly about 50% of the time, while in the same year, DeepMind's AlphaProof system achieved silver medal performance at the International Mathematical Olympiad (IMO), solving complex mathematical proofs that challenge expert human

CHAPTER 8   PHYSICS OF LARGE LANGUAGE MODELS

mathematicians. This raised a very lively discussion about the limitations of generalization in a LLM; essentially, AI systems excel within their designed parameters but may fail at seemingly simpler tasks outside their optimization space.

That is, you can ask GPT-4 to do parity checks, for instance, "Was Joe Biden born in an odd year or even year?" Or like you can ask GPT-4 to, for instance, compare the birth dates of two celebrities like Donald Trump versus Nancy Pelosi. And it's actually going to produce errors almost all the time. The chance that it gives a correct answer is like flipping a random coin. So, in order to study really scientifically like what is happening behind the scene, I believe that it really requires us to do very careful controlled studies, to see why exactly this happens.

So could it be because the knowledge is not properly stored in the model? Or could it be because maybe the parity test is too hard, maybe the model doesn't know what even or odd means? Or could it be something else entirely? So, actually, as we will see, the reason is because of "something else." Therefore, we need full control of the data; if you only play with a pre-trained model, it's very hard for you to make scientific discoveries about what's exactly happening. Another concern I want to point out is that just by studying individual models may not be scientific enough either. For instance, you know this means we have bugs for GPT-4, but does that only apply to the July version of GPT-4 of this year? Does it apply to the August version or maybe the version of next year, right? So ideally speaking we want to identify big issues with language models, not only to a specific version of a language model, but we want to develop general universal principles that can apply to all the possible language models. So this is the hope—we hope that statements can be (validated) regardless of how you pre-train or how you fine-tune parameters or model sizes.

A third concern is that people are nowadays talking about data contamination, so we can no longer maybe rely on benchmarks. A very celebrated example is the GSM8k dataset, which only has 8K number of math problems. So if a model is like very good at solving those 8K problems, could it be because of data contamination, right? I'm pretty sure that nobody will intentionally cheat to put this data into your pre-train data, but what if imagine like tomorrow I translate all of the problems into French, into German, into Chinese, I put it on my MIT website. Because MIT websites are very likely to be crawled by the language models, then could it be that from tomorrow onward then all of the models will be cheating, just because of this action? By the way I haven't done this, but if I do this, imagine, right? Then it's no longer a trustable benchmark.

The fourth concern here—I think the biggest concern—is that just by playing with those models, you really see nothing about the internals of how those language models work. And if things work then, how do they work? And if things fail, then why do things fail? So we want to study this more scientifically. So to this extent I think like ethology or the idea of just playing with GPT-4 is more like maybe geocentrism in you know 400–200 BC that is like just by watching maybe two models like a sun and a moon like going up and down every day, you can form theories, but maybe the theory you can create may not be the most comprehensive and the most real (canonical) theory behind the scene. To this extent, we really put forward this initiative that we call the physics of language models, that is, we are emphasizing four different things. Number one, we really wish to decompose the concept of intelligence into building blocks and then to study them one by one, like language structures or knowledge or reasoning and so on. Let's study them like one by one. Do not mix everything together; that will be too complex. And two, let us build synthetic data to study everything in a controlled setting, in an idealized environment so that you can tweak the data's difficulty, the data's type, the amount of data, or the data's formats, and to see like how those individual things affect the model's performance, and in this way you can start to make a very informed knowledge about what you should do, if you're going to train tomorrow's next generation of language models. The third thing we're advocating is to really make the experiments highly repeatable. So,

CHAPTER 8   PHYSICS OF LARGE LANGUAGE MODELS

if pre-training a model costs like 10 million US dollars, then that would be too expensive—you cannot afford doing repeated experiments. If you have like, say, seven different things you want to try, you cannot afford like tuning each of them up and down to do controlled experiments to figure out what exactly is causing like the final outcome.

So therefore we propose to study smaller models, maybe models of only 100 million parameter sizes. And as you will see throughout this chapter just by studying those smaller models, you can also derive very universal laws about language models. The reason here is because we're not focusing on the entire concept of intelligence altogether, we're focusing on just individual building blocks. And also we're building synthetic data, so we are in a very idealized setting; in this setting you do not need a model size to be super huge. And finally like we're advocating for doing probing, that is, to see the inner workings of language models. So here is the structure of this chapter: I'm going to cover three main parts, respectively, regarding how language models learn language structures, reasoning, as well as knowledge. So I'm going in actually the reverse direction, that is, I will start with Part 3 that's about knowledge.

Part 3: Knowledge in Language Models

So this part is the joint work with Professor Yuanzhi Li from Mohamed bin Zayed University of Artificial Intelligence (MBZUAI). So I will begin with this counterexample I showed you a few slides ago, that is, large language models just generally fail on doing the parity test for the person's birth years or maybe comparing the two celebrities' birth dates. And you can keep getting counterexamples like this very easily. Now how to study this type of counterexamples, right? You can of course test it upon like a model to see like how accurately it performs, but I claim that before you even attempt to do this, there is a prerequisite that you need to keep in mind. That is, if the model fails on such a problem, then could

CHAPTER 8   PHYSICS OF LARGE LANGUAGE MODELS

it be because the model cannot extract the birth year of celebrities? Or maybe more specifically, could it be because the model did not see, for instance, Joe Biden's biography in its pre-train data? Or if the model has seen such biography, could it be because the model cannot extract the birthday information of celebrities, or could it be because the model can extract the birthday about certain celebrities and not others? So in fact we spent an entire paper to study under what conditions a language model can extract knowledge that it has seen in the pre-train. So this itself is already like an area that deserves performing some controlled experiments, so this what we will review first. So once we are certain that the model is capable of, for instance, extracting the birth dates of every single celebrity on Wikipedia, for instance, now we can start to test the model's performance on manipulating knowledge, such as like performing knowledge classification, like the parity test, is it even or odd. But I claim, even here, there are still a lot of subtleties, so if the model successfully answered the question of like "if Joe Biden was born in an even year," could this be because of data contamination? So this was a counterexample we discovered at the end of last year; if today the model succeeds on this specific question (the parity test), could it be because we have put the paper on arXiv and therefore this question got revealed to the newer generations of the language models? So we need to exclude the possibility of this (data contamination) in order to study this question properly. And similarly, if the model fails to answer this question, could it be because the model just does not know what even or odd means? Maybe it did not get fine-tuned enough to do the parity test properly. So to study the language models' true capability of manipulating knowledge, you have to also get rid of the scenarios B and D, so you have to do very careful and controlled experiments.

Scenario A: Model infers from "1946 is even" and "Biden was born in 1946," making the final answer based on a function of certain knowledge it sees during training

Scenario B: Model sees training data of equivalent form such as "Is Joe Biden's birth year even?"

Scenario C: Model does not know what "even" means.

Scenario D: Model knows what "even" means and can answer questions like "Is 1946 even?" but cannot answer "Was Joe Biden born in an even year?"

The following is a brief summary of studying language models:

Knowledge capacity: LLMs store knowledge at an estimated rate of 2 bits per parameter under sufficient pre-training. This provides a theoretical upper bound for the maximum knowledge retention achievable by LLMs.

Memorization versus extraction: Memorization does not equate to knowledge extraction. Models can perfectly memorize knowledge word for word while still being unable to extract and use that knowledge effectively.

Knowledge augmentation: Without knowledge augmentation, models struggle to effectively extract stored knowledge. This is a fundamental limitation even when the knowledge is demonstrably stored in the model.

Enhancing extraction: Training models with multiple rephrased versions of the same information significantly enhances knowledge extraction accuracy. This approach transforms how knowledge is stored within the model's parameters.

So I will begin with Part 3.1, that is, under what conditions language models can extract knowledge. So I'm going to divide it into some sub-results. To study this properly, as I mentioned I need to design the knowledge dataset. I need to design some synthetic dataset. What is the knowledge that comes to your mind that's the most natural one? (To answer the parity test.) So to me, it's biography, right. People's biography is some sort of knowledge, and indeed we build synthetic biography data of fake random people, and we either use maybe a set of sentence templates before we generate the biographies or we use some LLMs to help us to generate the biographies. And for now imagine that we have N individuals and we generate one biography entry per person. This is the

CHAPTER 8   PHYSICS OF LARGE LANGUAGE MODELS

biography data that we created as synthetic data. And at the same time we also prepared QAs. This is like instruction fine-tuning data, that is, each person has six attributes: the birth date, the birth city, the university, the major, the employer, and the work city. We prepared six questions for each person, corresponding to the six attributes of the person, so these are the QA data. And here is the experiment setup: we only reveal half of the QA data to the training and then evaluate the model out of the distribution on the remaining half of the individuals. So in this way we can do a controlled experiment by separating out really the training set from the test set. And if the model is capable of getting high accuracy on the test set, then we say this is the skill of knowledge extraction. So if the model is capable of extracting knowledge for people only in the training set, that's not knowledge extraction; that's only memorization. But if it can generalize the skill of the QAs onto the other half of the individuals based on their biography data, then we say this is knowledge extraction. Okay, this is how we define knowledge extraction, and now comes the first result: Suppose you do mix-training, that is, you put both the biography data and the QA data into the pre-training process and, then, test it on the out-of-distribution dataset; the accuracy is high. In short, if you do mix-training, you get knowledge extraction to a very good accuracy, but this is not what people do in practice.

In practice, people first pre-train the data on (a source such as) Wikipedia and so on, and then they instruct fine-tune the model and finally reveal the model to the users who evaluate and use it out of distribution. So if you follow this procedure, and even if you perfectly pre-train and say close to perfectly like instruct fine-tune, we discovered that the model will perform very bad on extracting knowledge. So this is actually a universal statement. It's independent of how large the model or which architecture you use; you can use like GPT (GPT-2) or Llama, Mistral, and so on. It's independent of the data size; you can try different data sizes. It's also independent of the training parameters or fine-tuning parameters; you can use LoRA of different ranks. And in all of the cases, we

CHAPTER 8   PHYSICS OF LARGE LANGUAGE MODELS

actually tried more than I think 500 possibilities here, all of them give you like a 0% accuracy (close to 0% accuracy). This was really mind-blowing the first moment I did this experiment until I realized one catch, that is, we only have one biography per person. What if you had more biographies? This is what we call knowledge augmentation. So suppose you augment the pre-train data to make sure that the knowledge is not described only once but described multiple times using different writing styles—maybe the sentences are permuted; maybe like you change, you do translation, from English to French; or maybe you just rewrite the biography of each person, say, using some small model. Then the accuracy suddenly increases. For instance, if you have five biography entries per person using different writing styles, you get 96% test accuracy. To summarize, unless you do mix-training, **it's absolutely necessary for you to knowledge augment the pre-train data before the knowledge can be become extractable**. Okay so in this controlled setting we actually discovered this. But why does this happen? Right, the main theme of this chapter's tutorial is not only to discover phenomenon, but also to discuss why. So we did probing (position-probing). We used probing techniques to actually exactly study where and how knowledge is stored inside a language model. For instance, if you pre-train a language model like GPT-2 in this biography data and try to do probing by feeding a biography entry as the input to the transformer, so now it's already pre-trained; we feed the input once again to the model, and we look at the hidden states of the last layer. We tried to do probing to see how much knowledge of this person's biography is stored in those probing positions. Let's take one example. Suppose we care about the knowledge about this person's employer name, in this case Meta Platforms. Then if you probe from position 4, of course like that position's hidden state should encode like what is this person's employer name because you know the training task is auto-regressive, right. It's about predicting the next token, so therefore the hidden states at this point definitely should encode at least the token of "Meta" and therefore very likely "Meta Platforms." So what we are more interested in is, from those previous token positions, do the hidden states actually also encode the knowledge of this person? So the answer is very striking, that is, if you do not do knowledge augmentation, then from all of the previous token positions, the probing accuracy is very close to zero; but if you do knowledge augmentation, that is, once you have multiple different writing styles, the model stores knowledge in a very different way by satisfying that, at right after the person's name, the hidden states already store knowledge about this person's employer name. So let me elaborate on this, that is, if you do not do knowledge augmentation for the pre-train data, then the model tends to learn the wrong logic; it may not learn like it was Anya who works for Meta Platform. You may learn the wrong logic, that is, it's someone who was born on October 2, 1996, in Princeton, New Jersey, who studied commutations at MIT works for Meta. Or in the mathematical form, it could happen that the knowledge of value 5 is jointly stored in this tuple, which is defined by the key as well as all of the values before it. But if you do knowledge augmentation, because the values can be permuted, it may not be always in the same order; in this way, the model tends to store knowledge in the right format, that is, it is Anya who works for Meta. Or in the mathematical form, value 5 will be directly stored onto the key; in this case it's the person's name. **To summarize, we discovered that, if you pre-train a language model with knowledge augmentation, this changes the behavior of how knowledge gets stored inside the language model, and this in turns affects whether or not the knowledge can be further extracted via instruction fine-tuning.**

This is what you can discover if you do controlled experiments. Now we know that it's important to augment knowledge, but what's the fraction of knowledge that we have to augment? Do we have to augment everybody? It turns out you don't. So let's consider the following controlled experiment, that is, you have some major celebrities and some minor celebrities (minorities). For the major celebrities, their biographies are very rich on the Internet, for instance, you see at least five biographies of the same person written in different writing styles. Now for the minor celebrities, you may only have one biography entry for each. In this case, suppose you pre-train the two kinds of data all together and now also fine-tune the model with respect to the QAs on the celebrities. First of all, we saw that the model out of distribution generalized to the rest of the celebrities, but what's more interesting here is how does this affects the knowledge extraction for the minorities. It turns out, the accuracy is pretty high. Let's take a moment to appreciate why this is significant, because for the minorities their biographies have no knowledge augmentation, and on top of that the minorities did not even appear in the instruction finding data. **The mere inclusion of the celebrity data in the pre-training actually enhances the model's knowledge extraction for the minorities**. We also did probing here and discovered that the mere inclusion of celebrity data teaches the model to store knowledge in the right format, and that causes the model to also perform well under minorities. For instance, Donald Trump's biographies have been appearing so many times on the Internet, and the mere existence of those biography data actually helped all of the language models' capability of extracting knowledge about biographies for the minorities. **So as a result, it's really sufficient for you to augment only part of the people, and that will give you knowledge extraction for all of the people.**

So to summarize on this Part 3.1, I showed you that there's a distinction between knowledge storage versus knowledge extraction, that is, even if a model can 100% word by word memorize knowledge such as biographies, it does not mean that the knowledge can be always extractable. And to make sure knowledge is extractable, you either do mix-training or make sure the knowledge is augmented. So the last result, which I didn't show you in this chapter, is that if you use bidirectional models like BERT or the DeBERTa, all of them will fail. They do not give you knowledge extraction, even if you do mix-training together with knowledge augmentation. For like language modeling, for like GPT, if you do one of the two (mix-training or knowledge augmentation), you get knowledge extraction, but for bidirectional models, even if you do both of them, you do not get knowledge extraction.

CHAPTER 8   PHYSICS OF LARGE LANGUAGE MODELS

Let me now jump to Part 3.2 about knowledge manipulation. For this part, I'm going to assume that the knowledge is already fully extractable, and I want to study further the skills of language models regarding how much they can manipulate knowledge. There are a lot of different ways to manipulate knowledge, and the simplest possible task I can imagine is knowledge classification. Suppose you have a model that you pre-train on the biographies and then you'll fine-tune it, to make sure that all of the birth dates of everybody can be extractable. Further, suppose you have already done this either using mix-training or knowledge augmentation. Let's try to study the task of knowledge classification, and maybe the simplest possible classification task is classifying 12 months into even or odd, into two categories. Here we not only consider the knowledge classification like without CoT; we also consider a version with chain of thought where the model first spells out explicitly the birth month of this person, followed by yes or no. Now suppose you do fine-tuning sufficient enough to get the perfect accuracy. Then let's once again evaluate the model's classification accuracy on the remaining half of the individuals. We found something very striking, that is, if you do this procedure, the accuracy for the out-of-distribution people, for the remaining half of them, is extremely low if you do not use CoT. In other words, we discovered that in knowledge manipulation (even in the simplest single order knowledge manipulation task; in this case it's knowledge classification, but you can try others like ranking or comparisons), if you do not use CoT, the performance is roughly equivalent to a random guess. In fact, what is even worse here is that the inclusion of CoT in your training does not help the accuracy during evaluation without CoT (training with CoT does not help inference without CoT). So this means you both need to include CoT in your training data and when you're deploying the model; you have to encourage the model to use chain of thought, that is, to explicitly spell out knowledge, before it can manipulate knowledge. Universal law: Knowledge manipulation is impossible without CoT. This CoT is very different from CoT in reasoning, which I will cover later in this chapter. That is, you can imagine GPT-4 is very capable of, for instance, answering the sum of two numbers (even or odd) without actually writing down the sum A plus B explicitly, so you can skip steps; but for knowledge manipulation tasks, a language model cannot skip steps. It always has to write down the explicit knowledge before it can do any simple operations on the knowledge. This is a very strong statement, and in fact it's a statement that you can only derive from doing controlled experiments. So that's about knowledge manipulations such as classification or comparison and ranking and so on. Another manipulation task we studied was inverse search, that is, we try to find the model to answer like who was born on this date, in this city, and works for a particular employer. Let's again test this out of distribution on the remaining half of the individuals. And here's what we discovered: zero accuracy. **So our conclusion is that knowledge inverse search is literally just impossible**. This is once again a universal law, so I'm stating this regardless of the model size, regardless of the data size, regardless of the training method. You can use like mix-training or fine-tuning, whichever you like. You can like fully argument your data, by asking GPT to rewrite your data several times. You can also change your fine-tuning method. And so on. In all of them, knowledge reversal fails. So only when the pre-train data is already knowledge reversed can you do inverse knowledge search. With my colleagues from Meta, we wrote a separate paper regarding how to practically, very easily reverse knowledge, but the key point here is that if you reverse knowledge in the fine-tune stage, that would be too late—you really have to reverse knowledge in the pre-train stage. You cannot hope for like changing from, say, unidirectional models like GPT to bidirectional models like BERT; if you do that, it also doesn't solve this issue. Okay, so some negative examples regarding a language model's knowledge manipulation capabilities, and let's also connect this to practice. We also tested the same thing on GPT-4 or Llama and realize that if you try to ask, "Was Joe Biden like born in an even year or odd year?", you can try it with all of the celebrities on Wikipedia, and the accuracy of the answer is like flipping a random coin, if you do not use CoT, but if you

CHAPTER 8   PHYSICS OF LARGE LANGUAGE MODELS

use CoT, then the accuracy will greatly improve. Another thing we tested is inverse search. You can design different types of inverse search, but to me, my favorite task was actually this Chinese idiom task. In Chinese, we have these Chinese idioms, which are like four-letter idioms that we use in our daily conversations. You can mask out the first letter out of a Chinese idiom, and they ask like GPT-4 like what is the missing letter. I can tell you very confidently at least one-third of the Chinese speakers in mainland China are able to answer this question very accurately, but not for GPT-4. This is another evidence that the large language models today just cannot do inverse knowledge search.

In order to state something strong, you have to do controlled experiments that can tell you that these bugs just cannot be easily fixed. We discovered those bugs last year in September, but still you can see these bugs showing up in every single language model of today. On the other hand, this also gives you a Turing test that can distinguish all the modern AI models from humans, because if you ask who was born earlier like for your mom and dad, you don't need to explicit explicitly state their birthday, but you can directly say yes or no. You can directly do the comparison, and you don't need to say the year out loud—you can do this mental calculation, but large language models cannot. This actually pretty much summarizes Part 3.2. I'm actually skipping one result, that is, knowledge partial search. We discovered that although a language model can fully extract knowledge, for instance, the birthday of a person, it may not be able to extract the last word of this knowledge, which is the birth year—so the accuracy of these two can also be very different. This is actually related to a paper from my colleagues at Meta, who proposed this idea of multi-token prediction: instead of predicting only the next token, you ask the model to predict multiple future tokens. This will actually change how the knowledge is stored in a language model, and they may improve its capabilities. This is actually a result I'm skipping today. The result I covered is that a language model just cannot say a birth year is even without saying the year explicitly. There is a concurrent work to ours that

CHAPTER 8 PHYSICS OF LARGE LANGUAGE MODELS

actually gives a name to this phenomenon. They call it reversal curse and summarized it as if you train a model on A is B, then the model cannot learn B is A, and that's the same thing we discovered here.

In the next part I'm going to tell you about scaling laws regarding knowledge capacities. The first result I'm going to tell you is regarding **all language models can store knowledge in this ratio that is 2 bits per parameter.** Before I do that, I need to define what do I mean by *bit*. So I mean information-theoretically, the number of bits in your data. So how to measure this? With the help from synthetic data, if you randomly generate synthetic knowledge data, then you can actually measure how many information bits are there in your dataset. For instance, if Anya's birthday is randomly generated, say, uniformly at random, from 12 months and 28 days and 200 years, then this is log2 of you know 12 * 28 * 200, which is like 6.21 bits of knowledge, and similarly like if Eugeo's birth city is Washington, DC and if this is randomly generated from 300 different cities, then this is 8.23 bits of knowledge. Therefore, if you design biography data with N people and with like, say, six attributes that are generated according to certain distribution, then you can compute exactly how much amount of information is representing this dataset. And this is by the way regardless of the writing styles: you can rewrite the biography of the same person like 40 different times, but it's capturing the same knowledge, so therefore the amount of knowledge in terms of information-theoretic bits is not changed. Another way to do the synthetic data is to create more hyperparameters. Instead of thinking about people biographies, let's make it more general. We can study knowledge that has a vocabulary size T and maybe some diversity D and so on. You don't need to read all the parameters, but the point here is that for any type of synthetic knowledge, you can actually create a formula to actually compute what is the amount of knowledge bits stored in this dataset. And now suppose you pre-train a language model on knowledge data that is synthetically generated, you can start to compute how much knowledge is stored in this learned language model. If the model achieves zero loss on this dataset, then of

273

course it has fully captured the knowledge, but what if the model is only, say, half-correct on this dataset? Then you have to be a little bit careful to compute what is the discount factor, that is, what's the exact amount of knowledge the model has learned. If you do that, you can start to derive scaling laws. This is a more scientific version of the scaling laws, compared with what you have previously seen. Our major discovery here is that all LLMs can consistently achieve 2 bits per parameter in terms of storing knowledge, if the data is sufficiently pre-trained. By universal, I mean that for a wide range of model sizes, hyperparameters, depths, and widths; regardless of the data types, as long as you study transformers of at least two layers, all language models converge to storing knowledge in 2 bits per parameter, regardless of how you rewrite the data and so on. From here, we made a conjecture about the amount of knowledge available to humankind, especially for all the English Wikipedia plus all the English textbooks. **We actually estimated how much information bits there are, and we predicted that a 7-billion-parameter language model should be sufficient in terms of storing all of such knowledge.** Of course we haven't reached there yet, but I'm claiming this is definitely very plausible, and maybe in two years, if we haven't reached there, then we need to rethink are we doing something wrong. Now let me explain what I mean by "sufficiently trained," that is, I claim if all the knowledge got exposed during the pre-training, if each piece of knowledge gets exposed for a thousand times, then we can reach the 2 bits per parameter capacity. By exposure, I do not mean to train a model for a thousand passes of the training data. I mean that each piece of knowledge is seen a thousand times. For instance, knowledge about the US capital being Washington, DC may have been exposed maybe a million times, if you do just one pass of the Internet pre-train data. Therefore, by exposure, I just mean the same knowledge having been exposed multiple times, using different writing styles. Let's do a controlled experiment, that is, suppose each piece of knowledge is exposed for the same number of times, all of them, say, a thousand times. Then we achieve this 2 bits per parameter scaling law.

CHAPTER 8   PHYSICS OF LARGE LANGUAGE MODELS

If you fix the data size, then when you increase the (size of the) model, you cannot learn more knowledge from the data. In this scenario, the interesting thing is, as you approach the upper limit of the knowledge a model can acquire, its capacity to store knowledge aligns closely with the 2 bits per parameter scaling law.

In contrast, insufficient training is where the knowledge is not exposed too many times, say, that each piece of knowledge is exposed only for 100 times or, equivalently speaking, rare knowledge may not appear enough number of times (in training data) on the Internet. For those kinds of knowledge, the knowledge capacity actually decreases to 1 bit per parameter. The more interesting thing is that if you focus now on such rare knowledge or equivalently insufficient training, then model architectures become relevant. If you use GPT-2, that's good, but if you use Llama or Mistral, the performance drops. You have a factor of 1.3 difference between using GPT-2 and using Llama, so the performance will actually get worse if you use Llama or Mistral. I'm going to explain why this happens, but before that, let me also tell you that even if you reduce the size of the MLP layers of GPT-2 by a factor 4 to make it smaller than the attention layer, you still do not have any capacity loss. But if you completely remove the MLP layers, then you're going to have capacity loss. So two disclaimers: This comparison is only for knowledge capacity; it's not reasoning and so on. And disclaimer number 2 is that it's for rare knowledge, so if you consider the knowledge that appears frequently on the Internet, with a thousand exposures, I told you that there's no difference across model architectures, but for the rare knowledge, there is a difference. So this is one of the good things about doing controlled experiments: you can exactly figure out for what type of data, for what kind of tasks, one model is better than another. You can do more controlled experiments to compare model architectures. So here, we exactly pinpoint to what caused Llama or Mistral to have a poor performance; that's because of GatedMLP. If you identify the differences between GPT-2 and Llama, there are seven total architectural differences such as different activation functions (SiLU versus

GELU) or maybe different layer norms, but you can systematically turn off each one and figure out it's the MLP layer. If you take Llama and replace its GatedMLP with a standard MLP, then the knowledge capacity improves back to the original 1 bit per parameter.

GatedMLP is an alternative to transformers without self-attention. It uses channel projections and spatial projections with static parameterization and near state-of-the-art results on NLP and computer vision tasks but uses a lot less trainable parameters than the corresponding transformer model.

The last thing I want to show you is that we also did a controlled experiment with data that has mixed qualities. Let's imagine that we not only have data that is rich in knowledge such as Wikipedia, but we also have data that is not so good in knowledge, such as the common crawls or Internet *junk*. Now, let's compile two scenarios. In scenario 1, you train your model only with respect to good data, the data that is rich in knowledge, and suppose you make sure each piece of data is exposed exactly 100 times during the pre-train. In the other scenario, you train both with the good data and with the bad data, but you still make sure that each piece of good data is exposed 100 times. Now you can start to quantify how much good knowledge is stored in a model for both scenarios, and you will see a big jump. There is 20× difference between the two scenarios. So this is not 20%; this is 20 times: in the first scenario, you may be able to retain 20 million bits of information, and in the second scenario, you can only memorize 1 million bits. Even if you increase the training time in the second scenario, so, say, that you made sure the good data got exposed 300 times (that's three times larger than before), you still have a very large loss, like three times loss. We summarize this as saying that **the mere existence of the junk data in the pre-train actually significantly harms LLM's knowledge capacity on the good data**, sometimes by a 20× factor. We also used control experiments to discover how to fix this. Let's consider adding a domain token in front of each piece of pre-train data. In the past, your pre-train data looks like concatenating all of the maybe Internet pages altogether, but now let's prepend each piece of Internet data with either the domain name or maybe the URL. And once you do that, things get fixed. For instance, with the addition of a domain token, the 20× worse performance becomes ten times better. As long as you add such domain tokens to the data, the LLMs can automatically detect the domains that are rich in high-quality knowledge and then prioritize learning from them. You don't need to teach the model which domains are good; all you need to do is to just place the domain name in front of the data. To summarize, in Part 3.3, I told you that if the data is sufficiently pre-trained, then you can hit this 2 bits per parameter of knowledge capacity regardless of the model architecture, and we use that to make some predictions about how large a language model needs to be in order to capture all of the human knowledge. We also studied scaling laws for insufficiently trained models, that is, what if the knowledge is rare? In such a case we see architecture differences, and it's better to use the original MLP implementation compared with GatedMLP.

And one thing I didn't cover today is about quantization and MoE. For instance, if you quantize a model into 8-bit parameters, that is, if you use int8, you can still achieve this 2 bits per parameter capacity. This means language models are very capable of achieving a compression ratio of knowledge being like 4-to-1, and that's extremely strong. Finally, I showed you this surprising result regarding how to deal with data of mixed qualities, and the trick is to add domain tokens. So that really summarizes Part 3.

Part 2: Reasoning in Language Models

I'm not going to be able to talk about all levels of reasoning and will focus only on reasoning at the level of grade school math. In this part our goal is to understand the hidden reasoning process of large language models. In order for us to study this, we propose to create a synthetic math dataset

CHAPTER 8 PHYSICS OF LARGE LANGUAGE MODELS

that can simulate GSM8k. And then we use that dataset to understand how large language models think, what is their mental process, what is the reasoning skill that they developed, and why language models make mistakes. This is the goal of Part 2.1. All of the statements I'm going to make are supported by probing.

The goal is to study how large language models solve grade school math problems. But we can't use GSM8k because the data is too small and risks contamination. We also cannot use GPT-4 to augment GSM8k because the generated problems may be too biased and use very few solution templates. If you use this approach to generate math data, it's not going to give you very hard math problems. For this reason, we really believe it's necessary to develop our own synthetic math dataset. But we also made some assumptions, that is, we try to develop a dataset so that you can directly pre-train the language model on such data. So this means we had to remove some commonsense reasoning, for instance, if a candle burns, its length shrinks (not increases). So this is some skill you have to learn from the entire Internet data, but it has nothing to do with the reasoning aspect of a language model. Therefore, we decide to remove that. But at the same time, we think it's necessary to keep at least the following things: Direct dependency between parameters, that is, if a parameter depends on, say, the sum of another two, we want to capture this type of math reasoning. And we also want to capture instance dependency, for example, if there are X classrooms and each classroom has Y messenger bags, then we want to understand that in total there are X times Y messenger bags. Also we want to capture implicit dependency, for instance, if Bob has three times more fruits than Alice and Alice has three apples, four eggs, and two bananas, then eggs are not fruits.

Let me give you a glimpse into what our data looks like. Here is an easy example. Each problem statement is related to two graphs. One is what we call the structure graph, which defines the possible parameters. For instance, one edge captures how many film studios are there in Riverview High School. This is a parameter that can be assigned, and the first sentence of the problem states that this parameter depends on five times the sum of two other parameters. That's one type of parameter. Another type of parameter we manage to capture is, for example, how many bags are there in this high school. This requires some implicit computation, such as figuring out how many film studios exist in the high school and how many bags are in each film studio and so on. That's a rough sense of what the parameters represent. Each sentence of the problem description captures a dependency. For instance, Riverview High School's number of film studios—this parameter—depends on five times the sum of two others. If that's the case, we draw a directed graph from those parameters to this parameter. Eventually, combining all the problem description sentences results in a directed acyclic graph (DAG). That's how we describe a problem. Now, each math problem needs to be followed by a solution. Here, we use the standard chain-of-thought solution to perform the computations. Let me walk you through this so you can better understand how our data looks. For instance, here the question is about how many backpacks are there in Riverview High School, which is represented by a parameter. We know that it equals the product of two other parameters, which in turn need to be derived from other parameters noted in the problem statement. Essentially, the solution is a step-by-step computation from the leaves of a topological graph to get the final answer. Throughout this section, I'm using modular arithmetic with mod 23. For example, if the computation is 7 times 22, I assume it's taken mod 23. The reason for this is that we want to focus on reasoning. By focusing on reasoning, we must eliminate other aspects of language models, such as multi-digit arithmetic. This ensures that if a language model fails on this type of task, it's not because of the arithmetic, but due to reasoning.

Okay, so that's a very rough description of how the data looks. There are many subtleties, but only two things are important for this chapter. First, the sentences in the problem description are randomly shuffled. This means that for a model to learn how to generate solutions, it's not just a line-by-line translation of the problem. It has to figure out what the first step is, what the second step is, and so on, essentially performing a topological sort. Secondly, there's this parameter called "op," which captures the number of operations needed in the solution. For instance, even if the solution has six steps, one of them might involve summing three things, so the total number of operations would be seven. This quantity measures how challenging the reasoning problem is. These are the two key points to focus on. Now, let's pre-train a language model, for instance, GPT-2, on this data. In principle, this data is infinite in size, but we restrict it to two families of data. The first family contains medium-level math problems where the number of solution operations is no more than 15. In the second case—the hard dataset—we focus on problems where the number of operations is no more than 21. We conduct pre-training on these types of data. To give you an idea of how challenging the data is, if op=21, the problem isn't extremely hard but is at least non-trivial. Even for humans, it requires some mental calculation to figure out the first step and so on.

We also computed how many solution templates exist for each dataset. For medium-level problems, there are at least 7 billion solution templates. For hard problems, there are at least 90 trillion templates. This means that if a language model learns from this data, it's not simply memorizing templates—it has to genuinely develop problem-solving skills. So we trained the model and tested it. What's particularly interesting is that we didn't just test the model's performance on problems of the same difficulty as the training set (in distribution). We also tested its ability to solve out-of-distribution problems—problems that are harder than those in the training set. The results showed that language models can generalize out of distribution. **This leads me to an initial claim: language models are indeed capable of learning the skills needed to solve math problems, and they don't do this by memorizing solution templates.** There's an ongoing debate about whether models like GPT-4 solve math problems by memorizing templates. You can't certify this when you don't have full control of the data. But in our case, we have complete control. During

CHAPTER 8   PHYSICS OF LARGE LANGUAGE MODELS

training, the problems are limited to a specific difficulty level, and during testing, the problems are entirely different—longer and more complex. This allows us to conclude that language models genuinely have the ability to learn reasoning skills.

But the real question is, what exactly did they learn? What skills did they develop? That's what I care about for the rest of this chapter. The first thing we discovered is that, for instance, the GPT-2 model—or even models like Llama or Mistral—if trained on this data, immediately develops something we call a "level 1" reasoning skill. Let me explain. When presented with a math problem like this, there are at least two strategies for solving it. One is "level 0" reasoning, where you brute-force your way through all the possible parameters that are mentioned in the problem statement and try to just compute them maximally. For example, you might start with one parameter—if it's not computable, you move to the next one. If it is computable, you compute it. By going through this process in a few loops (say, four or five), you can eventually compute the values for all the parameters and solve the problem, arriving at the correct answer. However, a "level 1" reasoning skill is smarter. "Level 1" reasoning involves performing a topological sort and completely ignoring parameters that are unnecessary for answering the final question. We discovered that language models can truly learn this "level 1" reasoning skill. We provided the models with math problems and ensured their solutions were the shortest possible. Interestingly, the models not only solved the problems but also almost always produced the shortest solutions. If this doesn't surprise you, let me point out why this is a significant advancement. To generate the shortest possible solutions, the model must first understand which parameters are necessary before it even begins generating the first sentence. If the model doesn't recognize the unnecessary parameters, it might compute those in the first steps, resulting in a longer solution. The fact that the language models achieved this means they mentally processed the entire problem before speaking out the first sentence. This is highly non-trivial. **One might assume that using a chain of thought**

simply breaks math problems into simpler steps. But here, I'm saying that deciding the first step itself requires considerable mental processing. I'll use probing to convince you that this is indeed what the language model did.

The first thing we probed was whether, before generating the first sentence of the solution, the model knew if a parameter A was necessary for answering the question. For every possible parameter A, we tried to probe this. We also probed whether, during the generation of solution sentences—say, between consecutive pairs of sentences—the model knew if a parameter A could be computed next. Of course, the model knows which parameter can be computed next, but there could be multiple such parameters. We wanted to see if the model had a complete list of them hidden in its internal states. Even more intriguingly, we tested whether, before a question was even asked, the model already knew which parameter A depends on which parameter B. **After performing these probes, we discovered that the model had already mentally computed all these dependencies with over 99% accuracy. This demonstrates that the model developed a "level 1" reasoning skill.** For instance, if it mentally knows which parameters are necessary and also knows which parameters can be computed next, it can logically deduce the next parameter that is both necessary and computable. Following this logic allows the model to generate the shortest possible solution. This is how language models achieve "level 1" reasoning. But there's something even more surprising here. The model has secretly developed a "level 2" reasoning skill. In particular, even before the question is asked, we discovered that the model has already precomputed the all-pair dependency graph among all the parameters mentioned in the problem statement. This is a skill that isn't strictly necessary for solving the math problems. It's also worth noting that this is definitely a skill humans don't use. Humans typically start from the question and work backward to identify the necessary parameters. But language models have developed a "level 2" reasoning skill by precomputing all-pair parameter dependencies.

CHAPTER 8   PHYSICS OF LARGE LANGUAGE MODELS

I'm not saying this is inherently smarter, but it is undoubtedly a larger amount of computation than what humans perform. We view this as a preliminary signal of where the "G" in AGI (Artificial General Intelligence) might come from. The "G" implies that language models can generalize to skills not explicitly taught in the training set. This is exactly what we observed here. **The model learned to precompute all dependencies among a set of objects after being exposed to their relationships, even before being presented with the actual question. It developed this skill on its own.**

This ability to figure out the dependency graph is critical for the model to later be fine-tuned for other tasks. Once the model has this ability to understand the dependency graph, it can answer questions like "What parameter depends on what?" or even assess the connectivity between various elements. It can leverage this skill to develop additional capabilities, making this a significant piece of evidence for where generalization in AGI might originate. That covers the internal reasoning skills we observed in how language models solve math problems. Now, let's shift focus to how they make mistakes.

I've summarized that language models, at least on our dataset, tend to make two types of mistakes. The first type is occasionally computing unnecessary parameters. While this happens rarely, it becomes more likely when the problems are extremely difficult, with the number of operations (op) pushed to the maximum possible. For example, our GPT-2 model pretrained on this dataset sometimes generates unnecessary parameters. We observed the same behavior in GPT-4 and GPT-4.0 when we tested them last month. This is the first kind of mistake. The second type of mistake occurs when the model starts to compute something—perhaps by defining a parameter—but then gets stuck because the parameter isn't actually ready for computation. These two types of mistakes are the most common ones we've found, at least with the data we've developed. Let's now dive deeper into understanding what causes the models to make these errors.

283

CHAPTER 8   PHYSICS OF LARGE LANGUAGE MODELS

For the first type of mistake, recall that before the model starts generating solutions, it mentally precomputes which parameters are necessary. We can conduct a correlation test to examine the relationship between these errors and whether the model incorrectly marks a necessary parameter as "true" when the correct label is "false." Let me repeat: before the model begins generating solutions, it precomputes the entire set of necessary parameters. By comparing this precomputed set to the actual parameters it uses in the solution, we observe a very high correlation. **This indicates that some mistakes can be identified even before the model begins generating its output. By probing the model's internal states, we can detect errors that are bound to occur. This finding tells us that some math mistakes are systematic rather than random.** While one might assume that errors result from the randomness of the generation process, this evidence shows otherwise. The model's internal state, even before it generates anything, often predicts that a mistake will occur. The second type of mistake also shows a correlation between probing results and errors. If the model mentally determines that a parameter is ready for computation when it actually isn't, the model is very likely to make this error. Improving the model's reasoning thus requires enhancing its ability to compute what we call the "can_next" quantity. I'll discuss this further in Part 2.2, where I'll explain how improving this aspect can enhance the model's reasoning capabilities.

We conducted further probing to link how models make mistakes with the internal states of a language model. The final point I want to discuss in this section, Part 2.1, concerns scaling laws. Starting with OpenAI's original scaling laws, it was suggested that only the size of the model matters, while network width and depth may not. Additionally, as I mentioned in Part 3.3, for knowledge-based tasks, only the model size matters, provided you have at least two transformer layers. **However, for reasoning tasks, depth matters a lot.** To illustrate, consider an experiment comparing a smaller, tall-and-skinny model (20-layer and 9-head) to a larger, shallow-and-wide (4-layer, 30-head) model. Even though the shallow-and-wide model has more parameters, its reasoning accuracy on our dataset is much lower than that of the tall-and-skinny model. The reason for this lies in the mental processing, or precomputation, happening internally. For instance, if you plot the accuracy of the probing task (such as determining necessary parameters) with respect to how far a parameter is from the question, you'll see that **accuracy decreases as the distance increases**. Think about it: if a parameter is, say, eight steps away from the question, the **model must perform at least eight reasoning steps to determine that this parameter is necessary. This is why transformers require deep networks to handle such tasks effectively.** Using probing, we can explain why having more layers improves a language model's reasoning skills. When the number of layers increases, the probing accuracy for parameters far from the question improves and approaches nearly 100%. This leads us to conclude that the **depth of a language model is crucial for reasoning because of this mental computation requirement**. This need for depth cannot be mitigated by using the chain-of-thought framework alone. While chain of thought can break complex operations into simpler steps, it still relies on the model's ability to mentally compute the first step before generating a solution. This preliminary mental processing demands depth in the network. To conclude Part 2.1, we created a synthetic math dataset to simulate GSM8k, using it to study the model's hidden reasoning processes. We discovered that language models exhibit a level 2 reasoning skill that goes beyond human capabilities. We used probing to uncover how they make mistakes and found a connection between a model's depth and the reasoning length of a math problem. This level of insight isn't possible with pre-trained language models sourced from the Internet—you need controlled experiments to make such discoveries.

One finding not yet mentioned, but included in our paper, is that you can also test our dataset with models like GPT-4. When we tested GPT-4 and GPT-4.0 a few weeks ago, we observed that they cannot reliably perform reasoning tasks with more than ten steps. Most of you may already know that GPT-4 struggles with long reasoning tasks, and we systematically confirmed this using our dataset. This highlights that if we aim to improve the reasoning capabilities of large language models in the future, synthetic math datasets will be crucial for advancing these abilities.

This brings us to Part 2.2. Another way to improve reasoning is by teaching language models to learn from their mistakes. Here's an interesting discovery: **language models often know when they've made a mistake.** For instance, consider when a model begins defining a parameter for computation but realizes part-way through that the parameter isn't ready. This typical error can cascade into further issues. By probing the model at specific points—such as the moment it processes a particular word—we can determine whether the model internally recognizes its mistake. Surprisingly, we found that models often do. Their internal states exhibit a kind of regret, as though they want to go back and fix the error but cannot. What happens if we allow the model to go back and correct itself? There are two outcomes. First, if the model is pre-trained on correct data, it essentially becomes an automatic error detector. You can use probing or fine-tuning to help it identify errors. Second, if you let the error detector assist during the generation process—by allowing the model to go back and regenerate after detecting a mistake—you achieve a modest accuracy improvement, around 2%. However, there are downsides. This approach changes how data is generated, requiring two models: one for generation and one for error detection. More importantly, the accuracy improvement is limited because this method relies on randomness to correct errors. For example, when the model goes back and regenerates, it's essentially retrying the computation without truly learning from its mistake. To enable models to genuinely learn from errors, you need data that includes both mistakes and their corrections. In our synthetic setting, we implemented this by generating solutions with deliberate mistakes. For instance, at the end of each sentence, we introduced a mistake with a probability p. Each mistake was simple: it involved a parameter that wasn't ready for computation, followed by a special text token "BACK" to indicate an attempt to correct the error. This approach allows the model to learn

CHAPTER 8 PHYSICS OF LARGE LANGUAGE MODELS

through auto-regressive language modeling, gaining access to its previous mistakes and learning to correct them. Using this data, we observed significant accuracy gains. Interestingly, the improvement was greater when p was higher—that is, **when more mistakes were introduced during training**. Even when half the sentences included mistakes, the model's test-time accuracy continued to improve. This suggests that incorporating mistakes and corrections into training data is a powerful way to enhance a model's reasoning capabilities. An interesting property of this approach is that even if you insert many mistakes into the pre-training data, it doesn't mean the model will make mistakes during inference. For example, even if p=0.5 (where mistakes are inserted with 50% probability during training), the model can still use techniques like temperature zero or beam search to find the most likely next sentence during inference. Although we introduce random errors during training, each of these errors has a very small probability of being generated. The most likely next sentence remains the correct one. If you calculate this, you'll see that the model is still encouraged to use correct sentences in its solutions. Therefore, you don't need to worry about a model trained on this data suddenly generating numerous errors during inference—it won't.

Another discovery is that you don't need label masking. In PyTorch, label masking involves setting ignore_index to −100. You might think that when working with math data containing errors, you'd need label masking to prevent the model from learning from the mistakes and only focus on the corrections. But we found that label masking isn't necessary, and not using it doesn't significantly affect performance. A third point to highlight is that even though the solutions in the pre-training data are longer due to mistakes and corrections, the model still uses level 1 and level 2 reasoning skills during inference to produce the shortest solutions. The main takeaway here is that this is a very safe method. **It's safe to include math data with mistakes and corrections in training, and, in fact, the more mistakes you include, the better the results**. This doesn't require any changes to the pre-training or inference procedures, which remain auto-regressive. There are two key comments to make here. First, how do you obtain such data in practice? I'll address that shortly. Second, what training process is necessary to achieve these accuracy gains? In our experiments, we pre-trained models on math data with mistakes and corrections. But what happens if you fine-tune a model that was pre-trained only on perfectly correct math data, using data with mistakes and corrections? Can such a model perform well? **The answer is no.** Despite extensive testing with different parameters and fine-tuning methods, the accuracy improvement was negligible—and in most cases, accuracy decreased. The reason is simple: **It's crucial to include math data with mistakes during the pre-training stage. Adding it during fine-tuning is too late.** Unlike error detection, which is relatively easy to train for via probing or fine-tuning, error correction is significantly harder. It requires the model to understand the mistake it made and determine the next corrective step. This is a much more complex skill that must be learned during pre-training. For instance, if you use a pre-trained model like Llama-70B that wasn't trained on math data with errors and corrections, fine-tuning it with such data won't yield good results. Our controlled experiments confirm this.

Finally, how do you prepare this kind of data in practice? In our synthetic setting, generating this data is straightforward since we have full access to the dependency graphs and can manipulate the data as needed. But in real-world practice, we explored two ideas: a "dumber" approach and a "smarter" approach. The dumber idea involves creating fake mistakes by randomly inserting future sentences from a solution into earlier parts of the solution. For example, if you're midway through a math solution and want to introduce a mistake, you randomly select a sentence that appears later in the solution and place it earlier, treating it as a mistake. While some of these sentences may not truly be mistakes (since they might already be computable at that point), this approach is very cheap and easy to implement. On our synthetic data, this method produced significant accuracy gains. Although it doesn't perform as

CHAPTER 8 PHYSICS OF LARGE LANGUAGE MODELS

well as perfect math data with genuine mistakes, it still delivers decent improvements. The smarter idea involves creating fake mistakes by selecting random parameters from the problem statement and treating them as mistakes. However, this approach is harder to implement in practice and yields weaker results. Thus, the dumber idea—being easier and more practical—turns out to be more effective for improving reasoning capabilities. We even coined a slogan for this approach: *"Pre-train with fake mistakes, no more regret."*

To summarize Part 2.2, I explained how language models often know when they've made mistakes. They exhibit a kind of regretful behavior, as though they want to correct themselves but can't because they lack the capability. To give the model this capability, you need to include pre-training data with mistakes and corrections. This approach teaches the model how to correct itself—a capability that can't be achieved through beam search or fine-tuning alone. You have to incorporate such data at the pre-training stage. Additionally, you can create fake mistakes quite easily, and based on our synthetic data, we predict this method will yield decent accuracy gains. Reflecting on the broader theme of this chapter, in Part 2, I focused entirely on the reasoning capabilities of language models. We designed synthetic grade school math datasets and worked with models as small as 100 million parameters. You don't need a large model for this because the focus is on developing specific skills using clean, structured math data. Within this setup, we experimented with tweaking various elements: the difficulty of the data, the types of mistakes, and the training process, observing how these factors influenced the model's reasoning skills. We also conducted extensive probing to understand how models reason, how they make mistakes, and how different levels of parameter difficulty connect to model depth and reasoning length. This ties back to this chapter's main theme, as we explore these fundamental reasoning processes.

CHAPTER 8   PHYSICS OF LARGE LANGUAGE MODELS

Part 1: Language Structures in Language Models

Now, moving forward, I'll transition to Part 1 of the chapter, which focuses on language models learning language structures. This section has two primary goals. The first goal is to interpret large language models (LLMs) beyond the token level. We already have strong token-level interpretations, such as the "induction head" concept, where seeing "AB" allows the model to predict "B" when it later encounters "A." While useful, this interpretation is relatively simple. We want to push beyond this to explore harder, hierarchical algorithms and give precise interpretations of how language models learn and implement such algorithms. For example, we aim to go beyond tasks like topological sorting, which might still be considered easy for you readers. The second goal is to understand how language models learn structures. There's something I've deliberately avoided mentioning until now: I haven't explained how language models learn formats. In Part 3, I discussed how they acquire knowledge, and in Part 2, I covered how they develop reasoning skills. But how do they learn the correct formats for outputs? Why do they consistently adhere to these formats? This ties into the concept of "hallucination," often mentioned in discussions of language models. **To me, hallucination reflects the fact that models learn formats faster than the underlying tasks.** If a model learns the format quickly, it will confidently produce outputs in the correct format—such as answering "Yes" or "No" to a parity test—even if it hasn't yet mastered the task itself. This raises a challenge: to push the limits of language models, we need to create more hierarchical and complex language structures. This allows us to explore how well models can handle truly difficult language structures.

To address these two goals, we studied how language models learn context-free grammar (CFG). We designed long, synthetic CFGs that are intentionally very challenging. For instance, we developed over 20

CFGs, each involving rules where generation begins at a root, followed by random rule application at each level, until reaching the leaves. The characters at the leaves form sentences generated by the CFG tree.

Context-free grammar (CFG) is a set of rules or instructions for building sentences in a formal language. It tells you how to start with a basic idea (like a starting symbol) and expand it step by step into a full sentence using these rules. Here, CFG is being used to create sentences that would be analyzed by a language model. Given the complexity of sentences generated by CFG, we can probe how language models learn correct output formats.

In our synthetic data, we intentionally kept the vocabulary size small, resulting in patterns like "123–321." This setup makes the task extremely difficult because analyzing consecutive tokens, even looking at groups of ten, it is hard to derive where a token is coming from or any clear indication of their parents or grandparents in the tree structure. While CFG includes "grammar" in its name, it's important to distinguish it from English grammar. Parsing English grammar can often rely on greedy methods—such as pairing an adjective with a noun. By contrast, our synthetic CFG requires dynamic programming to identify correct segmentations and parent relationships. Moreover, the number of possible samples generated by this CFG tree is $\sim 10^{80}$, making it impossible for a language model to memorize the data. So what happens if you pre-train a language model like GPT on this CFG data? We measured accuracy in three aspects. First, after pre-training, we provided the model with a valid prefix it hadn't seen during training (since there are far too many possible samples to cover in training) and observed whether it could generate a valid CFG-compliant sentence, potentially hundreds of tokens long. The results were striking: **models using relative attention or rotary attention achieved high accuracy, while vanilla GPT models with absolute positional embeddings performed much worse**. We also analyzed other perspectives, including diversity and distribution differences, and measured KL divergence. All these metrics showed similar results: **using relative attention or rotary attention significantly outperformed absolute positional embeddings**.

Rotary attention is a technique used in transformer models to help them understand the order or position of tokens in a sequence by encoding positional information into the attention mechanism through rotation of token embeddings. The process relies on positional embeddings, where each token in a sequence is associated with a vector representing its position (such as "first" or "second"). The core mechanism applies a mathematical rotation to these embeddings using trigonometric functions like sine and cosine, which allows the model to incorporate positional information directly into its computations. Unlike traditional absolute positional embeddings, rotary attention naturally captures relationships between tokens based on their relative positions in the sequence. This approach enables the model to better understand and process sequential information by maintaining awareness of how tokens are positioned in relation to each other.

Relative attention offers an alternative approach for encoding positional information into transformers by explicitly modeling relationships between tokens based on their distances. Rather than assigning fixed positions to tokens, this method computes the distance between each pair of tokens in the sequence—for instance, token AAA might be "two tokens away" from token BBB, and this relative distance is encoded into the model. These distances are then incorporated as embeddings during the attention calculation, enabling the model to focus on relationships rather than absolute positions. This approach offers several advantages: it enhances the model's understanding of context by emphasizing relationships like "this token depends on the token two steps back" rather than absolute positions like "this token is at position 3." Additionally, relative attention demonstrates strong adaptability, performing particularly well in tasks where relative positioning carries more importance than absolute placement, such as understanding hierarchies or sequences with repeating patterns.

CHAPTER 8   PHYSICS OF LARGE LANGUAGE MODELS

Absolute positional embeddings represent the simplest approach, where each position in a sequence is assigned a fixed vector indicating its absolute location (e.g., position 1, position 2, etc.). While straightforward to implement, this method can struggle with longer sequences and has difficulty generalizing to positions not seen during training.

This aligns with the fact that relative attention mechanisms, like those used in Llama and Mistral models, have become standard in state-of-the-art architectures. Let me highlight the conclusion: by comparing accuracies across different setups, we see a **strong connection between rotary embeddings, relative attention, and their effectiveness compared with absolute positional embeddings**. This insight explains why relative attention is now the standard in many leading models. **By experimenting with this synthetic CFG data, we discovered that relative distance-based attention mechanisms, such as those in relative attention and rotary attention, are highly beneficial for learning language structures**. However, a surprising result emerged when we conducted a controlled experiment using a simplified architecture we called "GPT Stupid," which employed uniform attention. In GPT Stupid, we maintained multiple attention heads. For example, the first head always looked back at the previous token, the second head looked back at the previous three tokens with uniform weight (1/3), the third head looked back at seven tokens, and the fourth head looked back at fifteen tokens. The attention spans increased exponentially, but all attentions were uniform. Surprisingly, GPT Stupid performed much better than vanilla GPT with positional embeddings. This finding suggests a valuable lesson: If we ever want to move away from traditional attention mechanisms—for example, as seen in approaches like Mamba—it might still be **beneficial to retain some form of uniform attention**.

CHAPTER 8   PHYSICS OF LARGE LANGUAGE MODELS

Uniform attention is a simplified attention mechanism that assigns equal attention weights to all tokens in a sequence, effectively creating a uniform distribution across all positions. Unlike standard attention mechanisms that compute dynamic attention weights based on query-key interactions, uniform attention simply assigns the same fixed weight ($1/n$, where n is the sequence length) to every token. This approach drastically simplifies the computation since no learned parameters are needed for the attention weights, making it much faster to compute than traditional attention mechanisms.

This setup is cheap to implement and powerful for learning language structures, making it useful for certain tasks. While I won't go into the technical details here, the key takeaway is that even a simplified GPT Stupid architecture can outperform vanilla GPT. **Another conclusion we reached is that relative attention outperforms rotary embedding**. This fact may not be widely recognized because rotary embeddings are preferred in practice due to their efficiency—they only offer about a 1% accuracy improvement over relative attention but with a significant reduction in runtime. However, it's important to acknowledge that relative attention technically performs better. Now let's delve into how and why language models learn from this data. Recapping briefly, a language model trained on CFG data only sees sequences like "123321"— superficially ambiguous. The underlying CFG tree that generates these sequences is hidden from the model. After pre-training, we probed whether the model had implicitly learned to parse CFG trees. Specifically, we examined whether the hidden embeddings in the transformer's last layer encoded information about the parsing tree behind the sequence. The answer is yes. Not only does the model encode this information, but it also stores it in the correct locations. For example, knowledge about nodes in a sub-tree— such as node 11 or node 7—is linearly encoded in the hidden states near their respective positions. Information about a node's parent, grandparent, and even great-grandparent is also stored locally in these hidden states. However, as a unidirectional decoder model, the transformer cannot

CHAPTER 8   PHYSICS OF LARGE LANGUAGE MODELS

encode future node information. Still, all parsable information is stored within the model's hidden states, given the constraints of language modeling. In summary, GPT does not merely learn from synthetic CFG data; it also implicitly learns the CFG trees themselves. The precise finding is that although the CFG trees were hidden from pre-training, information about each sub-tree root is linearly encoded near the ending position of that sub-tree. **While this might seem natural for all language models, it's worth noting that encoder-based models like BERT or DeBERTa do not exhibit this capability**. Encoder-based models rely on masked language modeling (MLM), which involves masking 15% of tokens and predicting their values using nearby tokens. This task is relatively easy, as the model only needs to analyze local contexts. In contrast, language modeling (LM) requires parsing sequences from the root to predict the next token, making LM significantly harder than MLM. This also explains why decoder-based models are more suited for extracting knowledge and reasoning.

To understand how GPTs achieve this, consider how humans parse CFGs using dynamic programming (DP). For humans, DP involves defining a state like DP(i,j,a) representing whether a symbol A can generate a sub-sequence from i to j. This process combines smaller subsequences to verify if larger sequences can be generated. Remarkably, we found that these DP states are locally stored in the hidden states of GPTs. Moreover, the attention mechanisms in transformers serve as DP transition functions, connecting smaller DP states into larger ones. This alignment between transformer attention and dynamic programming is precise and critical for CFG parsing. But CFG parsing is only one side of the problem. GPTs must also learn to generate sequences from CFGs, requiring another level of dynamic programming. This involves computing which prefixes can be extended by certain nodes and their probabilities. Again, this relies on DP states and transition functions, which are encoded in the attention mechanisms after pre-training. **Transformers effectively simulate dynamic programming for both parsing and generation tasks**. To summarize Part 1, GPTs can learn complex, synthetic CFGs, which require

CHAPTER 8 PHYSICS OF LARGE LANGUAGE MODELS

non-trivial planning (must use rotary/relative attention) and computations far beyond tasks like topological sorting. **We used probing to show that DP states are encoded in the hidden states and DP transition functions are encoded in the attention mechanisms, providing strong interpretability for language models.** Importantly, encoder-only models like BERT cannot achieve this due to their reliance on MLM. One additional result, which I didn't discuss here but is detailed in the paper, explores how GPTs can learn implicit or corrupted CFGs. This study highlights further lessons in language model capabilities. The two-step dynamic programming process required for CFGs is extremely complex. Even among software engineers and competitive programmers, many are unfamiliar with this specific DP method. Personally, I first encountered a variant of it at the 2005 International Olympiad in Informatics, where I failed to solve the problem as a participant. In some sense, GPT-2 has surpassed the 17-year-old version of myself.

What's most fascinating is that GPT-2, trained only on sequences like "123321," independently learns the best algorithms for parsing and generating such data. This inspired my interest in studying the "physics" of language models. Looking ahead, I view this as a form of future science. A year ago, working on synthetic data for machine learning might have been ridiculed, but it's now recognized as essential. Real-world data is finite, and even models like GPT-4.0, trained on vast Internet datasets, struggle with reasoning tasks requiring more than ten steps. To surpass these limitations, we must develop and refine synthetic datasets for training future models like GPT-5 or GPT-6. This raises critical questions: What is the optimal format for knowledge data to maximize learning? What reasoning problems should we include to extend a model's reasoning capabilities? These are the challenges we must address to move closer to AGI.

Conclusion

This chapter is a very deep dive into language models with the help of synthetic data. It explores foundational aspects of knowledge storage and extraction, reasoning in language models, and hierarchical language structures. The key takeaways are bolded throughout the chapter.

To fully grasp the depth and nuances presented, a re-read might be necessary. This chapter serves as both a technical guide and a testament to the power of using carefully designed synthetic data for understanding how advanced language models are progressing toward AGI.

CHAPTER 9

Contemporary Decentralized Organizations

Decentralized autonomous organizations (DAOs) represent a rapidly evolving form of an organization built on top of a blockchain. These entities aim to facilitate collective decision-making "from the bottom up," without relying on centralized authorities such as directors, vice presidents, or a hierarchical system of administrators. Instead, DAOs allow all members to vote on topics of resource allocation and future directions with the rationale that collective decision-making often leads to better outcomes, provided the group works cohesively. However, this inherently utopian concept has garnered both excitement and skepticism. Historically, decentralized organizations such as guilds and labor unions have excelled in coordinating specific activities but struggled in areas requiring centralized authority—such as conflict resolution, direct competition, or adapting to an evolving environment. Therefore, the effectiveness of a DAO heavily depends on its purpose and the alignment of its members' goals and worldviews.

The emergence of DAOs is deeply rooted in the cypherpunk movement of the 1990s and early 2000s. This heterogeneous group of computer hackers and software engineers, primarily communicating through the

CHAPTER 9   CONTEMPORARY DECENTRALIZED ORGANIZATIONS

cypherpunk mailing list, advocated for self-governance and political decentralization through technology. Their vision emphasized creating peer-to-peer participatory systems with immutable rules that couldn't be manipulated for political control. Bitcoin, the first public blockchain and cryptocurrency, emerged from this movement, effectively functioning as the first DAO. The term "decentralized autonomous corporations" was first coined by Dan Larimer, in 2013, and later popularized as "decentralized autonomous organizations," by Vitalik Buterin, co-founder of Ethereum. Buterin envisioned DAOs as these meta-systems combining algorithmic automation for low-level tasks with human oversight for higher-order judgments. Over the years, DAOs have realized this vision by maturing into a set of programs for collective self-governance and automated organizational functions while preserving human judgment for higher-order decision-making.

The Public DAO: Inception and Collapse

The DAO, launched in April 2016, represented the first large-scale implementation of a decentralized autonomous organization on the Ethereum blockchain. Built by the team at Slock.it, it was designed as a decentralized venture capital fund where token holders could vote on investment proposals. The project attracted significant attention and raised approximately 12.7M ether (worth about US$150 million at the time) during its crowdfunding period, making it the largest crowdfunding event in history at that point. Slock.it, founded by Christoph Jentzsch and other Ethereum veterans in 2015, focused on the sharing economy by creating a network of smart locks controlled through Ethereum smart contracts. The core vision was to enable a fully decentralized version of platforms like Airbnb or car-sharing services, eliminating the need for intermediaries in rental transactions. The company's primary innovation was the "Ethereum Computer," a combination of hardware and software

CHAPTER 9   CONTEMPORARY DECENTRALIZED ORGANIZATIONS

that would connect physical locks to the Ethereum blockchain. This device was designed to serve as a bridge between smart contracts and real-world assets (RWAs), enabling autonomous rental operations. For example, an apartment door would automatically unlock when a user sent the appropriate payment through a smart contract, and the lock would remain accessible for the duration specified in the contract.

While Slock.it initiated the DAO's creation, they positioned themselves as just one of many potential recipients of DAO funding. Their proposal to the DAO, known as the "Universal Sharing Framework," requested funding to develop their sharing economy infrastructure. The proposal included detailed technical specifications, development milestones, and a comprehensive business plan for scaling their technology. The team's dual role as both the DAO's creators and potential funding recipients later drew criticism, with some arguing it represented a conflict of interest. However, Slock.it maintained that the DAO's decentralized voting mechanism would ensure objective evaluation of their proposal alongside others.

Its complexity and novelty also made it a prime target for scrutiny and exploitation. Shortly after its launch, vulnerabilities in the DAO's smart contract code were discovered. On June 17, 2016, a hacker exploited one of the vulnerabilities, siphoning off approximately 3.6 million ETH (valued at around US$60 million at the time). Although the funds were moved into a child DAO and couldn't be immediately accessed due to a 28-day holding period coded into the contract, the incident threw the Ethereum community into crisis. The exploit not only highlighted the risks of poorly audited smart contracts but also raised questions about immutability and governance in blockchain-based organizations. More formally, the DAO's smart contract architecture was based on a "split function" that allowed members to withdraw their funds and create a "child DAO" if they disagreed with any investment decisions. This feature, while designed to protect minority stakeholders, ultimately became its Achilles' heel. On June 17, 2016, an attacker exploited a recursive call vulnerability in the split function's code, allowing them to repeatedly withdraw ETH before the contract could update its balance. The technical specifics of the exploit involved the following:

```
// Vulnerable split function
function splitDAO(
    address _childDAO,
    uint256 _amount
) public returns (bool) {
    // First transfer tokens
    Token.transfer(_childDAO, _amount);

    // Then transfer ETH
    if (!_childDAO.call.value(_amount)()) {
        throw;
    }

    return true;
}
```

The attacker exploited this split function by creating a recursive call pattern that allowed multiple withdrawals before the balance was updated, draining approximately 3.6M ETH ($50 million) into a child DAO. The DAO hack left the Ethereum community with a significant dilemma: should the blockchain remain immutable and let the consequences of the hack persist, or should it intervene to recover the stolen funds? The community was divided, leading to extensive debates about the principles of decentralization and governance. Ultimately, a controversial decision was made to implement a hard fork to reverse the effects of the hack. This fork occurred on July 20, 2016, creating two parallel blockchains:

CHAPTER 9   CONTEMPORARY DECENTRALIZED ORGANIZATIONS

1. **Ethereum (ETH)**: This chain followed the hard fork, effectively rolling back the stolen funds to their original holders. The majority of the community and developers supported this chain, ensuring its continuity as the main Ethereum blockchain.

2. **Ethereum Classic (ETC)**: This chain retained the original, unaltered transaction history, upholding the principle of immutability. A smaller portion of the community, including some developers and miners, chose to support Ethereum Classic as an alternative vision of the platform.

As of now, both blockchains continue to operate independently, each with their own community and development trajectory. Notable updates to the Ethereum blockchain are detailed Chapter 7, and on December 11, 2017, the total supply of ether on Ethereum Classic was permanently capped at 210,700,000 ETC through the Gotham hard fork upgrade. In response to the DAO hack and similar exploits, the Ethereum ecosystem has developed several critical security improvements that have become standard practice for modern DAOs. OpenZeppelin's ReentrancyGuard has emerged as an industry standard for preventing reentrancy attacks, implementing a mutex pattern that blocks recursive calls to protected functions. Sophisticated time-lock mechanisms for treasury management have also become essential, placing mandatory waiting periods before significant transactions can be executed, giving stakeholders time to evaluate and potentially reject malicious proposals. Most advanced DAOs now utilize multi-signature wallets, particularly for treasury management, requiring approval from multiple authorized members before funds can be transferred. Additional protective measures include implementing the checks–effects–interactions pattern, which ensures state changes occur before external calls, and comprehensive testing frameworks specifically designed to simulate attack scenarios. These combined security practices have significantly reduced the vulnerability surface of modern DAOs while maintaining their decentralized operational capabilities.

Technical Foundations of a DAO

Smart contracts form the operational backbone of DAOs, implementing organizational rules and procedures through deterministic code execution. These self-executing contracts, written primarily in Solidity for Ethereum-based DAOs, encode the organization's constitution, voting mechanisms, and treasury management protocols. Smart contracts automatically execute predetermined actions when specific conditions are met, eliminating the need for manual intervention and reducing operational friction. A prototypical DAO can be designed with five core technical components; however, to enable advanced features, contemporary DAOs can be comprised of up to 12 technical "organs." Let us examine each component through the lens of practical examples and lessons learned from years of deployment:

1. The **treasury management system** handles all financial operations and asset control. This component requires integration with multi-signature wallets, usually encoded by Gnosis Safe or similar protocols, and includes modules for transaction batching, spending limits, and asset diversification. To be versatile, this system needs practical considerations such as automated rebalancing of assets, yield generation through lending protocols, and emergency shutdown mechanisms. For instance, BitDAO implements a

treasury system that automatically allocates assets across different yield-generating protocols while maintaining predetermined risk parameters.

2. The **asset management framework** provides sophisticated treasury operations capabilities. This component implements portfolio rebalancing, risk-adjusted return optimization, and liquidation management. Enzyme Finance demonstrates this with its vault management system, implementing sophisticated investment strategies, risk management, and performance tracking.

3. The **governance engine** manages the entire proposal lifecycle and voting mechanisms. This component handles proposal creation, voting periods, vote counting, and execution of approved decisions. In practice, this means implementing time-locks for proposal activation, quorum calculations, vote delegation capabilities, and result execution triggers. Uniswap's governance engine provides a practical example, where proposals require a minimum token threshold for submission, undergo a two-day delay period, and need to meet specific quorum requirements for execution.

4. The **governance simulation system** enables impact analysis of proposed changes. This component implements agent-based modeling, economic simulations, and governance outcome prediction. For instance, Element Finance's governance system also includes simulation capabilities for testing parameter changes before implementation, helping predict outcomes of governance decisions.

5. The **integration framework** enables interaction with external protocols and services. This component manages connections to oracles for price feeds, bridges for cross-chain operations, and interfaces with other DeFi protocols, for example, implementing Chainlink oracle integration for price-dependent decisions or Layer 2 bridges for cost-efficient operations. Aave's cross-chain governance implementation demonstrates this by enabling governance actions across multiple networks while maintaining security and consistency.

6. The **analytics and monitoring system** tracks DAO operations and provides visibility into organizational activities. This component includes event logging systems, performance metrics tracking, and reporting mechanisms. In practice, this means implementing subgraphs for data indexing, monitoring systems for treasury performance, and dashboards for member activity. For instance, MakerDAO's monitoring infrastructure tracks liquidation events, collateral ratios, and governance participation rates in real time, enabling informed decision-making by stakeholders.

7. The **reputation system** implements soulbound tokens and credential verification mechanisms. This component manages member reputation scores, skill attestations, and contribution history. In practice, this involves implementing ERC-1155 contracts for multiple credential types, zero-knowledge proofs for private attestations, and reputation scoring algorithms.

8. The **dispute resolution system** handles conflicts and governance challenges. This component implements arbitration mechanisms, challenge periods for decisions, and appeal processes. For instance, Kleros provides a decentralized court system where token holders serve as jurors, implementing complex selection algorithms and incentive mechanisms for fair judgments. The framework includes smart contracts for evidence submission, juror selection, and automated penalty enforcement.

9. The **tokenomics system** manages token distribution, vesting, and economic incentives. This sophisticated component handles dynamic token emission rates, liquidity mining programs, and staking mechanisms. Curve DAO exemplifies this with its vote-escrowed tokenomics model (veCRV), implementing time-weighted staking rewards, boost multipliers, and gauge-weighted emissions across multiple pools.

10. The **task management system** facilitates decentralized work organization. This component manages bounty creation, task allocation, and compensation distribution. For example, Coordinape implements peer-to-peer reward distribution mechanisms, allowing members to allocate points to contributors based on perceived value creation. The system includes smart contracts for escrow management, milestone verification, and automated payments.

11. The **risk management system** monitors and manages organizational risks. This component implements circuit breakers, exposure limits, and risk assessment algorithms. Nexus Mutual's implementation includes sophisticated risk assessment models for smart contract coverage, implementing automated premium calculations, claim assessments, and capital adequacy monitoring.

12. The **compliance system** handles regulatory requirements and organizational documentation. This component manages audit trials, regulatory reporting, and compliance verification. For example, Syndicate DAO implements compliance checking for investment DAOs, including accreditation verification and reporting generation for regulatory requirements.

Ethereum's role in enabling DAOs extends beyond merely providing a platform for smart contract deployment. The Ethereum Virtual Machine (EVM) offers a Turing-complete environment that enables complex computational operations necessary for sophisticated contract-organizational logic and deployment of the technical "organs" discussed above. The platform's account abstraction capabilities, transaction processing mechanisms, and gas fee structure create a robust framework for DAO operations. The Ethereum network's security model, maintained by thousands of nodes through proof-of-stake consensus, also ensures the integrity of DAO operations and protects against unauthorized modifications. Token standards have also played a crucial role in DAO implementation, with ERC-20 and ERC-721 serving distinct purposes within the ecosystem. ERC-20 tokens typically represent governance rights and voting power within the DAO. These fungible tokens enable

CHAPTER 9 CONTEMPORARY DECENTRALIZED ORGANIZATIONS

proportional representation in decision-making processes and can be traded on secondary markets, providing liquidity for DAO participants. Compound Protocol, for example, utilizes COMP tokens to enable stakeholder participation in governance decisions. ERC-721 tokens, being non-fungible, serve specialized purposes such as representing unique assets, membership credentials, or specific voting rights within the organization.

Asset management, especially with regard to decentralized governance in DAOs, represents one of the most complex technical challenges and warrants a thorough discussion. The core infrastructure centers around a multi-signature wallet implementation. Gnosis Safe has emerged as the industry standard, implementing m-of-n signature schemes with configurable thresholds. For instance, Uniswap's treasury implements a 4-of-7 multi-signature requirement, providing resilience against private key compromises while maintaining operational efficiency. The technical implementation includes time-locks for large transactions, veto capabilities for emergency situations, and modular guard contracts that enforce spending policies. Since the 2016 DAO hack, modern treasury implementations now incorporate reentrancy guards and comprehensive state validation mechanisms. Contemporary treasury management implementations utilize sophisticated asset diversification strategies. MakerDAO's treasury system demonstrates this through its Protocol-Owned Vault (POV) strategy, implementing automated rebalancing mechanisms based on market conditions. The technical architecture here includes oracle integration for price feeds, algorithmic portfolio management, and risk assessment modules that adjust positions based on market volatility. Treasury monitoring is another critical component of assent management, and Yearn Finance is a good use case for implementing comprehensive monitoring through event emission and indexing services. Their tech stack includes real-time balance tracking, automated alerts for large transactions, and performance analytics using the graph for data indexing and retrieval of treasury operations.

CHAPTER 9   CONTEMPORARY DECENTRALIZED ORGANIZATIONS

A notable failure occurred in the Parity multi-signature wallet incident, where a vulnerable library contract was accidentally destroyed, freezing approximately $150 million in treasury funds. This highlighted the importance of real-time balance-tracking mechanisms in the contract. Modern implementations now commonly use proxy patterns for upgradability while maintaining clear separation of concerns in contract architecture. Successful treasury diversification can be observed in BitDAO's implementation, which maintains a sophisticated asset allocation strategy across different chains and protocols. Their architecture includes cross-chain bridges, automated yield farming strategies, and risk management systems that monitor exposure across different protocols. The implementation utilizes adapters for different DeFi protocols, enabling flexible treasury management while maintaining security boundaries.

Risk management systems also play a crucial role in treasury protection. Aave's treasury implements sophisticated risk assessment models that monitor protocol health and adjust treasury allocations accordingly. The technical implementation includes automated circuit breakers, exposure limits, and collateralization ratio monitoring. These systems helped prevent significant losses during market volatility events. ENS DAO demonstrates successful treasury management through its implementation of structured investment strategies such as time-locked governance for major treasury decisions, automated yield generation through lending protocols, and sophisticated reporting mechanisms for transparency. The implementation successfully manages both ETH and stablecoin holdings while maintaining operational efficiency.

Note A significant challenge in treasury management and executing the advanced features mentioned above is gas optimization and network congestion due to frequent operations. Compound's treasury management system implements batch processing

CHAPTER 9   CONTEMPORARY DECENTRALIZED ORGANIZATIONS

mechanisms for multiple transactions, reducing operational costs. Their implementation includes transaction batching contracts, optimal timing mechanisms for execution, and gas price monitoring systems.

Recent innovations in asset management include the implementation of streaming payments and vesting mechanisms. Superfluid's protocol enables real-time treasury distributions, implementing sophisticated payment streams through super-tokens. This technical approach reduces the need for manual treasury management while ensuring consistent resource allocation. Security vulnerabilities in treasury management often arise from complex interaction patterns between multiple protocols, for instance, the Harvest Finance incident, resulting in a $34 million loss, demonstrated the risks of flash loan attacks against treasury management systems. Modern implementations now incorporate price impact checks, flash loan detection mechanisms, and sophisticated validation of complex transaction sequences. Balancer's treasury implementation demonstrates effective Layer 2 integration, utilizing Polygon and Arbitrum for cost-efficient operations while maintaining security through bridge monitoring and validation systems. The technical implementation includes automated bridging mechanisms and risk-adjusted threshold management. Looking forward, treasury management systems are evolving to incorporate more sophisticated DeFi strategies, for instance, Curve's treasury management demonstrates this through its implementation of concentrated liquidity positions and yield optimization strategies. Their technical architecture includes automated position management, impermanent loss protection mechanisms, and sophisticated rebalancing algorithms.

Connecting hobbyists, developers, artists and like-minded individuals across various DAOs poses a technical as well as a social challenge, spanning multiple protocols, messaging systems, and cross-chain architectures. Most interoperability research and development for DAOs focuses on some form of cross-chain messaging protocols. LayerZero emerged as a prominent solution in this space, implementing a lightweight message-passing protocol that enables secure cross-chain communication. Their approach includes Ultra Light Nodes (ULNs) for message verification, oracle networks for block confirmation, and relayers for message delivery. For instance, Aave's cross-chain governance leverages LayerZero to enable proposal execution across multiple networks while maintaining atomic transaction guarantees. However, over the years, a few other protocols and supportive mechanisms have also emerged:

1. The **Cross-Chain Interoperability Protocol (CCIP)** implements standardized message formats and verification mechanisms. The technical architecture includes message serialization standards, cross-chain identifiers, and protocol-specific adapters. Chainlink's CCIP implementation demonstrates this through its standardized message-passing interface, enabling consistent communication patterns across different blockchain networks.

2. **Bridge protocols** enable asset and state transfer between different DAO instances. Multichain (formerly Anyswap) implements sophisticated bridge contracts with standardized interfaces for asset transfer. The technical implementation includes lock-and-mint mechanisms, liquidity pools for instant transfers, and validator networks for transaction verification. However, the Wormhole bridge exploit, resulting in a $320 million loss, highlighted the importance of robust validation mechanisms and secure bridge architectures.

3. **State synchronization systems** maintain consistency across different chain deployments.

CHAPTER 9   CONTEMPORARY DECENTRALIZED ORGANIZATIONS

Polygon's state sync mechanism implements checkpointing and fraud-proof systems for secure state transfer. The technical architecture includes Merkle trees for state verification, challenge periods for fraud detection, and optimistic rollup patterns for efficient processing. This enables DAOs to maintain consistent state across different scaling solutions while preserving security guarantees.

4. **Governance action execution** across chains requires sophisticated coordination mechanisms. Compound's cross-chain governance implementation demonstrates this through its time-locked execution system. The technical architecture includes proposal queuing mechanisms, cross-chain execution verification, and rollback capabilities for failed actions. The implementation ensures governance decisions can be consistently applied across multiple chain deployments.

5. **Protocol standardization** efforts like EIP-4824 (Common Interfaces for DAOs) implement consistent interfaces for cross-DAO interaction. The technical specification includes standardized function signatures, event formats, and data structures. This standardization enables better tooling support and simplified integration patterns between different DAO implementations.

6. **Identity and reputation systems** across chains also present unique challenges. As briefly

mentioned above, the Ethereum Name Service (ENS) implements cross-chain identity resolution through its name service protocol. The technical implementation includes universal resolvers, cross-chain verification mechanisms, and cached resolution systems for efficiency. This enables consistent identity management across different DAO deployments.

7. **Message queue systems** handle asynchronous communication between chain deployments. Axelar's General Message Passing (GMP) implements reliable message delivery with ordering guarantees. The technical architecture includes sequenced message delivery, failure recovery mechanisms, and gas management systems for cross-chain execution.

8. **Oracles** play a crucial role in cross-chain coordination. Chainlink's Cross-Chain Interoperability Protocol implements secure price feed aggregation and message-passing. The technical implementation includes decentralized oracle networks, off-chain computation systems, and robust consensus mechanisms for data validation.

9. **Error handling and recovery systems** manage failed cross-chain interactions. Arbitrum's retry buffer system implements sophisticated recovery mechanisms for failed messages. The technical architecture includes message queuing, automated

CHAPTER 9　CONTEMPORARY DECENTRALIZED ORGANIZATIONS

retry logic, and manual intervention capabilities for critical failures.

10. **Protocol-specific adapters** enable standardized interaction patterns. 1inch's cross-chain aggregation protocol implements adapters for different DEX protocols. The technical implementation includes standardized interfaces, protocol-specific optimization strategies, and unified error handling mechanisms.

Note An interesting recent innovation in cross-chain governance is optimistic governance systems, implemented by Optimism, a Layer 2 Ethereum application that features a bicameral (two-house) structure. The Token House is composed of OP token holders who make decisions on protocol upgrades, project incentives, and treasury allocations. Voting power in this house is proportional to the number of OP tokens held, allowing stakeholders to influence decisions based on their economic stake. Complementing this, the Citizens' House operates on a one-person-one-vote basis and focuses on retroactive public goods funding. Membership in this house is granted through non-transferable "soulbound" non-fungible tokens (NFTs), which represent individual contributions and reputation within the community. This dual-house system is designed to balance short-term economic incentives with long-term community values, fostering a governance framework that is both holistic and resilient.

Looking ahead, emerging standards like the Hyperlane protocol are implementing more sophisticated interoperability patterns with improved security guarantees and efficiency. At large, we expect the DAO community to focus on reducing complexity while maintaining robust security properties for cross-chain coordination.

Governance Models

Contemporary decentralized organizations built on the blockchain have evolved past basic voting mechanisms and embracing novel governance models that prioritize distribution of decision-making power, fairness, and community engagement. Over the years, the following governing models have been developed:

- **Token-weighted voting** is the original and most common governance structure, implemented since the DAO in 2016 and more recently by MakerDAO as well as Uniswap, where voting power directly correlates with token holdings. MakerDAO's implementation became the gold standard, requiring 40,000 MKR (~$100,000) to submit proposals, with a five-day voting period and an executive delay of 48 hours. Uniswap refined this model with a 2.5 million UNI threshold (1% of total supply) for proposal submission, implementing a two-phase governance process: temperature check followed by formal proposal. This structure proved effective for major protocol decisions but faced criticism for plutocratic control during the Optimism retroactive funding proposal where just 18 wallets controlled over 50% of the voting power.

CHAPTER 9   CONTEMPORARY DECENTRALIZED ORGANIZATIONS

- **Quadratic voting** implemented by Gitcoin DAO and clr.fund aims to mitigate plutocratic control by making vote weight proportional to the square root of tokens committed in Gitcoin and has demonstrated remarkable success in grant distribution efficiency. Over 15 rounds, the system has distributed more than $50 million across 3,000+ projects. Their implementation uses BrightID for Sybil resistance and has processed over 2.5 million individual votes. Technical challenges included managing gas costs for on-chain vote calculation—solved by implementing snapshot-based off-chain voting with on-chain execution. However, the system faced manipulation attempts in Round 9 (2021), leading to the implementation of fraud detection algorithms and identity verification requirements. Success metrics show 62% higher distribution efficiency compared with linear voting systems.

- **Reputation-based systems (RBS)** implemented by DAOstack, where voting power is earned through contributions and can't be transferred, have evolved significantly over the last few years. Their Genesis protocol introduced continuous reputation decay (1% per week) to ensure active participation. Colony's implementation further subdivided reputation into domains (development, marketing, operations) with sophisticated scoring algorithms based on task completion and peer review. Technical challenges included managing state bloat from reputation tracking—solved through periodic checkpointing and Merkle proofs for efficient verification. Success rates show 3× higher proposal quality compared with token-weighted systems, but participation rates remained challenging at 15–20% of eligible voters.

- **Holographic consensus**, also developed by DAOstack, implements prediction marks along with governance decisions where voters can stake tokens on proposal outcomes, creating economic incentives for thorough proposal evaluation. The DAOstack implementation saw prediction markets accurately forecast 89% of proposal outcomes, with stakers earning an average 8–12% APR on correct predictions. However, gas costs for market creation and settlement limited adoption. The system processed over 2,000 proposals across various DAOs, with an average time to decision 40% faster than traditional voting. Technical challenges included oracle manipulation risks and market liquidity issues.

- **Optimistic governance** implemented by protocols such as Compound and Aave where proposals automatically pass after a time delay unless explicitly challenged achieved significant efficiency gains. The architecture includes challenge periods, semi-automated dispute resolution mechanisms, and automated execution systems. This structure significantly reduced gas costs for routine governance actions while maintaining security through challenge capabilities. Compound's implementation reduced governance gas costs by 86% through delayed execution with challenge periods. The system processed over 175 successful proposals with only 3 challenges, demonstrating effective incentive alignment. Aave's variation added tiered challenge periods based on proposal impact—2 days for minor changes, up to 14 days for critical protocol modifications. Success metrics show 99.7% proposal execution rate with zero successful attacks.

- **Multi-tiered governance** is implemented by protocols such as Curve, where different levels of token locking (veCRV) grant varying levels of voting powers and rewards. The system locks over $6 billion worth of CRV (60% of circulating supply) for an average of 3.6 years. Technical implementation includes weekly reward epochs, boost calculations based on ve-token balance, and gauge weight voting for liquidity incentives. The model proved so successful it was adopted by multiple protocols including Frax and Balancer. However, the system has faced criticism for high complexity and barrier to entry.

- **Skin-in-the-game voting** implemented by Nexus Mutual, where voters must stake assets that can be slashed for incorrect decisions, has proven out to be highly effective for claim assessment. The system processed over 500 claims with 97% accuracy, requiring assessors to stake NXM tokens that get slashed for incorrect votes. Technical implementation includes a sophisticated claims assessment module that weighs votes by stake size and assessor historical accuracy. The system successfully handled several high-profile claims, including the Celsius collapse, with zero successful governance attacks.

CHAPTER 9   CONTEMPORARY DECENTRALIZED ORGANIZATIONS

- **Category-weighted voting** is implemented by Element Finance where different proposal categories require different voting thresholds and participation requirements. They define four broad categories (Emergency, Core, Framework, General) with different quorum requirements (40%, 30%, 20%, 10%) and approval thresholds. Technical challenges included managing state complexity for different proposal types—solved through modular executor contracts. The system processed 70+ proposals with a 100% successful execution rate.

- **Futarchy** is an experimental governance structure implemented by Gnosis, where prediction markets determine which proposals will best achieve specified metrics. Technical challenges included oracle reliability and market manipulation risks. While the theoretical framework was sound, practical implementation faced liquidity constraints and high operational overhead.

- **Liquid democracy** was implemented by DAOstack and others, allowing dynamic delegation of voting power with the ability to override specific votes. DAOstack's deployment increased participation rates by 45%; however, complexity of delegation chains created technical challenges for vote counting. Success metrics show improved proposal quality, but it faced challenges with delegation market concentration—top ten delegates controlled 60% of delegated votes.

- **Pod-based governance** implemented by organizations like MetaCartel, where small working groups (pods) have autonomy over specific decisions within their domain. The technical architecture includes pod creation mechanisms, resource allocation systems, and inter-pod coordination protocols.

- **Time-weighted voting**, similar to Curve's veCRV model but implemented by other DAOs, where longer token lock periods grant proportionally more voting power. The technical implementation includes vote escrow contracts, decay mechanisms, and sophisticated reward distribution systems based on lock duration.

- **Qualified majority voting** implemented by multiple DAOs, requiring super-majority thresholds for critical decisions. The technical architecture includes proposal categorization systems, dynamic threshold calculations, and sophisticated quorum requirements based on proposal impact.

- **Permission-based voting** implemented by specialized DAOs like investment DAOs, where voting rights are tied to verified credentials or qualifications. The technical implementation includes credential verification systems, role-based access control, and sophisticated permission management mechanisms.

- **Rage quit mechanisms** implemented by MolochDAO and derivatives, allowing members to exit with their share of assets if they disagree with governance decisions. The technical implementation includes asset withdrawal mechanisms, share price calculations, and sophisticated treasury management systems to handle exits.

CHAPTER 9   CONTEMPORARY DECENTRALIZED ORGANIZATIONS

Along with the choice of governance mechanisms, another fundamental architectural decision in DAO implementation is whether to do governance on-chain or off-chain. This significantly impacts operational efficiency, security, and participant engagement. On-chain governance, pioneered by Tezos with their self-amending ledger, implements fully automated decision execution through smart contracts. Their system established a sophisticated four-stage voting process encompassing proposal, testing, testing vote, and promotion vote periods, enabling automated protocol upgrades based on voting outcomes. While this system successfully processed multiple protocol upgrades, it revealed inherent challenges with gas costs and voter participation that would influence future governance implementations. Compound's on-chain governance implementation through their Governor Alpha/Bravo contracts showcases the evolution of this approach, incorporating sophisticated technical components including time-lock contracts, proposal queuing systems, automated vote counting mechanisms, and delegate tracking with checkpointing. Their implementation successfully processed over $1 billion in treasury allocations, though the system's requirement for significant gas expenditure for voting transactions highlighted the ongoing challenge of balancing security with accessibility.

Off-chain governance, exemplified by Snapshot's widely adopted implementation, emerged as a response to these challenges by implementing signature-based voting without requiring blockchain transactions. The technical architecture leverages IPFS for proposal storage, EIP-712 signatures for vote verification, and sophisticated space management contracts for configuration. This approach has achieved remarkable adoption, processing over 300,000 proposals across 10,000+ DAOs while significantly reducing participation costs through off-chain aggregation. Hybrid governance systems evolved to combine the strengths of both approaches, as demonstrated by SushiSwap's implementation that integrates off-chain signaling through Snapshot with on-chain execution via time-lock contracts and cross-chain governance coordination. Similarly, Aave's governance system implements a sophisticated multi-tiered approach with varying time-lock periods based on proposal criticality, combining off-chain discussion forums with on-chain execution mechanisms protected by guardian oversight. The trade-offs between these approaches highlight the complexity of governance design and the increased barriers to entry for participants. On-chain systems provide automated execution guarantees, transparent state transitions, and immutable voting records, but suffer from high gas costs and limited flexibility. Conversely, off-chain systems enable minimal participation costs and rapid iteration capability but introduce additional coordination overhead and complex verification requirements. Recent innovations in governance implementation demonstrate a trend toward optimistic systems that leverage the strengths of both approaches. Synthetix's hybrid implementation exemplifies this evolution, combining off-chain proposal submission and voting through Snapshot with on-chain execution contracts protected by challenge periods. This approach introduces sophisticated technical challenges in cross-chain message-passing, state synchronization, and signature aggregation, but offers a promising balance of security and efficiency. The emerging pattern in governance implementation gravitates toward a layered architecture encompassing social, coordination, execution, and security layers. This modular approach enables DAOs to adapt to changing requirements while maintaining robust security guarantees.

Use Case for DAOs: Decentralized Science (DeSci)

In the hyper-competitive landscape of public and private funding for biotechnology research, a portion of proposals are rejected each grant cycle. Even if the proposals are novel, current funding mechanisms cannot account for the large volume. To that end, micro-grants can be immensely useful in getting preliminary data from a high-risk, high-reward project. Molecule is a decentralized protocol and a platform for biotech research funding via micro-grants. The protocol has already shown some success reflected by the adoption of fractional intellectual property (IP) ownership (Molecule's IP-NFT framework). More recently, Molecule launched bio.xyz, a biotech DAO and DeSci launchpad that can incubate new ideas and provide a tokenized DeSci meta-governance layer from the parent DAO. In essence, this is a meta-DAO. Current initiatives include the development of novel therapeutics for rare diseases, where their micro-grants program has enabled early-stage research that traditional funding mechanisms might have overlooked. Since 2018, Molecule's initiatives have garnered significant attention and investment, exemplified by a successful seed funding round that raised $12.7 million. This capital infusion is being utilized to expand their marketplace with numerous research projects and further develop their protocol into open infrastructure.

The IP-NFT framework tokenizes intellectual property (IP) rights and encapsulates them within non-fungible tokens (NFTs). This approach allows intellectual property—such as patents, research data, and licensing agreements—to exist as a tradable digital asset on the blockchain. Each IP-NFT is unique and represents the legal rights and ownership of the underlying intellectual property, making it transferable, divisible, and accessible to a broader pool of stakeholders, such as researchers, investors, and organizations. At its core, the **ownership layer** records the ownership and transfer of the IP-NFT on a blockchain, ensuring transparent and immutable proof of ownership. This tokenization enables fractional ownership, meaning multiple stakeholders can co-own a single IP-NFT, facilitating collaborative funding for research projects. The **access control layer** integrates tools like Lit Protocol to secure sensitive data, allowing only authorized IP-NFT holders to access the underlying intellectual property. The framework also incorporates a **decentralized storage layer**, using platforms like IPFS or Arweave to store research data, patents, and agreements securely and permanently. This ensures the integrity and accessibility of critical research materials. Additionally, the **application layer** facilitates the creation and negotiation of agreements, such as licensing contracts or research partnerships, directly linked to the IP-NFT. This layer integrates real-world legal frameworks into the blockchain ecosystem, bridging traditional IP systems with decentralized technology. One of the key advantages of the IP-NFT is its liquidity and discoverability. By tokenizing IP, Molecule creates a marketplace where researchers can auction their IP-NFTs or license them to interested parties, unlocking new funding sources. For example, researchers can sell a portion of their IP rights to fund their projects while retaining a stake in the potential future profits. This system democratizes access to funding, empowering smaller research teams and institutions that might lack traditional financial backing. Multiple other use cases have emerged in the biotech space:

1. VitaDAO emerged as one of the first prominent biotech DAOs, focused on funding longevity research and democratizing biotech investment. Their technical implementation includes a sophisticated proposal system for research funding, with proposals categorized into different research stages. They've successfully funded multiple research projects, including work on senolytics and longevity biomarkers. Notable achievements include funding research at institutions like Buck Institute and establishing intellectual property frameworks for decentralized research ownership. Additionally, in collaboration with VitaDAO, Molecule facilitated the transfer of an IP-NFT containing longevity research from the Scheibye-Knudsen lab to the DAO. This enabled the lab to secure funding while allowing VitaDAO members to collectively own and govern the research's development.

CHAPTER 9   CONTEMPORARY DECENTRALIZED ORGANIZATIONS

2. BioDAO focuses on democratizing access to biotech investment opportunities, implementing a unique governance structure for research selection. Their technical implementation includes specialized voting mechanisms for scientific assessment, with token-weighted voting modified by expertise credentials. They've funded several early-stage research projects including AthenaDAO (advancing women's health research and education), HairDAO (R&D on new hair-loss treatments), ValleyDAO (synthetic biology research), and CerebrumDAO (neurodegeneration focused).

3. PsyDAO specializes in psychedelic medicine research, implementing governance mechanisms specific to clinical trial funding and development. Their technical architecture includes milestone-based funding releases and specialized proposal assessment frameworks. Notable successes include funding several preclinical studies, though they've faced regulatory challenges in different jurisdictions.

4. LabDAO is focused on open source drug discovery and developed infrastructure for decentralized laboratory services, implementing smart contracts for equipment sharing and service provision. Their technical implementation PLEX is a software platform that interacts with Lab exchange where users can purchase lab or computational resources needed for experiments, and the DAO also includes reputation systems for service providers and quality assurance mechanisms.

CHAPTER 9   CONTEMPORARY DECENTRALIZED ORGANIZATIONS

5. Protocol DAOs such as Uniswap and Aave represent a transformative use case for decentralized governance in the realm of DeFi (decentralized finance). These DAOs allow stakeholders, typically token holders, to propose and vote on changes to the underlying protocol, such as adjusting interest rates, liquidity incentives, or introducing new features. Uniswap, for instance, leverages its governance token (UNI) to enable community-led decision-making on its liquidity pools and fee structures. Similarly, Aave uses its AAVE token to govern lending and borrowing parameters across its ecosystem. These protocol DAOs not only decentralize control but also align incentives between developers, users, and liquidity providers, fostering an open, collaborative environment for continuous improvement.

6. Investment DAOs like Flamingo DAO are reshaping how investments are made and managed, particularly in the realm of digital assets such as NFTs and cryptocurrencies. Flamingo DAO pools funds from its members to collectively invest in high-value NFTs and other blockchain-based assets, with each member having a say in the investment decisions. This model reduces barriers to entry for individuals who might otherwise lack the capital or expertise to participate in such markets. The DAO structure also ensures transparency and trust, as all transactions and decisions are recorded on the blockchain, enabling members to track and validate the use of pooled resources. By democratizing access to investment opportunities,

investment DAOs are creating new avenues for wealth generation and community-driven asset management.

7. Service DAOs like Developer DAO showcase how decentralized communities can coordinate to offer specialized services in a more democratic and transparent manner. Developer DAO, for example, is a community of developers, designers, and blockchain enthusiasts who collaborate on building open source projects, creating educational resources, and contributing to the broader Web3 ecosystem. Members can propose and work on projects, earning tokens or other rewards for their contributions. This model decentralizes the traditional service industry by enabling professionals to work directly with clients or organizations, bypassing intermediaries, and ensuring fair compensation through tokenized rewards.

Automated Market Makers (AMMs) and Real-World Asset (RWA) Protocols

Automated market makers (AMMs) have undergone substantial evolution since their inception, introducing innovations that enhance capital efficiency and user experience. The initial constant product model, implemented by Uniswap v2, utilized a straightforward formula where the product of two asset quantities remained constant, ensuring continuous liquidity. However, this approach was capital-inefficient, as assets were distributed across all price ranges. The advent of concentrated liquidity,

CHAPTER 9   CONTEMPORARY DECENTRALIZED ORGANIZATIONS

notably implemented in Uniswap v3, allowed liquidity providers to allocate capital within specific price ranges, significantly improving capital efficiency. This advancement, while beneficial, introduced complexities in position management and risk assessment. Further developments include the creation of stable AMMs, tailored for assets that trade at near-equal values, such as stablecoins. These systems employ sophisticated mathematical models that integrate multiple pricing strategies, facilitating efficient trades between similarly valued assets while maintaining tight price ranges. Some implementations have incorporated dynamic fees that adjust based on market volatility and liquidity depth, enhancing adaptability to changing market conditions. In 2024, the introduction of auction-managed AMMs (am-AMMs) marked a significant innovation. These systems conduct on-chain auctions to determine temporary pool managers who set swap fee rates and manage liquidity pools. This approach aims to reduce losses from informed order flow and maximize revenue from uninformed order flow, ultimately benefiting liquidity providers.

Real-world asset (RWA) protocols have also advanced, striving to bridge traditional assets with blockchain technology. Successful implementations often utilize a layered architecture that separates legal compliance, asset custody, and tokenization processes, enabling regulatory adherence while leveraging blockchain's benefits. A notable innovation in this domain is the development of hybrid validation systems, which combine traditional legal frameworks with on-chain governance. This fusion allows for efficient dispute resolution while maintaining decentralization where feasible. Additionally, sophisticated oracle systems have been implemented to verify real-world events and trigger smart contract executions, automating processes such as rental payments or dividend distributions. The tokenization of real-world assets has gained momentum, with various projects emerging in 2024. For instance, Ondo Finance specializes in tokenizing US Treasury bonds and money market funds, providing investors with blockchain-based access to low-risk, income-generating assets. Since its launch, Ondo has experienced rapid growth, with its Total Value Locked (TVL) surpassing $600 million across its products.

The success rates of these innovations vary. AMMs have achieved widespread adoption, with certain protocols handling billions in daily volume. The most successful implementations balance innovation with usability, attracting both liquidity providers and traders. However, experimental AMM designs that attempt to optimize for specific trading patterns have sometimes struggled to gain traction due to increased complexity. RWA protocols have encountered mixed results. While the technology holds promise, regulatory challenges and the intricacies of managing real-world assets have impeded widespread adoption. Nonetheless, focused implementations in real estate tokenization and trade finance have demonstrated promising outcomes, with successful pilot programs and increasing transaction volumes. The market for tokenized real estate, for example, is projected to grow significantly, potentially reaching a value between $2 trillion and $16 trillion by 2030.

Regulatory Landscape and Future Directions

The rapid emergence of DAOs has outpaced existing legal and regulatory frameworks, leading to a complex compliance landscape. In the United States, several states have taken significant steps to provide legal recognition and protections for DAOs, recognizing the unique nature of these blockchain-based entities and the need for tailored regulatory frameworks. These state-level initiatives aim to offer DAOs legal clarity, promote innovation, and mitigate risks associated with operating outside traditional structures:

CHAPTER 9   CONTEMPORARY DECENTRALIZED ORGANIZATIONS

1. Wyoming led the charge in July 2021, becoming the first state to officially recognize DAOs as legal entities. By amending its existing limited liability company (LLC) laws, Wyoming introduced a framework that allows DAOs to register as DAO LLCs, providing liability protections similar to traditional LLCs, subject to specific conditions and limitations outlined in the state's regulatory framework. This legal recognition helps establish operational guidelines while maintaining accountability. Wyoming's DAO legislation also allows these organizations to specify in their operating agreements whether their governance will be algorithmically managed or member-managed, ensuring flexibility that aligns with the ethos of decentralization.

2. Tennessee followed Wyoming's example by enacting its own legislation to grant legal recognition to DAOs. Under Tennessee law, DAOs can operate under existing LLC structures but with a distinct "decentralized organization" status. This status ensures that DAOs in Tennessee enjoy the same protections and operational benefits as other LLCs while accommodating the decentralized governance mechanisms that define these organizations. Tennessee's strategy highlights the growing acknowledgment that DAOs require a regulatory framework distinct from traditional corporate structures to thrive within the existing legal system.

CHAPTER 9   CONTEMPORARY DECENTRALIZED ORGANIZATIONS

3. Utah took a more comprehensive approach with the passage of the Utah Decentralized Autonomous Organizations Act (HB0357) in 2023. This law introduced the concept of Limited Liability Decentralized Autonomous Organizations (LLDs), providing an innovative legal structure designed specifically for DAOs. The legislation goes beyond basic recognition by addressing critical aspects of DAO operations, such as ownership guidelines and anonymity protections. For example, Utah's law allows DAOs to maintain member anonymity while ensuring compliance with the bylaws specified in their governing smart contracts. Additionally, the Act incorporates quality assurance protocols to provide greater transparency and trustworthiness in DAO operations.

Other states, including Vermont and Nevada, have begun exploring similar legislation, signaling a growing recognition of DAOs' importance in the evolving digital economy. These emerging frameworks often build upon lessons learned from early adopters while adapting to their specific state contexts. The market response to these state initiatives has been notable, with several prominent DAOs choosing to register under these new frameworks. However, many DAOs continue to operate without formal registration, highlighting the ongoing tension between traditional legal structures and decentralized governance models. Despite these advancements, DAOs face significant regulatory challenges:

1. The Commodity Futures Trading Commission (CFTC) v. Ooki DAO in 2022 was the first to highlight the legal challenges DAOs face. Ooki DAO operates as the governance structure for bZx Protocol, a blockchain-based platform offering margin trading.

CFTC alleged that the DAO facilitated unregistered trading of leveraged and margined retail commodity transactions, violating the Commodity Exchange Act (CEA), without proper registrations and safeguards. The court classified the DAO as an unincorporated association, making it liable for regulatory enforcement actions. This case demonstrated that DAOs could be treated as legal entities, subjecting them and their participants to regulatory scrutiny. Moreover, it emphasized that DAO members might face personal liability for the organization's actions, especially in the absence of formal legal recognition.

2. In 2023, the case of *Sarcuni v. bZx DAO* presented similar concerns. Following a hack of bZx Protocol, a negligence claim was filed against the DAO and its token holders. The court treated the DAO as a general partnership, holding individual token holders liable for the organization's actions. This case revealed the risks associated with DAOs being classified as general partnerships and exposed participants to significant personal liability. It underscored the importance of formal legal structuring, such as incorporating as a limited liability company (LLC), to shield members from such risks.

3. In 2024, the US District Court heard a case against Lido DAO, where the organization and its venture capital backers were accused of selling unregistered securities. The court ruled that Lido DAO and its backers could be held liable, reinforcing the need for DAOs issuing governance or utility tokens to

ensure compliance with securities laws. This case also highlighted the potential legal exposure of investors and backers, emphasizing the importance of due diligence and legal safeguards.

To mitigate legal risks identified in cases like CFTC v. Ooki DAO and Sarcuni v. bZx DAO, modern DAOs are implementing several protective measures. First and foremost is establishing formal legal recognition through entity registration. A DAO-specific entity (DSE) provides a legal structure designed to seamlessly integrate with decentralized autonomous organizations, automatically recognizing token holders as members while providing limited liability protection. Legal wrappers—conducting DAO activities through incorporated legal entities—create separation between individual members and organizational liability, enabling DAOs to open bank accounts, enter contracts, and interact with traditional legal systems. For DAOs operating in regulated sectors such as DeFi and real-world assets (RWAs), implementing KYC and AML verification procedures for treasury management has become essential for regulatory compliance. Some forward-thinking DAOs are exploring decentralized identity solutions that allow users to prove identity without revealing unnecessary personal information, maintaining decentralization principles while satisfying legal requirements.

Establishing a well-designed legal structure has proven valuable for DAOs seeking to attract serious investors, access loans or government incentives, and expand into markets requiring formal legal identity.

Summary

Decentralized autonomous organizations represent a fundamental shift in how entities are governed, transcending traditional hierarchical structures via blockchain technology and smart contract automation. Their evolution from simple token-weighted voting systems to sophisticated multi-layered

CHAPTER 9   CONTEMPORARY DECENTRALIZED ORGANIZATIONS

governance frameworks demonstrates the maturation of decentralized decision-making. Through implementations like Compound's delegation mechanisms, Curve's vote-escrowed tokenomics, and Molecule's IP-NFT framework, DAOs have proven their capacity to handle complex organizational challenges while maintaining decentralized principles. The innovation continues with cross-chain governance solutions, reputation-based systems, and specialized frameworks for different industries, from DeFi to biotech research. However, the true testament to their potential lies in their ability to balance technical innovation with practical governance needs, regulatory compliance with decentralized ideals, and individual agency with collective decision-making. As these organizations continue to evolve, incorporating lessons from both successes and failures, they will establish new paradigms for human coordination and resource allocation in the digital age.

Bibliography

Buterin, V. (2023). The rise of decentralized autonomous organizations: Theory and practice. MIT Press.

Zetzsche, D. A., Arner, D. W., & Buckley, R. P. (2024). Decentralized finance (DeFi) and the law: Legal and regulatory challenges of crypto-assets. *Journal of Financial Regulation*, 10(1), 23–47. https://doi.org/10.1093/jfr/fjad009

OpenZeppelin. (2024). Smart contract security and best practices. https://docs.openzeppelin.com/contracts/security-considerations

Sarcuni v. bZx DAO, No. 22-cv-0618-LAB-DEB (S.D. Cal. Mar. 27, 2023).

Yermack, D. (2024). Corporate governance and DAOs: Comparative analysis of traditional and decentralized governance models. *Journal of Corporate Finance*, 78, 102321. https://doi.org/10.1016/j.jcorpfin.2023.102321

Molecule. (2024). IP-NFT framework: Tokenizing biotech intellectual property. https://docs.molecule.to/documentation/ip-nft-framework

Wyoming Decentralized Autonomous Organization Supplement, Wyo. Stat. § 17-31-101 et seq. (2021).

MakerDAO. (2024). Technical documentation: Protocol-owned vault strategy and treasury management. https://docs.makerdao.com/smart-contract-modules/core-module/vault-module

Gnosis Safe. (2024). Multi-signature wallet implementation for DAOs. https://docs.gnosis-safe.io/introduction/gnosis-safe-multisig

Curve Finance. (2024). veCRV tokenomics: Time-weighted governance implementation. https://resources.curve.fi/governance/voting-escrow

CHAPTER 10

Biological Large Language Models

Beyond traditional NLP applications, LLMs are now being applied to healthcare, biological modeling, and the biopharmaceutical industry, where their ability to maintain long context and understand complex relationships within datasets is proving immensely valuable. In a clinical context, LLMs are driving personalized medicine and medical education. By training on vast amounts of clinical data, these models can assist in identifying patterns and providing decision support, ultimately enhancing patient care. From clinical note generation to conversational agents for mental health, LLMs are reshaping how language-based interactions occur in healthcare and other critical fields. Their role in synthesizing and summarizing medical literature is also becoming indispensable for clinicians and researchers. Efficient extraction of insights from unstructured text (for instance, electronic health records) will become a significant part of daily clinical practice in the near future. In biological modeling, LLMs are being applied to DNA, RNA, and protein sequences, treating these biological molecules as a form of language. Models trained on genomic and proteomic datasets are uncovering intricate gene regulation patterns, predicting protein structures, and designing novel biomolecules, showcasing the potential of LLMs in computational biology. By integrating molecular, genomic, and clinical data, LLMs facilitate the identification of drug targets, prediction of molecular interactions,

CHAPTER 10   BIOLOGICAL LARGE LANGUAGE MODELS

and accelerating drug discovery. This chapter explores the multifaceted applications of LLMs, with a focus on their impact in healthcare, biological modeling, and biopharmaceutical research. We will review the technical foundations of biological language models, the practical applications, and lessons learned in the development of such models. Finally, we will conclude the chapter by presenting topics that will be the focus of upcoming research in the field.

A comprehensive LLM framework for biology and bioinformatics involves three critical stages: data tokenization, model pre-training, and subsequent downstream analyses. Due to the inherent differences between bioinformatics and conventional NLP data, researchers have been pioneering adaptations to the LLM architecture to better suit bioinformatics applications. At its core, the fundamental difference between traditional NLP data and bioinformatics data lies in their structural organization and complexity. While NLP deals with human language that follows linguistic rules and patterns, biological data presents unique challenges due to its highly structured nature and complex interdependencies. In the genomic context, biological sequences are treated analogously to language, where each nucleotide in a sequence read functions like a character, each read operates like a sentence, and the entire genome corresponds to a full article. One significant contribution in handling biological data is the development of new techniques to tokenize genome sequences. For instance, models like DNABERT and Nucleotide Transformer use overlapping fixed-length k-mers as tokens, while more advanced versions like DNABERT-2 and GROVER employ Byte Pair Encoding (BPE) for more efficient representation. This tokenization strategy allows the models to capture biological patterns similar to how language models capture linguistic patterns. RNA analysis presents additional complexities compared with DNA, requiring more sophisticated preprocessing strategies. While models like RNABERT mirror DNA approaches using k-mer methods, others like SpliceBERT, RNA-MSM, and RNA-FM opt for single nucleotides (one-mers) due to the

CHAPTER 10   BIOLOGICAL LARGE LANGUAGE MODELS

typically shorter RNA sequences. These different tokenization strategies present trade-offs that influence model performance and applicability. K-mer tokenization offers greater computational efficiency but results in more fragmented representations compared with single-nucleotide embeddings, which preserve complete sequential information at the cost of increased computational demands. Byte Pair Encoding (BPE) produces compact representations that reduce memory requirements but may sacrifice biological details important for certain analyses. In practice, these tokenization methods have demonstrated domain-specific advantages: single-nucleotide tokenization works best for DNA/RNA sequence tasks requiring precise base-level information, k-mers excel at capturing motifs and functional domains where context is crucial, and BPE has shown particular effectiveness for protein sequences where compressing redundant patterns improves efficiency without sacrificing performance on structure prediction tasks.

These models often incorporate additional metadata during preprocessing, such as RNA-RBP labeling sequences based on RNA-binding protein regions and RNA-MSM enhancing input by including multiple sequence alignments (MSAs) to preserve evolutionary history. At the gene product level, LLMs handle single-cell RNA sequencing (scRNA-seq) data, which presents a unique challenge as it comes in a count matrix format rather than sequential data. Different strategies have emerged to adapt this data for LLM processing: Cell2Sentence, tGPT, and Geneformer employ ranked sequences of gene symbols by expression level, while scGPT and scBERT discretize gene expressions into tokens. Some methods utilize transformer-based architectures that can handle non-discrete inputs more flexibly, such as CIForm's approach of segmenting gene expression vectors into equal-length sub-vectors.

Language models have also been adept in understanding non-coding regions of the genome. Models like EpiGePT have addressed previous limitations by enabling predictions in diverse cellular contexts and incorporating 3D chromatin interaction data. These models typically consist of four key components: a sequence module for DNA analysis, a transcription factor module for cellular context encoding, a transformer module for examining long-range interactions, and a prediction module for outputting context-specific gene regulation insights. In protein-level analysis, LLMs have demonstrated remarkable success in processing mass spectrometry–based proteomics data. Tools like PROTEUS leverage foundational LLMs to automate proteomics data analysis and hypothesis generation. Various protein language models have emerged, differing in architecture, training strategies, and application scope, each designed to address distinct bioinformatics challenges in protein modeling, structure prediction, and functional annotation. The success of these adaptations lies in how LLMs have been modified to handle the hierarchical and interconnected nature of biological data. While traditional NLP models process linear sequences of text, bioinformatics LLMs must account for multiple levels of biological organization, from molecular interactions to cellular systems. The attention mechanisms in these models have been specially adapted to capture long-range dependencies in biological sequences, similar to how certain DNA regions can influence gene expression from a distance.

In the application of LLMs to biology, a broader conceptual framework is necessary to systematically understand the complexity of long-range dependencies. A recent review by Ruan et al. introduces such a concept, Life Active Factors (LAFs), a new bioinformatics "language" that encapsulates the fundamental building blocks of biology in a framework designed to serve as training data for biological language models. LAFs include tangible molecular entities like DNA, RNA, proteins, genes, and drugs, as well as abstract biological components such as biological pathways, regulatory networks, and protein interactions. They also incorporate biological measurements like phenotypes and disease biomarkers. What makes LAFs particularly powerful is their ability to reconcile conceptual differences across various bioinformatics subfields while respecting the complex interrelationships between biological components. This framework

CHAPTER 10 BIOLOGICAL LARGE LANGUAGE MODELS

aligns with foundational models by emphasizing the connections between sequence, structure, and function while treating each LAF as an interconnected node within broader biological networks. Our discussion of biological models will follow the central dogma, starting with DNA foundational models, then RNA models, and finally protein models.

DNA Language Models

DNA language models represent a transformer-based approach to genomic sequence analysis, evolving from traditional sequence alignment methods to sophisticated deep learning architectures. These models fundamentally differ from protein and RNA language models due to the unprecedented length of genomic sequences and the complex, hierarchical nature of genomic (and epigenomic) regulation. The development of DNA-LLMs has been particularly challenging due to the need to capture both local sequence motifs and long-range regulatory interactions that can span millions of base pairs. The architectural foundation of DNA-LLMs typically employs modified transformer architectures optimized for extremely long sequences. Standard transformer architectures, with their quadratic attention complexity, become computationally intractable for genomic-scale sequences. Consequently, several innovations have emerged, including linear attention mechanisms, hierarchical transformers, and sparse attention patterns. These modifications enable the models to process sequences of hundreds of thousands to millions of nucleotides while maintaining computational efficiency. Common implementations include the Enformer architecture, which uses dilated attention patterns, and Genomic-BERT models, which implement sequence chunking strategies.

Training data for DNA-LLMs primarily comes from genome databases such as ENCODE, GenBank, and species-specific genome projects. The preprocessing pipeline typically involves careful consideration of sequence representation, with strategies ranging from simple one-hot encoding of nucleotides to more sophisticated approaches that incorporate evolutionary conservation scores, chromatin accessibility data, and other genomic annotations. A crucial aspect of data preprocessing involves handling the inherent asymmetry of DNA sequences, as regulatory elements can function on either strand and in various orientations. The training objectives for DNA-LLMs often extend beyond simple masked language modeling. While masked nucleotide prediction serves as a foundational pre-training task, models typically incorporate multiple auxiliary objectives. These can include predicting chromatin accessibility, transcription factor binding sites, enhancer–promoter interactions, and other functional genomic features. Multitask learning frameworks are commonly employed to simultaneously learn these diverse aspects of genomic function. A particular challenge in DNA-LLM development lies in handling the hierarchical nature of genomic organization. Models must capture information at multiple scales: from individual nucleotide sequences that form transcription factor binding sites (typically 6–12 base pairs) to regulatory elements spanning hundreds of base pairs and to topologically associating domains extending over millions of base pairs. This multiscaled nature has led to the development of hierarchical attention mechanisms and multi-resolution architectures that can efficiently process genomic information at different scales. The application scope of DNA-LLMs is remarkably broad. These models have demonstrated success in predicting regulatory element function, identifying disease-associated variants, and understanding the impact of genomic variations on gene expression. They have proven particularly valuable in interpreting non-coding regions of the genome, which traditional methods often struggle to analyze. Advanced applications include predicting three-dimensional chromatin organization, identifying long-range regulatory interactions, and predicting the impact of genetic variants on complex traits.

CHAPTER 10 BIOLOGICAL LARGE LANGUAGE MODELS

Technical optimization of DNA-LLMs focuses heavily on memory efficiency and computational scalability. Common strategies include gradient checkpointing, mixed precision training, and efficient attention implementations. Many models employ sophisticated chunking strategies that allow them to process long sequences while maintaining contextual information across chunks. Some implementations use hierarchical compression schemes where the sequence is processed at multiple resolutions, with fine-scale analysis reserved for regions of particular interest. Performance evaluation of DNA-LLMs typically involves multiple benchmark datasets and metrics. These include prediction accuracy for transcription factor binding sites, enhancer activity, chromatin accessibility, and other functional genomic features. Models are often evaluated on their ability to predict the effects of genetic variants, particularly in non-coding regions. Cross-species generalization and the ability to capture evolutionary constraints are also important evaluation criteria. Current limitations and challenges include the computational resources required for training and inference on genomic-scale sequences, the difficulty of interpreting model predictions in biological terms, and the challenge of incorporating three-dimensional genomic organization. Future directions include the integration of multimodal data (such as combining sequence information with chromatin state data), improved interpretability methods, and the development of more efficient architectures for handling genome-scale sequences. Ethical considerations in DNA-LLM development include privacy concerns related to genetic information, potential biases in training data (particularly regarding the representation of different populations), and the responsible use of these models in clinical applications. There are also significant considerations regarding the environmental impact of training these large-scale models, given their substantial computational requirements. The following is an overview of the widely used DNA language models:

1. Among the pioneering models, **DNABERT** stands out for its adaptation of the BERT architecture to genomic sequences. Its distinctive feature lies in the k-mer tokenization strategy, processing overlapping sequences of nucleotides rather than individual bases. This model employs a standard transformer encoder architecture with 12 layers, 768 hidden dimensions, and 12 attention heads, trained through masked k-mer prediction and next sentence prediction tasks on the human reference genome.

2. DeepMind's **Enformer** represents a significant advancement in handling long-range genomic interactions, capable of processing sequences up to 196,608 base pairs. The model implements a hybrid architecture that combines convolutional layers with transformer blocks, featuring a convolutional stem for sequence length reduction, transformer blocks with relative positional embeddings, and dilated attention patterns. This sophisticated design, incorporating 1,536-dimensional embeddings across 11 transformer layers, enables efficient capture of long-range dependencies while maintaining computational feasibility.

3. The **Genomically Aware Transformer** (GAT) introduces several innovations specifically tailored to genome-scale sequence processing. Its architecture implements hierarchical attention mechanisms operating at multiple genomic scales, incorporating custom positional encodings that account for genomic coordinate information. The model integrates evolutionary conservation scores

CHAPTER 10   BIOLOGICAL LARGE LANGUAGE MODELS

in its input representation and employs sparse attention patterns focused on biologically relevant interactions, supplemented by auxiliary training objectives including enhancer–promoter interaction prediction.

4. **Nucleotide Transformer** scales up the approach with 600M parameters across 24 transformer layers, implementing a hybrid tokenization strategy that handles both individual nucleotides and k-mers. The model distinguishes itself through the integration of chromatin accessibility data during pre-training and a multitask learning framework that encompasses various genomic prediction tasks. Its specialized attention mechanisms are designed to handle sequence symmetry, accounting for both forward and reverse strands of DNA.

5. **GenSLMs** (Genomic-Scale Language Models) specifically targets the challenge of processing extremely long genomic sequences through linear attention mechanisms and hierarchical compression schemes. The architecture incorporates multiscale feature extraction through interleaved convolutional layers and custom pre-training objectives focused on regulatory element prediction. A notable feature is its integration of phylogenetic information in the input representation, enabling better capture of evolutionary constraints.

6. **GENA** (Genomic Native Attention) advances the field through several technical innovations, including rotary positional embeddings adapted for genomic coordinates and attention patterns informed by known chromatin interaction data. The model implements multi-resolution processing of genomic sequences and integrates epigenetic modifications in its input representation, supported by custom loss functions for different genomic prediction tasks.

These models differ significantly in their approaches to key technical challenges. Sequence length handling varies from DNABERT's k-mer tokenization to Enformer's dilated attention and GenSLMs' linear attention mechanisms. Input representation strategies range from simple k-mer–based tokenization to sophisticated integrations of multiple data types. Attention mechanisms span from standard self-attention to complex hierarchical and biologically informed patterns. Training objectives vary from basic masked prediction tasks to sophisticated multitask frameworks incorporating various genomic features.

RNA Language Models

RNA language models use the transformer architecture with attenuated attention mechanisms, designed to capture long-range dependencies in sequential data. These models are pre-trained on extensive RNA sequence datasets using self-supervised learning techniques, such as masked language modeling (MLM). In MLM, certain nucleotides in the RNA sequence are masked, and the model learns to predict these masked positions based on the surrounding context. This approach enables the model to grasp the underlying patterns and structures inherent to RNA and help in downstream secondary analysis. There are three relevant

CHAPTER 10 BIOLOGICAL LARGE LANGUAGE MODELS

applications including secondary structure prediction, functional annotation (of existing and newly discovered RNA molecules), and designing RNA sequences for therapeutic and biotech applications. The following are some of the most popular RNA language models:

1. **RiboNucleic Acid Language Model (RiNALMo)** is the largest RNA language model to date, with 650 million parameters. It was pre-trained on 36 million non-coding RNA sequences from several databases, enabling it to capture the underlying structure information implicitly embedded within RNA sequences. The model architecture consists of 33 layers, each with a hidden size of 1,280, 20 attention heads, and an intermediate size of 5,120. RiNALMo has achieved state-of-the-art results on several downstream tasks, notably demonstrating superior generalization capabilities in RNA secondary structure prediction, even on unseen RNA families. The model's ability to extract hidden knowledge from RNA sequences represents a significant potential for advancing our understanding of RNA structures and function.

2. **RNA-FM** is a foundation model for RNA sequence analysis, pre-trained on an extensive dataset of over 1 billion RNA sequences. It employs a BERT-style transformer encoder architecture, enabling it to capture long-range dependencies and structural cues within RNA sequences. The pre-training objective is masked language modeling (MLM), where the model learns to predict masked nucleotides based on their context. RNA-FM has been successfully applied to various RNA-related

tasks, including secondary structure prediction, functional annotation, and RNA–protein interaction analysis.

3. **ERNIE-RNA** is a BERT-style model pre-trained on a large corpus of non-coding RNA sequences in a self-supervised fashion. The model was trained on the raw nucleotides of RNA sequences only, with an automatic process to generate inputs and labels from those texts. The pre-training objective used was masked language modeling (MLM), where 15% of the tokens are masked, and the model learns to predict these masked tokens based on the surrounding context. The model architecture consists of 12 layers, each with a hidden size of 768, 12 attention heads, and an intermediate size of 3,072, totaling approximately 85.67 million parameters. ERNIE-RNA was pre-trained on a dataset of 20.4 million non-redundant RNA sequences from RNAcentral, with sequences longer than 1,024 nucleotides excluded. The model has demonstrated SOTA performance in RNA feature extraction and secondary structure prediction tasks compared with existing models.

4. **Gener-RNA** is a transformer-based model designed for the de novo generation of RNA sequences. It utilizes a generative framework to produce entirely new RNA sequences with desired properties, such as forming specific secondary structures or binding to target molecules. The model was trained on extensive RNA datasets to learn the patterns governing sequence–structure relationships,

enabling it to generate sequences optimized for specific functions. This capability is particularly valuable in synthetic biology and therapeutic RNA design, where novel RNA molecules with tailored functionalities are in demand.

5. **RNA-MSM** (RNA Multiple Sequence Alignment-based Language Model) is an unsupervised RNA language model that utilizes multiple sequence alignments (MSAs) of homologous RNA sequences to generate embeddings and attention maps for various downstream tasks, such as RNA secondary structure prediction. The model employs multiple layers of attention mechanisms to capture intricate relationships between aligned RNA sequences. By focusing on conserved regions and co-evolutionary signals within the MSAs, RNA-MSM learns representations that are highly informative for structural and functional inference. The model was pre-trained on the Rfam 14.7 database, which includes 4,069 RNA families. To avoid overfitting, RNA-MSM excluded RNA families with experimentally determined structures, such as ribosomal RNAs, transfer RNAs, and small nuclear RNAs, narrowing the dataset to 3,932 RNA families. The median number of sequences per MSA in the dataset was 2,184. The RNAcmap3 pipeline was employed to identify and align homologous sequences, integrating tools like BLAST-N, INFERNAL, Easel, RNAfold, and evolutionary coupling analysis. The pre-training objective was masked language modeling (MLM), in which 15%

of the nucleotides were randomly masked, and the model was trained to predict these masked positions based on the surrounding context. RNA-MSM's attention maps and embeddings exhibit strong correlations with RNA secondary structures and solvent accessibility, even without supervised fine-tuning. When fine-tuned, the model demonstrates significantly improved performance in these tasks compared with state-of-the-art methods such as SPOT-RNA2 and RNAsnap2. Moreover, RNA-MSM outperforms models like RNA-FM in predicting base pairs and solvent-accessible surface areas.

6. **LncRNA-BERT** is a novel RNA language model specifically designed for classifying RNA sequences as either coding or long non-coding. The model demonstrates SOTA performance in RNA classification while utilizing a more efficient architecture compared with existing approaches. The model's architecture is based on the BERTmedium transformer framework, consisting of 12 transformer blocks with a dimensionality of 768, 3,072 nodes in feedforward layers, and 12 attention heads. A notable innovation is the introduction of Convolutional Sequence Encoding (CSE), which directly embeds nucleotide sequences into a high-dimensional space using convolution, providing an efficient alternative to traditional encoding methods. The model has approximately 85M trainable parameters in total. The training data is primarily sourced from human RNA sequences, including 297,724 coding and 238,470 non-coding

RNA sequences from GENCODE (v46), NONCODE (v6), and RefSeq (v255) databases. This is a key differentiation from other RNA language models that typically use RNAcentral as their main data source. The model undergoes pre-training using masked language modeling (MLM) with a 15% masking probability (of which 80% is masked and 10% randomly replaced), followed by fine-tuning on a carefully curated dataset of 101,270 coding and 48,785 non-coding RNAs. The researchers used the CD-HIT algorithm with a 90% sequence identity threshold to ensure non-redundancy and test set independence. A significant finding is that LncRNA-BERT can distinguish between coding and non-coding RNA sequences even during the pre-training phase, without requiring labeled data, indicating that coding potential is an intrinsic sequence characteristic. The distinction between coding and non-coding RNA is complicated by biological ambiguity—some lncRNAs contain short ORFs that translate into small peptide chains, while some pcRNA genes can have non-coding isoforms. The model's success in classification is attributed to its ability to recognize three-base periodicity patterns in coding RNA, which aligns with biological reading frames. For optimal performance, the researchers found that a context length of 2,304 nucleotides is sufficient for classifying coding potential. The model's performance matches or exceeds state-of-the-art classifiers on standard test sets while maintaining a smaller model size compared with alternatives like RiNALMo. On the GENCODE/

RefSeq test set, it achieves macro-averaged F1 scores of 0.940, with particularly strong performance in precision for protein-coding RNA (0.965) and recall for non-coding RNA (0.926).

BEACON (BEnchmArk for COmprehensive RNA Task and Language Models) is a recently introduced RNA benchmarking framework that comprehensively addresses a gap in standardized evaluation methods for RNA models. The benchmark consists of 13 distinct tasks derived from extensive RNA research, encompassing 967,000 sequences with lengths ranging from 23 to 1,182 nucleotides. The structural analysis component of BEACON comprises four key tasks. Secondary structure prediction (SSP) employs a target matrix to identify paired regions within RNA molecules, utilizing the bpRNA-1m database containing over 100,000 single-molecule RNA structures. Contact map prediction (CMP) focuses on binary classification of nucleotide pairs within an 8 Å distance threshold, while distance map prediction (DMP) extends this to a regression problem for precise inter-nucleotide distance prediction. The fourth task, structural score imputation (SSI), addresses missing structural information prediction using icSHAPE sequencing data from HEK293 cell lines, implementing carefully controlled masking protocols with 30% of nucleotides randomly masked during training. The functional studies domain of BEACON encompasses four sophisticated tasks. The splice site prediction (SPL) task implements a three-way classification system for acceptor, donor, or neither sites, utilizing Jaganathan's dataset and evaluated using Top-k accuracy. The non-coding RNA function classification task categorizes RNAs into 13 distinct classes using data from GENCODE, circBase, and Rfam. The modification prediction task covers 12 different RNA modification types from 15 base-resolution technologies, while the mean ribosome loading task predicts mRNA translation activity using 91,519 5' UTR sequences. For engineering applications, BEACON incorporates four critical tasks. Vaccine degradation prediction forecasts stability under various environmental conditions using Stanford

OpenVaccine competition data covering 6,043 RNA constructs. The programmable RNA switches task analyzes ON/OFF states activity across 91,534 toehold switches. CRISPR on-target and off-target prediction tasks assess sgRNA efficiency and specificity using weighted Spearman correlation coefficients, evaluating approximately 15,000 sgRNAs targeting 1,071 genes.

The benchmark also introduced **BEACON-B**, a new baseline model incorporating single-nucleotide tokenization and ALiBi positional encoding, based on a BERT backbone with 12 layers. BEACON's comprehensive evaluation revealed several crucial insights about RNA model architectures. Pre-trained RNA language models demonstrated superior performance over previous task-specific state-of-the-art approaches on 8 out of 13 tasks. Single-nucleotide tokenization significantly outperformed alternative tokenization methods across 11 out of 13 tasks, while ALiBi positional encoding showed particular advantages for shorter sequences. The BEACON-B baseline achieved competitive performance while requiring significantly fewer computational resources—just 3.58 GPU days compared with up to 240 GPU days for some competitors. Overall, the benchmark includes extensive preprocessing pipelines, standardized training protocols, and task-specific evaluation metrics. The technical infrastructure supports both sequence-level and nucleotide-level predictions, with specialized processing for structural tasks requiring nucleotide–nucleotide-level predictions.

Protein Language Models

Protein language models differ from DNA and RNA models in several fundamental ways, primarily due to the inherent differences in the complexity and information content of their respective sequences. While DNA and RNA models work with a relatively simple alphabet of just four nucleotides (A, T/U, G, C), protein models must handle 20 different amino acids as their basic units, creating a substantially larger vocabulary

CHAPTER 10   BIOLOGICAL LARGE LANGUAGE MODELS

space and more complex relationships to model. The three-dimensional structure of proteins is also far more crucial to their function than in nucleic acids, requiring protein language models to capture intricate spatial relationships and structural motifs that DNA and RNA models typically don't need to consider to the same degree. Protein sequences tend to be more conserved across species due to the critical nature of their functions, and protein language models can rely on evolutionary information effectively. In contrast, DNA and RNA sequences, especially non-coding regions, can be more variable, posing challenges for language models to capture meaningful patterns without extensive evolutionary data. Proteins also exhibit more complex context dependencies, where the function and behavior of an amino acid sequence can vary dramatically based on its surrounding residues and overall structural context. Despite the challenges, remarkable progress has been made for protein language models, as we discuss below:

1. **ProGen** is a transformer-based model designed for generating novel protein sequences with desired properties, making it a powerful tool for protein engineering and design. Its architecture leverages the transformer framework to analyze and learn the syntax and semantics inherent in large protein sequence databases. By doing so, it can generate protein sequences that not only adhere to biological rules but also exhibit specific functional or structural attributes.

2. The **xTrimoPGLM** model is a large-scale transformer-based framework tailored for protein sequence understanding and generation. Its purpose spans critical tasks such as protein structure prediction and de novo protein design. The architecture integrates dual pre-training

CHAPTER 10 BIOLOGICAL LARGE LANGUAGE MODELS

objectives—autoencoding and auto-regressive modeling—within a unified framework, allowing the model to excel in both understanding and generating protein sequences. With 100 billion parameters trained on a dataset comprising 1 trillion tokens, xTrimoPGLM demonstrates unprecedented capacity in modeling complex protein-related phenomena.

3. **ProLlama** is a cutting-edge model designed for multitask protein language processing. Its applications include sequence generation, property prediction, and functional annotation, making it a versatile tool for protein-related research. Built on the Llama architecture, ProLlama employs a two-stage training approach enhanced by low-rank adaptation (LoRA). This strategy enables the model to efficiently learn from diverse protein-related tasks while minimizing computational overhead.

4. **ProtLLM** is a specialized model designed for tasks that bridge protein-centric analysis and protein-language interactions. Its purpose includes predicting protein–protein interactions, annotating functions, and interpreting protein-related literature. The architecture introduces a dynamic protein mounting mechanism to handle mixed inputs of natural language text and protein sequences seamlessly. Employing a "protein-as-word" modeling approach, ProtLLM learns from a large-scale interleaved protein-text dataset, enabling it to process and contextualize protein sequences within the framework of linguistic patterns.

CHAPTER 10   BIOLOGICAL LARGE LANGUAGE MODELS

ESM-3

ESM-3 implements a sophisticated multimodal architecture that processes three parallel tracks (sequence, structure, and annotation) within a unified transformer framework. The model utilizes discrete tokenization across all modalities, with sequence tokens representing individual amino acids, structural tokens derived from a specialized discrete autoencoder, and function tokens encompassing GO terms and InterPro annotations. The architecture leverages 216 transformer blocks in its largest 98B parameter configuration, processing input through geometric attention and modality-specific embedding layers before fusion in a shared latent space. The model operates on 2.78 billion proteins and 771 billion unique tokens, with training conducted across three scales: 1.4B, 7B, and 98B parameters. The token embeddings are processed through transformer blocks that incorporate geometric attention mechanisms, allowing cross-modal interaction while maintaining modality-specific information through specialized attention patterns. The model achieves representation fusion through a combination of self-attention mechanisms and cross-modal attention, enabling joint reasoning across sequence, structure, and function spaces.

The training methodology employs a sophisticated masked language modeling objective that operates simultaneously across all modalities. A masking scheduler is implemented to vary masking rates across training, allowing the model to learn dependencies at different levels of information availability. This is combined with a preference optimization loss during fine-tuning that encourages the model to assign higher likelihood to high-quality samples. The training process incorporates both conditional and unconditional generation capabilities, with the model learning to predict tokens given any combination of masked inputs across modalities. The objective function factorizes the probability distribution over all possible predictions, enabling the model to handle missing or partial information across any combination of tracks. Spatial information processing in ESM-3 is implemented through a sophisticated geometric attention mechanism and processes structural information through transformation matrices that allow local frames to interact globally, implementing this through a series of attention operations that maintain rotational and translational invariance. This enables incorporation of both backbone and side-chain atomic coordinates, processing them through specialized attention layers that handle both local and global structural relationships.

In silico protein language models do not explicitly work within evolutionary constraints. However, for ESM-3 to solve the training task of predicting the next masked token, the model must learn how evolution moves through the space of potential proteins. In the ESM-3 publication, the developers show that the model reasoned in a chain of thought to generate candidates of new green fluorescent proteins (GFPs) called esmGFP. Given the conserved identity of naturally occurring GFPs, it is estimated that esmGFP represents an equivalent of over 500 million years of natural evolution performed by an evolutionary simulator.

AlphaFold

AlphaFold 1, introduced in 2018, marked DeepMind's entry into the protein structure prediction domain. It utilized a combination of evolutionary sequence analysis and machine learning to predict pairwise residue distances and torsion angles, which were then used to construct protein structures. The model relied heavily on multiple sequence alignments (MSAs) to extract evolutionary information and integrate physics-based constraints to guide structure prediction. While it outperformed traditional methods, its accuracy and efficiency were limited, setting the stage for more advanced approaches.

The next iteration, AlphaFold 2, employs a sophisticated neural network architecture centered around the novel "Evoformer" block, which processes protein information through two parallel tracks: a multiple sequence alignment (MSA) representation and a pair representation.

Dual-track processing allows the system to simultaneously reason about both evolutionary conservation patterns and spatial constraints. The architecture's input processing begins with extensive feature engineering, incorporating multiple sequence alignments, position-specific scoring matrices, template information when available, and various chemical and physical properties of amino acids. These inputs undergo transformation through a series of specialized attention mechanisms, including MSA row attention, MSA column attention, and triangular attention operations that help capture both local and global relationships within the protein sequence. The Evoformer block, which forms the backbone of the network, contains several sophisticated operations (row-wise and column-wise attention over the MSA, transition layers with feedforward networks, etc.) that are repeated 48 times in the full model. This deep processing allows the model to build up increasingly refined representations of the protein's structure through iterative refinement. The structure module, which follows the Evoformer blocks, employs an Invariant Point Attention (IPA) mechanism to generate and refine 3D coordinates. This module operates by predicting backbone atom positions and torsion angles, gradually building up the protein structure while respecting physical constraints and amino acid properties.

Training the model involved several sophisticated techniques, including masked MSA prediction, distogram prediction, and end-to-end coordinate refinement. The training data comprised publicly available protein structures from the Protein Data Bank (PDB), with careful consideration given to preventing information leakage between training and test sets. The model was trained using a multitask loss function that incorporated various structural and evolutionary objectives. A key innovation in AlphaFold 2's training process was the implementation of equivariant operations that ensure predictions remain consistent under rotations and translations in 3D space. This architectural constraint helps the model learn meaningful structural features rather than arbitrary

CHAPTER 10 BIOLOGICAL LARGE LANGUAGE MODELS

spatial relationships. The training process also employed sophisticated data augmentation techniques and carefully designed loss functions that balance different aspects of structural prediction.

Note In October 2024, the Nobel Prize in Chemistry was awarded to Demis Hassabis and John Jumper of Google DeepMind, along with David Baker of the University of Washington, for their groundbreaking work in protein structure prediction and design. Hassabis and Jumper were recognized for developing AlphaFold, a model capable of accurately predicting the three-dimensional structures of proteins based solely on their amino acid sequences.

AlphaFold 3 (AF3), the newest iteration, is designed to predict the structures of protein complexes involving DNA, RNA, ligands, ions, and post-translational modifications. A notable innovation in AF3 is the introduction of the "Pairformer" module, a deep learning architecture inspired by transformers. The Pairformer processes input sequences to capture intricate relationships between amino acids and other molecules, effectively modeling interactions within complexes. Following this, AF3 employs a diffusion-based generative model to construct the three-dimensional structures. This approach starts with a random configuration and iteratively refines it, akin to techniques used in advanced image generation models. To accommodate the expanded scope, AF3 was trained on an extensive dataset comprising diverse biomolecular interactions. This training regimen enabled the model to learn the structural nuances of various complexes, enhancing its predictive accuracy across a wide range of biological scenarios. Benchmarking studies have demonstrated that AF3 achieves a minimum 50% improvement in accuracy for predicting protein interactions with other molecules compared with previous methods. In specific cases, such as DNA interactions, the accuracy has more than doubled, underscoring AF3's enhanced predictive performance.

CHAPTER 10 BIOLOGICAL LARGE LANGUAGE MODELS

In November 2024, Google DeepMind released the source code for AlphaFold 3 (AF3), making it accessible for academic research. While the source code is openly available, access to the model parameters (weights) requires permission from the company.

scGPT

Beyond the central dogma of molecular biology, the next generation of biological language models are tackling the single-cell domain. scGPT is an advanced foundational model tailored for single-cell RNA sequencing (scRNA-seq) and multi-omics analysis. Based on the architecture of generative pre-trained transformers (GPTs), scGPT is designed to process and analyze large-scale single-cell datasets with unprecedented precision and efficiency. The research is led by Dr. Bo Wang at the University of Toronto. The model was pre-trained on an extensive dataset of over 33 million human cells from 51 organs and 441 studies, sourced from the CELLxGENE collection. This large-scale pre-training enables scGPT to learn intricate patterns in gene expression, providing a comprehensive understanding of cellular functions and heterogeneity. The training of scGPT is divided into two phases: pre-training and fine-tuning. During pre-training, a self-supervised approach is employed to model the non-sequential nature of gene expression data. The model uses a specially designed attention mask and a generative training pipeline to predict complete gene expression profiles based on cellular states and existing cues. The transformer architecture enables simultaneous learning of cell and gene representations, effectively capturing the complex relationships inherent in single-cell data. The fine-tuning phase adapts the pre-trained model to specific tasks using smaller, targeted datasets, enhancing performance in areas such as batch correction, cell type annotation, multi-omics integration, genetic perturbation prediction, and gene regulatory network inference. The training objectives for scGPT include integrating multi-omics data to provide a

CHAPTER 10 BIOLOGICAL LARGE LANGUAGE MODELS

unified view of transcriptomics, epigenomics, and proteomics, annotating cell types with high accuracy to reveal cellular heterogeneity, predicting the effects of genetic perturbations to aid therapeutic research, and inferring gene–gene interactions for deeper insights into regulatory networks. Its applications span multiple domains: correcting batch effects for multi-dataset integration, achieving precise cell type classification, predicting cellular responses to genetic modifications using Perturb-seq datasets, and constructing gene regulatory networks at single-cell resolution. Despite its remarkable capabilities, scGPT faces challenges such as addressing batch effects more effectively and incorporating spatial omics data. Future improvements aim to expand its training datasets to include diverse omics and spatial data, further enhancing its robustness.

Evo

Evo is a multi-omic language model designed to handle tasks like protein function prediction, gene expression analysis, and generating coherent genome-scale sequences. Built on the StripedHyena architecture, it employs convolutional operators equipped with rotary position embeddings (RoPE) for sequence handling. Compared with its predecessor, HyenaDNA, Evo boasts a 1,000× larger model size and leverages 100× more training data, achieving a context length of up to 131K tokens using single-nucleotide, byte-level tokenization. Its hybrid architecture interweaves 29 layers of data-controlled convolutional operators with 3 layers of multi-head attention, a deliberate balance that capitalizes on the strengths of each component: Hyena layers excel in sequence processing, while attention layers enhance information recall from the input context. This design enables Evo to excel in filtering noisy DNA patterns and aggregating nucleotides into motifs, outperforming the Transformer++ architecture in scaling performance. Evo combines data-controlled convolutional operators and multi-head attention to handle sequences up to 131,000 tokens in length. The model's training relied on the OpenGenome dataset, encompassing over 80,000 bacterial and archaeal genomes and millions of predicted prokaryotic phage and plasmid sequences, totaling 300 billion nucleotide tokens. Sourced from GTDB and IMG/VR databases, the dataset's taxonomic composition included Pseudomonadota (N = 21,693), Bacillota (N = 17,264), Actinomycetota (N = 11,500), and Bacteroidota (N = 8,813), alongside other phyla, with 60,789 bacterial and 4,418 archaeal genomes. The training process took roughly four weeks and unfolded in two stages. The first phase utilized an 8K-token context length for pre-training, later extending to 131K tokens in the second phase. During pre-training, Evo learned genome data distributions and biological sequence motifs without explicit supervision or annotations. The model was trained on 300 billion nucleotides, with researchers estimating 250 billion tokens as the compute-optimal number for Evo 7B based on the FLOP budget. This equated to a 17% offset from the compute-optimal model size during the initial pre-training phase.

Evo exhibited advanced sequence analysis capabilities, excelling in multiple benchmarks. It outperformed nucleotide models in protein function prediction using DMS datasets of *E. coli* proteins and achieved competitive results with protein-specific language models. Evo effectively predicted gene essentiality across 58 bacterial studies without task-specific fine-tuning. In generation tasks, Evo demonstrated the ability to create sequences up to 650 kb in length. When fine-tuned on 82,430 CRISPR-Cas loci, it generated coherent complexes, with 15–45% matching Cas coding sequences as long as 5 kb. The researchers observed stable training across all model sizes and learning rates, further validating their estimation of 250 billion tokens as the compute-optimal limit for Evo 7B. The developers acknowledged that genome-scale sequences generated by Evo resembled "blurry images," lacking some finer details of natural genomes. They highlighted ethical considerations, such as excluding eukaryotic viruses from training data for biosecurity reasons, and identified technical challenges, including limited human protein fitness predictions and incomplete genomic feature generation. Future improvements may stem from increased scale, extended context lengths, and more diverse training datasets, drawing parallels to advancements in natural language models.

In the remainder of this chapter, we will cover various translational healthcare and scientific applications where a LLM or a LLM-powered service is being used to assist in scientific discovery.

Drug Discovery with LLMs

Drug discovery is an intensive process, typically requiring between 7 and 15 years from initial development to market approval, with drug–target interaction (DTI) identification being a crucial initial step. Pre-trained language models like PharmBERT, BioBERT, and ProteinBERT excel at extracting meaningful representations from molecular data. DTI language models address the cold-start problem by utilizing pre-trained models to predict DTIs based solely on molecular and protein sequences. For instance, ConPLex generates co-embeddings of drugs and target proteins, achieving broad generalization to unseen proteins with significantly faster inference compared with traditional sequence-based methods—specifically ten times faster. TransDTI is another example that employs a transformer-based language model to classify drug–target interactions into active, inactive, or intermediate categories. A few other drug–target interaction models are as follows:

1. DrugLAMP employs Pocket-Guided Co-Attention (PGCA) and Paired Multi-Modal Attention (PMMA) to fuse molecular graphs with sequence data.

2. PGraphDTA incorporates 3D contact maps alongside protein sequences, demonstrating superior performance compared with sequence-only methods.

3. DrugChat combines prompt-based learning with sequence data and textual inputs, trained on three datasets to predict indications, mechanisms of action, and pharmacodynamics while generating dynamic textual outputs in response to user prompts.

Knowledge graph–based approaches represent another significant advancement. Y-Mol enhances biomedical reasoning by integrating multiscale biomedical knowledge and using Llama2 as its base LLM. It learns from publications, knowledge graphs, and synthetic data, enriched by three types of drug-oriented prompts: description-based, semantic-based, and template-based. Similarly, the DrugAgent framework advances drug repurposing by combining AI-driven DTI models, knowledge graph extraction from databases (including DrugBank and CTD), and literature-based validation. Biologyn LMs have shown remarkable capabilities in processing various data types, including scientific literature, patent databases, and specialized datasets. These models integrate diverse sources to provide comprehensive analyses of protein sequences, structures, binding pockets, and interaction sites.

In molecular docking, LLMs have been adapted to enhance various aspects of structure prediction, binding affinities, and binding site identification. DrugChat demonstrates the ability to generate insights from compound molecule graphs when provided with appropriate prompts. LaMPSite, powered by the EMS-2 protein language model, represents an advancement in binding site prediction, requiring only protein sequences and ligand molecular graphs as inputs, achieving comparable performance to methods requiring 3D protein structures. Recent developments in protein–ligand binding prediction have further enhanced screening efficiency. RTMScore integrates Graph Transformer for extracting structural features of proteins and molecules, using 3D residue graphs of proteins and 2D molecular graphs as inputs. This approach has outperformed traditional docking software including AutoDock Vina, DeepBSP, and DeepDock in virtual screening tasks. LLMs can also automate data extraction and normalization for drug property predictions, particularly in ADMET (Absorption, Distribution, Metabolism, Excretion, and Toxicity) analysis. Systems like PharmaBench exemplify this through their multi-intelligence approach to extracting ADMET-related data from multiple public databases. These advancements significantly reduce both time and resources needed for drug discovery while improving the likelihood of identifying successful drug candidates.

Public Health with LLMs

In disease prediction and vaccine efficacy analysis, LLMs like GPT-3 and GPT-4 have demonstrated significant capabilities in processing vast biomedical datasets. Neural networks combined with logistic regression have achieved notable accuracy in predicting influenza vaccination outcomes based on demographic and clinical data. ChatGPT has been utilized to generate insights for reducing severe post-COVID-19 cases, while machine learning algorithms have been validated for predicting influenza infection in patients with influenza-like illness (ILI).

For vaccine adherence and risk prediction, LLMs facilitate the analysis of large datasets to identify demographic and social determinants of health impacting vaccination rates. Machine learning models have been applied to assess low adherence to influenza vaccination among adults with cardiovascular disease, offering insights into vaccination barriers for high-risk groups. Real-time data analysis from online self-reports and social media posts has been instrumental in tracking influenza vaccine uptake and public sentiment trends. In biomarker analysis and antigen prediction, LLMs have been crucial in analyzing genetic relationships and autoimmune markers to understand vaccination outcomes and disease susceptibility. Differential network centrality analysis and feature selection techniques have been employed to identify key susceptibility hubs within biological networks. For influenza vaccines, particularly influenza A (H3N2), statistical analyses of antigenic similarity have demonstrated the potential of machine learning models in mapping antigenic drift and optimizing strain selection for seasonal vaccines.

The MAIVeSS platform exemplifies how LLMs streamline the selection of high-yield, antigenically matched viruses for seasonal influenza vaccines. For populations with specific health conditions, such as HIV, LLMs have been applied to predict the immunogenicity of trivalent inactivated influenza vaccines, revealing key biomarkers and immune signatures for personalized vaccination strategies. Sentiment analysis and public attitude research on social media have also benefited significantly from LLM techniques in identifying factors contributing to vaccine hesitancy or acceptance. In epidemiology and public health data analysis, machine learning and large datasets have revolutionized understanding of disease patterns, risk factors, and vaccination responses. Studies integrating socioeconomic, health, and safety data have examined how these factors affect COVID-19 spread, revealing the influence of demographics like income and healthcare access on infection rates. The Human Vaccines Project leverages large datasets to map immune responses across populations, enhancing understanding of vaccine design and immunology.

A novel example of AI-driven data analysis is the use of wearable sensors in epidemiological studies where the WE SENSE protocol facilitated early detection of viral infections by analyzing real-time health metrics. Additionally, studies like those by the CAPNETZ group highlight unmet needs in understanding disease mechanisms, emphasizing the necessity for targeted data collection and analysis in developing effective treatment and intervention strategies. Continued development of LLMs in the field of public health sentiment analysis will be crucial for addressing future public health challenges and improving vaccination strategies across marginalized populations.

Clinical Foundational Models

The following are foundational models trained for clinical use cases as decision support tools:

1. **ClinicalBERT** represents major progress in domain-specific language modeling, built upon the BERT architecture with modifications optimized for clinical text processing. Its pre-training process involves masked language modeling and next sentence prediction tasks on a massive corpus of clinical narratives, including discharge summaries, progress notes, and radiology reports. The model maintains BERT's core 12-layer transformer architecture but incorporates specialized vocabulary augmentation with clinical terms and implements context-aware token masking that considers medical entity relationships during pre-training. The model utilizes a domain-specific tokenizer trained on clinical text, resulting in a vocabulary of 30,000 word pieces that better represent medical terminology. The attention mechanism is enhanced with a clinical entity-aware module that assigns higher weights to medically relevant terms and their contextual relationships. The model implements gradient checkpointing to reduce memory requirements during training and employs a specialized loss function that balances general language understanding with clinical domain expertise.

2. To address the challenge of processing lengthy clinical notes, **Clinical-Longformer** and **Clinical-BigBird** extend the core BERT architecture and incorporate novel attention mechanisms. Clinical-Longformer employs a sliding window attention pattern combined with global attention tokens, enabling efficient processing of sequences up to 4,096 tokens while maintaining $O(n)$ complexity instead of the quadratic complexity of traditional transformers. Clinical-BigBird, meanwhile, implements a unique sparse attention mechanism that combines random, window, and global attention patterns, allowing it to process similar sequence lengths but with potentially better performance on tasks requiring cross-document understanding. Clinical-Longformer's architecture includes a specialized positional encoding scheme that better captures long-range dependencies in clinical narratives, while its attention mechanism employs dilated sliding windows that expand receptive fields without increasing computational cost. Clinical-BigBird enhances its sparse attention patterns with medical entity-aware attention heads that dynamically adjust attention weights based on the clinical relevance of tokens. Both models implement gradient accumulation techniques to handle large batch sizes on limited hardware and utilize specialized caching mechanisms to optimize memory usage during inference.

3. **BioGPT**, developed by Microsoft Research, utilizes a decoder-only transformer architecture pre-trained on 15 million biomedical research papers. Its unique

feature lies in its domain-specific pre-training objectives, which include both traditional language modeling and specialized biomedical relation prediction tasks. The model implements a modified Top-k sampling strategy optimized for biomedical text generation, incorporating medical knowledge constraints during the generation process to improve factual accuracy. BioGPT's architecture also includes an adaptive layer normalization scheme that adjusts to the complexity of medical content, and its attention mechanism incorporates a hierarchical medical knowledge graph that guides the model's understanding of biomedical relationships. The model employs a specialized vocabulary of 50,000 tokens optimized for biomedical terminology and implements a dynamic temperature scaling mechanism that adjusts generation parameters based on the required precision of medical information.

4. **PubMedBERT** distinguishes itself through its "domain-specific pre-training from scratch" approach, eschewing the common practice of starting from general-domain models. This methodology involves pre-training on 21B words of biomedical text using a customized WordPiece vocabulary derived purely from PubMed, resulting in more precise biomedical term representations. The model implements a modified attention mechanism that gives higher weight to domain-specific terms and incorporates a biomedical entity-aware masking strategy during pre-training. Its architecture includes

specialized biomedical entity recognition heads that operate in parallel with the main transformer layers, enabling simultaneous processing of general language understanding and entity identification. PubMedBERT implements a novel continual pre-training approach that allows for periodic updates with new medical literature while maintaining stability on existing knowledge. The model utilizes a hierarchical learning rate scheme that applies different optimization parameters to domain-specific and general language components.

5. **Med-PaLM** represents a significant advancement in medical AI, building upon Google's PaLM architecture with specialized medical knowledge integration. The model implements a novel multitask learning framework that combines traditional language modeling with specific medical reasoning tasks. It incorporates a medical knowledge verification system that cross-references generated content against a curated database of medical facts, enhancing the reliability of its outputs. Med-PaLM's architecture includes a specialized medical reasoning module that implements symbolic logic operations alongside neural processing, enabling more precise handling of medical inferences. The model employs a unique attention mechanism that incorporates medical temporal awareness, allowing it to better understand and represent the progression of medical conditions and treatments. It implements

CHAPTER 10   BIOLOGICAL LARGE LANGUAGE MODELS

a sophisticated few-shot learning framework optimized for medical scenarios and includes a specialized medical entity grounding system that links generated content to standardized medical ontologies.

6. **GatorTron**'s architecture is notable for its scale and specialized training approach, utilizing over 82 billion words of clinical text in its pre-training phase. The model implements a modified transformer architecture with additional attention heads specifically designed to capture clinical temporal relationships and incorporates a hierarchical attention mechanism that prioritizes clinically relevant terms based on their context within medical documentation. GatorTron includes a novel pre-training objective that explicitly models the hierarchical nature of medical documentation, from individual symptoms to complete patient histories. The model implements a specialized tokenization strategy that preserves the structure of medical abbreviations and numerical values and employs a context-aware pooling mechanism that better captures the relationships between different sections of clinical documents. It utilizes a dynamic batch scheduling system that optimizes training efficiency across varying lengths of clinical narratives and implements gradient checkpointing with automated mixed precision training to manage its large parameter count efficiently.

7. **Clinical-T5** adapts the T5 framework with several medical domain-specific modifications. Its text-to-text approach allows for unified handling of various clinical NLP tasks through a consistent interface. The model incorporates a specialized prefix-tuning mechanism for different clinical tasks and implements a medical entity-aware vocabulary that improves its handling of clinical terminology. Its architecture includes task-specific adapters that can be fine-tuned independently while maintaining a frozen base model. Clinical-T5 employs a novel prompt engineering system specifically designed for medical tasks, incorporating standardized medical terminologies and formatting conventions. The model implements a hierarchical decoder architecture that generates structured medical documentation while maintaining natural language fluency and includes a specialized loss function that balances general language modeling with adherence to medical documentation standards. It utilizes an advanced caching mechanism that optimizes performance on repetitive medical terminology and implements a dynamic vocabulary expansion system that adapts to new medical terms while maintaining model stability.

8. **SapBERT** introduces a novel self-alignment pre-training approach that explicitly optimizes biomedical entity representations. The model implements a specialized loss function that combines traditional masked language modeling with synonym alignment objectives, utilizing

structured knowledge from medical ontologies. It incorporates a hierarchical attention mechanism that considers both local context and global ontological relationships when processing medical terms. SapBERT's architecture includes a sophisticated entity alignment module that maintains consistency across different medical terminology systems and implements a contrastive learning framework specifically designed for medical entity relationships. The model employs a specialized pooling strategy that creates more robust medical entity embeddings and includes a novel fine-tuning approach that preserves entity alignment while adapting to specific downstream tasks.

9. **BlueBERT**'s dual-domain architecture enables effective processing of both clinical and biomedical text through a specialized domain adaptation layer. The model implements a domain-aware attention mechanism that adjusts its parameters based on the input text type, allowing for optimal performance across different medical text genres. It incorporates a modified tokenization strategy that better handles the varying linguistic patterns between clinical notes and research literature. BlueBERT employs a novel domain mixing strategy during pre-training that optimizes the balance between clinical and biomedical knowledge acquisition. The model implements a specialized feature fusion mechanism that combines domain-specific representations at multiple levels of the

network and includes an adaptive normalization scheme that adjusts to different medical text styles. It utilizes a sophisticated curriculum learning approach that gradually increases the complexity of domain adaptation tasks and implements efficient parameter sharing between domain-specific components while maintaining specialized processing pathways.

10. **ClinicalGPT** differentiates itself through its comprehensive multitask medical training framework, incorporating both general medical knowledge and specific clinical scenarios. The model implements a hierarchical decision-making system that combines pattern recognition with explicit medical reasoning steps. Its architecture includes a specialized verification module that cross-references generated content against established medical guidelines and literature. ClinicalGPT employs an advanced few-shot learning system optimized for diverse clinical scenarios and implements a novel attention mechanism that incorporates medical temporal awareness and causal relationships. The model includes a sophisticated medical reasoning framework that combines neural processing with symbolic logic operations, enabling more precise handling of complex medical scenarios. It utilizes a dynamic prompt engineering system that adapts to different clinical contexts and implements a specialized cache mechanism that optimizes performance on frequently encountered medical patterns.

11. **Colosseum 355B** employs a unique distributed training architecture optimized for deployment on private infrastructure. The model implements advanced parameter-efficient fine-tuning methods that allow for customization without full model retraining, crucial for adaptation to specific clinical settings. Its architecture includes built-in privacy-preserving mechanisms and specialized attention patterns that improve handling of sensitive medical information. Colosseum 355B incorporates a novel distributed training framework that enables efficient scaling across private computing clusters while maintaining data privacy. The model implements sophisticated encryption techniques for model weights and gradients during training and includes specialized modules for handling regulatory compliance requirements. It utilizes an advanced parameter sharing mechanism that optimizes performance across distributed systems and implements efficient gradient compression techniques for reduced communication overhead.

12. **DERA** represents an innovative approach to improving LLM outputs through a structured dialog system. The framework implements two specialized agents—a Researcher focused on information gathering and verification and a Decider responsible for final output generation. This dual-agent architecture incorporates a novel attention mechanism that weights information based on its source reliability and clinical relevance while maintaining a verification loop that ensures

adherence to medical accuracy standards. DERA employs a sophisticated agent communication protocol that optimizes information exchange between the Researcher and Decider components, implementing specialized attention mechanisms for each agent role. The framework includes an advanced verification system that maintains multiple hypothesis streams and implements a novel scoring mechanism for evaluating the reliability of medical information. It utilizes a dynamic memory management system that efficiently tracks the state of medical reasoning processes and implements specialized modules for handling uncertainty in medical decision-making.

Reducing Physician Burnout with LLMs

LLMs are being piloted as clinical assistants to help reduce the administrative burden on physicians, which is a major contributor to burnout. They can help draft clinical notes and documentation by generating initial versions that physicians can then review and modify. The following are some tools currently in development:

1. **Abridge's** medical conversation AI platform implements a sophisticated multimodal transformer architecture that processes both audio and text streams in parallel. Their speech recognition pipeline utilizes a specialized medical acoustic model trained on 500,000+ hours of clinical audio, combined with a medical language model incorporating over 2 million clinical terms. The system employs a three-stage NLP pipeline:

first, a medical named entity recognition (NER) transformer pre-trained on UMLS and SNOMED-CT taxonomies; second, a relationship extraction model using graph attention networks to map clinical entities and their interconnections; and finally, a SOAP note structuring model that employs hierarchical attention mechanisms to organize information into appropriate clinical sections.

2. **Nabla's** system architecture integrates a custom-built ambient listening system using beamforming arrays for enhanced audio capture in clinical settings. Their "medical context preservation" architecture implements a novel attention mechanism they call "temporal-clinical attention," which uses a sliding window approach with overlapping context to maintain consistency across long conversations. The backend employs a modified T5 architecture fine-tuned on over 10 million clinical notes, with special tokens for medical entities and relationships. Their EHR integration layer uses HL7 FHIR standards with custom middleware that handles real-time synchronization and conflict resolution.

3. **Karya's** "hierarchical attention" architecture implements a multi-level transformer model that processes clinical conversations at three distinct levels: utterance-level encoding, semantic chunking using a custom tokenization scheme optimized for medical terminology, and global context modeling. Their medical entity disambiguation system combines BERT-based models fine-tuned on

medical corpora with a knowledge graph containing over 5 million medical entity relationships, achieving 95+% accuracy through ensemble learning approaches.

4. **Nuance DAX's** platform utilizes an advanced far-field audio processing system with adaptive noise cancellation and multi-channel acoustic echo cancellation. Their speech recognition pipeline implements a hybrid CTC–attention model architecture, combining the benefits of CTC (Connectionist Temporal Classification) for alignment and attention mechanisms for context understanding. The system uses Azure's custom GPT-4 models fine-tuned on specialized medical datasets, with custom prompt engineering techniques for different medical specialties.

5. **Suki's** "clinical context injection" technique implements a novel architectural approach combining transformer-based language models with a Retrieval-Augmented Generation (RAG) system. This system maintains a vector database of previous patient encounters and relevant medical knowledge, using similarity search to inject relevant context into the generation process. Their adaptive learning system employs online learning techniques to continuously update provider-specific language models while maintaining HIPAA compliance.

6. **DeepScribe's** speaker diarization system implements a novel neural architecture combining spectral clustering with transformer-based

embeddings, achieving speaker separation accuracy above 95% even in noisy clinical environments. Their "medical reasoning verification" system uses a combination of knowledge graph validation and causal inference models to ensure logical consistency in generated documentation, cross-referencing against both general medical knowledge bases and specialty-specific guidelines.

7. **Notable Health's** computer vision integration uses a custom-trained YOLOv5 model for real-time processing of visual clinical findings, combined with a multimodal transformer that fuses visual and textual information. Their mobile-first architecture implements edge computing techniques to process sensitive patient information locally, with encrypted synchronization to cloud services for more computationally intensive tasks.

8. **Augmedix's** hybrid human–AI system implements a real-time assistance architecture where AI models provide suggestions and structured information to human scribes through a custom interface. Their "clinical context maintenance" system uses a combination of vector databases and attention mechanisms to maintain consistency across patient encounters, with specialized models for different medical specialties.

9. **Corti's** emergency care–focused system implements real-time speech analysis using a custom architecture optimized for low-latency processing. Their "urgency detection" system

uses a novel approach combining acoustic feature analysis (for detecting stress in voice patterns) with NLP-based content analysis, employing a custom-trained transformer model that can identify critical medical conditions with high accuracy. The system includes a real-time alerting mechanism that can flag potential emergency situations based on conversation patterns and medical context.

These platforms are increasingly adopting sophisticated security architectures to handle personal health information (PHI), including homomorphic encryption for processing sensitive data, secure enclaves for model inference, and federated learning approaches for model updates. The integration challenges with existing EHR systems are being addressed through specialized middleware layers that implement both HL7 FHIR standards and legacy integration protocols, with custom caching and synchronization mechanisms to maintain performance under high-load conditions.

AI and LLMs Powering Mental Health Services

LLMs are being cautiously explored as supplementary tools in mental health support, with strict limitations and oversight. Early research suggests they may help with initial screening and simple supportive interactions, but they cannot replace trained mental health professionals. Current applications focus on increasing accessibility to basic emotional support and psychoeducational resources, particularly in areas with limited access to mental healthcare. However, there are significant ethical concerns around privacy, the potential for harmful advice, and the risk of users forming inappropriate attachments to AI systems. Any deployment

CHAPTER 10 BIOLOGICAL LARGE LANGUAGE MODELS

of LLMs in mental health contexts requires careful consideration of safety protocols, clear disclosure of AI involvement, and escalation to human professionals when needed. The following are a few startups in this space:

1. **Aiberry** provides an AI-powered mental health assessment platform that conducts quick and objective screenings in various settings, including in-clinic, telehealth, or self-screening environments. The platform delivers real-time assessments of a patient's mental state, quantified risk scores, and health insights to enhance diagnosis and treatment. Aiberry's system is clinically validated and utilizes multiple modalities—voice, text, and audio—to ensure reliable and accurate mental health assessments.

2. **Talkspace** is an online and mobile therapy company that connects users with licensed therapists for virtual counseling sessions. The platform allows users to communicate with their therapist via video, audio, and text messaging. Depending on the plan, users may also have access to a number of 30-minute video conference sessions per month. Talkspace has grown to include over 1.5 million clients and includes therapists in all 50 states. The company uses machine learning and artificial intelligence tools to analyze anonymized transcripts of therapy sessions in order to improve services.

3. **Woebot** is an AI chatbot developed by a team of Stanford psychologists to provide mental health support through cognitive-behavioral therapy (CBT) techniques. The chatbot engages users in

CHAPTER 10 BIOLOGICAL LARGE LANGUAGE MODELS

text-based conversations, helping them manage their mental health by offering evidence-based strategies and coping mechanisms. Woebot utilizes natural language processing (NLP) to understand and respond to user inputs, aiming to deliver personalized support. Studies have shown that Woebot can form therapeutic bonds with users, comparable to human-delivered services.

4. **Wysa** is an AI-driven mental health chatbot that provides anonymous chat support to users dealing with stress, anxiety, and other mental health concerns. The platform employs evidence-based therapeutic techniques, including CBT, dialectical behavior therapy (DBT), and meditation, to assist users in managing their mental well-being. Wysa's AI is designed to offer empathetic listening and suggest appropriate coping strategies based on user interactions. Notably, Wysa's AI has been effective in detecting users in crisis, identifying 82% of such cases and providing appropriate support.

5. **Replika** is an AI companion designed to engage users in meaningful conversations, serving as a friend, therapist, or romantic partner. The platform uses natural language processing to simulate human-like interactions, aiming to improve emotional well-being and provide support. Replika adapts to user inputs over time, learning to offer more personalized responses and companionship.

6. **Troodi** is a mental health chatbot integrated into Troomi phones, specifically designed for children and adolescents. It uses AI to validate and respond

to children's concerns, offering support similar to that of a therapist, and is available 24/7. Troodi provides stress management tips and assists children with emotional issues, aiming to alleviate the youth mental health crisis and therapist shortage.

7. **Youper** is an AI-driven mental health assistant that combines cognitive-behavioral therapy (CBT) techniques with mood tracking and mindfulness exercises. It engages users in brief conversations to monitor emotional states and provides personalized insights to promote mental well-being. Youper's integration of therapeutic methods with AI allows for a tailored user experience.

8. **Tess** is an AI mental health chatbot designed to provide on-demand emotional support. It offers real-time conversations and utilizes evidence-based therapeutic approaches to assist users in managing stress, anxiety, and other mental health challenges.

9. **Kintsugi** is an AI-powered platform that uses voice biomarkers to detect signs of depression and anxiety during conversations. By analyzing vocal patterns, it provides real-time mental health assessments, enabling early intervention and support. This non-intrusive approach allows for continuous monitoring without explicit questionnaires.

10. **Clara** is an AI mental health companion that engages users in conversations to provide emotional support and coping strategies. It focuses on

building resilience and offers personalized activities to improve mental well-being. Clara's design emphasizes user engagement through interactive dialogues.

Summary

Biological large language models represent a paradigm shift in our understanding of the foundational molecules of life. In this chapter, we explored how these models are improving our understanding of biological sequences, from DNA and RNA to proteins, and beyond to single-cell regulation. DNA models like DNABERT and Enformer have pioneered new approaches to handling genomic-scale sequences, while RNA models such as RiNALMo and RNA-FM have advanced our understanding of RNA structure and function. The development of protein models, culminating in achievements like ESM-3 and AlphaFold 3, has dramatically improved our ability to predict and understand protein structures and interactions. These advances are particularly noteworthy given the fundamental differences in complexity between nucleic acid and protein sequences. Beyond the central dogma, we've seen how models like scGPT are pushing boundaries in single-cell analysis, while platforms like Evo are tackling multi-omic integration challenges. The translation of these technological advances into practical applications has been equally impressive. In drug discovery, LLMs are accelerating the identification of drug–target interactions and enabling more efficient screening processes. Clinical applications are showing promise in reducing physician burnout through automated documentation and providing mental health support services, though with appropriate caution and human oversight. However, the deployment of these technologies in clinical settings requires careful consideration of several critical factors. Regulatory concerns remain significant as many LLM-based clinical tools operate in a rapidly evolving landscape where formal approval frameworks are still developing. Bias risks present another substantial challenge, as AI-generated medical advice may perpetuate or amplify biases present in training data, potentially leading to disparate outcomes across different patient populations. Perhaps most crucially, the limited interpretability of complex biological models poses particular challenges in high-stakes medical decision-making, where clinicians need transparent explanations for AI-suggested interventions. Balancing these risks against the benefits of increased efficiency and accessibility will require thoughtful implementation strategies that maintain human medical expertise at the center of patient care while leveraging AI as a supportive tool rather than a replacement for clinical judgment.

Several challenges still remain. These include the need for more efficient architectures to handle the computational demands of biological sequence analysis; the challenge of integrating diverse data types while maintaining biological relevance; the importance of balancing automation with human expertise, particularly in clinical applications; privacy and security concerns in handling sensitive medical data; and the need for robust validation frameworks to ensure reliable and safe deployment. Looking ahead, new research and development will likely focus on enhanced integration of multimodal biological data, improved interpretability of model predictions, more sophisticated approaches to handling long-range dependencies in biological sequences, development of more efficient and environmentally sustainable training methods, and expanded applications in personalized medicine and therapeutic design. As these models continue to evolve, their impact on biological research and healthcare is likely to grow, completely transforming how we understand and treat diseases.

Bibliography

Jumper, J., Evans, R., Pritzel, A., Green, T., Figurnov, M., Ronneberger, O., Tunyasuvunakool, K., Bates, R., Žídek, A., Potapenko, A., Bridgland, A., Meyer, C., Kohl, S. A. A., Ballard, A. J., Cowie, A., Romera-Paredes, B., Nikolov, S., Jain, R., Adler, J., ... Hassabis, D. (2021). Highly accurate protein structure prediction with AlphaFold. *Nature*, 596(7873), 583–589. https://doi.org/10.1038/s41586-021-03819-2

Rives, A., Meier, J., Sercu, T., Goyal, S., Lin, Z., Liu, J., Guo, D., Ott, M., Zitnick, C. L., Ma, J., & Fergus, R. (2021). Biological structure and function emerge from scaling unsupervised learning to 250 million protein sequences. *Proceedings of the National Academy of Sciences*, 118(15), e2016239118. https://doi.org/10.1073/pnas.2016239118

Lin, Z., Akin, H., Rao, R., Hie, B., Zhu, Z., Lu, W., Smetanin, N., Verkuil, R., Kabeli, O., Shmueli, Y., dos Santos Costa, A., Fazel-Zarandi, M., Sercu, T., Candido, S., & Rives, A. (2023). Evolutionary-scale prediction of atomic-level protein structure with a language model. *Science*, 379(6637), 1123–1130. https://doi.org/10.1126/science.ade2574

Abramson, J., Ahdritz, G., Akant, L., Burke, J. M., Nordström, J., Aktulga, H., Alexandrova, A., Baldwin, C., Berchansky, M., Blaber, S., Bogard, N., Burke, E. K., Case, D. A., Chowdhury, R., Correia, B. E., Cortina, G. A., Davis, I. W., Dey, F., Dou, J., ... Chen, D. (2024). AlphaFold 3: Protein structure prediction with atomic accuracy at genomic scale. *Nature*, 630(8004), 493–500. https://doi.org/10.1038/s41586-024-07487-w

Cui, H., Wang, C., Maan, H., Pang, K., Luo, F., Duan, N., & Wang, B. (2024). scGPT: Toward building a foundation model for single-cell multi-omics using generative AI. *Nature Methods*, 21(8), 1470–1480. https://doi.org/10.1038/s41592-024-02201-0

Hayes, T., Evans, R., Kudo, T., Havens, S., McGrath, M., Lightman, D., McHardy, M., Liu, Y., Meyer, C., Koukos, P. I., Pham, T. H., Robertson, A., Kang, D., Wang, L., & Colwell, L. J. (2024). Evo: Evolution-inspired multimodal language model for genome-length sequences. arXiv preprint arXiv:2401.10780. https://doi.org/10.48550/arXiv.2401.10780

Zvyagin, M., Brace, A., Hippe, K., Deng, Y., Zhang, B., Ilie, I. M., Sanyal, A., Luo, Y., Jones, A. M., Judge, T., White, A. D., Li, K., Haas, K. R., Benmore, C., Prelesnik, A., Chung, L. S., Islam, K. A., Shukla, C., Tran, T., ... Esteva, A. (2023). RiNALMo: RNA language modeling with nucleotide-level tokenization. *Nature Machine Intelligence*, 5(10), 1159–1170. https://doi.org/10.1038/s42256-023-00711-8

Petti, S., Tohgasaki, T., Alrashid, S., Shin, J. E., Lin, Y. R., MacWilliams, A., Wang, J., Qi, Y., & Yang, K. K. (2023). RNA-MSM: An accurate RNA language model enables comprehensive homology-based RNA design. *Proceedings of the National Academy of Sciences*, 120(26), e2300397120. https://doi.org/10.1073/pnas.2300397120

Lin, Y. R., Kang, D., Wu, R., Zhang, H., Esvelt, K. M., & Das, R. (2023). BEACON: A comprehensive benchmark for biological sequence foundation models. *Nature Methods*, 20(10), 1513–1523. https://doi.org/10.1038/s41592-023-01899-8

Rives, A., Goyal, S., Meier, J., Guo, D., Ott, M., Zitnick, C. L., Ma, J., & Fergus, R. (2024). ESM3: Simulating 500 million years of evolution with a language model. Science, 385(6683), 637–644. https://doi.org/10.1126/science.adl7384

Szałata, A., Hrovatin, K., Becker, S., Tejada-Lapuerta, A., Cui, H., Wang, B., & Theis, F. J. (2024). Transformers in single-cell omics: A review and new perspectives. *Nature Methods*, 21(8), 1430–1443. https://doi.org/10.1038/s41592-024-02353-z

Madani, A., Krause, B., Greene, E. R., Subramanian, S., Mohr, B. P., Holton, J. M., Olmos, J. L., Xiong, C., Sun, Z. Z., Socher, R., Fraser, J. S., & Naik, N. (2023). Large language models generate functional protein sequences across diverse families. *Nature Biotechnology*, 41(8), 1099–1106. https://doi.org/10.1038/s41587-022-01618-2

Zhang, H., Diacon, A., Xia, Z., Jiao, M., Yao, V., Zhong, E., Chen, B., Wang, X., & Zou, J. (2023). Gene expression programs: Generative pre-training for protein-gene interactions. *NPJ Systems Biology and Applications*, 9(1), 43. https://doi.org/10.1038/s41540-023-00288-3

Notin, P., Schols, E., Connors, J., Du, M., Zatmeh, S., Fusi, N., & Svistunova, P. (2023). BiomedCLIP: A foundation model for biomedical images and text. *Nature Medicine*, 29(12), 3211-3222. https://doi.org/10.1038/s41591-023-02504-3

Thirunavukarasu, D., Kong, Y., McGuire, A. M., Landgren, A. J., Lee, C., Wang, T., Yang, S., Alsentzer, E., Shafran, R., & Naumann, T. (2023). ClinicalBERT: Modeling clinical notes and predicting hospital readmission. ACM *Transactions on Computing for Healthcare*, 4(2), 1-28. https://doi.org/10.1145/3471259

Ruan, Wei, Yanjun Lyu, Jing Zhang, Jiazhang Cai, Peng Shu, Yang Ge, Yao Lu et al. Large Language Models for Bioinformatics. arXiv preprint arXiv:2501.06271 (2025).

CHAPTER 11

Blockchain in Scientific Reproducibility

Evidence-based clinical sciences are currently suffering from a paralyzing reproducibility crisis. From clinical psychology to cancer biology, recent meta-research indicates a rise in researchers' failing to replicate studies published by their peers. This problem is not just limited to benchwork that happens in a lab; it also plagues translational research where the transformation from bench to bedside happens. Treatments, tests, and technologies are converted from simple lab experiments to FDA-approved devices and assays that affect hundreds of lives. Therefore, replicability is crucial to converting scientific breakthroughs into pragmatic remedies.

The primary role of blockchain technology in the emerging landscape of open-access science is increasing the amount of transparency into these processes. To that end, three use cases and applications are presented in this chapter: the first one involving deposition of data in clinical trials, the second one involving a reputation system that can be developed for researchers and institutes committed to open research, and the third one involving the application of supply-chain management for tracking counterfeit drugs. In these use cases, we provide ample examples of ongoing work that will come to drastically shape the world of blockchain in

CHAPTER 11   BLOCKCHAIN IN SCIENTIFIC REPRODUCIBILITY

science. We will begin by discussing the current paradigms of the research method and the importance of negative data; our focus will mostly remain limited to the clinical sciences. Then, we will talk about traditional metrics and altmetrics systems presently implemented to measure the impact of published research. This will allow us to transition into the use cases that supplement traditional metrics and expand them to make open science a fundamental feature. Finally, we will end our discussion by looking at ongoing efforts to incorporate blockchain into the existing research infrastructure.

Blockchain Properties and Reproducibility

The following core properties of a blockchain become essential in addressing scientific reproducibility:

>**Immutability and scientific integrity**: Blockchain's immutable ledger provides a tamper-proof record of research activities that directly addresses the reproducibility crisis. By recording research data in a decentralized ledger, blockchain ensures that findings are immutable and transparent, enhancing trust and accelerating collaboration while preventing data manipulation after collection. This immutability creates an unalterable audit trail of research methods, protocols, and results, making it impossible for researchers to selectively report findings or manipulate data after experiments conclude.
>
>**Transparency and research verification**: Blockchain technology's transparent nature enables researchers to trace the origin and history

of scientific data, ensuring transparency and increasing trust in the scientific community. This transparency not only enables reproducibility but also facilitates the identification of potential errors. This capability directly counters the "publish or perish" culture described in the chapter by making the entire research process visible and accountable.

Decentralization and democratic science: By using blockchain technology and decentralized networks, decentralized science (DeSci) seeks to democratize access to scientific research, improve collaboration between researchers, and ensure greater transparency and reproducibility in scientific endeavors. Decentralization prevents any single authority from controlling research data, removing institutional biases and conflicts of interest that can compromise scientific integrity.

Reproducibility Crisis

Let's begin our discussion with what *reproducibility* means in the context of scientific discourse and investigation. One of the major cornerstones in research is the ability to follow written protocols from a study, using the documented methods to carry out experiments and arrive at the same conclusions as those given by that study. In other words, a published study can be independently verified by other researchers and replicated to achieve the same results. Recent meta-research in clinical sciences demonstrates that more and more published works are not rigorous experimentally so as to be replicated with ease. Leonard P. Freedman and colleagues estimate that over 50% of preclinical research cannot be translated from animal models to human clinical trials, thereby placing the approximate annual cost of irreproducibility at $28 billion in the United States alone. Consequently, as preclinical findings in animal models are rarely repeated in clinical trials, drug discovery has slowed down its pace, and the costs have risen dramatically. The economic costs are very debilitating, as close to $200 billion is wasted annually because the discovered targets cannot be reproduced. These problems are often inherent to the design of a particular study or due to very genuine intricacies and complications that arise in experiments on differing cell lines. To understand why, we have to look for answers in meta-research, which is a branch of investigation that statistically evaluates the claims, results, and experiments performed in a study.

A multitude of factors in academia are creating a vicious culture of "bad science," as Dr. Ben Goldacre refers to it: a vanishing funding landscape, a culture of "publish or perish," and an incredible amount of pressure on young researchers to get tenured push them to follow erroneous methods that lead to non-reproducible publications. In some cases, the slipshod research methods and manipulations have led to fraud and eventual retractions with serious consequences to the researcher.

Note Retraction Watch is a blog that recently came about to report on scientific misconduct happening at all levels, from editors working with journals to individual researchers at universities. The blog also tracks papers that have been retracted from journals due to fraudulent data or manipulation of experimental evidence. You can follow their website, which posts about 500–600 retractions per year.

Academic journals are also partly to blame for this mess, though there are signs of real change and improvement in the works. Over the past few years, it has been easier to publish studies with positive findings in journals regarding potential drug targets or effectiveness of a particular drug. But negative findings from experiments, such as a drug target not working even though it was expected to work, have been incredibly difficult to publish. On face value, it seems to make sense: why would someone want to know if an experiment failed? Negative data usually gets ignored because of similar reasoning, and from a marketing standpoint, a journal claiming that X didn't work as expected isn't a highlight that would sell. Let's take a closer look at positive and negative data in the context of how journals have shaped their use and publication.

Positive data is simply the confirmation of an initial hypothesis, where a researcher predicted a finding and the data validated it. On the other hand, negative data comes from the cases where the expected or wanted effect was not observed. If an experiment showed that no difference existed between the null and alternative hypotheses, the data and results would likely end up buried in the pile of unpublished results of the lab group. Figure 11-1 provides a very simplified overview of an erroneous research method for dealing with positive and negative data, a method that results from the pressures in academia. Replication is sacrificed in pursuit of highly demanding and attractive drug targets, which ultimately do not translate well into clinical trials and lead to more economic waste.

CHAPTER 11   BLOCKCHAIN IN SCIENTIFIC REPRODUCIBILITY

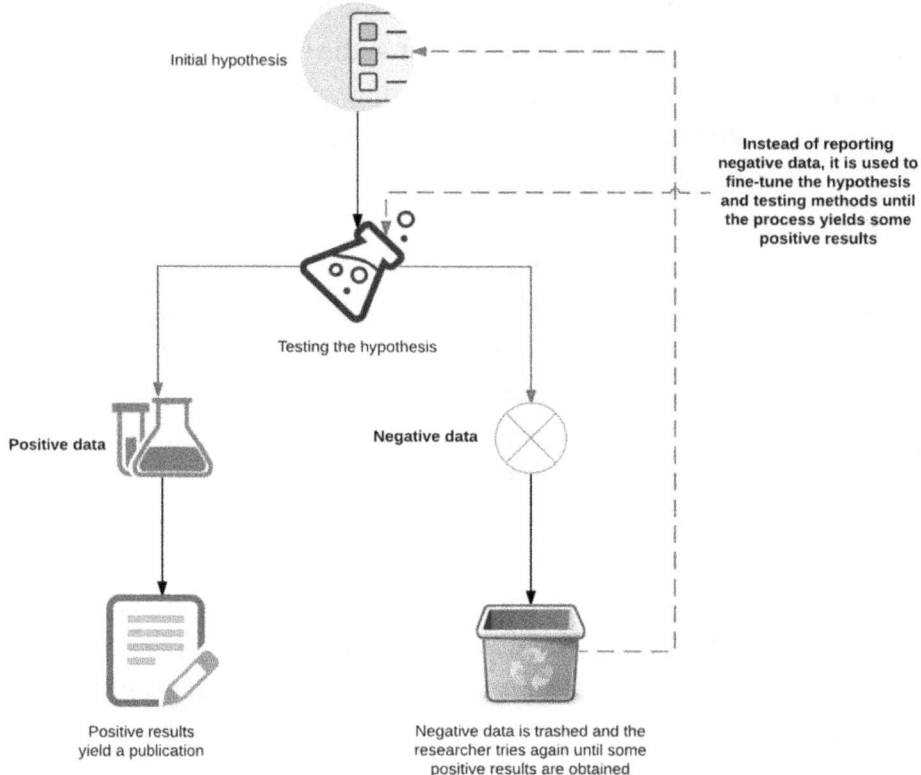

Figure 11-1. Overview of positive and negative data in the context of publishing a study

In Figure 11-1, we see a simple demonstration of hypothesis testing that leads to the publication of "flukes," which are non-replicable in translational research or scaled clinical trials. Due to the nature of publishing in academic journals, positive data usually implies that you're done. Most researchers will stop here and not bother to follow up with any appreciable fraction of all the data that was collected or generated while conducting the experiments. This could include potential negative data regarding an avenue of thought that didn't work or information that was omitted due to feedback from reviewers. Once a research paper has been accepted, the authors of a publication have no further incentives to release more data or put in more time to clean up and make available other results. This turns out to have some detrimental consequences, which we will discuss later in the chapter.

These trends have been observed by journals internationally, and publishers are beginning to take some action. A plethora of new initiatives are raising the standards for the data that can be included in a publication, as well as the design considerations that must be fulfilled to ensure replication. Let's talk about three of those efforts here:

- **Minimum publishing standards**: Print journals have specific requirements for space where only a certain number of pages can be allocated to each section of a research paper. In such scenarios, researchers focus more on making bold claims and showing data that provides evidence for their conjectures. Usually, this comes at the expense of the methods section, which provides instructions for other researchers to follow in order to replicate an experiment. Recently, most journals have moved online and space is a non-issue; however, supplemental materials are still lacking in quality even when they are made available. BioMed Central has released a checklist of minimum standards that must be met before a paper can be published. The purpose of this checklist is to provide a level of standardization so that researchers can write papers with specific criteria in mind that can enhance reproducibility. If all the standards are met, there is a high likelihood that a published study can be replicated to a greater degree.

CHAPTER 11   BLOCKCHAIN IN SCIENTIFIC REPRODUCIBILITY

Note   More prominent journals have added data-sharing disclosures that specify where datasets will be available and what type of data is being shared. For instance, Cell Press created a new journal to publish peer-reviewed, reproducible, and transparent research methods called *STAR Protocols*. Similarly, the EQUATOR Network has created structured guidelines for quality standards for data being published in a scientific report.

- **Data Discovery Index (DDI)**: One of the major problems mentioned earlier was the lack of incentives for researchers to make supplemental data available. The National Institutes of Health (NIH) has sought to create a new measure to credit researchers for uploading additional experimental data, called the Data Discovery Index. This is a citable data repository where researchers can make additional data points available related to their studies. For academic researchers, a huge incentive is to elicit additional citations for their work, which in turn becomes a measure of impact for a published study. By making the database citable, NIH created this new incentive for researchers to dedicate additional time and resources to upload unpublished databases.

- **Reproducibility project**: The Center for Open Science in collaboration with Science Exchange will be looking at high-impact studies in cancer biology from 2010 to 2012 and replicating each one with help from members of Science Exchange. Full-length reports on the attempts at replicating experiments, discovering drug

CHAPTER 11 BLOCKCHAIN IN SCIENTIFIC REPRODUCIBILITY

targets, and more will be made openly available along with detailed methods. This project is being done in two phases; the first phase culminates in a registered report that documents standardized protocols to carry out certain experiments. The second phase involves one of the member institutes of Science Exchange conducting the experiment using the registered report and documenting the results. Ultimately, both the reports and the data will be peer-reviewed by reviewers at the *eLife* journal and made available online.

These three initiatives are examples of a large-scale coordinated effort to enhance reproducibility, and many more are on the horizon. So far, we have discussed the problems in the academic environment leading to differing treatment of negative and positive data, the core of the reproducibility crisis, and the difficulties that arise as a result. Next, we will begin talking about the more serious consequences of data manipulation in the case of drug trials. The data points from clinical trials decide the fate of medications that will affect thousands of lives. Obtaining all relevant data is crucial not only for accurately prescribing medication but also to avoid pitfalls and avenues already tackled in the past.

Note Dr. Ben Goldacre gave a TED talk in which he told the story of the drug lorcainide, released in the 1980s. It was meant to be an anti-arrhythmic drug that could prevent abnormal heart rhythms in people who had had heart attacks. A small clinical trial was conducted in under 100 patients, and unfortunately ten of them died. The drug was regarded as a failure, and commercial development stopped. The data from this failed clinical trial was never published. Over the next few years, other drug companies had similar ideas for anti-arrhythmic drugs, which were brought to market. It is approximated that 100,000 people died because these new drugs also caused an increased instance of death. In 1993, the researchers who conducted the original 1980 study came forth and wrote an apology mentioning that they had attributed the increased death rate to chance in the initial trials and that had the data from this failed trial been published, it could have provided early warnings and prevented future deaths. This is just one example of the very serious consequences of publication bias. We'll tackle a generalized version of this scenario in the next section.

Clinical Trials

We have already described a few complications that can arise due to flawed data reporting from clinical trials, and here we will begin outlining a potential solution. In this section, we will focus on three specific issues and provide a use case for the integration of blockchain technology in each one:

1. **Trial registration**: Registering clinical trials when they begin, providing timely updates, and depositing the relevant results in a public database are crucial for offering clinical trials for new possible medications to patients for whom the standard drugs aren't effective. Even though large-scale clinical trials involving human participants should be registered, more often than not, these trials remain missing in action. The only indication of data coming from an unregistered trial is a publication or perhaps a few papers that contain experiments and results highly tailored toward proving the effectiveness of the drug candidate being proposed. This type of publication bias

CHAPTER 11 BLOCKCHAIN IN SCIENTIFIC REPRODUCIBILITY

can mislead clinicians in a dangerous manner; therefore, we need to incentivize investigators to send regular updates from registered clinical trials on progress and any relevant clinical protocols.

2. **Comparing drug efficacies**: Today, in most clinical settings, multiple drug options are increasingly becoming available to clinicians, but there is often a lack of evidence from head-to-head clinical trials that allows for direct comparison of the efficacy or safety of one drug over another. Computational models allow for parallel processing of large datasets in a type of analysis called Mixed Treatment Comparisons (MTCs). These models use Bayesian statistics to incorporate available data for a drug and generate an exploratory report comparing the drugs. This can become the foundation for automated comparisons as more data is liberated from unpublished or unavailable information silos. Recently, there has been more interest in using umbrella protocols for clinical trials. These protocols test multiple treatment interventions simultaneously for one disease and gather massive amounts of comparative data.

3. **Post-processing**: In some cases, when a trial is registered, and it does provide some supplemental data that goes along with a publication, the registry acts more like a data dump than an organized data deposit. Recently, we have seen more carefully prepared and published post-analysis summaries; however, this is often an exception, not the rule. The key here is that once clinical trial data is linked up to

CHAPTER 11   BLOCKCHAIN IN SCIENTIFIC REPRODUCIBILITY

the blockchain, it becomes available to be included in an automation workflow, and now post-analysis summaries/data can be generated by an algorithm rather than a person. A universal backend for the storage of data can foster the development of front-end clients that read the blockchain and, using the appropriate public–private keypair, download the appended data from an external source and locally do the post-processing. After that, the summary reports can be appended back to the blockchain.

Note   Soenke Bartling and some collaborators in Heidelberg, Germany, have been working relentlessly on open-science innovation using blockchain technology. Recently, they founded a think tank called Blockchain for Science to accelerate the adoption of blockchain technology in open science. You can find more on their website: `blockchainforscience.com`.

Let's talk about a prototypical solution that uses the blockchain for making clinical trials more transparent. We will use an implementation of colored coins to make supplemental data available from clinical trials on the blockchain. The scripting language of Bitcoin core allows for the attachment of small amounts of metadata to the blockchain. A colored coin takes advantage of this feature by attaching static metadata to the blockchain to represent assets with real-world value. In this sense, colored coins leverage the blockchain's capacity to hold virtual assets. We will be using colored coins as a mechanism to introduce scarcity and incentivize users of a network to upload auxiliary clinical data and provide regularly timed updates. For our purposes, there are three components that make colored coins special:

- **Coloring scheme**: The encoding method by which the colored coin data is encoded or decoded on the blockchain.

- **Asset metadata**: The actual metadata attached to a colored coin transaction that gets stored in blockchain; we will go over an example of it next. The new colored coin protocol allows for the attachment of a potentially unlimited amount of metadata to a colored coin transaction, by using torrent keys that provide a decentralized way to share and store data.

- **Rule engine**: In the past, the metadata just contained static information added to colored coins. But recently, a new rules section has been added that encodes an extra layer of logic supported by the rule engine that unlocks smart contracts' functionality to colored coins. Currently, four types of rules are supported that we will discuss.

Here's the generalized syntax for the metadata that can be added to a colored coin transaction:

```
{
  metadata: {...Static data goes here...},
  rules: {...Rule definitions go here...}
}
```

There are two rules from the rule engine that we will be using in our solution: the expiration rule and the minter rule. The expiration rule is used to loan an asset, and it dictates the lifespan of an asset. Upon expiration, the asset returns to the last output (a valid Bitcoin address) that had a valid expiration. The minter rule grants a recipient permission to issue more of the same asset. So a minter receiving colored coins can further issue more colored coins to others on the network. Both rules play

401

CHAPTER 11   BLOCKCHAIN IN SCIENTIFIC REPRODUCIBILITY

an important role in introducing scarcity in this instance of blockchain economics. What role does scarcity play? To understand this, we need to introduce one more rule: the holder. When an asset is issued, holders are described within the set of asset-issuing rules as the addresses allowed to hold this asset.

Figure 11-2 visually describes the interaction between a researcher and a minter. The researcher registers a clinical trial and provides periodic updates, while the minter acknowledges the updates, issues new colored coins, and requests future cooperation as the next phases of the trial begin. Let's walk through Figure 11-2 step by step. The clinical trial begins with our researcher registering the trial, which initiates a genesis colored coin transaction from the minter to the holder (our researcher). This transaction comes with an expiration rule attached, and this in a sense is the deadline for depositing data associated with one of the several phases of a given clinical trial. The researcher must send a colored coin transaction back to the minter, with URLs to metadata containing updates or new data. When the minter receives this transaction, an evaluation is performed on whether the asset was expired, and the result is exported. We will return to this result in the next section. After this return transaction, the minter issues more colored coins to the holder for the next phase, and the cycle repeats. Each phase of the trial results in more data URLs being appended to the metadata sent by the holder as a sign of continuous updates.

Tip   The rule engine of the colored coin protocol is also a part of the metadata not stored directly on the blockchain; instead, it is stored in plain JSON format using torrents. Torrents provide a decentralized mechanism to share data and make it possible for rules to interact with objects outside of the blockchain. We have abstracted the minter here as an oracle; however, the actual implementation would involve a hybrid of an automated evaluator and a smart contract.

CHAPTER 11 BLOCKCHAIN IN SCIENTIFIC REPRODUCIBILITY

The entire process visualized in Figure 11-2 can be considered analogous to the **SSL handshake** that forms the foundation of sure server-client interactions and symmetric encryption in our browsers. Perhaps in the future, one can extrapolate, if this type of interaction becomes common, it could become a feature of the colored coin wallet. The evaluation of data received by the minter can be carried out publicly using an add-on that returns the results to the wallet software. In the future, this modular add-on design will enable the integration of new protocols into the wallet client.

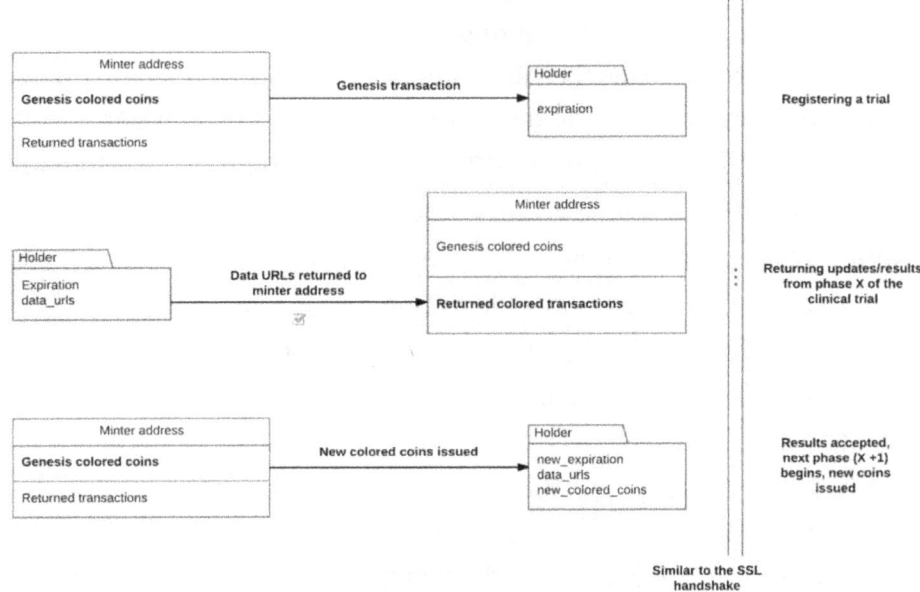

Figure 11-2. *Interactions between a minter and a holder*

The process shown in Figure 11-2 can create artificial scarcity by imposing the expiration rule. The holder (researcher) has to return a colored coin transaction with data URLs corresponding to the update. The minter performs an evaluation of the state of the holder and then acknowledges the receipt of updates. New coins are issued for the next cycle of updates, and the whole cycle begins anew. The evaluator result is exported and will be used to build a reputation system, which we will discuss shortly.

CHAPTER 11 BLOCKCHAIN IN SCIENTIFIC REPRODUCIBILITY

When implementing blockchain systems for clinical trials, scalability challenges can be addressed via off-chain storage. Modern implementations use decentralized storage systems such as InterPlanetary File System (IPFS) and save the main blockchain from becoming bloated while maintaining data integrity through cryptographic linking. Similarly, implementing privacy-by-design principles is essential when using blockchain for clinical trials. This includes pseudonymization or anonymization of patient-specific demographic data wherever possible, carefully considering data access protocols and restricting access to those who need it, and implementing robust security measures to protect sensitive data. Modern blockchain systems for healthcare data incorporate sophisticated encryption schemes, consent mechanisms, and self-sovereign identity (SSI) to protect privacy while maintaining data integrity.

Note Blockchain implementations in clinical trials must also navigate complex regulatory frameworks including the General Data Protection Regulation (GDPR) in the European Union (EU) and HIPAA in the United States. The Clinical Trials Regulation (EU No. 536/2014) harmonizes the conduct of clinical trials across the EU, ensuring participant safety, rights, and data protection compliance with GDPR. Similarly, in the United States, the application of HIPAA creates compliance requirements for the insurers and healthcare providers throughout the clinical trial process. Eventually, blockchain systems must mature to comply with every aspect of the regulatory frameworks, especially if large-scale deployments are to be considered.

Now that we have discussed the colored coin interactions, let's take a look at the entire clinical trials system in Figure 11-3.

CHAPTER 11 BLOCKCHAIN IN SCIENTIFIC REPRODUCIBILITY

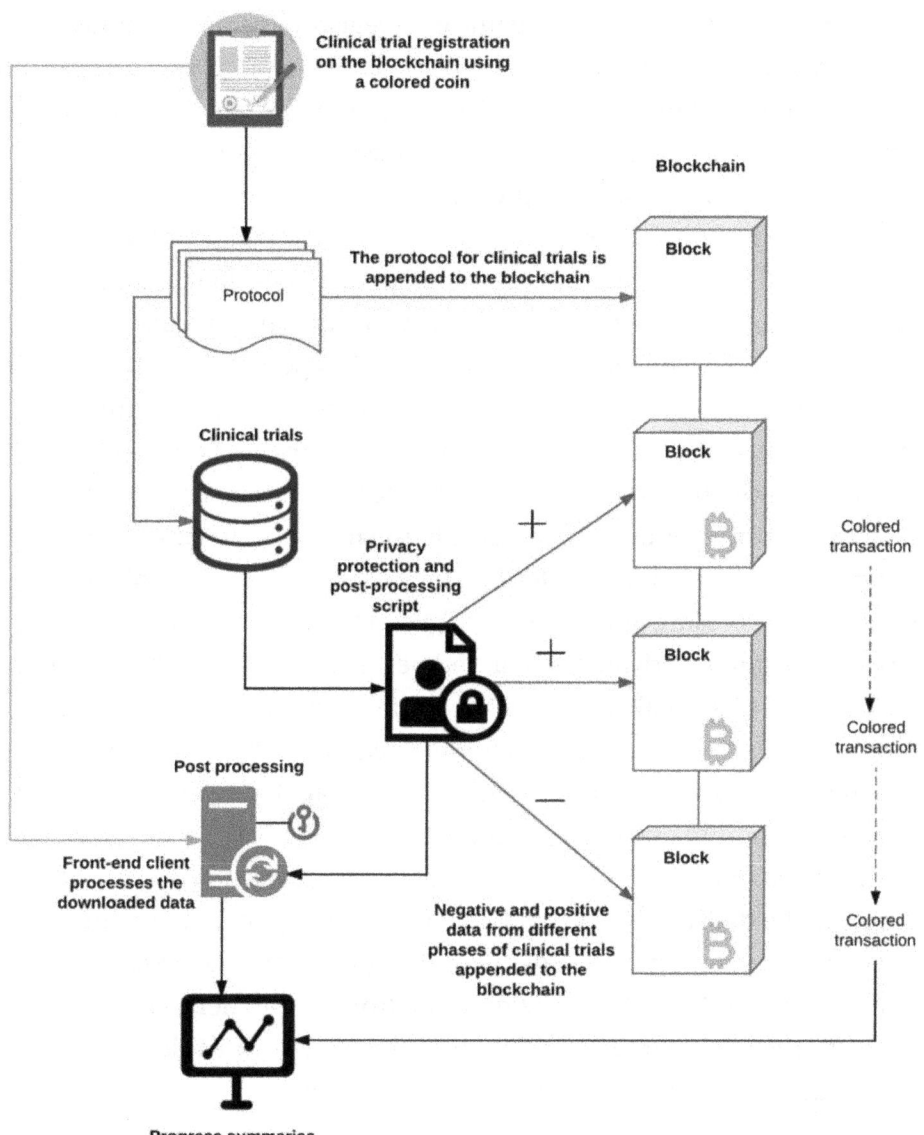

Figure 11-3. Summary of blockchain integration into the clinical trials workflow

CHAPTER 11   BLOCKCHAIN IN SCIENTIFIC REPRODUCIBILITY

In Figure 11-3, the process begins with registration and a proposed summary of what the clinical trial will entail, the methods being used, and what data/results can be expected. The summary information and the approved protocol are appended to the blockchain before the trial begins. This completes the registration process.

Colored coins and the rule engine are used to manage updates from researchers. These updates are appended to the blockchain after going through a light privacy protection check. Once the clinical data is on a common backend, the most important benefit is perhaps the shift of focus from backend clients that hold databases to simply developing frontend clients that can read the blockchain. The management of data will happen automatically within the blockchain—all we need is a mechanism to read the tags or breadcrumbs left over in the metadata to know what to pull from an external location for further processing. An example of this is the post-processing unit shown in Figure 11-3. This unit contains the appropriate public–private keypair and permissions to read the blockchain and access the external locations. The same script that appended data updates to the blockchain also contains a segment for post-processing that tells the post-processing unit how to integrate data from various third-party locations into one local collection.

After that, post-analysis statistical methods are used to determine the quality of the data appended, and an automated report can be generated that summarizes the progress of the trial at given intervals. The intervals at which data updates should be required from researchers, along with instructions on how to process that data once made available, are coded in a script made available to the post-processing unit.

Reputation System

Let's revisit the notion of scarcity. It was crucial for us to build the clinical trials system; however, the introduction of colored coins with the expiration rule also allows us to build another component: the reputation system. The premise of reputation is simply tracking adherence to the expiration rule. Recall that we built an export feature in the evaluator function, and here we can use the export function as a counting mechanism to reward researchers (or holder addresses in the colored coin protocol) who have been proactive in sending periodic updates. In a practical application, this export counter would become added to the metadata by the minter after periodic updates have been established. From here, establishing reputation is a straightforward task: higher export counter corresponds to better reputation.

It is important to note that for our clinical trials system, reputation simply emerged as a property of the design, but it has some far-reaching implications concerning reproducibility. High reputation indicates the commitment of an institution or a research group to quality control. Once a reputation mechanism is implemented network-wide on a blockchain, it can be referenced externally: third-party services can request the reputation score associated with a particular colored wallet. This can be as simple as an API call to return the rep_score of a wallet. Why would this be useful? Earlier in our discussion, we mentioned the Data Discovery Index (DDI), and here we want to expand the notion of DDI from just being a data repository to being a repository with rep_score tags. This can provide another layer of granularity into DDI: a tag of reputation scores (high or low) on datasets linked to clinical trials that are available to the public. Keep in mind that within this design, all the data from clinical trials or updates resides in the DDI repositories; however, the rep_score lives in the blockchain metadata through colored coin transactions. Figure 11-4 describes the sequential evaluation happening with each periodic update and the incremental addition of reputation in rep_score.

CHAPTER 11   BLOCKCHAIN IN SCIENTIFIC REPRODUCIBILITY

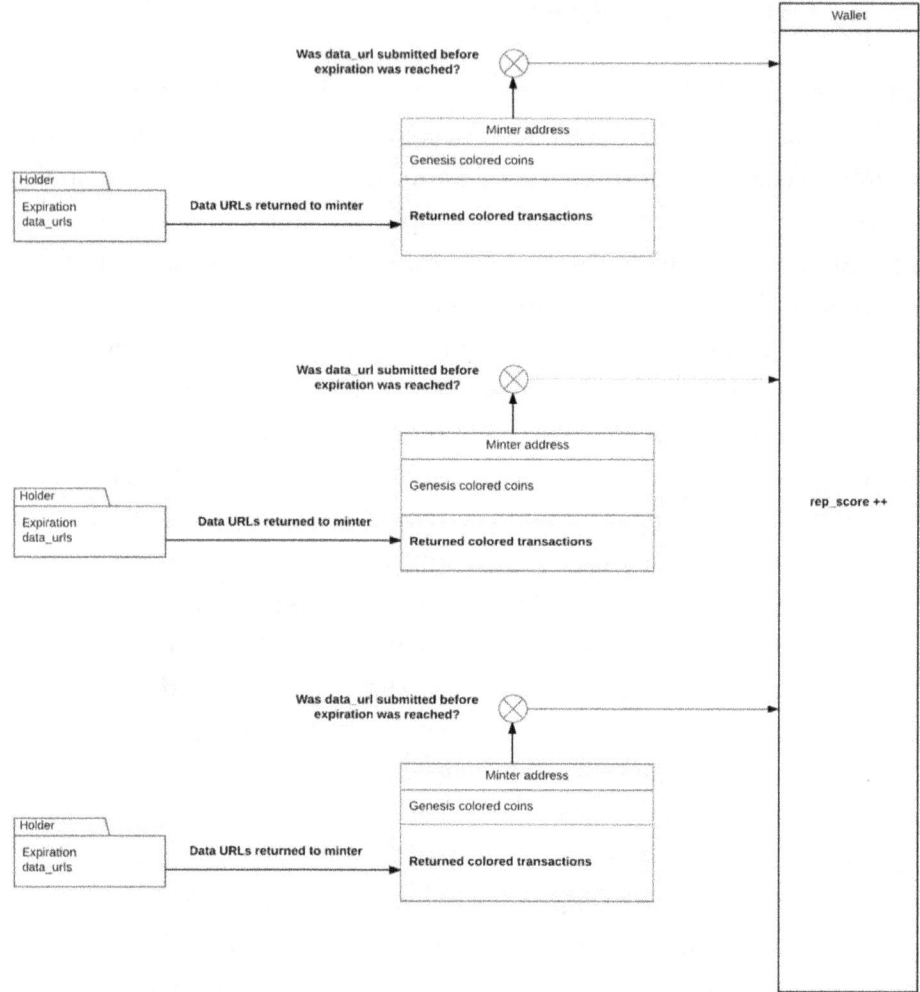

Figure 11-4. *Overview of rep_score increasing with each periodic update*

The evaluator function checks for the expiration rule and if the colored coin transactions made by the holder contain the URLs corresponding to updates in the metadata. If those two conditions are met, the rep_score is updated for the holder's wallet. This slow increase allows for the reputation to build over time, and the rep_score parameter can be referenced in a blockchain-agnostic manner from external services. API calls can become the default manner of attaching an up-to-date rep_score to databases deposited at DDI.

Now that we have a better understanding of the rep_score mechanism, let's look at the complete reputation system. Figure 11-5 provides a comprehensive depiction of a reputation system, as well as its consequences for members network-wide.

CHAPTER 11 BLOCKCHAIN IN SCIENTIFIC REPRODUCIBILITY

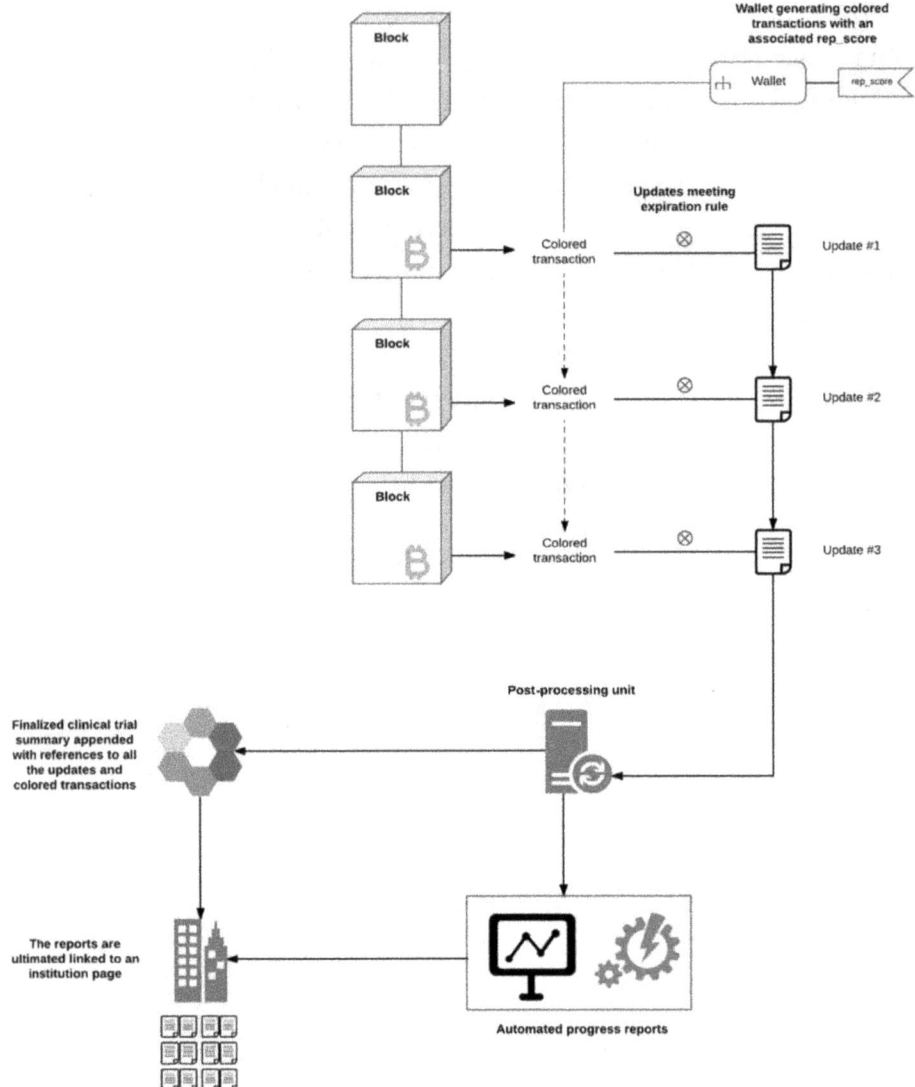

Figure 11-5. *The reputation system*

Figure 11-5 begins with the blockchain recording colored coin transactions happening between the minter and holder roles from the colored coin protocol. These colored coin transactions happen each time

CHAPTER 11   BLOCKCHAIN IN SCIENTIFIC REPRODUCIBILITY

the holder provides an update and the minter evaluates it. After the initial update, the minter sends a rep_score as a part of the returned colored coin transaction to carry on the update process for a clinical trial. The reputation now gets amended to the metadata with each exchange, and the rep_score gets revised each time. This score can eventually become an attribute of the holder's wallet, and in this manner it can be referenced externally from the blockchain. The post-processing unit becomes important after the clinical trial has matured to generate enough updates that can be compiled in one comprehensive overview. The purpose of this unit would be to automatically perform quality control statistical calculations and share the updates by following instructions in a script that was added to the blockchain in the beginning of the trial. In a similar fashion, the post-processing unit will compile a final summary and attach that to the institution's page, along with all the updates shared from the clinical trial.

Note   It must be noted that post-processing and data storage are all functions done off the blockchain. No calculations or data manipulations are performed on the blockchain. We want to limit the blockchain-executable code as much as possible to only the necessary primitives. The only tools that interact with transactions or metadata on the blockchain are in place to update the distributed state of a variable or parameter.

In the last few years, more significant progress has been made in building reputation systems that are specific for scientific efforts, including open publishing and data deposition. Three such efforts are reviewed here:

- Augur is a prediction platform built on top of the Ethereum blockchain as an ERC-20 token. Augur is powered by a token of reputation called REP that is earned as a reward for accurate reporting on the platform. Members of the network have an incentive to earn reputation (REP) by participating in accurate reporting on outcome of events. Over time, a record of REP building among users leads to the emergence of a reliable set of users that are more likely to make accurate predictions: a group-think model where wisdom of the crowd takes a productive shape in predicting outcomes. Augur has four components that allow for propagation of reputation on the network: a platform for members from the network to submit predictions toward an outcome, a scoring mechanism to reward points for accurate predictions, a consensus framework to gather the points into a long-term parameter such as reputation, and, finally, a group of overseers who maintain network security and integrity. These characteristics also make Augur suitable for a new generation of scientific hypotheses/predictions in a decentralized market.

- The Academic Endorsement System (AES) is built on the blockchain as a reputation system that uses Academic Endorsement Points (AEP), as compared with Augur, which uses REP. AEP are awarded to scientific works that are worthy of endorsement and public promotion. But compared with Augur, AES is more comprehensively built for scientific publications and endeavors. The amount of AEP awarded to a research item is based on AEP received in the past. This is a premium awarded to researchers who have produced works that received significant endorsements. In this manner, researchers who produce high-quality work receive more AEP and are incentivized to share more quality work. The use of AEP as a global reputation parameter can someday be used by journals along with more traditional citation metrics such as H-index.

- PEvO (Publish and Evaluate Onchain) is a Steem-based decentralized social media platform where content creators can communicate directly with authors of scientific studies. In this platform, authors can share updates, upload new content, reply to comments, and integrate reviews into continuous updates to the research. This creates an extension of a published paper so it becomes a living document, and updates can be tracked on the blockchain powering Steem. In addition, interactions on PEvO result in a payout (in the form of tokens) to the authors. This incentivizes authors to participate in discussions, and meaningful conversations are helpful to the broader scientific community.

Pharmaceutical Drug Tracking

The final use case in this chapter covers tracking pharmaceutical drugs via a supply-chain management framework. Prescription drug monitoring programs are an essential element for controlling drug shopping. The Mayo Clinic defines drug shopping as a patient obtaining controlled substances (most often narcotics) from multiple healthcare practitioners without the clinician's knowledge of the other prescriptions that the patient has. This leads to drug abuse or sales on a large scale. The Mayo Clinic attributes drug shopping to the following three factors:

- **Poor timeliness of data**: How often does a pharmacy or provider upload prescription data into their existing centralized system? A blockchain-based backend would make drugs associated with all transactions available instantly to all members of the network.

- **Reliability**: Centralized databases have a single point of failure, as compared with the blockchain, which is decentralized by nature, and therefore the data does not rest on a single database, making it more reliable.

- **Complexity of data retrieval**: The current model of data retrieval and compatibility with existing hospital systems is completely broken. Often times, hospitals are not synced up to the databases being used by pharmacies, and updating is an arduous task. Blockchain makes the process universal by providing a common backend to read for external services.

In this system, when a clinician writes a script for a prescription, the provider can check the blockchain to find the patient record for any currently active prescriptions. This can help the clinician determine whether the patient is asking for a prescription from multiple sources or whether another family member is getting the same prescription. An active prescription from a different provider would automatically invalidate the request for a new one, and this can be encoded in the network as a double-spending request. Otherwise, the transaction will go through, and the pharmacy will receive a request to provide medication to the patient. The requesting provider and patient can sign the transaction, allowing for better tracking all the way through the care of a particular patient.

Although this system seems simple, it fulfills most of the requirements for a Drug Supply Chain Security Act (DSCSA)–compatible system that can be implemented across providers. There are some efforts under way by major blockchain players such as IBM and Deloitte Blockchain Labs to control the opioid over-prescription epidemic. Recently, some startups have sprung up that are focused solely on pharma drug tracking using the blockchain.

Even though supply-chain management fits the blockchain infrastructure most closely and out of the box, this field is very new and the technology is immature. The future of drug tracking and open science looks much more promising with new technologies enabling layers of communication that were never possible before. Blockchain, if nothing more, has been an immense catalyst of new innovation in open scientific inquiry and discourse.

BRUINchain is a blockchain-based system developed by LedgerDomain in collaboration with UCLA Health to enhance the security and efficiency of the pharmaceutical supply chain, particularly addressing the requirements of the Drug Supply Chain Security Act (DSCSA). The system was initiated in response to the US Food and Drug Administration's (FDA) 2019 call for innovative solutions to combat counterfeit and suspect medications, aiming to ensure the delivery of authentic medications to patients. BRUINchain operates by scanning 2D barcodes on medication packages using commercial off-the-shelf (COTS) technology, such as iPhones, to capture essential data, including the Global Trade Item Number (GTIN), serial number, lot number, and expiration date. This information is recorded on a Hyperledger Fabric–based blockchain, providing an immutable, timestamped, and near-real-time auditable record of each transaction. The system tracks medications throughout their journey in the pharmacy, down to specific storage locations like individual refrigerators, and verifies the drug's authenticity directly with manufacturers. BRUINchain's architecture ensures that stakeholders in the supply chain have access to a single, reliable version of the truth, facilitating efficient tracking and tracing of

CHAPTER 11   BLOCKCHAIN IN SCIENTIFIC REPRODUCIBILITY

medications from manufacturers to patients. Additional functionalities include flagging expired products, verifying authenticity, and quarantining suspect or illegitimate products. In real-world applications at UCLA Health, BRUINchain achieved a 100% success rate in barcode scanning, expiration detection, and counterfeit detection, demonstrating its effectiveness in ensuring patient safety, reducing counterfeit risks, and streamlining processes, which also resulted in significant cost savings.

Updates in Blockchain for Science

Decentralized science (DeSci) movement: Since 2021, the DeSci movement has gained more momentum, aiming to democratize traditional scientific research by using blockchain and Web3 technologies. DeSci seeks to create a more transparent, equitable, and collaborative research ecosystem by redefining funding mechanisms, knowledge sharing, and the dissemination of published results. Several key protocols and platforms have emerged as leaders of this movement. VitaDAO is a decentralized autonomous organization (DAO) focused on funding longevity research. It raises and manages research funds through a DAO governance model, allowing researchers to apply directly for funding from the community, while token holders participate in decision-making. As of 2024, VitaDAO has funded more than 20 early-stage research projects related to longevity and has attracted collaboration with pharmaceutical companies like Pfizer. ResearchHub is another notable platform that incentivizes the sharing and discussion of academic content. By rewarding users with tokens for their contributions, it aims to accelerate the pace of scientific research and foster a more open and collaborative environment. DeSci Labs is working to rebuild the infrastructure of science using Web3 tools, addressing current pain points by creating decentralized ecosystems that empower scientists. Their efforts focus on enhancing transparency, collaboration, and efficiency in scientific research. The impact of DeSci on research funding models is significant. Traditional funding often involves

416

CHAPTER 11   BLOCKCHAIN IN SCIENTIFIC REPRODUCIBILITY

centralized institutions with significant overhead and opaque processes. In contrast, DeSci utilizes DAOs and tokenized economic models to provide micro- and macro-grants for research projects that may be too risky for traditional funding mechanisms.

NFTs in scientific review and publishing: The idea of repurposing lab notebooks as NFTs represents a unique approach of scientific record-keeping, where researchers can create immutable, timestamped records of their experimental procedures and findings. This ensures data integrity and establishes clear provenance and ownership of scientific discoveries. Such implementations should also allow for selective sharing of research data while maintaining verifiable authenticity, addressing a long-standing challenge in scientific collaboration and reproducibility. Digital twins for scientific equipment and samples, when coupled with NFT technology, create a unique bridge between physical laboratory assets and their digital representations. This system enables detailed tracking of instrument usage, calibration history, and sample lineage. Research facilities have begun exploring this to maintain comprehensive records of expensive equipment maintenance and to trace biological or chemical sample histories through their complete experimental lifecycle. The integration of NFTs into peer review processes has emerged as a potential solution to incentivize quality peer review in scientific publishing. Some platforms have experimented with awarding reviewers NFTs that represent their contributions, building a verifiable portfolio of review expertise. These tokens can potentially carry value within academic communities, whether for professional recognition or more tangible benefits within scientific publishing ecosystems. Regarding data ownership and sharing, NFTs provide a framework for scientists to maintain control over their research data while facilitating secure sharing. This model allows researchers to grant specific access rights while tracking how their data is used throughout the scientific community. Some institutions have begun implementing systems where datasets are tokenized, creating clear audit trails of fair data usage and attribution. In terms of scientific artifact preservation, one notable example is that the University of California, Berkeley, auctioned off an NFT based on research documents belonging to James Allison, a Nobel Prize–winning immunotherapy researcher, and raised over $50,000 to fund further scientific endeavors. Molecule is another key player, offering a platform that connects researchers with funding through the tokenization of intellectual property (IP). By minting IP as non-fungible tokens (IP-NFTs), Molecule facilitates decentralized ownership and governance of scientific projects, allowing for community-driven funding and decision-making.

Smart-contract driven science on the blockchain: Novel frameworks are being developed to integrate smart contracts into scientific processes. For instance, the Decentralized Virtual Research Environment (D-VRE) offers a scalable and adaptable decentralized model that enhances data sharing and collaboration within research and grant lifecycles. It incorporates custom sharing policies, secure asset management, and research activity tracking, all without centralized oversight. Integrated into JupyterLab, D-VRE supports custom collaboration agreements and smart contract–based automated execution on the Ethereum blockchain. Smart contracts can also facilitate the automated distribution of research funds by encoding funding agreements that release resources upon the completion of predefined milestones. This automation ensures timely payments and reduces administrative burdens, allowing researchers to focus more on their work. For example, DeSci Labs is exploring the use of smart contracts to manage funding allocations, ensuring that funds are disbursed automatically when specific research milestones are achieved. Managing access to shared laboratory equipment can also be automated using smart contracts. A system proposed by Ghaffer et al. on the Ethereum blockchain creates a peer-to-peer network where researchers can share and access laboratory resources securely. Smart contracts manage permissions and usage rights, ensuring that only authorized individuals can access specific equipment or data, thereby enhancing collaboration while maintaining security. The peer review process can also directly benefit from decentralization on a blockchain. A system proposed by Morales-Alarcón can use a blockchain to create an immutable and transparent record of the peer review process, enhancing trust and accountability. Smart contracts can automate reviewer assignments and track the review process, ensuring that all actions are recorded and verifiable, thereby improving the integrity of scientific publications. Ensuring the integrity of scientific data across different blockchain networks is crucial for collaborative research. Cross-chain verification mechanisms are being developed to allow data to be authenticated and shared securely between disparate blockchain systems. This interoperability ensures that researchers can trust and utilize data from various sources without compromising security or validity.

Clinical trial innovations with blockchain: Timely recruitment of participants is crucial for successful completion of clinical trials. Blockchain offers a secure, decentralized backend where patient data can be securely shared among stakeholders. For instance, a blockchain model put forth by Zhuang et al. utilizes multiple trial-based smart contracts for trial management and patient engagement. A master smart contract automates subject matching and recruitment by evaluating inclusion and exclusion criteria, thereby streamlining the recruitment process and ensuring patient privacy. Ensuring the integrity and authenticity of clinical trial data is paramount. Blockchain's immutable ledger provides a tamper-proof record of all transactions and data entries. In clinical trials, a peer-to-peer network can be established using blockchain to record data interactions, enabling real-time data verification and enhancing trust among stakeholders. This approach ensures that once data is recorded, it cannot be altered, providing a reliable audit trail. Smart contracts can automate various phases of clinical trials by executing predefined actions when specific conditions are met. For example, they can manage patient enrollment by automatically verifying eligibility criteria and obtaining informed consent. Additionally, smart contracts can facilitate the secure sharing of data among authorized parties, ensuring compliance with regulatory requirements and enhancing operational efficiency. Decentralized identifiers (DIDs) offer a secure and user-centric way to manage identities in clinical trials. By integrating DIDs with blockchain, patients can have greater control over their personal information, deciding when and with whom to share their data. This integration enhances privacy and security, fostering trust between patients and researchers. A blockchain-based decentralized identity management system proposed by Torongo et al. for healthcare demonstrates how DIDs can be utilized to improve data security and patient autonomy.

Pharmaceutical supply chain: The Drug Supply Chain Security Act (DSCSA) mandated the development of an interoperable system to trace prescription drugs in the United States. The use of blockchain as an immutable ledger and its decentralized nature make it a suitable technology to meet DSCSA requirements, offering a secure method to track drug products and prevent counterfeiting. By recording each transaction in the supply chain, blockchain ensures that all stakeholders have access to a tamper-proof source of truth, facilitating compliance with DSCSA's traceability mandates. As noted above, BRUINchain was a pilot example of a DSCSA-compatible blockchain, with MediLedger by Chronicled and PharmaLedger coming after as new DSCSA-compliant supply chains. Most pharmaceutical companies are actively exploring blockchain to enhance supply chain integrity. For instance, Pfizer and other major firms have participated in blockchain pilot programs to improve drug traceability and combat counterfeit products. These initiatives aim to create a more transparent and secure supply chain, ensuring that medications reaching patients are authentic and safe.

Citations on chain: Efforts are underway to track academic citations and impact metrics on blockchain networks. By doing so, the transparency of citation records is enhanced, providing a more accurate and tamper-proof method of assessing research impact. This approach addresses issues like self-citation and disciplinary biases, offering a more nuanced analysis of academic influence. Blockchain-based reputation systems are

CHAPTER 11   BLOCKCHAIN IN SCIENTIFIC REPRODUCIBILITY

also being proposed to evaluate and record researchers' contributions. By utilizing tokens to represent reputation scores, these systems aim to provide a transparent and decentralized method for assessing a researcher's credibility and impact within the scientific community. Blockchain tokens are being utilized to create decentralized knowledge markets, where researchers can exchange data, methodologies, and findings. These markets incentivize the sharing of valuable information by providing tokens as rewards, thereby accelerating the dissemination of knowledge and fostering innovation. The SCIENCE-index, developed by Adams et al., is a blockchain-based metric designed to assess a researcher's scientific contributions. By analyzing data from sources like the Microsoft Academic Graph and incorporating machine learning techniques, it predicts a researcher's progress over their career. The index also includes parameters for data-sharing activities, encouraging researchers to share datasets with peers. Ants-Review, a blockchain-based protocol from Trovo et al., is designed to incentivize open peer reviews. Submitting authors can issue bounties for anonymous peer reviews on the Ethereum blockchain. If the reviews meet specified requirements, they are accepted and compensated proportionally to their assessed quality. The system also incorporates a gamified mechanism, allowing the community to evaluate and vote on the best reviews, thereby building trust and reputation among reviewers. Another peer review mechanism designed by Finke et al. incentivizes reviewers for their efforts, publishes anonymized reports for community scrutiny, tracks reviewer reputations, and provides digital certificates.

Data sovereignty: Zero-knowledge proofs (ZKPs) are cryptographic protocols that enable one party to prove to another that a statement is true without revealing any additional information. In scientific research, ZKPs can be utilized to verify data authenticity and integrity without exposing the underlying sensitive information, thereby maintaining confidentiality while ensuring trust in the data's validity. Privacy-preserving computation techniques, such as homomorphic encryption and secure multi-party computation (SMPC), allow multiple parties to collaboratively analyze data without revealing their individual inputs. In the context of scientific research, these methods enable collaborative studies and data analysis across institutions while safeguarding sensitive information, thereby promoting data sharing and collective analysis without compromising privacy. SMPC is particularly valuable in clinical trials, where multiple stakeholders may need to compute functions over their private data inputs without revealing them to each other. This approach ensures that sensitive patient data remains confidential while allowing for the aggregation and analysis necessary for trial outcomes, thereby enhancing data security and compliance with privacy regulations. Blockchain technology facilitates patient-centric data ownership models by enabling individuals to have control over their personal health information. Through self-sovereign identity (SSI) frameworks, patients can manage access to their medical records, granting permissions to healthcare providers as needed. This decentralized approach ensures that patients retain ownership of their data, enhancing privacy and autonomy. Compliance with regulations like the General Data Protection Regulation (GDPR) is crucial in handling personal data. Blockchain's immutable nature poses challenges for data erasure requirements; however, solutions such as off-chain storage combined with on-chain hash references, along with the use of ZKPs and SMPC, can help in designing systems that comply with GDPR by ensuring data privacy and enabling data subject rights.

Enhancing reproducibility: In addition to secure data storage, blockchain can facilitate automated off-chain replication attempts by enabling the sharing of computational workflows. By recording detailed metadata and methodology of experiments on the blockchain, other researchers can access and execute these workflows, ensuring that replication studies follow the exact procedures of the original research. Projects like HyperProv leverage blockchain to manage data provenance in edge computing environments, ensuring that data collected and processed across decentralized nodes is accurately tracked and verifiable.

Integrating version control systems with blockchain further enhances research transparency. By combining traditional version control with a blockchain, researchers can maintain comprehensive and tamper-proof records of all changes to their code and data, ensuring that evolution of a research project is fully reproducible. Moreover, blockchain can enforce pre-registration of studies by timestamping research plans and hypotheses before data collection begins. This practice prevents selective reporting and p-hacking by ensuring that researchers adhere to their original study designs, thereby enhancing the credibility and reproducibility of scientific findings.

Cross-chain scientific infrastructure: Interoperability protocols are essential for enabling seamless communication and data exchange between disparate blockchain networks used in scientific research. Projects like Polkadot facilitate such interoperability by allowing multiple blockchains to operate within a unified network, enabling them to share data and resources efficiently. Bridge protocols play a crucial role in transferring assets and data between different blockchain networks. For instance, blockchain bridges enable the movement of digital assets and information across various blockchains, ensuring that scientific data and resources can be shared and accessed universally. This capability is vital for collaborative research projects that require the integration of data from multiple sources, enhancing the scope and depth of scientific investigations. Managing researcher identities across multiple blockchain platforms necessitates robust multichain identity solutions. Decentralized identifiers (DIDs) offer a framework for creating and managing digital identities that are interoperable across different blockchains. This approach ensures that researchers can maintain a consistent identity across various platforms, facilitating seamless collaboration and access to resources while preserving privacy and security. Establishing cross-chain verification standards with protocols such as the Cross-Chain Interoperability Protocol (CCIP) aims to provide a universal connection between various blockchain networks, enabling the verification of data and transactions across different chains. This ensures that scientific data remains trustworthy and verifiable, regardless of the originating blockchain. Oracle networks are necessary for integrating real-world data into blockchain-based scientific applications. They act as intermediaries that fetch and verify data from external sources, providing it to smart contracts on the blockchain. In scientific research, oracle networks can supply experimental data, environmental readings, or other relevant information to blockchain applications, ensuring that smart contracts operate with accurate and up-to-date data. Collectively, these cross-chain enhancements to the scientific infrastructure are making it possible for decentralized collaborative research.

Institutional adoption: Prominent research institutions are exploring the use of blockchain to improve data sharing and experimental reproducibility and investing heavily in blockchain-based applications for scientific discovery. In collaboration with IBM, Columbia University established a center dedicated to blockchain research, education, and entrepreneurship. This initiative aims to explore innovative applications of blockchain across various sectors, including science, to enhance data sharing, health data security, and real-time multi-institutional collaboration. Stanford's Center for Blockchain Research focuses on interdisciplinary studies of blockchain technology, encompassing fields such as cryptography, distributed systems, and their applications in scientific research. The center brings together experts from engineering, law, and economics to address technical challenges and explore blockchain's potential in science. The University of Wyoming's Advanced Blockchain Lab, supported by state and university matching funds, concentrates on formal verification, smart contracts, and secure hardware related to real-world blockchain applications. The lab's research includes developing blockchain solutions to ensure the integrity and security of scientific data and computations. ASU's Blockchain Research Lab aims to advance the development of blockchain-based technologies for use in business, finance, economics, mathematics, and computer science.

CHAPTER 11   BLOCKCHAIN IN SCIENTIFIC REPRODUCIBILITY

The lab's mission includes exploring how blockchain can be applied to scientific research to enhance data management and security. Carnegie Mellon's Secure Blockchain Initiative is a multi-year, interdisciplinary research program that rethinks blockchain across enterprise ecosystems.

Environmental considerations: The shift from proof-of-work (PoW) to proof-of-stake (PoS) consensus mechanisms has led to a 99.99% decrease in energy usage, significantly lowering its carbon footprint. In scientific computing, energy efficiency is paramount. PoS-based blockchains offer a more sustainable alternative to PoW systems, consuming substantially less energy. Blockchain also facilitates sustainable scientific computation by enabling decentralized networks that optimize resource utilization. By distributing computational tasks across a network of nodes, blockchain can reduce the need for centralized data centers, which are often energy-intensive. Moreover, blockchain is also being used as a ledger service to track carbon footprint. By recording carbon emissions data on a transparent and tamper-proof ledger, organizations can monitor and verify their environmental impact more effectively. This approach enhances accountability and supports efforts to reduce carbon footprints. Green blockchain initiatives are emerging to address environmental concerns associated with traditional blockchain operations. Projects are focusing on developing energy-efficient consensus mechanisms, integrating renewable energy sources, and promoting carbon offsetting practices within blockchain networks.

Post-quantum world: The emergence of quantum computing poses significant challenges to current cryptographic systems, as quantum algorithms could potentially break widely used encryption methods. In response, the field of post-quantum cryptography (PQC) is developing cryptographic systems that are secure against both quantum and classical computers. The National Institute of Standards and Technology (NIST) has been leading efforts to standardize post-quantum cryptography, recently releasing a set of algorithms designed to withstand attacks by quantum computers. Companies like Microsoft and IBM are actively researching quantum-safe cryptographic algorithms to prepare for the quantum era. These efforts include developing new cryptographic protocols and integrating them into existing communication systems to ensure data security in a future where quantum computers are prevalent.

Augmented reality (AR)/virtual reality (VR) technologies: The metaverse—a collective virtual shared space—holds promise for various scientific applications. In medical education and healthcare, the metaverse offers new opportunities for medical education, on-job training, and patient outcome improvement. Augmented reality (AR) and virtual reality (VR) are transforming scientific collaboration by providing immersive environments that enhance data visualization and interaction. These technologies enable researchers to explore complex datasets in three dimensions, facilitating a deeper understanding of intricate scientific phenomena. For instance, in biomedical science education, VR and AR applications have been developed to teach concepts such as pharmacology and medicinal chemistry, allowing students to interact with 3D models of molecules and biological systems, thereby enhancing comprehension and retention. Blockchain technology serves as a foundational element in the metaverse for facilitating secure micropayments. In these virtual environments, users engage in various economic activities, such as purchasing digital assets, accessing premium content, and compensating creators for their contributions. Cryptocurrencies, operating on blockchain networks, enable swift and low-cost transactions, allowing users to make small payments without the high fees associated with traditional financial systems. This capability is crucial for the metaverse's economy, where numerous small transactions occur frequently. Moreover, blockchain's ability to handle micropayments efficiently supports a vibrant and dynamic virtual economy.

Summary

This chapter started with a broad description of the reproducibility problem and its serious economic consequences in evidence-based sciences. Then, we moved into discussing the current solutions and their shortcomings in the science community. After that, we described the idea of building reputation systems using blockchain and covered three use cases: clinical trials, reputation networks, and finally pharmaceutical tracking of drugs from the point of manufacturing. Finally, we went over updates in the application of blockchain to scientific research, as well as new technologies that have emerged over the last three to four years. All the use cases highlighted the strengths of blockchain in tracking and accountability, as opposed to traditional methods.

Bibliography

Benchoufi, M. & Ravaud, P. (2017). Blockchain technology for improving clinical research quality. *Trials*, 18(1), 335. https://doi.org/10.1186/s13063-017-2035-z

Leiva, V. & Castro, C. (2025). Artificial intelligence and blockchain in clinical trials: Enhancing data governance efficiency, integrity, and transparency. *Bioanalysis*, 17(3), 161-176. https://doi.org/10.1080/17576180.2025.2452774

Benchoufi, M., Altman, D., & Ravaud, P. (2019). From clinical trials to highly trustable clinical trials: Blockchain in clinical trials, a game changer for improving transparency? *Frontiers in Blockchain*, 2, 23. https://doi.org/10.3389/fbloc.2019.00023

Wong, D. R., Bhattacharya, S., & Butte, A. J. (2019). Prototype of running clinical trials in an untrustworthy environment using blockchain. *Nature Communications*, 10(1), 917. https://doi.org/10.1038/s41467-019-08874-y

CHAPTER 11   BLOCKCHAIN IN SCIENTIFIC REPRODUCIBILITY

Nugent, T., Upton, D., & Cimpoesu, M. (2016). Improving data transparency in clinical trials using blockchain smart contracts. *F1000Research*, 5, 2541. https://doi.org/10.12688/f1000research.9756.1

Hang, L., Choi, E., & Kim, D. H. (2022). Blockchain for applications of clinical trials: Taxonomy, challenges, and future directions. *IET Communications*, 16(6), 640–655. https://doi.org/10.1049/cmu2.12488

Jayabalan, M. & Jeyanthi, N. (2022). Scalable blockchain model using off-chain IPFS storage for healthcare data security and privacy. *Journal of Parallel and Distributed Computing*, 164, 202–214. https://doi.org/10.1016/j.jpdc.2022.02.013

Khan, S. I. & Hoque, A. S. M. L. (2020). Ensuring protocol compliance and data transparency in clinical trials using blockchain smart contracts. *BMC Medical Research Methodology*, 20, 256. https://doi.org/10.1186/s12874-020-01109-5

Krittanawong, C., Rogers, A. J., Aydar, M., Choi, E., Johnson, K. W., Wang, Z., & Narayan, S. M. (2020). Blockchain technology applications in healthcare. *Future Healthcare Journal*, 7(1), 65–69. https://doi.org/10.7861/fhj.2019-0037

Kumar, R. & Tripathi, R. (2021). Decentralized secure storage of medical records using blockchain and IPFS: A comparative analysis with future directions. *Security and Privacy*, 4(2), e162. https://doi.org/10.1002/spy2.162

Zhuang, Y., Sheets, L., Shae, Z., Tsai, J. J. P., & Shyu, C. R. (2018). Applying blockchain technology for health information exchange and persistent monitoring for clinical trials. *AMIA Annual Symposium Proceedings*, 2018, 1167–1175.

Omar, I. A., Jayaraman, R., Salah, K., Simsekler, M. C. E., Yaqoob, I., & Ellahham, S. (2021). Ensuring protocol compliance and data transparency in clinical trials using blockchain smart contracts. *BMC Medical Research Methodology*, 21(1), 1–17. https://doi.org/10.1186/s12874-021-01271-4

Bhuiyan, M. Z. A., Zaman, A., Wang, T., Wang, G., Tao, H., & Hassan, M. M. (2020). Blockchain and big data to transform the healthcare. *Proceedings of the International Conference on Data Processing and Applications*, 62–68. https://doi.org/10.1145/3378016.3378041

Cruz, M. M. P., Cofino, C. L., Balogo, K. M., & Dandan, D. G. (2024). A proposed distributed off-chain medical health record management using blockchain technology and IPFS for HEIs. *International Journal of Scientific Engineering and Science*, 8(3), 25–31.

Ghaffar, Abdul, Muhammad Azeem, Zain Abubaker, Muhammad Usman Gurmani, Tanzeela Sultana, Faisal Shehzad, and Nadeem Javaid. (2020) Smart contracts for research lab sharing scholars data rights management over the Ethereum blockchain network. In Advances on P2P, Parallel, Grid, Cloud and Internet Computing: Proceedings of the 14th International Conference on P2P, Parallel, Grid, Cloud and Internet Computing (3PGCIC-2019) 14, pp. 70-81. Springer International Publishing.

Morales-Alarcón, C.H., Bodero-Poveda, E., Villa-Yánez, H.M. and Buñay-Guisñan, P.A., 2024. Blockchain and Its Application in the Peer Review of Scientific Works: A Systematic Review. Publications, 12(4), p.40.

Torongo, Arnaf Aziz, and Mohsen Toorani. (2023). Blockchain-based Decentralized Identity Management for Healthcare Systems. arXiv preprint arXiv:2307.16239.

Adams, Kacy, Fernando Spadea, Conor Flynn, and Oshani Seneviratne. (2023). Assessing scientific contributions in data sharing spaces. In Companion Proceedings of the ACM Web Conference 2023, pp. 826-833.

Trovò, Bianca, and Nazzareno Massari. (2020). Ants-review: A privacy-oriented protocol for incentivized open peer reviews on Ethereum. In European conference on parallel processing, pp. 18-29. Cham: Springer International Publishing.

Finke, Andreas, and Thomas Hensel. Decentralized peer review in open science: A mechanism proposal. arXiv preprint arXiv:2404.18148 (2024).

CHAPTER 12

Large Reasoning Models

The release of open source reasoning models as the next generation of LLMs represents a significant leap forward in how machines approach complex problem-solving tasks. These models introduce new architectures, design decisions, and training methodologies and demonstrate remarkable capabilities in tackling reasoning challenges while maintaining computational efficiency. The democratization of such advanced AI capabilities through open source initiatives has accelerated progress in the field, enabling researchers and developers worldwide to build upon existing frameworks. Moreover, with new advances, new avenues for research become available to researchers, even in low-compute resource settings.

A pivotal shift necessary for this next generation of AI models is the concept of test-time compute, which allows models to harness additional computational resources during inference, systematically generating and evaluating multiple potential solutions. This approach mirrors human cognition—where quick intuition is complemented by deliberate analytical thinking—enhancing both the accuracy and robustness of AI-generated reasoning. This chapter begins by introducing the concept more formally as well as optimization techniques, and then we present a deep technical dive into a promising open source model: DeepSeek-R1.

CHAPTER 12   LARGE REASONING MODELS

Test-Time Compute

Test-time compute represents a paradigm shift in how LLMs approach reasoning and problem-solving. Instead of relying solely on knowledge acquired during pre-training, models are given additional computational resources during inference to generate multiple potential solutions, systematically evaluate each option, and select the most promising path forward. This algorithmic approach implements a form of Monte Carlo Tree Search (MCTS) with importance sampling, allowing for efficient exploration of the solution space. This process mirrors human problem-solving behavior, where we spend more time thinking through difficult problems rather than providing immediate answers, analogous to System 1 versus System 2 thinking.

Test-time compute operates through two main mechanisms. The first mechanism involves refining what's called the "proposal distribution"—essentially the model's set of possible answers and their likelihood. The model iteratively improves these answers through guided self-revision, using a mathematical technique called Sequential Monte Carlo (SMC) sampling, which is a way to estimate complex probability distributions by generating random samples in sequence. During this process, the model generates a sequence of revisions, with each attempt building on insights from previous ones. It does this using two key techniques: gradient-based optimization (which systematically adjusts the model's parameters to minimize errors) and learned update rules (patterns the model has discovered for how to improve answers). This sequential approach is particularly effective when the base model has a reasonable initial understanding but needs refinement to reach the correct answer, gradually converging on better solutions through repeated improvements. The model can dynamically modify its output distribution (its range of possible answers) based on previous attempts using two sophisticated sampling methods: adaptive importance sampling (which focuses computational resources on the most promising solutions) and rejection sampling (which filters out poor solutions). These techniques can achieve up to 4× improvement in efficiency compared with simpler approaches that try many solutions in parallel.

The second key mechanism focuses on optimizing what's called "verifier search" through process reward models (PRMs). While traditional verification only checks if the final answer is correct, PRMs evaluate the correctness of each step along the way, using learned value functions (which score how good each intermediate state is) and uncertainty quantification (which measures how confident the model is in each step). These detailed, step-by-step reward signals enable sophisticated search algorithms like beam search and lookahead search. Beam search keeps track of multiple promising solution paths simultaneously (typically 4–16 paths, called the "beam width") using a priority queue to track the best candidates. Lookahead search, on the other hand, tries to anticipate future steps (typically looking two to four steps ahead) to make better current decisions, similar to how a chess player thinks several moves ahead. The effectiveness of these search strategies varies with problem difficulty— beam search, which maintains multiple candidate solutions at each step using a priority queue implementation, often outperforms simpler approaches on harder problems but can lead to over-optimization on easier ones. Meanwhile, lookahead search, which simulates future steps to evaluate current decisions using dynamic programming techniques, helps prevent the model from getting stuck in local optima but requires more computational resources.

The combination of these mechanisms leads to a powerful hybrid optimization approach—meaning it combines multiple strategies to find the best solutions. While refining the proposal distribution (the model's set of possible answers) helps generate better initial solutions through iterative importance sampling (repeatedly testing and refining potential answers), the verifier search ensures these improvements are systematic and well-directed by using two key tools: learned value functions (which score how good each solution is) and uncertainty estimates (which measure how confident the model is in each solution). Research has shown that finding the right balance between these approaches depends heavily on how difficult the problem is. This difficulty can be measured in two ways: entropy-based metrics (which measure how uncertain or chaotic the possible solutions are) and model confidence scores (how sure the model is about its answers). For easier problems, it's often better to focus on sequential revisions—making a series of improvements to the initial answer. This typically works well with 10–20 attempts at refinement. However, harder problems need a more thorough search of possible solutions. This means using beam search with wider beams (keeping track of more than eight possible solutions at once) and deeper lookahead (checking more than three steps ahead to anticipate future consequences). Advanced versions of these systems can automatically adjust their approach based on how well they're performing. They use adaptive scheduling algorithms (which automatically adjust how computational resources are used) with exponential backoff strategies (a technique that progressively reduces how often certain approaches are tried if they're not working well). This allows the system to efficiently allocate its computational resources based on what's working best for each specific problem.

The theoretical advances in test-time inference are being applied in practical reasoning models like DeepSeek-R1. By integrating test-time compute with sophisticated architectures—such as Mixture of Experts (MoE) and Multi-head Latent Attention (MLA)—the DeepSeek family of models achieves a high degree of balance between computational efficiency and advanced problem-solving. This integration fundamentally reshapes how AI systems refine their reasoning during inference, ensuring more systematic and well-directed improvements. The combination of structured optimization, reinforcement learning, and adaptive compute mechanisms represents a significant leap in the AI reasoning landscape, one that is broadly accessible for development of domain-specific reasoning models.

CHAPTER 12 LARGE REASONING MODELS

DeepSeek Architecture

DeepSeek-R1 uses a multi-stage training pipeline designed to enhance reasoning capabilities while maintaining efficiency. This process includes distinct phases, each guided by task-specific loss functions and reward mechanisms, ensuring progressive refinement in performance. The key stages are supervised fine-tuning (SFT), RL, rejection sampling, and an additional RL phase for generalization. Before we review each stage of model development, we need a firm grasp of the underlying architecture.

Mixture of Experts (MoE) Architecture

The MoE mechanism in DeepSeek-R1 is designed to significantly reduce computational costs during inference by selectively activating only a subset of experts per input token, rather than using the entire network for every task. In practical terms, when running inference, only specific experts most relevant for a given task are activated, while the full model (including all experts) must still be loaded into memory. This architectural design creates a distinction between "sparse parameters" (total model size) and "active parameters" (parameters used during computation). DeepSeek-R1 refines the framework by introducing dynamic expert routing, reinforcement learning–based load balancing, and enhanced sparsity constraints, making it one of the most efficient and scalable open source MoE models available. The reasoning model implements dynamic expert assignment, where experts are allocated based on contextual embeddings. A softmax temperature scaling mechanism is used to prevent expert over-specialization. In addition, the model employs a reinforcement learning–guided routing system that introduces policy-based optimization to guide expert selection, with a feedback loop specifically designed to optimize computational load balancing. It also implements sparse activation constraints through hierarchical Top-k gating to enforce sparsity constraints and adjusts token-level entropy metrics to reduce unnecessary activations.

CHAPTER 12 LARGE REASONING MODELS

Looking at the architectural foundations from DeepSeek-V2, the DeepSeek-MoE architecture consists of 236B total parameters, but only 21B parameters are activated per token. This strikes a balance between model scalability and computational efficiency. The system implements Device-Limited Routing (DLR), where tokens are assigned only to a subset M of available devices to reduce communication overhead. The routing mechanism uses affinity-based device selection, where the top M devices with the highest token–expert affinity scores are selected before choosing the Top-k experts within them. To maintain efficiency, DeepSeek-V2 introduced three auxiliary loss functions: Expert-Level Balance Loss, which ensures uniform expert usage across different training batches; Device-Level Balance Loss, which ensures equal computational load distribution across GPUs; and Communication Balance Loss, which ensures balanced information flow between GPUs. This optimizes efficiency by capping communication between GPUs, reducing MoE-related synchronization costs and leading to faster training convergence.

The expert selection process in DeepSeek-R1 follows a gating function that uses a trainable weight matrix. The final output is computed by combining the outputs of the Top-k selected experts, weighted by their gating probabilities. To ensure equal utilization of experts, the system applies a load balancing loss that considers the number of tokens assigned to each expert relative to the total number of tokens in a batch and the number of active experts per token. Additionally, an entropy regularization term is implemented to prevent excessive reliance on specific experts. For inference efficiency, DeepSeek-R1 implements FP8 quantization to reduce memory overhead while maintaining precision and Multi-head Latent Attention (MLA) to compress KV cache size as well as enabling larger batch sizes for inference time. To make sure the workload is evenly spread across GPUs, the system uses an eight-way expert parallel setup. Additionally, the model can adjust the number of active experts for each token based on how complex the sequence is.

Floating-Point 8 Quantization

DeepSeek-R1 uses 8-bit floating-point (FP8) quantization for efficiency during both training and inference. The system implements a learned dynamic scaling factor that adapts per layer, which helps reduce quantization errors and improve numerical stability. The model extends FP8 quantization to inference operations, reducing latency and optimizing GPU memory usage for more efficient deployment. A key technical feature is the adaptive clipping mechanism that introduces per-token dynamic clipping thresholds, ensuring values remain within FP8 representable limits (between –127 and 127), which prevents numerical overflow.

Block-wise FP8 quantization is specifically designed for the Mixture of Experts (MoE) layers, which reduces computational and memory overhead for large-scale models. The system is specifically designed to fully use NVIDIA H800 Tensor Cores, ensuring efficient low-precision computation without sacrificing accuracy. DeepSeek-V3 was among the first models to adopt FP8 mixed precision training, integrating it with other numerical formats like BF16 in a hybrid precision approach to maintain training stability while benefiting from lower-precision computations.

By using per-tensor scaling factors, the model maintains numerical stability even under extreme compression. For training efficiency, the system quantizes activations and gradients before transmission across distributed computing nodes. This approach, combined with block-wise quantization, significantly reduces memory bandwidth requirements and accelerates training by decreasing inter-GPU communication overhead. DeepSeek-R1 refined the scaling-based transformation used for numerical stability. Unlike DeepSeek-V3's static scaling factors, DeepSeek-R1 incorporates a learned dynamic scaling factor optimized based on loss gradients. This enables per-layer adaptive precision adjustments, significantly reducing quantization-induced errors. The implementation extends FP8 quantization to inference, involving selective quantization of attention layers, feedforward layers, and key–value cache storage.

The model also introduces an advanced clipping mechanism that ensures values remain within the representable range, preventing numerical overflow and maintaining precision during gradient accumulation and weight updates.

A significant enhancement in DeepSeek-R1 is its improved handling of FP8 quantization within reinforcement learning processes. The model dynamically adjusts per-layer precision needs by adapting scaling factors throughout RL-based optimization, reducing the risk of gradient vanishing and ensuring more stable policy learning. The system further optimizes low-precision storage and computation through block-wise quantization strategies for MoE models, ensuring that expert activations and gradients are efficiently compressed. This results in more efficient expert selection and routing, reducing MoE-related computational overhead. The transition from DeepSeek-V3 to DeepSeek-R1 marked a significant advancement in FP8 quantization by improving training stability, expanding FP8's role in inference, introducing per-layer adaptive scaling, and enhancing RL robustness. Despite these advancements, DeepSeek-V3 faced challenges in ensuring numerical stability at extreme precision reductions, particularly during RL and fine-tuning phases, which required additional refinements to FP8 scaling and adaptive precision handling to prevent degradation in model accuracy.

Multi-head Latent Attention (MLA)

MLA enhances training efficiency by projecting key–query–value (KQV) matrices into a lower-dimensional latent space, which significantly reduces computational and memory costs. By utilizing low-rank compression techniques, MLA minimizes the storage overhead of the key–value cache, ensuring faster inference and supporting longer context lengths or larger batch sizes. With these refinements, DeepSeek-R1 achieved SOTA performance in long-context tasks while maintaining extremely low memory overhead.

DeepSeek-R1 introduces several key innovations in its MLA implementation. It includes decoupled rotary position embeddings (RoPE) that separate RoPE application from the compressed latent KV pairs, allowing efficient positional encoding without interfering with key–value compression. This eliminates redundant KV recomputation during inference and improves processing speed. The system also features adaptive attention scaling with a self-adjusting attention weight mechanism that dynamically modulates attention scores based on token entropy and positional significance. The compression efficiency in DeepSeek-R1's MLA extends beyond previous versions, reducing KV cache size by more than 93.3% and boosting inference speed by 7.2× compared with DeepSeek 67B. The system implements predictive KV caching and parallelized computation, precomputing frequently accessed KV projections to reduce on-demand inference latency. This enables faster batch processing for long sequences. Additionally, the system expands supported context length from 128K to 160K tokens, leveraging MLA's compression and caching optimizations to maintain high efficiency and responsiveness across extended sequences.

DeepSeek-R1 further enhances MLA by implementing a hierarchical caching approach for efficient retrieval. This includes a primary latent KV cache that stores compressed latent vectors to minimize memory footprint and uses a hierarchical lookup table for fast retrieval. The system features context-aware retrieval where tokens appearing in similar contexts reuse cached latent vectors, and a similarity-based indexing system dynamically retrieves the most relevant cache entries. The implementation also includes latency reduction through prefetching, which predicts future attention patterns and precomputes required latent keys and values. The technical implementation in DeepSeek-R1 focuses heavily on optimization for long-context scenarios by using adaptive attention scaling that dynamically adjusts the importance of different tokens, ensuring critical tokens receive more attention while redundant information is downweighted. The system also implements careful token importance weighting, which helps maintain coherence and relevance across extended sequences while keeping computational demands manageable.

Multi-token Prediction

MTP in DeepSeek-R1 fundamentally changes how language models generate text by enabling the prediction of multiple tokens in parallel, rather than the traditional token-by-token generation approach. Unlike traditional models that predict tokens one by one, MTP in DeepSeek-R1 extends the auto-regressive framework to predict multiple tokens simultaneously within the same context window. This is accomplished through a sophisticated architecture of independent prediction heads (each specializing in different future positions), shared embedding layers (ensuring consistent representations), and a linear projection mechanism that combines previous hidden states with new token embeddings. The practical benefits are substantial: throughput improvements of up to 3× for code generation and 2.7× for text via self-speculative decoding, enhanced output coherence through better capturing of text structure and flow, computational complexity reduction from $O(T)$ to $O(T/k)$ where k is the adaptive prediction depth, parallel validation of multiple token sequences, and improved memory efficiency through selective caching. DeepSeek-R1 achieved approximately 1.8× increase in tokens per second compared with standard auto-regressive models, demonstrating MTP's real-world performance advantages. What makes this particularly sophisticated is its dynamic prediction horizon feature, which intelligently adjusts the number of tokens predicted per step based on the model's confidence level, ensuring both speed and accuracy. MTP's ability to maintain or improve output quality while reducing computational demands represents a significant advance in model efficiency for large-scale deployments. The implementation in DeepSeek-V3 used a sequence of transformer modules, with each module predicting subsequent tokens while preserving context

CHAPTER 12   LARGE REASONING MODELS

from previous steps. The system employed shared embedding layers to ensure consistent representations across different prediction depths. This was achieved through a linear projection that combines the hidden state of the previous depth with the embedding of the next token, allowing the transformer block to process a well-structured representation. The system achieved an impressive 85–90% acceptance rate for predicted tokens, demonstrating its effectiveness in minimizing unnecessary recomputations. DeepSeek-R1 enhanced the MTP mechanism by addressing limitations of DeepSeek-V3's static approach. Instead of using a fixed number of predicted tokens per step, it introduced an adaptive mechanism to determine the prediction depth dynamically. The system implements speculative decoding with verification, generating and validating multiple token sequences in parallel before finalizing outputs. This is combined with a reinforcement learning–based selection system that prioritizes sequences based on fluency, coherence, and factual accuracy. The consequences of implementing MTP are significant. The system reduces computational complexity from $O(T)$ to $O(T/k)$, where k is the adaptive prediction depth, leading to substantially faster inference speeds. Memory efficiency is achieved through selective caching of representations instead of storing complete causal chains. The training combines traditional cross-entropy loss with reinforcement learning rewards, creating a system that can generate text both quickly and accurately. In practice, this led to approximately 1.8× increase in tokens per second compared with standard auto-regressive models.

DeepSeek-R1's implementation was also novel in its verification process. It uses a hierarchical token verification process where multiple candidate token sequences are generated and evaluated for coherence before predictions are finalized. If a low-confidence token is identified, the model dynamically re-evaluates and adjusts its predictions. The training methodology for MTP in DeepSeek-R1 combines cross-entropy-based training with reinforcement learning objectives. The loss function includes both the standard MTP-based cross-entropy loss from DeepSeek-V3 and a reinforcement-driven term that rewards high-quality token sequences. Through enhanced verification and adaptive prediction, DeepSeek-R1 achieved even greater improvements in inference speed compared with DeepSeek-V3 while maintaining output quality and coherence. Now that we understand the basic architecture, let us review the four stages.

Stage 1: Cold Start with Supervised Fine-Tuning (SFT)

DeepSeek-R1-Zero was the first open source model trained autonomously with very large-scale reinforcement learning instead of SFT as the initial step. This approach enabled the model to independently explore chain-of-thought reasoning, solve complex problems, and iteratively refine its outputs. However, the model's practical use was limited by challenges such as repetitive reasoning steps, poor readability of the output and reasoning steps, and language mixing. The solution was to pre-train the model with a curated dataset containing detailed reasoning examples before applying reinforcement.

To that end, DeepSeek-R1 begins the first stage by fine-tuning the DeepSeek-V3-Base model with a carefully curated dataset of high-quality chain-of-thought (CoT) examples. This is a called a cold start. The examples here are designed to guide the model through step-by-step reasoning processes, promoting clarity and coherence in its outputs. The dataset is relatively small, consisting of thousands of samples, but each is meticulously crafted to ensure quality. The sources for these CoT examples include

- **Few-shot prompting**: Utilizing large-scale pre-trained models to generate detailed reasoning paths.

- **Manual annotation and refinement**: Human reviewers filter and refine reasoning steps to enhance clarity and correctness.

CHAPTER 12 LARGE REASONING MODELS

- **Post-processing outputs from DeepSeek-R1-Zero:**
  Extracting well-structured reasoning paths from the
  RL-trained precursor model.

To further enhance readability and consistency, the fine-tuning process enforces a structured output format. Each response from the model is organized into distinct sections, typically delineated by special tokens, such as

- <reasoning_process>: This section contains a step-by-step explanation of the problem-solving approach.

- <summary>: This part provides the final answer or conclusion.

By adhering to this structured format, the model's outputs become more predictable and easier to interpret, aligning closely with human expectations. During supervised fine-tuning, the model is trained to minimize the cross-entropy loss between its predictions and the target outputs in the CoT dataset. This loss function encourages the model to generate token sequences that closely match the target reasoning paths, thereby reinforcing accurate and coherent outputs. By the conclusion of stage 1, DeepSeek-R1 achieves a foundational proficiency in structured reasoning. The model's outputs exhibit improved readability and coherence, effectively addressing the shortcomings observed in DeepSeek-R1-Zero. This supervised fine-tuning stage further ensures that the model is well-prepared for subsequent training phases, particularly reinforcement learning, by providing a stable and structured starting point.

CHAPTER 12 LARGE REASONING MODELS

Stage 2: Reinforcement Learning and Policy Evolution

Reinforcement learning is the backbone of DeepSeek-R1's reasoning evolution. In stage 2, the model learns to optimize its reasoning trajectories based on reward-driven feedback mechanisms, leading to significant improvements in accuracy and coherence. Before getting into model reasoning, we need to first review the concept of policy optimization.

Policy optimization is a cornerstone of modern machine learning, particularly in training LLMs. At its core, policy optimization is about teaching AI systems to make better decisions over time by adjusting their behavior—or "policy"—based on the outcomes of their actions. This approach is crucial for LLMs because it helps them learn to generate more accurate, contextually appropriate responses through trial and error, rather than simply memorizing patterns from training data. Traditional policy optimization methods like PPO (Proximal Policy Optimization) have been widely successful in robotics and game playing, but their application to language models presents unique challenges due to the vast, discrete nature of text generation. In this context, DeepSeek's approach to reinforcement learning parallels self-play in games like chess. Rather than relying on fixed datasets, the system begins with fundamental rules and develops through autonomous exploration. This mirrors how an AI system learns chess through iterative self-play—starting with basic moves and gradually developing sophisticated strategies through trial and error. While traditional supervised learning is like studying a grandmaster's chess book, reinforcement learning through self-play is more akin to discovering winning strategies through countless practice games. This self-play concept proved particularly powerful when adapted for reasoning-intensive domains, especially mathematical problem-solving, through the development of GRPO (Group Relative Policy Optimization).

CHAPTER 12   LARGE REASONING MODELS

GRPO's primary innovation lies in its elimination of the separate critic model traditionally required in policy optimization techniques. In standard reinforcement learning, the critic acts like a chess evaluator, assessing how good a particular position or move might be. However, maintaining an accurate critic for language models is exceptionally challenging due to the complexity of evaluating text quality. Instead of relying on this traditional approach, GRPO estimates baselines from groups of generated outputs, creating a more efficient yet stable training process. This concept went through three distinct phases, each addressing specific challenges in language model training. The initial phase with DeepSeekMath focused primarily on mathematical reasoning, employing structured evaluation metrics and reward functions based on mathematical correctness—similar to how a math teacher might grade solutions based on both the final answer and the solution process. The second phase emerged with DeepSeek-R1-Zero, where GRPO was applied without any supervised fine-tuning, allowing the model to develop reasoning capabilities purely through reinforcement learning, though this revealed challenges with readability and language mixing. The final phase, implemented in DeepSeek-R1, introduced a multi-stage reinforcement learning pipeline that incorporated cold-start fine-tuning before applying GRPO, along with expanded reward models and additional language consistency rewards.

The architecture of GRPO rests on three fundamental components that work in concert, each addressing a critical aspect of language model training. First, it ensures the updated policy improves upon previous iterations in expectation—imagine this as ensuring each new version of the model performs better than the last across a wide range of tasks. Second, it employs a clipping mechanism that acts as a safeguard against excessive updates, maintaining training stability. This is particularly important in language models, where small changes in parameters can lead to dramatic shifts in output quality. Third, it uses KL divergence regularization to keep the new policy from straying too far from the

445

CHAPTER 12 LARGE REASONING MODELS

original distribution, essentially preventing the model from "forgetting" its basic language understanding while learning new reasoning skills. This sophisticated yet elegant design is implemented through a process that samples multiple outputs per query, computes rewards over groups, and uses mean and standard deviation of rewards for normalized training baselines, all while carefully balancing policy improvement with control mechanisms. GRPO's efficiency stems from several key innovations that address common challenges in language model training. By eliminating the critic model, it significantly reduces memory consumption compared with traditional approaches—a crucial advantage when training large-scale models that already push the limits of available compute. The system implements batch computation for group sampling and maintains stable iterative reinforcement learning refinement, while its group-based reward normalization ensures consistent training progress across diverse types of queries and responses. These efficiency gains proved particularly valuable in practice, as the system demonstrated exceptional performance in mathematical reasoning and general problem-solving tasks, ultimately outperforming similar-scale models on various benchmarks. The ability to maintain stable training while reducing computational requirements made GRPO suitable for training LLMs, contributing significantly to DeepSeek-R1's performance across a wide range of reasoning tasks, from basic arithmetic to complex logical deduction. In DeepSeek-R1-Zero, GPRO demonstrated that reinforcement learning alone could develop sophisticated reasoning capabilities, though with some limitations in output quality. When implemented in the full DeepSeek-R1 model with its multi-stage approach, GRPO proved especially effective at refining reasoning skills while maintaining output coherence and readability.

The model after stage 2 demonstrated impressive performance in mathematical reasoning and general problem-solving tasks, outperforming other models of similar scale on various benchmarks.

Stage 3: Rejection Sampling and Expanded Supervised Fine-Tuning

This stage addresses limitations observed in earlier phases, such as the model's occasional generation of incoherent or linguistically inconsistent outputs, by leveraging a combination of rejection sampling and supervised fine-tuning on a curated dataset.

Following the reinforcement learning phase in stage 2, the model developed enhanced reasoning abilities, but still had issues like language mixing and formatting inconsistencies. To mitigate these problems, stage 3 begins with rejection sampling, a process designed to filter and select high-quality outputs from the RL-trained model. Specifically, the model generates multiple responses to a given prompt, and these responses are evaluated based on predefined criteria such as correctness, coherence, and adherence to the desired format. Responses that meet these standards are retained, while those that do not are discarded. For instance, in mathematical problem-solving tasks, only solutions that arrive at the correct answer through a clear and logical reasoning process are selected. This ensures that the dataset used for subsequent fine-tuning comprises only the most accurate and well-structured examples.

The rejection sampling process yields approximately 600,000 high-quality reasoning samples. To further enhance the model's versatility, an additional 200,000 examples covering non-reasoning tasks—such as writing, factual question answering, self-cognition, and translation—are incorporated. Some of these non-reasoning examples are augmented with chain-of-thought (CoT) reasoning, generated using the DeepSeek-V3 model, to provide a richer training context. This diverse dataset of around 800,000 samples is then used to fine-tune the DeepSeek-V3-Base model over two epochs. The fine-tuning process aims to balance the model's reasoning capabilities with its performance on general language tasks, ensuring that it can handle both complex problem-solving and more straightforward queries with equal proficiency. Prior to stage 3, the model might produce translations that, while contextually accurate, lack fluency or contain unnatural phrasing. After undergoing rejection sampling and expanded SFT, the model demonstrates improved fluency and coherence in translations, producing outputs that are more aligned with human expectations. Similarly, in tasks requiring factual question answering, the model's responses become more precise and informative, reflecting the enhanced training it received during this stage.

Stage 4: Secondary Reinforcement Learning

This stage is aimed at enhancing the model's alignment with human preferences, ensuring helpfulness, and minimizing harmful outputs. This stage builds upon the foundational reasoning capabilities established in earlier phases, addressing limitations such as the model's occasional generation of incoherent or linguistically inconsistent outputs. By using a combination of rejection sampling and supervised fine-tuning on a curated dataset, stage 4 refines the model's reasoning capabilities and broadens its applicability across diverse tasks. The necessity for a secondary RL phase arises from challenges inherent to LLM training. Initial training phases, including supervised fine-tuning and primary RL, focus on instilling fundamental reasoning abilities and basic alignment with human instructions. However, these stages may not fully capture the nuances of human preferences or effectively mitigate the risk of generating harmful or unhelpful content. The secondary RL phase specifically targets these areas by fine-tuning the model's behavior to be more aligned with human expectations.

In this phase, the model undergoes further training using reinforcement learning from human feedback (RLHF). Human evaluators assess the model's outputs, providing feedback on aspects such as relevance, coherence, and safety. This feedback is then used to adjust the model's parameters, reinforcing desirable behaviors and discouraging

CHAPTER 12　LARGE REASONING MODELS

undesirable ones. For example, if the model generates a response that is factually correct but presented in a confusing manner, human feedback can guide the model to produce clearer and more concise explanations in future iterations. A specific instance illustrating the impact of secondary RL is in the model's handling of sensitive topics. Prior to this phase, the model might generate responses that, while factually accurate, could be considered insensitive or inappropriate. Through targeted RLHF, the model learns to navigate such topics with greater care, providing information in a manner that is both accurate and considerate of user sensitivity. Moreover, secondary RL helps in fine-tuning the model's ability to refuse inappropriate requests. For instance, if prompted to provide information that could be harmful or unethical, the model, through reinforcement learning, becomes adept at declining such requests politely and firmly, thereby enhancing its safety and ethical alignment.

Note During the development of DeepSeek-R1, a particularly intriguing phenomenon emerged, often referred to as an "aha moment." This occurred when the model, while solving complex problems, demonstrated the ability to reassess its initial approach and allocate additional cognitive resources to derive a more accurate solution. For instance, in one scenario, DeepSeek-R1 began solving a mathematical problem but then paused, indicating, "Wait, wait. That's an aha moment I can flag here." This self-reflective behavior allowed the model to identify potential errors in its initial reasoning and correct them autonomously. This "aha moment" is a testament to the efficacy of reinforcement learning (RL) in training large language models. By utilizing RL, DeepSeek-R1 was not explicitly programmed to solve specific problems; instead, it was provided with incentives to develop advanced problem-solving strategies on its own. The emergence of such self-corrective behavior underscores the potential of RL to unlock new levels of intelligence in artificial systems. It highlights the model's capacity for autonomous adaptation and self-improvement, paving the way for more advanced and reliable AI applications in the future.

Distillation

DeepSeek-R1's advanced reasoning capabilities were successfully transferred to smaller models via a systematic distillation process. Qwen-7B and Llama-8B were the main targets of distillation, using an optimized training pipeline designed to maintain the depth of reasoning capabilities while significantly reducing the computational requirements. The process followed a teacher–student paradigm, where DeepSeek-R1 served as the teacher model, guiding the training of smaller student models. These smaller models underwent fine-tuning using a massive dataset of 800,000 reasoning-related samples that were generated by DeepSeek-R1, ensuring the transfer of complex reasoning patterns.

The training methodology for distilled models differed significantly from the original DeepSeek-R1 training process. Instead of using reinforcement learning, the distilled models primarily relied on supervised fine-tuning (SFT). The training dataset was carefully curated and consisted of 600,000 samples focused specifically on reasoning-based tasks, covering mathematics, logical reasoning, and coding problems. To ensure the models maintained general capabilities alongside their reasoning skills, an additional 200,000 general-purpose samples were included in the training data. This balanced approach helped create well-rounded models that could handle both specialized reasoning tasks and general applications. The effectiveness of the distillation approach became particularly evident when compared with alternative training methods. Experiments showed that distilling reasoning behaviors from DeepSeek-R1 was significantly

CHAPTER 12 LARGE REASONING MODELS

more efficient and effective than attempting to train smaller models from scratch using reinforcement learning. This was demonstrated clearly when comparing a directly RL-trained Qwen-32B model against its distilled counterpart, DeepSeek-R1-Distill-Qwen-32B. The distilled version consistently outperformed the RL-trained model, highlighting the superiority of the distillation approach in preserving complex reasoning patterns. These results suggest that knowledge transfer via distillation is more effective at capturing and reproducing sophisticated reasoning capabilities than developing them from scratch through reinforcement learning.

The success of the distillation process demonstrates that complex reasoning capabilities can be effectively compressed and transferred to more compact models without significant loss of functionality. This process has important implications for deploying advanced reasoning capabilities in resource-constrained environments, as it shows that smaller models can achieve impressive performance levels when properly trained through distillation. The process effectively democratizes access to advanced reasoning capabilities by making them available in more computationally efficient packages, allowing for broader deployment and application of these capabilities across different scales of hardware and computational resources. The distilled versions demonstrated competitive performance on various benchmarks when compared against other models (including some larger language models), showcasing their ability to maintain high-level reasoning capabilities despite their reduced size. For instance, the distilled 7B model achieves 55.5% on first attempt with AIME 2024, outperforming GPT-4o (9.3%) at a fraction of the cost. This suggests that the distillation process successfully captured and transferred the essential aspects of DeepSeek-R1's reasoning abilities, making them accessible in more compact and efficient forms.

CHAPTER 12   LARGE REASONING MODELS

Training Costs

DeepSeek's R1 model has garnered significant attention for its reasoning capabilities and the relatively low reported training cost of approximately $6 million. This figure is notably lower than the estimated $100 million spent on training models like OpenAI's GPT-4. However, it's important to delve deeper into these numbers to understand the full context.

The $6 million cost attributed to DeepSeek R1 primarily accounts for the direct expenses associated with a single training run, utilizing 2,048 NVIDIA H800 GPUs. This calculation focuses on the computational resources required for that specific training iteration. However, this figure does not encompass several other significant expenditures inherent in developing such a sophisticated model. For instance, the costs associated with training the teacher model, DeepSeek-R1, are not published or available. Additionally, expenses related to data acquisition and preparation, infrastructure maintenance, and personnel costs are excluded. These elements collectively contribute substantially to the overall investment in the model's development. Moreover, the development of advanced AI models typically involves numerous training runs and extensive experimentation to fine-tune performance and validate architectural innovations. Each of these iterations incurs additional costs, further elevating the total financial commitment beyond the initial $6 million cited. In summary, although the reported training cost highlights DeepSeek's efficiency in resource utilization, it only represents a portion of the complete cost required to develop reasoning capabilities in a model of R1's caliber.

Summary

The evolution of open source reasoning models, noted by the release of the DeepSeek family of models, marks a significant milestone for LLMs. Most remarkably, DeepSeek-R1 demonstrates that human supervision may not be essential in certain aspects of model training, particularly in developing reasoning capabilities through reinforcement learning. Unlike traditional models that rely heavily on supervised fine-tuning (SFT) with human-labeled datasets, DeepSeek-R1-Zero showed that large-scale reinforcement learning alone could enable the model to autonomously develop structured reasoning and problem-solving abilities. While human oversight remains important for ethical alignment and safety, DeepSeek-R1's training approach suggests that AI can develop strong reasoning skills autonomously, significantly reducing the need for direct human supervision in certain areas of training. The emergence of "aha moments" during training and the effective transfer of reasoning capabilities through distillation suggest promising directions for future research and development in artificial intelligence.

Bibliography

Lepikhin, D., Lee, H., Xu, Y., Chen, D., Firat, O., Huang, Y., Krikun, M., Shazeer, N., & Chen, Z. (2020). GShard: Scaling giant models with conditional computation and automatic sharding. arXiv. https://doi.org/10.48550/arXiv.2006.16668

Fedus, W., Zoph, B., & Shazeer, N. (2021). Switch transformers: Scaling to trillion parameter models with simple and efficient sparsity. arXiv. https://doi.org/10.48550/arXiv.2101.03961

Shazeer, N., Mirhoseini, A., Maziarz, K., Davis, A., Le, Q., Hinton, G., & Dean, J. (2017). Outrageously large neural networks: The sparsely-gated mixture-of-experts layer. arXiv. https://doi.org/10.48550/arXiv.1701.06538

Gloeckle, F., Youbi Idrissi, B., Rozière, B., Lopez-Paz, D., & Synnaeve, G. (2024). Better & faster large language models via multi-token prediction. arXiv. https://doi.org/10.48550/arXiv.2404.19737

DeepSeek-AI. (2024). DeepSeek-V2: A strong, economical, and efficient mixture-of-experts language model. arXiv. https://doi.org/10.48550/arXiv.2405.04434

DeepSeek-AI. (2024). DeepSeek-V3 technical report. arXiv. https://doi.org/10.48550/arXiv.2412.19437

DeepSeek-AI. (2024). DeepSeek-R1: Incentivizing reasoning capability in LLMs via reinforcement learning. arXiv. https://doi.org/10.48550/arXiv.2501.12948

Ainslie, J., Tur, G., Silva, A., Lee, C., Gu, Y., Peng, B., & Brunk, C. (2023). Grouped-query attention for long context understanding. arXiv. https://doi.org/10.48550/arXiv.2305.18654

Kahneman, D. *Thinking, Fast and Slow*. Farrar, Straus and Giroux, 2011.

Jiang, A. Q., Sablayrolles, A., Mensch, A., Bamford, C., Singh, D., Haziza, D., Snell, J., Szlam, A., Sanh, V., Scialom, T., Karamcheti, S., Kasai, J., Park, D., Tow, J., Webson, A., & Lachaux, M. A. (2024). Mixtral of experts. arXiv. https://doi.org/10.48550/arXiv.2401.04088

Wei, J., Tay, Y., Bommasani, R., Raffel, C., Zoph, B., Borgeaud, S., Yogatama, D., Bosma, M., Zhou, D., Metzler, D., Chi, E. H., Hashimoto, T., Vinyals, O., Liang, P., Dean, J., & Fedus, W. (2022). Emergent abilities of large language models. *Transactions on Machine Learning Research*.

Riquelme, C., Puigcerver, J., Mustafa, B., Neumann, M., Jenatton, R., Susano Pinto, A., Keysers, D., & Houlsby, N. (2021). Scaling vision with sparse mixture of experts. *Advances in Neural Information Processing Systems*, 34, 8583–8595.

Du, N., Huang, Y., Dai, A. M., Tong, S., Lepikhin, D., Xu, Y., Krikun, M., Zhou, Y., Yu, A. W., Firat, O., Zoph, B., Fedus, L., Bosma, M., Zhou, Z., Wang, T., Wang, Y. E., Webster, K., Pellat, M., Robinson, K., ... & Le, Q. V. (2022). GLaM: Efficient scaling of language models with mixture-of-experts. In *International Conference on Machine Learning* (pp. 5547–5569). PMLR.

Zoph, B., Bello, I., Kumar, S., Du, N., Huang, Y., Dean, J., Shazeer, N., & Fedus, W. (2022). ST-MoE: Designing stable and transferable sparse expert models. arXiv. https://doi.org/10.48550/arXiv.2202.08906

Rajbhandari, S., Rasley, J., Ruwase, O., & He, Y. (2022). DeepSpeed-MoE: Advancing mixture-of-experts inference and training to power next-generation AI scale. In *International Conference on Machine Learning* (pp. 18332–18346). PMLR.

CHAPTER 13

Technological Revolutions and Financial Capital Markets

Carlota Perez's seminal book titled the same as this chapter, *Technological Revolutions and Financial Capital*, presents a comprehensive theory of how technological revolutions drive long-term economic cycles and social transformation. The central theme argued by the book is that modern civilization has been shaped by five distinct technological revolutions starting from the Industrial Revolution, each following a similar three-phase pattern of installation, deployment, and maturity. Each technological revolution in Perez's framework begins with a breakthrough innovation that opens new opportunities for profit. For instance, the Industrial Revolution began with mechanized cotton factories; the age of steam and railways with the Liverpool–Manchester railway; the age of steel and heavy engineering with the Bessemer steel process; the age of oil, automobiles, and mass production with Ford's Model T; and the age of information with the Intel microprocessor.

CHAPTER 13   TECHNOLOGICAL REVOLUTIONS AND FINANCIAL CAPITAL MARKETS

Perez provides a detailed analysis of how financial capital and production capital interface during a technological revolution. She describes how each revolution goes through a "frenzy" phase where financial speculation dominates, often leading to a bubble and crash, followed by a "synergy" phase where the technology's benefits spread more widely through society. This pattern explains phenomena like the 1990s dot-com bubble and the follow-up maturation of technology in the two decades since. The book also introduces "techno-economic paradigms" that extend far beyond the intended industry where a technology emerged, for instance, mass production principles that were designed for automotive manufacturing spread to adjacent verticals and beyond to unrelated industries. In her framework, Perez describes four distinct phases: irruption, frenzy, synergy, and maturity. During irruption, new technologies emerge and begin displacing old ones. The frenzy phase sees intense financial speculation and investment in the new technologies. After a turning point (often a financial crash), the synergy phase begins, characterized by more balanced growth and broader social benefits. Finally, maturity sets in as technologies become standardized and returns diminish. These technological revolutions often become catalysts for institutional change. New technologies don't just need physical infrastructure—they need appropriate financial systems, regulatory systems, skills, and social structures. The tension between old and new institutional frameworks, for instance, Uber and traditional taxi systems, helps explain why technological transitions can be socially turbulent.

Leadership often shifts between revolutions, as established regions may be too invested in old ways of doing things to rapidly adopt new paradigms. Perez suggests we're in the deployment period of the information technology revolution, moving from the installation phase (characterized by the dot-com bubble) to a period where the benefits could become more broadly distributed—though this requires appropriate institutional innovations and policy choices.

CHAPTER 13   TECHNOLOGICAL REVOLUTIONS AND FINANCIAL CAPITAL MARKETS

Blockchain

The trajectory of blockchain closely mirrors the patterns Perez identified, offering insights into both its current state and potential future development. Blockchain's irruption phase began with the launch of Bitcoin in 2008, emerging during a time of global financial crisis. This timing was significant, as it introduced a novel solution for trustless digital transactions when trust in traditional financial institutions was at a low point. Blockchain technology initially attracted a small but dedicated community of cryptographers, computer scientists, and individuals interested in alternative financial systems. This early period was characterized by experimentation, technical development, and the establishment of fundamental protocols that would later enable broader applications. Blockchain entered its frenzy phase around 2014, marked by an explosion of interest and investment. The launch of Ethereum in 2015 represented a crucial evolution, expanding blockchain's potential beyond digital currency to include smart contracts and decentralized applications. This period saw the emergence of numerous competing platforms and protocols, each attempting to solve different aspects of scalability, security, and functionality. The ICO boom of 2017 exemplified the speculative fervor that Perez describes as typical of this phase, with billions of dollars flowing into blockchain projects at unprecedented rates. The frenzy phase reached its peak during 2020–2021 with the DeFi summer and the NFT explosion. This period demonstrated both the innovative potential of blockchain technology and the speculative excesses that Perez identifies as characteristic of installation periods. New financial instruments and models emerged rapidly, while speculation drove asset prices to unsustainable levels. The market exhibited classic bubble behavior, with investors rushing to participate regardless of underlying value or utility.

The market corrections of 2022 represent what Perez calls the "turning point"—a critical period of institutional reconfiguration. This phase has been characterized by increased regulatory scrutiny, a focus on practical applications, and the beginning of meaningful institutional adoption. Major corporations and financial institutions have begun integrating blockchain technology into their operations, while governments have started seriously exploring central bank digital currencies (CBDCs) and regulatory frameworks. The technology appears to be transitioning from pure speculation toward practical utility, mirroring Perez's description of the movement from installation to deployment periods. This shift is evident in the growing focus on enterprise blockchain solutions, supply chain applications, digital identity systems, and cross-border payment networks. These developments suggest blockchain is beginning to find its place within existing institutional frameworks while simultaneously pushing those frameworks to evolve. The broader implications of blockchain technology align with Perez's concept of techno-economic paradigm shifts. Blockchain is fundamentally changing how we think about trust in digital systems, the nature of financial intermediation, and organizational structure. The emergence of decentralized autonomous organizations (DAOs) represents a novel form of human coordination that can transform how society organizes economic work.

The interaction between blockchain and other emerging technologies adds another layer of complexity to this analysis. As blockchain technology combines with artificial intelligence, it could either represent a continuation of current blockchain development or possibly signal the early stages of a new technological surge. The key challenge ahead lies in managing the transition from installation to deployment in a way that maximizes social benefit while minimizing potential negative impacts. Looking forward, Perez's framework suggests that blockchain's successful transition to a deployment period will require significant institutional innovation. This includes developing appropriate regulatory frameworks, achieving standardization and interoperability between different systems, and finding ways to create genuine economic value beyond speculation. Blockchain must move beyond cryptocurrencies, from being primarily a vehicle for financial speculation to a tool for solving practical, high-impact problems.

CHAPTER 13   TECHNOLOGICAL REVOLUTIONS AND FINANCIAL CAPITAL MARKETS

Large Language Models

The development of LLMs mirrors blockchain's developmental trajectory while introducing its own unique patterns of technological revolution. Like blockchain, AI has gone through distinct phases of development, but its acceleration has been notably more dramatic, compressing what might have been decades of evolution into a few intense years. The initial phase of modern AI development can be traced to the breakthrough of deep learning and neural networks in the early 2010s. However, the true irruption phase for LLMs began with the release of GPT-3 in 2020, marking a fundamental shift in what was possible with language models. This mirrors how Bitcoin represented a breakthrough moment for blockchain, though AI's impact has been more immediately apparent across a broader range of industries and applications.

The frenzy phase for AI arrived remarkably quickly, essentially exploding with ChatGPT's release in late 2022. Unlike blockchain's frenzy, which was primarily characterized by financial speculation, AI's frenzy has manifested in a massive surge of business adoption, research advancement, and product development. Companies across every sector began integrating AI capabilities, while investment in AI startups and infrastructure reached unprecedented levels. The current phase of AI development shows signs of both frenzy and early maturity simultaneously. While investment and development continue at a breakneck pace, we're also seeing the emergence of serious regulatory frameworks and institutional adaptation. The EU's AI Act, various US executive orders on AI safety, and China's AI regulations represent early attempts to create governance structures for this technology, coming much earlier in AI's development cycle than similar regulations did for blockchain. The economic implications of AI's evolution differ significantly from blockchain's. While blockchain primarily challenged financial and organizational structures, AI is fundamentally altering the nature of work itself. LLMs are being integrated into existing business processes much more rapidly than blockchain, suggesting a different pattern of adoption and institutional change. This rapid integration is creating immediate pressure for regulatory and social adaptation.

The development of AI capabilities has also followed a different capital structure than blockchain. While blockchain's development was largely funded through speculative token investments, AI development has been dominated by large tech companies and venture capital. This has led to a more concentrated development pattern, raising concerns about AI capability inequality between large and small organizations. The relationship between research and commercialization in AI has also been distinctive. Unlike blockchain, where commercial applications often led development, AI has maintained a strong connection between academic research and commercial deployment. This has created a different dynamic in how AI evolves, with breakthroughs often coming from research labs rather than purely commercial enterprises. Governance challenges for AI are proving more complex than those faced by blockchain. While blockchain's regulatory challenges primarily concerned financial oversight and securities law, AI regulation must address a broader range of issues including safety, ethics, liability, and fundamental human rights. This suggests that the institutional adaptation required for AI might be more far-reaching than what was needed for blockchain technology. A crucial difference in the evolution of these technologies lies in their impact timeframes. While blockchain's effects on society have been relatively gradual, AI's impact is immediate and widespread. This rapid pace of change is forcing faster institutional adaptation and raising urgent questions about governance and control. The challenge is creating regulatory frameworks that can effectively govern the technology while remaining flexible enough to adapt to its rapid evolution. Looking forward, both AI and blockchain technologies appear to be entering new phases of development. For AI, the current challenge is managing the transition from pure capability advancement to responsible deployment and societal integration. This includes addressing issues of bias, safety, and open access.

Most significantly, the development of AI capabilities appears to be accelerating rather than stabilizing, unlike the more cyclical pattern seen in blockchain and other technological revolutions. This suggests we might need new frameworks for understanding this technology's evolution, as it may not follow the same installation–deployment–maturity cycle that Perez identified in earlier technological revolutions. The continuing advancement of AI capabilities, particularly in areas like multimodal models and Artificial General Intelligence, suggests we may still be in the early stages of understanding how this technology embeds into society.

AI Models as Smart Contracts

As blockchain and artificial intelligence separately follow the development patterns described by Perez, their integration creates entirely new paradigms. This integration manifests in three key areas that are reshaping how decentralized systems process information, noted below.

Decentralized AI training platforms distribute computing workloads across blockchain networks, allowing participants to contribute resources while maintaining control of their data. This approach democratizes AI development, making it more accessible while enhancing data security and integrity. These systems typically operate through specialized smart contracts that coordinate model training across nodes in the network, with token incentive structures that reward quality contributions and participation. Companies like SingularityNET and Ocean Protocol exemplify this model, creating marketplaces where AI developers can monetize algorithms and datasets in a decentralized ecosystem.

AI-enhanced smart contracts represent another powerful convergence of these technologies. Traditional smart contracts execute based on predefined conditions, but AI integration adds advanced decision-making capabilities. For example, in insurance, AI can automatically assess claims and trigger payment processing through the blockchain, significantly reducing processing times and minimizing human error. This advancement enables more complex and adaptive automated agreements that can respond to changing conditions in natural language while maintaining the security and transparency of blockchain.

On-chain content validation represents a third critical integration area. Platforms like CertiK combine AI with formal verification techniques to secure blockchain applications and smart contracts, automatically identifying vulnerabilities and ensuring code integrity. The Internet Computer Protocol (ICP) has demonstrated AI inference running directly on-chain, allowing for deterministic verification of AI outputs that can be trusted by all network participants. This capability is particularly valuable for grounding hallucinations as LLMs can generate content, while blockchain provides an immutable record of verification results, establishing traceability of digital assets.

ICOs

Initial Coin Offerings (ICOs) emerged around 2013–2014 as a new fundraising mechanism for blockchain projects, with Mastercoin (now Omni) conducting one of the first ICOs. The concept gained significant traction as a way for projects to raise capital directly from supporters while simultaneously distributing their tokens. The early ICO landscape was largely unregulated, allowing projects to raise funds with little more than a whitepaper and a compelling vision, which led to innovative successes and scams. The ICO boom reached its peak in 2017–2018, with projects raising billions of dollars. Notable examples included EOS raising $4.1 billion and Telegram's $1.7 billion offering. This period demonstrated both the potential and pitfalls of ICOs. While some projects like Ethereum (which conducted its ICO in 2014) went on to create significant value, many others failed to deliver on their promises or turned out to be outright frauds. The regulatory landscape began shifting dramatically in 2017 when the Securities and Exchange Commission (SEC) issued its DAO Report, indicating that many tokens sold in ICOs could be considered securities under US law by applying the Howey Test. This marked a crucial turning point, as it meant ICOs needed to either register with the SEC or qualify for an exemption. The SEC's subsequent enforcement actions against numerous ICO projects sent a clear message about the need for regulatory compliance.

The Howey Test, established by the US Supreme Court in "SEC v. W. J. Howey Co." (1946), is a legal standard used to determine whether a transaction qualifies as an "investment contract" under US securities laws. If a transaction meets the Howey Test criteria, it is classified as a security and must comply with federal securities regulations. The test consists of four key elements: (1) an investment of money, meaning individuals contribute funds or assets; (2) involvement in a common enterprise, where investors' money is pooled together and their success is tied to a larger collective entity; (3) an expectation of profits, where investors anticipate financial returns; and (4) profits that are derived from the efforts of others, meaning the financial gains depend primarily on third parties such as developers, managers, or promoters. The Howey Test plays a crucial role in the regulation of Initial Coin Offerings (ICOs), as the SEC frequently applies it to determine whether a token sale qualifies as a securities offering. If a token meets all four criteria, it is legally considered a security, requiring the ICO to register with the SEC or qualify for an exemption. Additionally, the project must comply with disclosure and reporting requirements, and in some cases, investors must meet accreditation criteria. Many ICOs have failed the Howey Test, leading to SEC enforcement actions, fines, and shutdowns. To avoid security classification, some token projects attempt to design their tokens primarily for utility purposes rather than as investment vehicles.

CHAPTER 13   TECHNOLOGICAL REVOLUTIONS AND FINANCIAL CAPITAL MARKETS

Several ICO-related legal cases have tested the application of the Howey Test, with significant implications for cryptocurrency regulation. In United States v. Zaslavskiy, Maksim Zaslavskiy was charged with promoting two ICOs—REcoin and Diamond Reserve Club (DRC)— which he claimed were backed by real estate and diamonds. The court determined that these offerings met the Howey Test criteria, as investors contributed funds with the expectation of profits based on Zaslavskiy and his team's efforts. This case reinforced that simply labeling a product as a cryptocurrency does not exempt it from securities laws. Another notable case, Securities and Exchange Commission (SEC) v. Blockvest, LLC, involved allegations that Blockvest's ICO constituted an unregistered securities offering. Initially, the court denied the SEC's motion for a preliminary injunction due to insufficient evidence that the tokens were securities. However, upon reconsideration, the court ruled that the SEC had presented enough evidence to proceed, highlighting the fact-specific nature of applying the Howey Test to ICOs. In response to increased regulatory scrutiny, the market evolved toward Security Token Offerings (STOs) and Initial Exchange Offerings (IEOs) around 2018–2019. STOs explicitly acknowledged their status as securities and complied with relevant regulations, while IEOs conducted token sales through established cryptocurrency exchanges, which provided some level of project vetting and built-in compliance mechanisms.

The emergence of DeFi in 2020 introduced new token distribution methods like liquidity mining and yield farming, which effectively served as alternatives to traditional ICOs. These mechanisms allowed projects to distribute tokens based on user participation rather than direct investment, potentially avoiding some securities law complications while creating different regulatory challenges. Current regulations vary significantly by jurisdiction. In the United States, most token sales must either register with the SEC or qualify for exemptions like Regulation D (for accredited investors) or Regulation A+ (which allows limited retail participation). The European Union has developed the Markets in Crypto-Assets (MiCA) regulation, providing a more comprehensive framework for token offerings. Meanwhile, countries like Singapore and Switzerland have created specific frameworks for token sales that aim to balance innovation with investor protection.

The regulatory evolution has had both positive and negative impacts. On the positive side, increased oversight has reduced the number of fraudulent offerings and provided clearer guidelines for legitimate projects. Professional investors now have more confidence in compliant token offerings, and there's generally better protection for retail investors. However, compliance costs have increased significantly, potentially limiting access to funding for smaller projects and pushing some innovation offshore to more permissive jurisdictions. Recent developments include the rise of Initial DEX Offerings (IDOs) and Fair Launch models, which attempt to create more equitable token distribution mechanisms while navigating regulatory requirements. These approaches often involve gradual token distributions through decentralized exchanges or earned allocations based on community participation, rather than traditional fundraising.

The infrastructure supporting token offerings has also matured significantly. Legal frameworks, technical standards, and best practices have emerged for conducting compliant token sales. Specialized service providers now assist with various aspects of token offerings, from legal compliance to technical implementation. This makes it easier for legitimate projects to conduct token sales while raising the barriers for potential bad actors. Looking forward, the token offering landscape appears to be moving toward more regulated, transparent offerings with stronger investors as well as consumer protection.

CHAPTER 13   TECHNOLOGICAL REVOLUTIONS AND FINANCIAL CAPITAL MARKETS

Regulatory Updates for Blockchain Platforms in 2025

The US regulatory framework for blockchain technology represents a complex interplay of multiple federal and state-level authorities, each with distinct jurisdictional claims and enforcement approaches. Given that the regulatory landscape evolves rapidly, the following are some major updates from the last three years:

1. The Securities and Exchange Commission's application of the Howey Test has evolved significantly since the 2017 DAO Report, which first established that digital tokens could be classified as securities. In practice, this has led to enforcement actions against numerous projects, including the landmark cases against Ripple Labs (alleging XRP as an unregistered security), Telegram's GRAM token (resulting in a $1.7 billion refund to investors), and Kik's KIN token offering (concluding with a $5 million settlement). More recently, in June 2023, the SEC filed charges against Binance and Coinbase for operating unregistered securities exchanges. Additionally, in July 2023, a district court ruled that XRP was not a security in secondary market sales, marking a significant development in the Ripple case. The SEC has also expanded its focus to decentralized finance (DeFi) protocols, arguing that automated market makers (AMMs) and liquidity pools may constitute investment contracts, particularly when platform tokens are distributed to liquidity providers.

CHAPTER 13   TECHNOLOGICAL REVOLUTIONS AND FINANCIAL CAPITAL MARKETS

2. The CFTC's jurisdiction has been reinforced through several court decisions, most notably CFTC v. McDonnell and CFTC v. My Big Coin Pay, Inc., which affirmed cryptocurrencies as commodities under the Commodity Exchange Act. This classification has significant implications for derivative products, requiring platforms like CME Group and Bakkt to register and comply with comprehensive regulatory requirements. These include maintaining substantial financial resources, implementing risk management systems, and establishing customer protection mechanisms. For instance, CME's Bitcoin futures must maintain initial margin requirements typically ranging from 35% to 40% of contract value, significantly higher than traditional commodity futures.

3. The regulatory framework for decentralized applications has become increasingly sophisticated, with FinCEN's guidance extending beyond traditional cryptocurrency exchanges to encompass various DeFi protocols. For example, decentralized exchanges (DEXs) implementing automated market maker protocols must navigate complex compliance requirements if they meet the definition of a money transmitter. This includes implementing know-your-customer (KYC) procedures, even in architecturally decentralized systems. Uniswap's introduction of a limited front-end screening mechanism for certain addresses illustrates the practical challenges of balancing regulatory compliance with decentralization principles. FinCEN's

requirements extend to maintaining comprehensive transaction records for five years, filing Suspicious Activity Reports (SARs) for transactions exceeding $5,000 where suspicious activity is detected, and implementing risk-based customer due diligence programs.

4. Node operators face varying compliance obligations based on their network participation level. In proof-of-stake networks like Ethereum 2.0, validators must maintain minimum stake requirements (32 ETH for Ethereum) and ensure high uptime to avoid penalties. The SEC's scrutiny of staking services, shown by the investigation into Kraken's staking program (resulting in a $30 million settlement), has created regulatory uncertainty for node operators offering pooled staking services. Technical requirements for node operators often include maintaining specific hardware configurations (minimum CPU cores, RAM, and storage specifications), implementing secure key management systems, and ensuring network connectivity meets minimum bandwidth requirements. Ethereum validators must maintain at least 99% uptime and face slashing penalties for malicious behavior or extended downtime.

5. The European Union's Markets in Crypto-Assets (MiCA) regulation represents the most comprehensive regulatory framework globally, establishing detailed requirements for different types of crypto-assets. Asset-referenced tokens must maintain a reserve of assets at a 1:1 ratio,

with specific liquidity requirements and stress testing protocols. E-money tokens must be issued only by authorized credit institutions or e-money institutions with minimum capital requirements of €350,000 or 2% of average outstanding e-money. Crypto-asset service providers must maintain professional indemnity insurance or comparable guarantees, with coverage requirements based on the nature and size of their operations. Technical standards under MiCA mandate specific cybersecurity measures, including regular penetration testing, vulnerability assessments, and incident response protocols.

6. Smart contract development faces increasingly stringent requirements under various regulatory frameworks. The EU's GDPR compliance necessitates innovative technical solutions, such as the implementation of state channels for private data processing or zero-knowledge proofs for verification without data exposure. Smart contract auditing requirements are becoming standardized, with major jurisdictions requiring formal verification processes, security audits by accredited firms, and ongoing monitoring systems. For example, the Dubai Financial Services Authority (DFSA) requires smart contracts deployed within its jurisdiction to undergo independent security audits and maintain clear upgrade mechanisms for bug fixes.

7. Decentralized autonomous organizations (DAOs) face evolving regulatory frameworks across jurisdictions. Wyoming's DAO LLC law (Bill 38) provides specific requirements for DAO registration, including maintaining a registered agent in Wyoming and implementing specific governance mechanisms. More state-specific DAO regulation is discussed in Chapter 9. The law requires DAOs to specify their governance structure in smart contracts, maintain clear voting procedures, and establish dispute resolution mechanisms. Technical requirements include implementing multi-signature schemes for treasury management, maintaining transparent governance tokens, and ensuring voting mechanisms are resistant to manipulation. For example, Compound's Governor Alpha and Bravo smart contracts implement time-locked execution periods and quorum requirements for governance decisions.

8. The Financial Action Task Force's (FATF) Travel Rule implementation has spawned various technical solutions, including the InterVASP Messaging Standard (IVMS101) and the OpenVASP protocol. These standards require VASPs to exchange specific customer information for transactions exceeding 1,000 USD/EUR, including originator and beneficiary names, account numbers, and physical addresses. Technical solutions must ensure secure message encryption, maintain data privacy, and provide audit trails for compliance verification. The

CHAPTER 13   TECHNOLOGICAL REVOLUTIONS AND FINANCIAL CAPITAL MARKETS

development of decentralized identity solutions and zero-knowledge proof systems has become crucial for compliance while preserving privacy.

9. International tax reporting requirements have led to the development of sophisticated tracking systems. For example, the US Infrastructure Bill's expanded definition of broker includes various blockchain network participants, requiring them to issue 1099-B forms for transactions. This has spurred the development of automated tax reporting solutions that can track complex DeFi interactions, including liquidity provision, yield farming, and token swaps. Technical requirements include maintaining detailed transaction histories, calculating cost basis across multiple protocols, and generating compliant tax documents.

10. In the realm of technical compliance, blockchain networks must implement specific security measures based on regulatory requirements. This includes maintaining NIST-compliant cryptographic standards, implementing key rotation procedures, and ensuring secure backup systems. Network operators must often maintain ISO 27001 certification, SOC 2 Type II attestations, and specific disaster recovery capabilities. For example, custody solutions must implement multi-signature schemes with specific threshold requirements (typically n-of-m where m > n), maintain geographically distributed key fragments, and implement time-locked recovery procedures.

CHAPTER 13   TECHNOLOGICAL REVOLUTIONS AND FINANCIAL CAPITAL MARKETS

11. The emergence of central bank digital currencies (CBDCs) has introduced additional regulatory considerations for blockchain networks. Technical requirements for CBDC integration include implementing specific consensus mechanisms (often permissioned variants), maintaining predetermined transaction throughput capabilities, and ensuring interoperability with existing payment systems. For example, China's Digital Currency Electronic Payment (DC/EP) system requires participating nodes to maintain specific hardware security modules (HSMs) and implement real-time monitoring capabilities.

12. With the introduction of new technologies like zero-knowledge proofs, Layer 2 scaling solutions, and cross-chain bridges, new regulatory frameworks must be designed. These innovations require specific compliance frameworks addressing issues like transaction privacy, asset portability, and cross-jurisdictional transfers. Technical standards are emerging for cross-chain communication protocols, oracle services, and bridge security mechanisms. For example, the development of zkEVM solutions requires compliance with both existing smart contract regulations and new requirements for zero-knowledge proof generation and verification.

13. Cross-border payment systems utilizing blockchain technology must comply with the Bank for International Settlements (BIS) principles for Financial Market Infrastructure (FMI). These requirements include maintaining real-time gross

settlement (RTGS) capabilities, implementing specific liquidity saving mechanisms, and ensuring payment finality. For instance, Ripple's RippleNet must maintain compliance with these principles while operating across multiple jurisdictions, implementing specific protocol-level features like partial payments, escrow mechanisms, and multi-hop payment routing. The technical requirements include maintaining deterministic transaction ordering, implementing Byzantine fault tolerance up to n/3 faulty nodes, and ensuring transaction settlement finality within predefined timeframes.

14. The regulation of stablecoins has become increasingly stringent, particularly following the collapse of algorithmic stablecoins like Terra/LUNA. The Basel Committee's proposed prudential treatment of stablecoin exposures requires banks to maintain risk-weighted assets based on the underlying reserve assets' composition. For example, stablecoins backed entirely by high-quality liquid assets (HQLA) face lower capital requirements compared with those with more volatile reserves. Technical requirements for stablecoin issuers include implementing real-time reserve monitoring systems, maintaining automated rebalancing mechanisms, and ensuring transparent attestation procedures. The New York Department of Financial Services (NYDFS) guidance on stablecoins mandates specific reserve composition requirements, monthly attestations, and redemption capabilities within 24 hours.

15. Privacy-focused blockchain networks face particular regulatory scrutiny under various anti-money laundering (AML) frameworks. The Financial Action Task Force's updated guidance on virtual assets specifically addresses privacy coins and enhanced anonymity services. Networks implementing privacy features must maintain specific transaction monitoring capabilities while preserving user privacy. For example, Monero's implementation of ring signatures and stealth addresses must be balanced against regulatory requirements for transaction tracing. Technical solutions include implementing view keys for voluntary disclosure, maintaining specific mining algorithms resistant to ASIC centralization, and implementing robust network analysis tools for detecting suspicious patterns.

16. The regulation of oracle services, which provide external data to blockchain networks, has emerged as a critical area of focus. The European Securities and Markets Authority (ESMA) has proposed specific requirements for oracle providers, including maintaining data quality standards, implementing redundancy mechanisms, and ensuring transparent price discovery processes. Technical requirements include implementing fault-tolerant consensus mechanisms for data validation, maintaining specific node operator requirements for data providers, and implementing cryptographic proof systems for data authenticity. Chainlink's decentralized oracle networks, for instance, must

maintain specific security deposits, implement minimum node operator requirements, and ensure data source diversity.

17. Governance token regulations have evolved to address the specific challenges of decentralized protocol management. The SEC's framework for analyzing digital assets has been expanded to consider governance tokens' specific characteristics, including voting rights, value accrual mechanisms, and protocol revenue distribution. Technical requirements for governance systems include implementing time-locked execution periods, maintaining specific quorum requirements, and ensuring vote delegation capabilities. For example, Aave's governance framework must implement specific proposal threshold requirements, maintain voting periods of predefined lengths, and ensure transparent execution of approved proposals.

18. Layer 2 scaling architectures also face regulatory requirements concerning transaction finality, fund security, and cross-layer communication. The technical specifications include maintaining specific fraud-proof systems for optimistic rollups, implementing zero-knowledge proof generation and verification for ZK-Rollups, and ensuring secure state transition mechanisms. Arbitrum's optimistic rollup implementation, for instance, must maintain a challenge period of specific length, implement secure bridge contracts, and ensure transaction data availability on the base layer.

CHAPTER 13   TECHNOLOGICAL REVOLUTIONS AND FINANCIAL CAPITAL MARKETS

19. The regulation of cross-chain bridges has become increasingly important following several high-profile security incidents. Technical requirements include implementing specific security measures for custody of bridged assets, maintaining secure signature schemes for cross-chain message-passing, and ensuring proper validation of cross-chain state transitions. For example, bridging solutions must implement specific threshold signature schemes, maintain secure key management systems, and ensure proper validation of cross-chain messages through relay networks.

20. Insurance requirements for blockchain networks have evolved to address specific risks associated with smart contract failures, oracle malfunctions, and network attacks. Technical requirements include implementing specific monitoring systems for detecting anomalous behavior, maintaining audit trails for claims processing, and ensuring proper coverage validation through on-chain mechanisms. For instance, Nexus Mutual's smart contract coverage system must implement specific risk assessment models, maintain capital adequacy ratios, and ensure transparent claims processing procedures.

21. The emergence of regulated DeFi platforms has introduced new compliance requirements for automated market makers and lending protocols. Technical specifications include implementing specific risk management systems, maintaining proper collateralization ratios, and ensuring

CHAPTER 13   TECHNOLOGICAL REVOLUTIONS AND FINANCIAL CAPITAL MARKETS

transparent price discovery mechanisms. For example, Compound's money market protocol must maintain specific interest rate models, implement automatic liquidation procedures, and ensure proper oracle price feed integration.

22. NFT marketplaces face increasing regulatory scrutiny regarding intellectual property rights, royalty enforcement, and transaction monitoring. Technical requirements include implementing specific metadata standards, maintaining proper royalty distribution mechanisms, and ensuring compliance with copyright laws. For instance, OpenSea's implementation must maintain specific creator verification systems, implement royalty enforcement mechanisms, and ensure proper tracking of secondary market sales.

23. The regulation of blockchain-based identity systems has evolved to address specific privacy and security requirements. Technical specifications include implementing specific credential issuance procedures, maintaining proper revocation mechanisms, and ensuring compliance with data protection regulations. For example, the European Self-Sovereign Identity Framework requires specific technical standards for credential formats, maintains trust registry requirements, and ensures proper verification procedures.

24. Metaverse platforms utilizing blockchain technology face emerging regulations concerning virtual asset ownership, interoperability standards,

and user protection. Technical requirements include implementing specific asset standardization protocols, maintaining proper transfer mechanisms between virtual worlds, and ensuring secure storage of digital assets. For instance, platforms must implement specific protocol standards for virtual land ownership, maintain proper rendering engines for NFT display, and ensure secure communication between different metaverse instances.

25. EU's Markets in Crypto-Assets (MiCA) framework entered into force on June 29, 2023, with stablecoin provisions implemented on June 30, 2024, and the full regulation becoming applicable on December 30, 2024. This comprehensive framework requires crypto-asset service providers (CASPs) to apply for licenses starting January 2025, with a grandfathering period allowing existing providers up to 18 months to achieve full compliance. In response to these requirements, industry leaders including Hedera, Aptos Foundation, and Ripple formed the MiCA Crypto Alliance in September 2024 to help service providers streamline compliance with the new regulations.

26. Most recently, the regulatory landscape in the United States has also been dramatically reshaped by the SEC v. Ripple Labs case that we touched in the beginning of this list and the subsequent developments. In July 2023, a federal judge ruled that XRP sales (on public exchanges) were not securities, while institutional sales were subject to securities regulations—an important distinction

CHAPTER 13   TECHNOLOGICAL REVOLUTIONS AND FINANCIAL CAPITAL MARKETS

that clarified how cryptocurrencies are classified based on their method of distribution rather than their inherent nature. In March 2025, the SEC ended its appeal of this ruling, and these changes signal a more accommodating regulatory approach with clear frameworks for legitimate blockchain innovation while maintaining appropriate investor protections.

Summary

The integration of blockchain with AI might represent a new paradigm of technological revolution that diverges from the Perez framework. Relatively speaking, LLMs are still in nascency, the next five to ten years; as the race toward artificial general intelligence gets more heated, a new paradigm will emerge, completely making the World Wide Web a footprint in history.

Bibliography

Perez, C. (2010). Technological revolutions and techno-economic paradigms. *Cambridge Journal of Economics*, 34(1), 185–202. https://doi.org/10.1093/cje/bep051

Perez, C. *Technological Revolutions and Financial Capital: The Dynamics of Bubbles and Golden Ages*. Edward Elgar Publishing, 2002.

Yang, S., Guo, M., Liu, B., & Li, H. (2024). AI-powered blockchain technology in industry 4.0: A review. *International Journal of Technology Management*, 2(1), 1–15. https://doi.org/10.1016/j.ijtm.2024.000015

Coluccia, B., Di Noia, A., & Melegoni, E. (2023). An analysis of the MiCA regulation and its impact for the blockchain-based economies. In *Smart Data and Digital Technologies for Sustainable Development* (pp. 285–294). Springer Nature.

De Filippi, P. & Wright, A. *Blockchain and the Law: The Rule of Code*. Harvard University Press, 2018.

Teslya, N. & Smirnov, A. (2024). On the integration of artificial intelligence and blockchain technology: A perspective about security. *IEEE Access*, 12, 21958–21975. https://doi.org/10.1109/ACCESS.2024.3355428

Kshetri, N. & Voas, J. (2023). Blockchain-enabled decentralized artificial intelligence. *IEEE Computer*, 56(4), 60–69.

Dillenberger, D. N., Novotny, P., & Zhang, Q. (2019). Blockchain analytics and artificial intelligence. *IBM Journal of Research and Development*, 63(2), 1–10.

Teichmann, F. M. J., Boticiu, S. R., & Sergi, B. S. (2024). The EU MiCA directive—chances and risks from a compliance perspective. *Journal of Money Laundering Control*, 27(2), 275–283. https://doi.org/10.1108/JMLC-02-2023-0030

Mazzucato, M. & Perez, C. (2015). Innovation as growth policy: The challenge for Europe. In The *Triple Challenge for Europe: Economic Development, Climate Change, and Governance* (pp. 229–264). Oxford University Press.

CHAPTER 14

Blockchain-as-a-Service

Blockchain-as-a-Service (BaaS) represents a cloud-based architectural paradigm that democratizes blockchain technology by abstracting away the underlying infrastructure for new startups and businesses. This model allows organizations to experiment with the blockchain ecosystem without having to develop and maintain their own infrastructure. BaaS platforms usually provide pre-configured blockchain networks and nodes, APIs, and toolkits that allow enterprises to deploy decentralized applications (DApps), smart contracts, as well as various blockchain-based consensus mechanisms. Modern BaaS implementations operate on a three-tier architecture: infrastructure layer (handling computation, storage, and networking), blockchain protocol layer (managing consensus, smart contracts, and chain state), and application layer (providing APIs, development tools, and monitoring capabilities). This abstraction allows enterprises to focus on business logic and application development while the platform handles complex tasks such as node provisioning, network security, and blockchain protocol updates. The following is a technical overview of the major players in the BaaS marketplace.

CHAPTER 14   BLOCKCHAIN-AS-A-SERVICE

Updates on BaaS Providers

1. Amazon Web Services (AWS) offers Amazon Managed Blockchain, a fully managed service that supports Hyperledger Fabric and Ethereum. Hyperledger Fabric is an enterprise-focused blockchain framework that allows businesses to create permissioned networks with configurable governance, while Ethereum on AWS provides a decentralized environment for public and private Ethereum networks. AWS handles node provisioning, network security, and scalability while integrating with other AWS services such as Amazon S3, AWS Key Management Service (KMS) for encryption, and AWS Identity and Access Management (IAM) for access control. It supports auto-scaling, cross-region deployment, and monitoring via Amazon CloudWatch. For Amazon Managed Blockchain, AWS provides specific technical enterprise features to deploy sophisticated blockchains. When creating a Hyperledger Fabric network, organizations can configure up to five ordering nodes using RAFT consensus protocol, with each member able to create up to 50 peer nodes. These peer nodes support both LevelDB and CouchDB as state databases, with CouchDB enabling complex queries on JSON-formatted ledger data. For Ethereum networks, AWS supports Geth clients with customizable gas limits and mining difficulties. A practical example is a supply chain consortium where members deploy chaincode

CHAPTER 14 BLOCKCHAIN-AS-A-SERVICE

(smart contracts) using the Fabric SDK, with event listeners triggering lambda functions when specific transactions occur. Organizations can implement private data collections with collections_config.json to segregate sensitive data while maintaining a hash of that data on the main channel for auditing purposes.

2. Microsoft's Azure Blockchain Service (now part of the Web3 application platform) was a managed blockchain network that supported Ethereum, Hyperledger Fabric, Corda, and Quorum. Though Microsoft discontinued the standalone blockchain service in 2021, it still offers a scalable blockchain service via Azure Confidential Ledger and integrations with Ethereum-based applications using Azure Kubernetes Service (AKS). Companies can deploy Ethereum-based applications on Azure using Azure Virtual Machines and leverage Azure's security features, including Azure Active Directory (AAD) and Azure Key Vault for cryptographic key management. Organizations can deploy Ethereum nodes using Helm charts, with each node running in separate pods for improved isolation and scalability. Azure also provides Logic Apps, enabling integration with external data sources. A real-world implementation might involve a financial services company deploying a private Ethereum network using proof-of-authority consensus, where validator nodes run on Azure Virtual Machines with managed disks for persistent storage. Azure also offers the Confidential Consortium Framework (CCF), an open

source framework designed for building secure, high-performance, and confidential blockchain applications. CCF can instantiate trusted execution environments for a high degree of data integrity and confidentiality, making it suitable for enterprise scenarios requiring secure multi-party computations.

3. IBM's Blockchain Platform is built on Hyperledger Fabric, offering enterprise-grade security, scalability, and governance. Unlike fully managed services, IBM provides a Blockchain-as-a-Service model, where businesses can deploy blockchain networks on-premises, on IBM Cloud, or any other cloud provider. IBM's platform includes automated network deployment, decentralized governance, and APIs to integrate existing enterprise applications. It also supports IBM Cloud Kubernetes Service (IKS) and IBM Cloud Hyper Protect Crypto Services, offering confidential computing capabilities. IBM's Fabric implementation allows for pluggable consensus mechanisms, fine-grained permission control, and privacy-preserving channels for selective data sharing among network participants. IBM Blockchain Platform has a few unique Fabric-specific technical sophistications. The platform supports Certificate Authorities (CAs) for each organization, with separate CAs for TLS certificates and identity certificates. Organizations can define custom MSP (Membership Service Provider) configurations and implement attribute-based access control (ABAC) within chaincode.

CHAPTER 14 BLOCKCHAIN-AS-A-SERVICE

A practical application involves a healthcare consortium where each hospital runs its own peer nodes, with private data collections storing patient records. The platform's hardware security module (HSM) integration ensures secure key storage, while the smart contract lifecycle management allows for chaincode to be upgraded without network downtime. IBM's implementation supports both Raft and Kafka-based ordering services, with the ability to add or remove ordering nodes dynamically.

4. Oracle Blockchain Cloud Service (OBCS) is a fully managed Hyperledger Fabric implementation optimized for enterprise use cases such as supply chain tracking, financial transactions, and identity management. Oracle's blockchain service features REST APIs for integration with existing enterprise software, pre-configured smart contract templates, and on-chain identity management. It also supports high availability and disaster recovery, ensuring blockchain nodes remain operational even in failure scenarios. Oracle provides extensive monitoring via Oracle Cloud Infrastructure (OCI) logging and analytics tools. Among the enterprise features, the service implements a multi-layer architecture where each organization can maintain multiple peers with distinct roles (endorsing, committing, or anchor peers). The REST API also has endpoints for chaincode invocation, with custom event subscriptions that can trigger Oracle Functions (serverless compute). A common implementation

involves a trade finance network where banks use pre-built chaincode templates for letter of credit operations. The service supports dynamic channel creation and management, with the ability to implement private data collections using collection_config.json files. Organizations can leverage Oracle's blockchain tables for immutable off-chain storage and integrate with Oracle Integration Cloud for connecting with external systems.

5. Alibaba Cloud BaaS supports Hyperledger Fabric, Ant Blockchain Open Alliance, and Quorum, providing a high-performance environment for building and deploying blockchain applications. Alibaba's service is integrated with Alibaba Cloud Security, Database, and Artificial Intelligence services, making it a popular choice among enterprises operating in Asia-Pacific regions. It offers multi-cloud support, permissioned network management, and cross-chain interoperability. With Alibaba's AI-powered blockchain monitoring and anomaly detection, businesses also benefit from fraud prevention and improved security. The platform supports Hyperledger Fabric networks with customizable endorsement policies using JavaScript conditions. Organizations can implement channel-based privacy with the ability to create multiple channels for different business scenarios. A typical implementation might involve a logistics network where each participant runs multiple peer nodes with different roles. The platform's integration with Alibaba Cloud Container Service

CHAPTER 14 BLOCKCHAIN-AS-A-SERVICE

for Kubernetes (ACK) enables automatic scaling of blockchain nodes based on transaction volume. The service also supports cross-chain protocols for interoperability between different blockchain networks, with built-in monitoring using Prometheus and Grafana dashboards.

6. Google Cloud offers Blockchain Node Engine, a managed node hosting service for Ethereum and other blockchain networks. While Google Cloud does not provide a full BaaS solution like AWS or IBM, it focuses on streamlined node deployment, maintenance, and security enhancements. The service ensures high uptime, automatic syncing, and optimized network connectivity. Google Cloud also collaborates with projects like Polygon, Solana, and Hedera, offering blockchain analytics and AI-powered insights via BigQuery Public Datasets. Developers can integrate blockchain applications with Google Cloud's AI, ML, and data analytics services. The service supports both full and archive nodes, with customizable retention periods for historical data. Organizations can implement Virtual Private Cloud (VPC) Service Controls to restrict access to node endpoints. A practical example involves a gaming company deploying multiple Ethereum nodes across regions for low-latency access to their NFT marketplace. The platform integrates with Cloud KMS for key management and Cloud Armor for DDoS protection. Developers can use Cloud Functions to automate responses to smart contract events and implement Cloud Load Balancing for distributed access to node endpoints.

CHAPTER 14 BLOCKCHAIN-AS-A-SERVICE

7. ConsenSys, the company behind MetaMask and Infura, provides Quorum Blockchain Service (QBS), a managed service based on Quorum—an enterprise-grade version of Ethereum. Quorum enables privacy-enhanced smart contracts, permissioned governance, and on-chain identity management. QBS supports private transactions, enterprise-grade key management, and integration with MetaMask Institutional for secure enterprise wallet management. It is designed for financial services, supply chain tracking, and digital asset tokenization. The platform implements a privacy manager using Tessera, which handles private transaction data through secure enclave technology. Organizations can configure multiple privacy groups within a single network, each with its own private state database. Additionally, Quorum supports both Raft and IBFT (Istanbul Byzantine Fault Tolerance) consensus mechanisms, with configurable block times and gas limits. A typical implementation might involve a consortium of banks using private smart contracts for interbank settlements, where transaction details are only visible to participating parties. The platform integrates with MetaMask Institutional, providing hardware security module (HSM) integration for key management and custom approval workflows. Developers can leverage the platform's GraphQL API for efficient querying of blockchain data, while the privacy manager's P2P discovery mechanism enables dynamic node participation.

CHAPTER 14   BLOCKCHAIN-AS-A-SERVICE

8. R3 offers Corda Network as a Service, providing managed node hosting, workflow automation, and regulatory compliance features. R3's Corda is a permissioned blockchain designed for financial institutions, supply chain consortia, and regulated industries. It integrates with HSM-backed key management solutions and enterprise ERP/CRM systems. Unlike traditional blockchains, Corda operates on a transaction-based model whereby only relevant parties see the data. Instead of a global ledger, Corda implements a point-to-point architecture where data is shared only between relevant parties. The platform uses notary clusters for transaction validation, supporting both validating and non-validating notaries with pluggable consensus algorithms. This privacy-centric architecture is ideal for banking, trade finance, and insurance applications. A practical implementation might involve an insurance network where claims processing is automated through CorDapps (Corda Distributed Applications). The platform's flow framework enables complex multi-party workflows, with checkpoint serialization for flow durability. Organizations can implement custom serialization schemes for complex data types and utilize the attachment framework for storing reference data. Corda Enterprise supports Intel SGX for confidential computing, allowing sensitive transaction logic to execute in secure enclaves. The platform's network map service handles node discovery and certificate management, while the built-in Hibernate integration enables efficient data persistence.

CHAPTER 14   BLOCKCHAIN-AS-A-SERVICE

9. Kaleido, a ConsenSys-backed BaaS provider, offers a multi-protocol blockchain cloud service supporting Ethereum, Hyperledger Fabric, and Corda. It features one-click blockchain network setup, enterprise middleware, governance tools, and built-in tokenization frameworks. Kaleido enables hybrid blockchain deployments, allowing businesses to run permissioned chains alongside public Ethereum networks. It also provides integrated identity solutions, API gateways, and private transaction capabilities. The platform implements a unique "Consortium-as-a-Service" model where organizations can deploy full-stack blockchain environments with pre-integrated tools and services. The service supports HD wallet management with role-based access control and customizable approval workflows. A typical implementation might involve a media rights management consortium using Ethereum-based smart contracts for content licensing and royalty distribution. The platform's AppCreds feature enables secure API authentication for external systems, while the Built-for-Enterprise transaction manager handles private transaction orchestration. Organizations can also implement zero-knowledge proof protocols for selective disclosure of transaction data and utilize the platform's event streaming service for real-time data integration. Kaleido's FireFly integration enables multi-party workflows with support for both on-chain and off-chain data management.

CHAPTER 14 BLOCKCHAIN-AS-A-SERVICE

10. Hedera is not a blockchain but a directed acyclic graph (DAG)–based distributed ledger technology that offers high-speed consensus, low transaction fees, and enterprise-grade security. Hedera Consensus Service (HCS) allows enterprises to leverage decentralized trust and tamper-proof logging without running their own blockchain nodes. It provides public and private key cryptography, state proofs, and low-latency transactions. Hedera is used for supply chain tracking, IoT authentication, and real-time payments. Hedera Hashgraph's technical architecture provides distinct advantages through its asynchronous Byzantine fault tolerance (aBFT) consensus mechanism. Hedera Consensus Service enables applications to create topics for ordered message delivery with guaranteed finality in seconds. A practical example involves a supply chain network using HCS for track-and-trace operations, where each logistics event generates a timestamped message with cryptographic proof of ordering. The platform's state proof system enables lightweight clients to verify transaction status without maintaining a full network history. Hedera's token service (HTS) supports native token creation with configurable properties like pause/resume functionality and KYC requirements. Organizations can leverage the file service for decentralized content addressing and the smart contract service for Solidity-based application logic. The platform's mirror node network provides scalable access to historical data through gRPC and REST APIs, while the network's guardian node structure ensures security through institutional diversity.

CHAPTER 14   BLOCKCHAIN-AS-A-SERVICE

BaaS Providers in 2025: A Decision Tree Approach

In 2025, selecting a BaaS provider involves analyzing multiple technical and business factors, including the type of blockchain (public, private, or hybrid), required transaction throughput, security, compliance needs, interoperability, and specific use case requirements. Below is a multi-layered decision tree to guide the selection process.

Step 1: Core Business Requirements Assessment

Primary use case definition: What type of blockchain network do you need?

- Permissioned enterprise blockchain (private/consortium)
    - Do you require more than 2,000 TPS?
        - **Yes**: Consider IBM Blockchain Platform (3,000 TPS), Oracle Blockchain Cloud (2,000 TPS).
        - **No**: Amazon Managed Blockchain (Hyperledger Fabric), Alibaba Cloud BaaS.
- Public blockchain
    - Do you prioritize transaction speed or decentralization?
        - **Speed**: Hedera Hashgraph (10,000 TPS, 3–5-second finality).
        - **Decentralization**: Amazon Managed Blockchain (Ethereum), Google Blockchain Node Engine.

Industry-specific considerations

- Financial services

    - Do you need real-time settlement? → R3 Corda (financial institutions), Hedera Hashgraph (low-latency payments).

    - Do you require regulatory compliance? → Hyperledger Fabric (IBM, Oracle) for financial institutions and banking.

- Supply chain

    - Do you need private transactions with selective disclosure? → Hyperledger Fabric.

    - Do you require cross-border operations? → Alibaba Cloud BaaS (Asia-based enterprises), Oracle Blockchain Cloud (enterprise integration).

- Healthcare and identity

    - Is HIPAA compliance required? → IBM Blockchain Platform, Oracle Blockchain Cloud.

    - Do you need self-sovereign identity (SSI)? → Hyperledger Fabric (with Indy integration for decentralized identity management).

Step 2: Technical Architecture Requirements

Consensus mechanism: What are your consensus priorities?

- Is finality speed critical? (Under 5 seconds)

    - **Yes**: Hedera Hashgraph (3–5 seconds), Quorum IBFT (4 seconds).

- **No**: Standard Ethereum-based proof-of-stake models may suffice.

- Do you need Byzantine fault tolerance (BFT)?

  - **Yes**: Hyperledger Fabric with PBFT/IBFT, R3 Corda, Hedera Hashgraph.

  - **No**: Raft consensus via Hyperledger Fabric (simpler leader–follower model).

Smart contract capabilities: What smart contract functionality do you require?

- Do you need Solidity compatibility?

  - **Yes**: Choose Ethereum-based services (AWS, Google, ConsenSys Quorum, Kaleido).

  - **No**: Consider Hyperledger Fabric (chaincode using Go, Node.js, Java).

- Do you require custom chaincode languages?

  - **Yes**: Hyperledger Fabric (Go, Node.js, Java support).

  - **No**: Simple ledger solutions like Hedera (no traditional smart contracts, uses native services) may suffice.

Data privacy requirements: How critical is transaction privacy?

- Do you need zero-knowledge proofs (ZKPs)?

  - **Yes**: ConsenSys Quorum, R3 Corda (for financial and private transactions).

  - **No**: Private channels or Fabric's chaincode-level access controls may be sufficient.

- Do you require hardware-based privacy protection?

  - **Yes**: Choose platforms with HSM (hardware security module) support → IBM Blockchain Platform, Oracle Blockchain Cloud.

  - **No**: Software-based encryption (Fabric's TLS/SSL, Ethereum's private transactions) is sufficient.

Step 3: Infrastructure and Integration

What is your current cloud infrastructure?

- Are you heavily invested in AWS?

  - **Yes**: Amazon Managed Blockchain (Ethereum and Hyperledger Fabric) offers native integration with 60+ AWS services (IAM, S3, CloudWatch).

  - **No**: Consider multi-cloud options.

- Do you need multi-cloud or on-premise support?

  - **Yes**: Kaleido, IBM Blockchain Platform (hybrid and multi-cloud support).

  - **No**: Single-cloud BaaS solutions like Oracle Blockchain Cloud and Amazon Managed Blockchain may suffice.

What are your security priorities?

- Do you need FIPS 140-2 certification (high-security encryption)?

  - **Yes**: Choose IBM Blockchain Platform, Oracle Blockchain Cloud.

  - **No**: Standard cloud security (AWS, Google, Kaleido) may be sufficient.

- Is enterprise-grade key management critical?
  - **Yes**: Ensure the platform supports external HSM integration (AWS KMS, IBM Cloud Hyper Protect Crypto Services).
  - **No**: Built-in cloud key management is sufficient.

Step 4: Operational Considerations

Performance requirements

- Do you need guaranteed throughput SLAs?
  - **Yes**: Consider enterprise blockchain platforms with performance guarantees → IBM Blockchain Platform, Oracle, R3 Corda.
  - **No**: Public blockchain-based BaaS (AWS Ethereum, Google Blockchain Node Engine) may be sufficient.
- Is latency a critical factor? (Sub-second finality)
  - **Yes**: Hedera Hashgraph (optimized consensus for high-speed transactions).
  - **No**: Standard Ethereum and Hyperledger Fabric configurations are acceptable.

Cost structure preferences

- Do you need predictable transaction costs?
  - **Yes**: Consider Hedera Hashgraph ($0.0001 per transaction), Hyperledger Fabric (fixed operational cost).
  - **No**: Usage-based pricing (Ethereum gas fees, AWS pay-per-node) might be acceptable.

- Is infrastructure cost a primary concern?

  - **Yes**: Consider managed services (AWS, Google, Kaleido) to reduce operational complexity.

  - **No**: Self-managed blockchain deployments may be more cost-effective.

Step 5: Compliance and Governance

Regulatory requirements

- Is GDPR compliance required?

  - **Yes**: Consider R3 Corda, IBM Blockchain Platform, Oracle Blockchain Cloud (privacy-enhanced architectures).

  - **No**: Other providers may suffice.

- Do you need SOC 2 certification?

  - **Yes**: Choose enterprise-grade providers (IBM, Oracle, AWS).

  - **No**: Public blockchain solutions like Ethereum BaaS are acceptable.

Governance structure

- Do you need consortium-based governance?

  - **Yes**: Consider Kaleido (multi-party governance), Enterprise Hyperledger Fabric.

  - **No**: Single-organization blockchain governance is adequate.

- Is automated compliance monitoring required?
    - **Yes**: Choose platforms with built-in audit capabilities (IBM, Oracle, R3 Corda).
    - **No**: Manual compliance monitoring is acceptable.

Use Case Summary

Use Case	Recommended BaaS Provider
Financial services (DeFi, tokenization, trade finance)	ConsenSys Quorum, Amazon Managed Blockchain (Ethereum), R3 Corda
Supply chain tracking	IBM Blockchain Platform (Hyperledger Fabric), Oracle Blockchain Cloud, AWS (Hyperledger Fabric)
Healthcare data and identity	Hyperledger Fabric (IBM, AWS), Hedera Hashgraph (tamper-proof records)
Public blockchain applications	Google Blockchain Node Engine (Ethereum), Amazon Managed Blockchain (Ethereum)
High-speed transactions (IoT, gaming, real-time payments)	Hedera Hashgraph, Corda Enterprise

Security in BaaS

In this section, we briefly want to review the various attack vectors in BaaS deployments and the countermeasures developed. On BaaS platforms, safe implementation of key management is a major security priority. Modern hardware security module (HSM) platforms typically operate with dedicated cryptographic coprocessors that handle operations like key generation, digital signatures, and encryption without exposing private keys to the main system memory. For example, AWS KMS integrates with

CHAPTER 14   BLOCKCHAIN-AS-A-SERVICE

CloudHSM using PKCS#11 interfaces, allowing for automatic key rotation and versioning while maintaining FIPS 140-2 Level 3 compliance. The emerging secure multi-party computation (MPC) protocols, particularly Shamir's Secret Sharing scheme, distribute key fragments across multiple parties using polynomial interpolation, where a key can only be reconstructed when a threshold number of parties combine their shares. Regarding consensus-layer attacks, the 51% attack vulnerability in proof-of-work systems is particularly concerning due to the increasing centralization of mining pools. In Bitcoin, for instance, the theoretical cost of a 51% attack has been estimated based on hardware costs (ASICs) and electricity consumption. Proof-of-stake systems implement different security models, where the Casper FFG protocol in Ethereum 2.0 requires validators to lock up 32 ETH as collateral. The Nothing-at-Stake problem is addressed through slashing conditions that monitor equivocation (signing multiple blocks at the same height) and inactivity, with penalties that can result in the loss of up to 100% of staked assets.

Smart contract vulnerabilities represent a significant attack surface in BaaS platforms. Reentrancy attacks, famously exemplified in the 2016 DAO hack, exploit the fact that Ethereum's EVM continues execution before external calls are completed. These attacks occur when a malicious contract makes repeated external calls to a vulnerable contract before the first transaction completes, potentially draining funds through multiple withdrawals. To mitigate reentrancy risks, BaaS providers should implement the checks–effects–interactions pattern, which ensures all internal state updates occur before making external calls. Using reentrancy guards and mutex locks can prevent simultaneous access to critical functions. Integer overflow protection through SafeMath libraries implements modular arithmetic checks, adding gas costs but preventing catastrophic overflow scenarios. Modern Solidity versions (0.8.0+) include built-in overflow checking, though explicit SafeMath usage remains common for compatibility and clarity. Oracle manipulation has emerged as another significant vulnerability in BaaS environments. Oracles connect smart contracts to off-chain data (real-world events, price feeds, random number generation), but attackers can distort market prices through methods like spoofing, ramping, and wash trading. To address oracle issues, BaaS platforms should integrate decentralized oracle networks like Chainlink or Tellor and implement multi-oracle architectures to increase the difficulty and cost of manipulating input data. Unchecked external calls represent another critical vulnerability that BaaS providers must address. These occur when smart contracts fail to properly validate return values from external contract calls, potentially leading to unexpected behavior and security breaches. Smart contracts should always implement proper error handling for external calls and avoid making assumptions about external contract behavior.

Network-layer security in blockchain networks involves complex peer discovery and message propagation mechanisms. Eclipse attacks are particularly sophisticated, requiring attackers to manipulate the peer selection algorithm by flooding the network with malicious nodes. Kademlia-based peer discovery uses XOR metric distance calculations to maintain diverse peer connections, making it harder for attackers to isolate honest nodes. The implementation of reputation systems in PoS networks often involves scoring mechanisms based on uptime, response latency, and validation accuracy, creating economic disincentives for Sybil attacks.

Despite growing awareness of quantum computing threats, enterprise readiness for post-quantum cryptography (PQC) remains insufficient. Many organizations understand the potential risks, but few have begun actively implementing PQC solutions, creating a significant preparedness gap. The most pressing concern is the "harvest now, decrypt later" (HNDL) attack, where adversaries capture encrypted data today to decrypt it when quantum computers become powerful enough—placing intellectual property, customer records, and confidential communications at risk. Industry experts estimate that some aspects of PQC migration will likely take nearly a decade, with significant implementation challenges and costs. The US government is adopting new PQC standards, but many

CHAPTER 14   BLOCKCHAIN-AS-A-SERVICE

organizations lack the necessary software development resources to implement such changes. NIST has announced plans to begin deprecating traditional public key cryptography (RSA and ECDSA) by 2030, with complete disallowance by 2035. This accelerated timeline creates urgency for BaaS providers and enterprises to develop comprehensive migration plans. Major technology companies like Meta are implementing hybrid approaches to PQC, combining traditional and quantum-resistant algorithms to maintain security during the transition period.

Post-quantum cryptography approaches like lattice-based systems use mathematical problems that remain hard even for quantum computers. CRYSTALS-Dilithium, for example, bases its security on the Module Learning With Errors (MLWE) problem, generating signatures that are significantly larger than current ECDSA signatures but resistant to quantum attacks. For effective PQC implementation, enterprises must develop detailed transition plans with clear timelines and evaluate their security plans comprehensively. Similarly, Blockchain-as-a-Service providers must prioritize cryptographic agility in their platforms, allowing customers to seamlessly transition between cryptographic algorithms as standards evolve. This includes developing modular security components, implementing hybrid cryptographic approaches, and ensuring infrastructure can support larger key sizes and signature formats required by post-quantum algorithms.

The regulatory landscape for BaaS platforms requires sophisticated technical solutions for compliance. Zero-knowledge proofs, particularly zk-SNARKs (Zero-Knowledge Succinct Non-interactive Arguments of Knowledge), enable privacy-preserving verification of transactions while maintaining regulatory compliance. These systems use elliptic curve pairings to create constant-size proofs regardless of computation complexity, though they require a trusted setup phase. GDPR compliance in blockchain systems often implements off-chain storage patterns where sensitive data is stored in traditional databases, with only hashes or encrypted pointers stored on-chain, combined with verifiable credential systems for selective disclosure.

CHAPTER 14   BLOCKCHAIN-AS-A-SERVICE

Summary

In this chapter, we highlighted the technical architecture of major BaaS providers and the new updates in 2025 and outlined a decision tree for how to select a BaaS provider. Finally, we went over some security vulnerabilities in BaaS deployments and the key countermeasures being developed. Although the field is rapidly evolving, this chapter should provide a good overview of BaaS as well as Consortia-as-a-Service deployments.

Bibliography

National Institute of Standards and Technology. (2024, August 13). NIST releases first 3 finalized post-quantum encryption standards. https://www.nist.gov/news-events/news/2024/08/nist-releases-first-3-finalized-post-quantum-encryption-standards

Nguyen, T. M., Pham, H. S., & Duong, T. Q. (2023). A survey of post-quantum cryptography: Start of a new race. *Cryptography*, 7(3), 40. https://doi.org/10.3390/cryptography7030040

Singhal, S., Bhatia, K., & Rajpoot, A. (2024, August). Smart contract vulnerabilities detection using deep learning. In *2024 Sixteenth International Conference on Contemporary Computing (IC3-2024)*. https://doi.org/10.1145/3675888.3676070

Varghese, J. (2025, January 21). OWASP top 10 2025 - Most critical weaknesses exploited/discovered in smart contract. CyberSecurityNews. https://cybersecuritynews.com/owasp-top-10-2025-smart-contract/

OWASP Foundation. (2024). OWASP smart contract top 10. https://owasp.org/www-project-smart-contract-top-10/

CHAPTER 14   BLOCKCHAIN-AS-A-SERVICE

Snagg, F., & Wildner, A. (2024, January 30). Quantum computing and the financial sector: World Economic Forum lays out roadmap towards quantum security. Cleary Cybersecurity and Privacy Watch. https://www.clearycyberwatch.com/2024/01/quantum-computing-and-the-financial-sector-world-economic-forum-lays-out-roadmap-towards-quantum-security/

Roese, J. (2024, September 30). Post-quantum cryptography: A strategic imperative for enterprise resilience. Dell Technologies. https://www.dell.com/en-us/blog/post-quantum-cryptography-a-strategic-imperative-for-enterprise-resilience/

Singh, P. (2024, June 12). How to prevent top smart contract vulnerabilities in 2024. Deftsoft. https://deftsoft.com/blog/how-to-prevent-smart-contract-vulnerabilities-in-2024/

Fox, J. (2024, December 26). Smart contract security risks: Today's 10 top vulnerabilities. Cobalt. https://www.cobalt.io/blog/smart-contract-security-risks

CHAPTER 15

Lean Blockchain and AI

For developers interested in building blockchain products, simply investing time in the technology is not enough. The blockchain stack comprises business logic integrated deeply into the technology models. As a result, an introductory level of familiarity with frameworks that formally describe the components of a startup and how to build a company around a product is necessary. This chapter begins with Lean methodology, a model created by Eric Ries that relies on three core principles: 1) transform the most basic version of your idea into a product that a customer can interact with; 2) talk to your potential customers early and often; and 3) iterate over that basic model with feedback from your customer to achieve a full product that aligns with customer needs. And we keep in mind this quote from Eric: "As you consider building your own minimum viable product, let this simple rule suffice: remove any feature, process, or effort that does not contribute to the learning you seek." Then, we present the business model canvas that breaks down Lean methodology into nine applicable components. In addition, we talk about Geoffrey Moore's approach to product–market fit for high-risk, high-reward technologies. Following this discussion, we apply the Lean framework to AI startups and how building an AI product vastly differs from traditional software approaches.

CHAPTER 15 LEAN BLOCKCHAIN AND AI

After reviewing Lean principles, we explore their application in building Lean AI startups. Unlike traditional software products, where features can be clearly defined and implemented, AI solutions often yield probabilistic outcomes and rely heavily on data availability for performance improvements. This inherent dependency on data creates a "cold-start" problem—AI startups need data to deliver value but require users to generate that data. Additionally, these startups face fierce competition for skilled machine learning engineers and data scientists. Successfully building the next generation of AI startups demands not only advanced technical expertise but also strong business acumen to address real-life consumer needs.

Lean Methodology

Lean methodology is a set of principles for developing products that aims to iteratively question whether a proposed business model solves a problem that the customers actually want, rather than planning for a product without any endpoint customer in mind. This is accomplished by shorter product development cycles followed by multiple releases to get customer feedback, business hypothesis experimentation, and validated learning. Eric Ries is the founder of Lean methodology. It provides a framework for bringing high-risk, high-reward technologies like the blockchain to market. For any organization trying to incorporate blockchain or experiment with new services that can be offered on blockchain, a rigorous framework is necessary to assess whether the organization will benefit from a blockchain. The practical application of Lean methodologies will provide such a toolset, and in this section we want to introduce the fundamentals of Lean to you:

CHAPTER 15   LEAN BLOCKCHAIN AND AI

1. **Minimum viable product (MVP)**: Arguably the most important aspect of Lean methodology. A minimum viable product is the earliest version of a product with a limited number of features designed only to draw in early adopters for the purpose of obtaining data and feedback on the core concept. MVPs must be designed with the least amount of effort directed into assembly and yield the most amount of data about your product and ideas. For instance, a service offering custom stickers does not need to spend months designing intricate stickers. Instead, a simple landing page with a few sticker designs is enough to ask the more important question: do customers want those stickers? A landing page can test this hypothesis, and our MVP can provide guidance on how to update the product such that it aligns with the needs of our customers. The features packed in MVPs are rudimentary, but the purpose here is not to showcase unique features, but rather to get in front of customers as soon as possible. Carefully defining an MVP to be actionable and mining for customer data is the first step in successfully bringing a high-risk, high-reward product to market.

2. **Pivot**: During the iterative development of an MVP, customer interactions will provide valuable guidance on new features and updates to build. However, some customer interactions may point to deficiencies in your product and the need for fundamental changes to your core concept. At this point, you have two choices: either pivot or

persevere. A pivot is the idea of changing a very limited set of product attributes and generating a new MVP to prove that your core concept is evolving in sync with the demands of your customer. Having a limited number of changes allows you to examine the direct effect that maximizes your reach to the customer. On the other hand, a persevere approach is a bold risk that further experimentation and tweaking of your product will satisfy the customer. Eric Ries suggests that a metric of bandwidth for a startup is not necessarily capital, but the number of pivots it can make before the product is ready for mass adoption. Decisions to pivot are crucial branch points and therefore pose risks. The use of split-testing can greatly help stratify and reduce the risk.

3. **Product–market fit**: This is a stage in your iterative design when the MVP has become feature-rich and the early adopters are convincing more pragmatic users to try your product. Product–market fit places your product just at the cusp of reaching mass adoption. At this stage, you have validated all the hypotheses regarding your product, and the product is in sync with what the market needs. However, your product needs additional support from marketing and sales engines to capture the market and generate revenue. Essentially, the other services in a startup need to be built and deployed.

4. **Business hypothesis experimentation**: Assumptions are ingrained in product development (especially when developing a high-risk, high-reward idea), and each assumption carries a

risk of failure. Lean reframes the assumptions as hypotheses that need to be proven or disproven before the cycle of product development can progress further. This reduces the cumulative risk by ensuring that our assumptions are internally consistent and validated by the customer. A popular technique for hypothesis testing in Lean startup is called split-testing (or A/B testing). In A/B testing, we present two different design decisions to end users wherein half of the early adopters are shown one design feature and the other half are shown a different feature. Data is collected from both user groups to help determine which design choice was better appreciated by users. In addition, this data collection provides opportunities for direct customer interviews to gain more insight into how the user interacted with the new functionality. There are two major benefits to using this approach. First, you can directly gauge the impact of your work on users. As developers, we may obsess over writing more sophisticated code or developing interesting features that end users ultimately may not care about. Second, A/B testing eliminates conflicts around the priority of feature development—new features can be added to the MVP with each iteration and followed up with A/B testing. We can let data inform us about the features that a user considers relevant. In this manner, if a limited number of changes are made to the MVP, gathering data can reflect whether the changes translate to increased user retention and other parameters.

5. **Validated learning**: A/B testing is helpful only if you and your team have the discipline to analyze the experiments rigorously and learn from them. Eric Ries talks about three properties that contribute to validated learning, summarized as the three As—actionable, accessible, and auditable:

    - **Actionable**: Well-designed experiments will reveal a causal relationship between changes made to an MVP and new users acquired. These experiments generate data that is actionable as they provide a direction for future development.

    - **Accessible**: The data collected and metrics used must be simple and accessible to every member on the team. In particular, metrics can become very misleading to anyone collecting the data. As such, what we're trying to measure and the importance of those data points should be stated in the simplest possible terms and be open to comments from any member of the team.

    - **Auditable**: This is analogous to an independent review of your validated learning and experimental design process. Anyone should be able to go through the raw data and trace the metrics to reach the same recommendations for each iteration of your MVP. This builds rigor in the Lean startup model and adds data-based justifications for pivot or persevere decisions.

CHAPTER 15   LEAN BLOCKCHAIN AND AI

Note   Lean startup was adopted and transformed by the National Science Foundation into a formal curriculum for university-based researchers who want to commercialize their technology. The Innovation Corps (I-Corps) program trains teams of researchers and entrepreneurs for 12 weeks and equips them with the customer discovery skills. Every week is an iteration of the MVP based strictly on customer interviews, and the teams receive feedback from a panel of experts at the site hosting the I-Corps program. Each team comprises a technical lead, an entrepreneurship lead, and an I-Corps mentor. The teams are required to log weekly customer interviews and present updates to their business model canvas (which we discuss next). Major decisions such as pivot points are made based on documented data trends from interviews, making the whole customer interview process very rigorous.

Identifying and building the appropriate MVP can be very challenging. Steve Blank shares a fantastic example on his blog about how difficult and potentially misleading this task can be:

> *I ran into a small startup at Stanford who wants to fly Unmanned Aerial Vehicles (drones) with a* Hyper-spectral camera *over farm fields to collect* hyper-spectral images. *These images would be able to tell farmers how healthy their plants were, whether there were diseases or bugs, whether there was enough fertilizer, and enough water. (The camera has enough resolution to see individual plants.) Knowing this means farms can make better forecasts of how much their fields will produce, whether they should treat specific areas for pests, and put fertilizer and water only where it was needed.*

513

(Drones were better than satellites because of higher resolution and the potential for making more passes over the fields, and better than airplanes because of lower cost.)

All of this information would help farmers increase yields (making more money) and reduce costs by using less water and fertilizer/chemicals by only applying where it was needed.

Their plan was to be a data service provider in an emerging business called "precision agriculture." They would go out to a farmer's fields on a weekly basis, fly the drones, collect and process the data and then give it to the farmers in an easy understandable form.

Customer Discovery on Farms

I don't know what it is about Stanford, but this was the fourth or fifth startup I've seen in precision agriculture that used drones, robotics, high-tech sensors, etc. This team got my attention when they said, "Let us tell you about our conversations with potential customers." I listened, and as they described their customer interviews, it seemed like they had found that—yes, farmers do understand that not being able to see what was going on in detail on their fields was a problem—and yes—having data like this would be great—in theory.

So the team decided that this felt like a real business they wanted to build. And now they were out raising money to build a prototype minimum viable product (MVP). All good. Smart team, real domain experts in hyper-spectral imaging, drone design, good start on customer discovery, beginning to think about product/market fit, etc.

Lean Is Not an Engineering Process

They showed me their goals and budget for their next step. What they wanted was a happy early customer who recognized the value of their data and was willing to be an evangelist. Great goal.

CHAPTER 15   LEAN BLOCKCHAIN AND AI

They concluded that the only way to get a delighted early customer was to build a minimum viable product (MVP). They believed that the MVP needed to 1) demonstrate a drone flight, 2) make sure their software could stitch together all the images of a field, and then 3) present the data to the farmer in a way he could use it.

And they logically concluded that the way to do this was to buy a drone, buy a hyper-spectral camera, *buy the software for image processing, spend months of engineering time integrating the camera, platform and software together, etc. They showed me their barebones budget for doing all this. Logical.*

And wrong.

Keep Your Eyes on the Prize

The team confused the goal of the MVP (seeing if they could find a delighted farmer who would pay for the data) with the process of getting to the goal. They had the right goal but the wrong MVP to test it. Here's why.

The team's hypothesis was that they could deliver actionable data that farmers would pay for. Period. Since the startup defined itself as a data services company, at the end of the day, the farmer couldn't care less whether the data came from satellites, airplanes, drones, or magic as long as they had timely information.

That meant that all the work about buying a drone, a camera, software and time integrating it all was wasted time and effort—now. They did not need to test any of that yet. (There's plenty of existence proofs that low cost drones can be equipped to carry cameras.) They had defined the wrong MVP to test first. What they needed to spend their time on was first testing whether farmers cared about the data.

CHAPTER 15   LEAN BLOCKCHAIN AND AI

So I asked, "Would it be cheaper to rent a camera and plane or helicopter, and fly over the farmer's field, hand process the data and see if that's the information farmers would pay for? Couldn't you do that in a day or two, for a tenth of the money you're looking for?"

Note   This post was taken from Steven Blank's blog and shared here to illustrate the importance of planning the stages necessary to define an MVP. The incorrect MVP will cost more resources and result in tangential data that does not validate your hypothesis directly. On the other hand, a properly constructed MVP will allow you to validate your core hypothesis rapidly without using any significant resources.

The Lean principles discussed here capture a market as the product gradually and iteratively matures through multiple stages. Product-market fit is the most important of the stages, and Geoffrey Moore, an organizational theorist, characterizes it as a chasm that products have to cross to be launched into mass adoption phases. Figure 15-1 summarizes the different phases of customer segments that a product can capture. Let us briefly review five of them here:

- **Innovators**: This segment is made of power users—a type of customer with some background and limited domain expertise in the vertical that your product falls under. Financial lucidity is a key property of this segment, as a low risk tolerance allows them to adopt technologies that may ultimately fail, but stable financial resources help absorb the failures. This customer is eager to try new products and will provide valuable technical insights as they have a vested interest in seeing new products succeed.

- **Early adopters**: This segment is very well connected with the innovators and has the highest amount of social capital to influence public opinion. More discrete in adopting new technologies and use this position to signal confidence in emerging trends. Early adopters play a huge role in helping a product appeal to broader audiences and achieve product-market fit.

- **Chasm**: A significant number of startups fail and never cross the chasm. The products developed never achieve product-market fit, and eventually the startup runs out of capital investment. Companies that manage to cross the chasm are now ready for mainstream market.

- **Early majority**: This is the first segment of the mainstream pragmatic consumers. Even though less social capital is invested at this level, word of mouth helps the product spread and reach very broadly.

- **Late majority**: This segment approaches new innovation with significant skepticism. A low financial lucidity plays a major role here, and although late, new product adoption happens long after the average member of society.

Note There are two sides of applying Lean principles. The first is an entrepreneur building out a product from scratch based on Lean and customer discovery methodology, and the second is an entrepreneur within a large organization trying to spin out a smaller company with potential resources and support for innovation. These two scenarios are drastically different in terms of resource allocation; however, the goal for a starting point is building an MVP. This should be done in such a way that minimizes resources used and therefore not be a cost-prohibitive experiment. Both examples also have varying degrees of flexibility in terms of how an entrepreneur operates and the culture of the larger organization. The core principles involving iterations of MVPs and customer interviews remain the same in both scenarios.

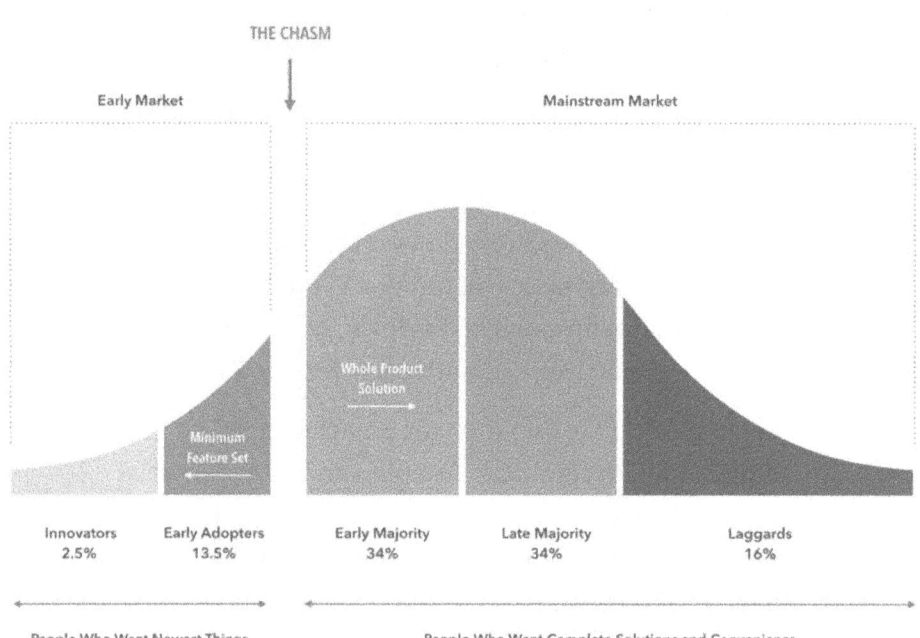

Figure 15-1. Chasm of product-market fit and customer segments. This figure was originally illustrated by Shah Mohammed from Prototypr.

Business Model Canvas

Alexander Osterwalder, a Swiss business theorist and entrepreneur, examined the structure of hundreds of companies and discovered that every company could be broken down into a model of nine basic components. To that end, new startups can be built following Lean methodologies that take the form of a canvas with these nine components, called a business model canvas. The idea is to work on a one-page canvas, frequently updating hypotheses about your business/product, and use customer interviews to fill out the nine components. This is opposed to the traditional model of creating lengthy business plans with projections on key metrics and user adoption without any validation from the customer. The canvas has two sides: the left side focuses on your product/business, and the right side focuses on the customer. The two sides converge on the value propositions, defined as the key points of value provided to the customer by your business or product. Let us go over each of the nine components here, followed by a visual representation of the business model canvas in Figure 15-2:

- **Customer segments**: This section lists the personas or archetypes of customers who will buy your product. In addition, this section should address the reasons why customers would want to buy from your company specifically. As such, it is your responsibility to interview customers belonging to each archetype and record how they interact with your products.

- **Value propositions**: This section contains the pain points that your customer is experiencing. Often times, the customer will try to solve a particular problem on their own with a patched-up solution. This method is usually inconvenient for a user, a "headache," so to speak, but a major source of value for the entrepreneur.

Building a simpler process to solve that very problem will serve as an instant "painkiller" and help your product appeal to the masses easier.

- **Channels**: This section defines the medium that you can use to communicate your value propositions to customers, make new sales, and obtain customer feedback from each of your customer segments. The output of this section is connecting each persona with the appropriate channel to reach them.

- **Customer relationships**: This section describes how you will interact with your customers and how your customers can reach you. This can be done through social media accounts, dedicated personal service, or forum communities.

- **Key activities**: The section represents the work you must perform to interact with your customers to deliver your value proposition. You need to create a list of key activities linked to your value proposition. It may include product distribution, research and development, strategy, etc.

- **Key resources**: The assets needed to build your value proposition and deliver it to your customers. This includes any equipment, software, and intellectual property in terms of proprietary knowledge, maintaining good relationships with your customers, and defining potential new revenue streams. The key resources should be mapped to your key activities in order to provide a clear roadmap of how to create value for your customers.

CHAPTER 15   LEAN BLOCKCHAIN AND AI

- **Key partnerships:** The key external actors that you need to rely on for carrying out all of the key activities. Without these partnerships, you will not be able to deliver on your value propositions. The output from this section is a list of partners and how they tie into your key activities.

- **Revenue streams:** The core financial feature covered by the business model canvas, answering a simple question of how your business will generate revenue. Traditional startups rely on three key revenue streams, including product sale, subscription fees, or licensing. Most blockchain companies have used the subscription fee model with a free tier, which allows users to try the platform before using it for any serious projects. The output of this section is to link customer segments with a potential revenue stream through value propositions.

- **Cost structure:** This section lists all the costs associated with keeping your startup running. Additionally, with careful planning, this section can help track the key activities or resources that are most expensive.

These nine components are arranged on the business model canvas, split into a left side and a right side, as shown in Figure 15-2, connected by the value propositions.

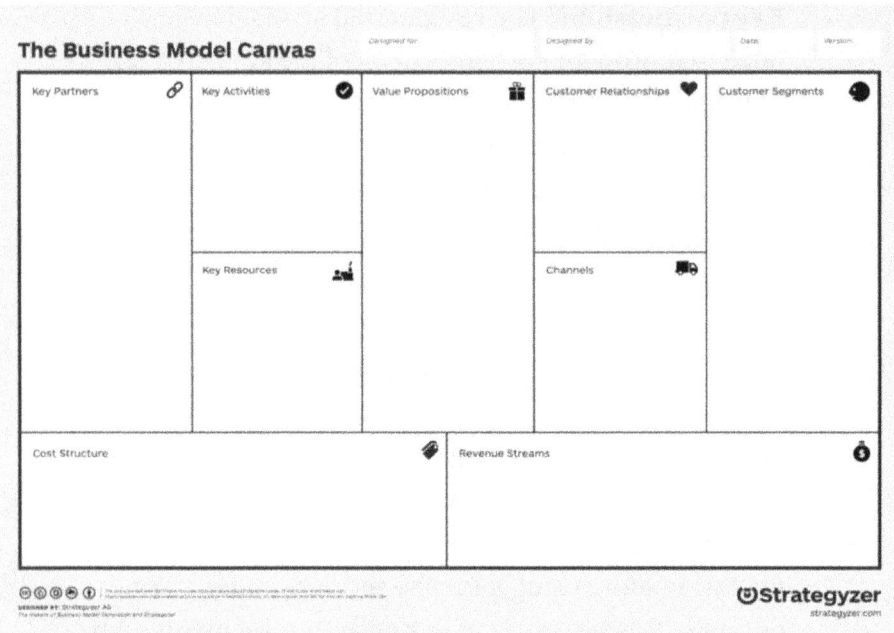

Figure 15-2. Overview of the business model canvas with nine core components, taken from Strategyzer

Applying Lean Methodology to AI Startups

When applying Lean principles to AI startups, one of the most critical variations from traditional startups lies in how minimum viable products (MVPs) are designed and measured. While a typical software MVP might focus on delivering a simplified set of features for rapid customer feedback, AI startups must deal with the significant pre-training requirements and have enough hardware (mostly GPUs) to train multiple generations of models. Startups such as Mistral often release a family of models at different parameter depth (8B versus 22B versus 123B). Over the years, the quality of data being used for model training has become the most crucial component. The release of the Phi family of models demonstrates this point, where the use of "textbook-quality" training data allows a 2.7B model to perform at the level of Llama and Mistral's 7B counterparts.

Customer discovery for AI products also has unique dimensions. Prospective users may have limited familiarity with how AI-driven systems differ from standard software. This knowledge gap can lead to misconceptions about the potential or limitations of machine learning. Educating early adopters—perhaps by explaining how a deep learning model identifies patterns in X-ray images—helps clarify expectations. Moreover, these discussions often reveal customer pain points that guide the model's development. For example, a startup building a computer vision system for warehouse automation might learn that customers specifically need accurate counting of irregularly shaped objects, prompting them to gather targeted data and tailor their labeling pipeline accordingly. Iterating on AI products involves more than just shipping a new code update. Each iteration typically requires data collection (or additional labeling) and model retraining. For example, a natural language processing (NLP) startup offering sentiment analysis might regularly gather new textual data from social media to capture evolving language usage, retraining the model to maintain accuracy. This cyclical process—collecting feedback, refining data, retraining the model—is central to the Lean "Build–Measure–Learn" loop in an AI context.

Establishing feedback loops for AI performance is essential for continuous improvement. These loops can include human-in-the-loop validation, automated model monitoring, and user-reported errors. Anomaly detection solutions, for instance, might incorporate real-time feedback on detected anomalies and update model parameters accordingly. The goal is to reduce time to learning so that each cycle of data gathering and model refinement quickly feeds into a new version of the AI product. Finally, managing customer expectations during early AI product development involves transparent communication about model maturity and potential failure modes. AI models—especially in their nascent stages—can misclassify inputs or generate suboptimal recommendations. Emphasizing pilot programs and proof-of-concept trials, paired with open discussions of error rates and ongoing improvements, helps maintain trust. A healthcare AI startup, for instance, might only deploy its model for non-critical tasks until it reaches a clearly documented performance threshold on clinically validated test sets.

AI-Specific MVP Considerations

1. **Creating MVPs with limited training data**
   AI startups in specialized domains often struggle with sparse or incomplete datasets in the early stages. A recommended approach is to begin with a narrowly scoped problem and a focused dataset that can demonstrate feasibility. For instance, a speech recognition startup might launch an MVP that supports only one or two languages or addresses a small domain of common commands, using just a few thousand labeled audio samples. This limited scope helps validate the core model architecture, and test if customers actually want the product, while keeping data requirements manageable.

2. **Using synthetic data for early prototypes**
   Synthetic data can accelerate AI development when real-world data is expensive or difficult to collect. Startups can employ generative adversarial networks (GANs) or simulation frameworks (e.g., Unity for 3D environments) to create realistic training examples. An autonomous driving startup could, for example, simulate various nighttime or rainy conditions to train object detection models

CHAPTER 15   LEAN BLOCKCHAIN AND AI

before gathering real driving data. This approach shortens the time to a working prototype and helps the team identify model weaknesses early.

Note The use of synthetic data presents multiple challenges for quality control, theory, and practical implementation. Models trained exclusively on synthetic data frequently encounter performance plateaus and may miss crucial real-world edge cases and nuances, while the "reality gap" between synthetic and real data can trigger unexpected model behaviors. Synthetic data may inadvertently encode biases or oversimplified patterns, raising fundamental questions about whether such data can truly capture the complexity of real-world distributions. This connects to deeper theoretical concerns about whether models can learn genuine insights from artificial data, the risk of "synthetic data overfitting" where models learn artifacts of the generation process, and philosophical questions about the authenticity of insights derived from synthetic data. These theoretical concerns are compounded by practical limitations, including the significant difficulty in generating high-quality synthetic data for complex domains, the computational overhead of maintaining synthetic data generation pipelines, the challenge of validating synthetic data quality without real-world references, and the persistent risk of propagating errors or biases from the generation process itself.

3. **Hybrid approaches combining rule-based systems and machine learning**
   In initial MVPs, merging rule-based logic with machine learning can help achieve predictable outcomes for simpler tasks while the ML components handle complex or less-defined scenarios. For instance, an AI chatbot might rely on a rule-based FAQ engine for straightforward questions (like "What are your business hours?") and an ML-based natural language understanding module for more nuanced requests ("What can I do if my device stops working unexpectedly?"). This hybrid strategy provides a fallback mechanism if the ML model underperforms and also allows a startup to quickly answer the question of whether consumers would find value from such a product.

4. **Importance of explainability in early AI products**
   Early adopters often demand explainability to understand how an AI system arrives at its decisions. Techniques such as Local Interpretable Model-Agnostic Explanations (LIME), SHapley values, or attention visualization in deep learning models can demonstrate which features or tokens the model focuses on. For instance, a credit-scoring startup may use heatmaps to show which customer attributes influenced a particular credit decision, thus building stakeholder trust and satisfying regulatory requirements.

5. **Methods for rapid AI prototyping**
   Leveraging pre-trained models, transfer learning, and robust machine learning frameworks (e.g.,

TensorFlow, PyTorch) can significantly shorten development cycles. An image recognition startup might begin with a pre-trained ResNet model and fine-tune the last few layers to classify specialized objects. This strategy accelerates experimentation, aligning with the Lean cycle of building, measuring, and learning from MVP iterations.

Business Model Canvas

For AI startups, each element of the business model canvas carries additional considerations:

- **Value propositions**: Demonstrating the AI advantage over traditional solutions means showcasing how ML-driven automation can allow for cost savings or revenue gains. For instance, a predictive maintenance startup might show how its ML models reduce equipment downtime by 30% through real-time anomaly detection.

- **Customer segments**: Early adopters typically have some familiarity with AI or show a willingness to experiment with new technology. AI healthcare applications might target technologically progressive clinics or research hospitals that can provide feedback and labeled data. In enterprise settings, data-savvy organizations often welcome pilot programs that promise a competitive edge and allow the company to test whether an emerging technology may be suitable for their use.

- **Key resources**: Beyond the usual startup resources, AI ventures require high-quality labeled datasets, computing infrastructure (e.g., GPU- or TPU-based clusters, cloud services for large-scale training), and specialized talent like data engineers, data scientists, and ML researchers. Partnerships with data providers or academic institutions can also be pivotal for obtaining domain-specific datasets (e.g., medical imagery or autonomous driving scenarios).

- **Key activities**: Core activities include data collection, data cleaning, labeling workflows, model training, hyperparameter tuning, and validation. Implementing best practices—such as continuous integration/continuous deployment (CI/CD) pipelines for models—enables repeated and reliable updates. For instance, a startup offering real-time fraud detection might have daily fine-tuning pipelines that incorporate the latest user transaction data.

- **Cost structure**: AI-specific expenses can quickly mount. Training large-scale neural networks can require considerable compute resources, often rented from cloud providers, with costs escalating based on GPU usage hours. Data acquisition or labeling costs can also be substantial. If a startup relies on specialized data—like annotated medical scans—labeling by domain experts may add significant overhead.

CHAPTER 15   LEAN BLOCKCHAIN AND AI

AI-Specific Success Factors

1. **Data cleaning and management**
    A robust data cleaning strategy is key to developing high-quality predictive models. Defining policies for data collection, labeling, governance, and privacy compliance is essential from day one. This includes strategies for dealing with data imbalance, data drift, and continuously updating the training dataset to reflect real-world changes. Tools such as data version control (DVC) can help keep track different dataset versions.

2. **Technical infrastructure choices**
    The choice of cloud platform, data pipeline tooling, and ML frameworks (TensorFlow, PyTorch, JAX) can affect scalability, performance, and cost. AI startups must balance the flexibility of managed services (like AWS SageMaker or Google Vertex AI) with the potential long-term benefits of building custom in-house solutions. Scalability planning is also important to avoid technical debt and expensive refactoring when demand grows.

3. **Ethics and responsibility frameworks**
    Ethical AI development involves addressing biases in training data, ensuring privacy protection, and maintaining transparency about model decisions. For instance, a facial recognition startup must proactively mitigate demographic biases by diversifying its training datasets and verifying model performance across different ethnicities, ages, and genders. Failure to consider this can

lead to regulatory scrutiny. Developers also need to implement continuous monitoring systems to detect drift from alignment in LLMs and have standard operating procedures for rectifying such discrepancies.

4. **AI regulatory compliance**
   The regulatory landscape for AI is rapidly evolving, with regulatory bodies demanding heightened algorithmic transparency, enhanced bias detection, clear compliance approaches, and risk management strategies. Organizations developing AI solutions must implement comprehensive governance frameworks that include establishing clear ethical and legal frameworks with guidelines for data collection, use, and sharing, as well as ensuring transparency, fairness, and accountability in AI decision-making processes. As AI regulation becomes more stringent globally, startups must proactively incorporate compliance measures into their development processes rather than treating them as afterthoughts.

5. **Scaling considerations**
   As the user base grows, data volume typically increases, requiring more efficient data ingestion, storage, and model training pipelines. AI startups should plan for distributed training and inference if rapid response times are critical. Implementing scalable microservices architectures can help isolate model serving from data collection, reducing bottlenecks during peak usage.

6. **Explainability and fairness**

    Explainability has become a critical requirement for AI systems, particularly in regulated industries. For an AI system to be considered trustworthy, it must demonstrate fairness through reduction of algorithmic bias, transparency about its inner workings, and the ability to explain decisions in comprehensible ways. Developers should implement techniques such as SHAP (SHapley Additive exPlanations) and counterfactual explanations to provide human-interpretable insights into AI decisions. Regular auditing processes should be established to evaluate model fairness across different demographic groups, with some organizations adopting practices like red team exercises and white-hat hacking to test AI systems for vulnerabilities.

7. **Risk management**

    AI involves distinct risks such as model drift (where real-world data evolves beyond the original training distribution) and catastrophic forgetting (when continual training overwrites learned information). Proactive and continuous monitoring of input data and model outputs is essential. Additionally, regulatory shifts around data usage—such as GDPR and HIPAA—can significantly impact startups if not anticipated.

CHAPTER 15   LEAN BLOCKCHAIN AND AI

Common Pitfalls in AI Startups

1. **Overpromising AI capabilities**
   Overstating what the model can do—even if it attracts attention—often leads to disillusionment when reality falls short. If a startup claims near-perfect object recognition but relies on a small training dataset, customers or investors may lose trust upon encountering too many misclassifications in real-world usage.

2. **Underestimating data requirements**
   Many new AI teams fail to appreciate the volume and quality of data needed to train robust models. Supervised learning in particular can demand thousands or millions of labeled examples to achieve reliable performance. Poor data labeling or data augmentation can stall progress, especially for complex tasks like natural language understanding in a real-life setting.

3. **Neglecting explainability**
   Lack of model transparency can alienate enterprise customers in highly regulated sectors such as finance, healthcare, or insurance. Techniques like feature importance analysis or heatmap visualizations not only address these requirements but also provide insight into model weaknesses, guiding further improvements.

4. **Focusing too much on model accuracy versus business value**

   A high-accuracy model that doesn't solve a meaningful business problem or is prohibitively expensive to run (e.g., requiring massive cloud compute for marginal accuracy gains) may not lead to commercial success. Balancing technical capabilities with solving a pain point for customers is crucial for startups operating within the Lean framework.

5. **Failing to consider edge cases**

   Edge cases—rare but high-impact events—can severely damage user trust if ignored. For example, an AI system for autonomous drones might excel in daylight but fail to detect obstacles in low-light conditions or in the presence of smoke or fog. Proactively simulating and testing these scenarios helps prevent catastrophic failures once the product is in the field.

Summary

In this chapter, we presented the Lean startup methodology to commercialize high-risk, high-reward research ideas into products that customers want. The Lean methodology was broken down into the business model canvas by Alexander Osterwalder and the chasm of product–market fit by Geoffrey Moore. To better understand the market for blockchain-enabled applications, we discussed customer discovery and then applied the Lean principles to AI startups. Given the distinct trajectory of AI startups, we also shared some hard challenges that current

CHAPTER 15   LEAN BLOCKCHAIN AND AI

AI startups are facing, as well as best practices to follow. We hope that you can take away practical and applicable tips from this chapter to develop your own ideas forward.

Bibliography

Birch, D., Brown, R. G., & Parulava, S. (2016). Towards ambient accountability in financial services: Shared ledgers, translucent transactions and the technological legacy of the great financial crisis. *Journal of Payments Strategy & Systems*, 10(2), 118–131. https://www.ingentaconnect.com/content/hsp/jpss/2016/00000010/00000002/art00002

Bender, E. M. et al. (2025, February 7). AI ethics: Integrating transparency, fairness, and privacy in AI development. *Applied Intelligence*. https://www.tandfonline.com/doi/full/10.1080/08839514.2025.2463722

IBM. (2024). Risk management in AI. IBM Think Insights. https://www.ibm.com/think/insights/ai-risk-management

IBM Developer. (n.d.). IBM blockchain 101: Quick-start guide for developers. https://developer.ibm.com/technologies/blockchain/tutorials/cl-ibm-blockchain-101-quick-start-guide-for-developers-bluemix-trs/

ISACA. (2024). AI and risk management: A strategic guide for CIOs and CISOs in financial services. ISACA Now Blog. https://www.isaca.org/resources/news-and-trends/isaca-now-blog/2024/ai-and-risk-management-a-strategic-guide-for-cios-and-cisos-in-financial-services

Koulaouzidis, G., Iakovidis, D., & Botsis, T. (2024). Challenges and efforts in managing AI trustworthiness risks: A state of knowledge. *Frontiers in Big Data*. https://pmc.ncbi.nlm.nih.gov/articles/PMC11119750/

Mökander, J., Schuett, J., Kirk, H. R., & Floridi, L. (2024). Auditing large language models: a three-layered approach. *European Journal of Risk Regulation*, 15(2). https://www.cambridge.org/core/journals/european-journal-of-risk-regulation/article/risk-management-in-the-artificial-intelligence-act/2E4D5707E65EFB3251A76E288BA74068

Moore, G. A. *Crossing the Chasm: Marketing and Selling Disruptive Products to Mainstream Customers* (3rd ed.). HarperCollins, 2014. https://www.harpercollins.com/products/crossing-the-chasm-3rd-edition-geoffrey-a-moore

Osterwalder, A. & Pigneur, Y. *Business Model Generation: A Handbook for Visionaries, Game Changers, and Challengers*. Wiley, 2010. https://www.strategyzer.com/books/business-model-generation

Palakurti, N. R. (2024). Ethical considerations of AI and ML in insurance risk management: Addressing bias and ensuring fairness. PhilArchive. https://philarchive.org/rec/NAGECO

Ries, E. (2011). The lean startup: How today's entrepreneurs use continuous innovation to create radically successful businesses. Crown Business. http://theleanstartup.com/book

SDG Group. (2024, July 10). Trustworthy & admissible AI: Trend #4 in SDG's 2024 data, analytics & AI trends. https://www.sdggroup.com/en-us/insights/blog/trustworthy-admissible-ai-trend-4-sdgs-2024-data-analytics-ai-trends

The Linux Foundation. (n.d.). Hyperledger. https://wiki.hyperledger.org/

The Linux Foundation. (n.d.). Hyperledger Fabric documentation. https://openblockchain.readthedocs.io/en/latest/

Wharton AI for Business. (2024, March 18). Artificial intelligence risk & governance. AI at Wharton. https://ai.wharton.upenn.edu/white-paper/artificial-intelligence-risk-governance/

Wüst, K. & Gervais, A. (2018). Do you need a blockchain? 2018 Crypto Valley Conference on Blockchain Technology (CVCBT). https://www.researchgate.net/publication/328820555_Do_you_Need_a_Blockchain

Zhang, J., Zeng, Y., Qiu, M., Xie, J., & Zheng, H. (2023). AI fairness in data management and analytics: A review on challenges, methodologies and applications. *Applied Sciences*, 13(18), 10258. https://www.mdpi.com/2076-3417/13/18/10258

Zouhair, S. & Abiad, D. (2023). Fairness and bias in artificial intelligence: A brief survey of sources, impacts, and mitigation strategies. *Sciences*, 6(1), 3. https://www.mdpi.com/2413-4155/6/1/3

CHAPTER 16

Beyond Large Language Models and Blockchain

This concluding chapter examines the future trajectories for research and product development in AI and blockchain technology. We reflect on two emerging topics that will become the center of future research: agents and LLM-powered robotics. Our discussion also extends to perspectives on the path toward Artificial General Intelligence (AGI), especially with the release of frontier models such as o3 and its potential implications for society.

Agentic AI

In the context of LLMs, an agent refers to an autonomous system that can use a LLM to reason through a problem prompted by the user, create a plan to solve the problem, and execute the plan with a help of built-in tools. In brief, agents are miniature complex reasoning systems with memory and programmatic capability to execute fixed tasks. The need for agents arises from the limitations of basic LLMs that are proficient in generating text and code but may struggle with tasks that demand multi-step reasoning or access to external tools and data. By incorporating components such as planning modules, memory systems, and tool interfaces, LLM agents can decompose complex problems into manageable sub-tasks, retrieve and process relevant information, and execute actions to achieve specific goals. The architecture of a LLM agent typically includes four key components:

1. Agent core: Acts as the central decision-making unit, managing the agent's goals, available tools, planning strategies, and relevant memory.

2. Planning module: Enables the agent to devise strategies for complex tasks, often involving the decomposition of tasks into sub-tasks and determining the sequence of actions required.

3. Memory module: Allows the agent to retain and recall past interactions and information, facilitating context-aware responses and learning from previous experiences.

4. Tools: External resources or systems that the agent can utilize to perform specific functions, such as accessing databases, executing software applications, or interfacing with other technologies.

Currently, four major platforms offer agent development capabilities, and many startups have agentic AI products in pipeline:

1. Amazon plans to develop advanced AI agents that can assist customers in making purchases. These AI agents, connected to a LLM named Rufus, will recommend products, add items to carts, and potentially even complete purchases for users. The company aims to create chatbots that proactively

CHAPTER 16   BEYOND LARGE LANGUAGE MODELS AND BLOCKCHAIN

suggest items based on users' preferences and broader trends, aiming for accuracy and non-intrusiveness. Amazon's AI-generated shopping guides, which provide detailed product insights and recommendations, have been introduced to enhance the online shopping experience. As the market for AI in ecommerce grows, Amazon's vast data repository (built from user comments and reviews) can serve as guide for improved customer service. In the near future, AI agents at Amazon could manage shopping needs from recognizing trends to automatic ordering, especially when combined with home automation services via Echo.

2. Google is advancing its AI capabilities with the development of AI agents powered by its Gemini model. These agents, including Astra and Mariner, are designed to process and respond to real-time queries across various formats, such as text, video, and audio. Astra operates via phone or smart glasses, providing users with on-the-go assistance, while Mariner functions within the Chrome browser, enhancing the browsing experience by offering contextual information and performing tasks like summarizing web content.

3. Anthropic has developed a LLM-based agent on top of Claude 3.5 Sonnet, which features a "computer use" capability. This allows Claude to manipulate a computer desktop environment, interacting with various software tools designed for human users. By taking screenshots and controlling a virtual mouse and keyboard, Claude navigates and operates

software applications as a human would, enabling it to perform tasks such as document editing and data entry autonomously.

4. OpenAI Swarm is a framework that enables the orchestration of multiple AI agents working in concert to achieve common objectives. It focuses on facilitating communication and coordination among agents, making it suitable for applications that require collaborative problem-solving and distributed intelligence.

5. CrewAI is an open source orchestration framework that employs a role-based architecture treating AI agents as a "crew" of "workers." At its core, the framework enables developers to use natural language to define specialized agents with specific roles, goals, and backstories while assigning them distinct tasks with clearly described responsibilities and expected outputs. These agents collaborate through either a sequential process, where tasks follow a preset order, or a hierarchical one, where a custom manager agent oversees task delegation, execution, and completion, allowing for complex workflows to be handled efficiently.

Note Traditional AI agents were primarily designed for executing specific tasks and making decisions in real-world environments through reinforcement learning and multi-agent systems, optimized for applications requiring real-time interaction such as robotics and autonomous vehicles. In contrast, LLM-powered agents can be described as systems that use a LLM to reason through a problem, create a plan to solve it, and execute that plan with the help of tools. LLM agents are distinguished by their ability to call on external tools and APIs to compensate for their limitations and utilize function calling to select and coordinate tools, critique and adjust their behavior, and demonstrate planning and reasoning abilities. Unlike LLMs, which are stateless and do not retain memory of previous interactions, agents incorporate memory mechanisms to remember past interactions and build upon them, allowing them to maintain continuity and coherence in long-term engagements.

Large Concept Models

Large Concept Model (LCM), a project from Meta, represents a fundamental shift from traditional LLMs by operating at a higher level of abstraction—working with "concepts" rather than individual tokens. While current LLMs like GPT, Claude, and Gemini process text token by token, LCMs operate in a semantic embedding space where each concept corresponds to a complete sentence. The research paper by Meta presents SONAR, a multilingual sentence embedding framework that supports 200 languages and speech input in 76 languages, as the foundation for representing these concepts. The core innovation lies in how LCMs process and generate text. Rather than predicting the next token in a sequence, LCMs predict entire sentence embeddings in the SONAR space. This better mirrors how humans process information—we typically think in complete ideas rather than individual words. When giving a talk, for instance, speakers don't memorize every word but rather plan a flow of key ideas. Similarly, when writing a research paper, authors typically start with an outline of main points before filling in details. LCMs attempt to model this higher-level thinking process.

CHAPTER 16   BEYOND LARGE LANGUAGE MODELS AND BLOCKCHAIN

The researchers explored several architectural variants to handle the challenges of working with continuous embeddings rather than discrete tokens. The Base-LCM uses direct MSE regression to predict the next embedding, but this proved insufficient for capturing the full distribution of possible next sentences. Then, the authors went on to explore diffusion-based One-Tower (a single transformer handling both context and denoising) and Two-Tower (split architecture with separate context-handling and denoising) and found the Two-Tower architecture to be promising. This was the final architecture implemented and scaled up to 7B parameters.

A major advantage of LCMs is their inherent multilingual capability. Since they operate in SONAR's language-agnostic embedding space, they can handle input and output in any of the 200 supported languages without requiring explicit translation or language-specific training. This allows for impressive zero-shot cross-lingual performance, outperforming even Llama-3.1-8B on languages it was specifically trained for. The model can take input in one language and generate output in another without ever being explicitly trained for translation. The researchers scaled their model to 7B parameters, training on 2.7T tokens across 142.4B concepts/sentences. They demonstrated its effectiveness on challenging tasks like summarization and summary expansion. The model showed particular strength in maintaining coherence across long documents, as it processes information at the sentence level rather than token by token. This reduces the effective sequence length the model needs to handle—where a traditional LLM might need to process thousands of tokens, an LCM works with hundreds of sentence-level concepts.

A particularly innovative aspect is the model's explicit planning capabilities. The researchers developed a Large Planning Concept Model (LPCM) that can predict higher-level concepts spanning multiple sentences, helping to maintain coherence in longer generations. This hierarchical approach—planning at both the paragraph and the sentence level—more closely mirrors human writing processes. They found this particularly helpful for tasks like summary expansion, where maintaining consistent narrative flow is crucial. The computational efficiency of LCMs presents interesting trade-offs. While they require more storage space for embeddings (15–20× the raw text size), they can process long documents more efficiently since they work with fewer, higher-level units. The researchers provide detailed comparisons of inference costs between LCMs and traditional LLMs, showing advantages for LCMs particularly when handling longer contexts. Despite these innovations, significant challenges remain. The continuous nature of the embedding space makes it harder to ensure generated embeddings correspond to valid, coherent sentences. The model struggles with factual accuracy, particularly for technical content or specific details. However, the researchers have open-sourced their implementation to foster further research in addressing these challenges.

Model Context Protocol

Model Context Protocol (MCP) serves as a universal connectivity standard for AI applications, much like how USB-C provides a standardized connection for electronic devices. This protocol transforms how LLMs interact with external data sources and tools by establishing a common language for these interactions. The central problem MCP addresses is the "M×N problem"—the exponential complexity that arises when integrating M different AI applications with N different data sources, which traditionally required building M×N custom integrations. By creating a standard protocol, MCP reduces this to an M+N problem, dramatically simplifying development and maintenance. The purpose of MCP extends beyond mere technical standardization. It aims to fundamentally enhance the capabilities of AI systems by granting them contextual awareness through access to real-time data and functional tools. Even the most sophisticated AI models are constrained by their training data,

CHAPTER 16 BEYOND LARGE LANGUAGE MODELS AND BLOCKCHAIN

which quickly becomes outdated and lacks personalized context. MCP bridges this gap by enabling AI systems to pull fresh information from databases, access user-specific files, interact with enterprise systems, and execute actions in the digital world—all through a consistent, secure interface. This transforms AI assistants from static information retrieval systems into dynamic, context-aware tools that can work with the most current and relevant information. MCP fulfills several critical needs in the AI ecosystem: It establishes trust boundaries between AI systems and external data sources, ensuring security and privacy through structured access patterns. It also enables incremental adoption, allowing organizations to connect their existing systems to AI applications without reimplementation. Most importantly, it creates an ecosystem where innovations in AI capabilities and data sources can progress independently yet remain compatible, accelerating development across the field. In a sense, MCP allows for oracle systems to interact with generative AI applications.

At an architectural level, MCP consists of hosts, clients, and servers. Hosts are the user-facing applications like Claude Desktop, AI-enhanced IDEs, or custom agents where users interact with AI systems. Within each host, multiple client instances can operate, with each client maintaining a dedicated one-to-one connection with a specific MCP server. This isolation pattern is intentional, enhancing security by ensuring that each server has limited access and cannot interfere with other connections. MCP servers represent the bridge between the AI world and specific functionality, whether accessing local files, querying databases, interacting with APIs, or controlling applications. Each server exposes a well-defined set of capabilities through the standardized protocol, handling authentication, resource management, and the actual business logic of the integration. This clear separation of responsibilities allows for a modular system where servers can be developed and deployed independently. The protocol itself is structured in layers, each addressing specific aspects of the communication. The base protocol layer

CHAPTER 16   BEYOND LARGE LANGUAGE MODELS AND BLOCKCHAIN

defines fundamental message types and formats, ensuring consistent interpretation across implementations. The transport layer manages the physical transmission of messages between clients and servers, supporting both local communication through standard input/output and remote communication through HTTP with Server-Sent Events. The features layer implements specific capabilities like tool invocation, resource access, and prompt management. One of the architectural innovations in MCP is its handling of message flows. Unlike traditional request–response patterns, MCP supports bidirectional communication, allowing servers to send notifications to clients without an explicit request. This enables real-time updates, progress reporting for long-running operations, and event-driven interactions. The architecture also supports streaming responses, enabling incremental data delivery for large outputs or continuous updates.

MCP defines three fundamental primitives that form the foundation of its functionality: tools, resources, and prompts. Each primitive addresses a different aspect of AI–world interaction, creating a comprehensive framework for context management. Tools represent dynamic, model-controlled functions that LLMs can discover and invoke. They enable AI systems to perform actions in the digital world, from searching databases to controlling applications or making API calls. Each tool is uniquely identified by a name and includes metadata describing its purpose and parameter requirements. The model can discover available tools through a standardized discovery mechanism and invoke them by providing the required arguments. This capability transforms AI systems from passive information providers to active agents capable of real-world interaction. Resources serve as the data access layer in MCP, allowing servers to expose structured content to clients. Unlike tools, which are primarily model-controlled, resources are typically application-controlled, meaning they're accessed based on specific requests rather than autonomous model decisions. Each resource is identified by a unique URI and can contain either text or binary data. Text resources include documents, code, logs, or other textual content, while binary resources encompass images, audio, video, or other non-text data. The protocol enables clients to discover available resources, read their contents, and even subscribe to updates when resources change. Prompts provide a way to standardize common interaction patterns between users, LLMs, and external systems. They define reusable templates and workflows that can be surfaced to users or automatically selected based on context. Each prompt includes a name, description, and optional parameters that customize its behavior. This primitive allows organizations to create consistent, optimized interaction patterns for common tasks, improving both user experience and model performance.

The protocol is based on the JSON-RPC 2.0 specification, which provides the foundation for all message exchanges. Every MCP message follows this format, ensuring consistent interpretation across different implementations. The protocol defines three fundamental message types: requests, responses, and notifications. Requests are bidirectional messages sent from client to server or vice versa, containing a unique identifier, a method name, and optional parameters. Each request expects a corresponding response with the same identifier, containing either a result or an error object. Notifications, in contrast, are one-way messages that do not require or expect a response, used for events like resource changes or progress updates. Every MCP connection also follows a structured lifecycle beginning with initialization. During this phase, the client sends an initialize request containing its protocol version and capabilities. The server responds with its own protocol version and capabilities, establishing the boundaries of their interaction. Once initialized, the client sends an initialized notification to acknowledge the connection, making it ready for use. This negotiation process ensures compatibility and prevents misunderstandings between components. An early success story for MCP has been IDE startups like Zed, Replit, Codeium, and Sourcegraph that have integrated MCP to power AI-assisted coding. These implementations now allow the AI assistants to understand project structure, access code files, interact with version control systems, and even execute commands—all through a standardized interface. This has transformed the coding experience, enabling more context-aware code suggestions, automated refactoring, and intelligent debugging assistance. On the horizon are applications in medicine, finance, and enterprise settings.

LLM-Powered Robotics

The integration of LLMs into robotics represents a new frontier of AI, aiming to enhance the capabilities of robots in understanding and executing day-to-day tasks through natural language processing. Major AI companies like OpenAI, Google's DeepMind, and several emerging startups are working to create systems that can comprehend and generate human-like language for more intuitive command execution and decision-making processes. One significant application is in robotic navigation and task planning, where researchers have developed methods for LLMs to interpret language-based instructions for multi-step tasks. For instance, robots can now understand and execute commands like "find a whiteboard" or "do the laundry," with the LLM breaking down these instructions into manageable steps. This advancement is particularly exemplified by startups like Skild AI, which has attracted substantial investment, including a SoftBank-led funding round valuing the company at nearly $4 billion. Established in Pittsburgh in 2023, Skild AI focuses on creating scalable foundation models for robotics that enable safe and dexterous human–robot interactions.

The integration of LLMs with other AI models, particularly vision-language models, has led to significant advances in multimodal robotics. This combination allows robots to process both visual and textual information simultaneously, enabling more sophisticated environmental interactions. Google's DeepMind has demonstrated this capability with their Gemini-powered robot, which can understand and execute complex commands in office environments by processing both text and video inputs. Companies like Agility Robotics are further advancing this field by exploring LLM integration to enhance communication with their humanoid robots. Their innovation team has developed interactive demonstrations showcasing how LLMs can make robots more versatile and faster to deploy. Meanwhile, MIT researchers have developed a framework called Grounding Language in DEmonstrations (GLIDE), which provides robots with commonsense reasoning abilities, enabling them to better understand how to interact with objects and their environment.

Notably, this integration also presents important challenges related to safety and reliability. Researchers are actively studying the robustness of LLM-driven robots against adversarial inputs, ensuring these systems can handle unexpected or malicious commands without compromising safety. Studies on "jailbreaking" LLM-controlled robots examine potential vulnerabilities and propose methods to enhance system resilience. The overall trajectory of LLM integration in robotics points toward more intelligent, adaptable, and user-friendly robotic systems. Ongoing research continues to focus on enhancing reasoning capabilities, safety protocols, and multimodal integration, with the goal of creating robots that can seamlessly understand and respond to human instructions while maintaining operational safety and reliability. Future advancements will likely focus on the development of larger and more complex LLMs with expanded capabilities that execute a plan generated by an agentic model in the real world. Multimodal AI with integration of text, image, and sensor data will enable more sophisticated home assistant robotics.

Note Despite impressive multimodal reasoning capabilities, real-world adaptability of LLM-powered robots remains particularly challenging: often generating plans lacking detailed actions and specific designs for complex environments. Additional challenges

CHAPTER 16   BEYOND LARGE LANGUAGE MODELS AND BLOCKCHAIN

include increased computational resources and energy consumption associated with embedding LLMs into robotic systems, as well as biases in language models and ethical considerations that need addressing in robotics applications.

Nuclear-Powered Data Centers

The energy demands of AI data centers have created a pressing challenge for major technology companies, leading them to explore nuclear power as a sustainable and reliable energy source. As the models become increasingly complex and computationally intensive, traditional energy sources like fossil fuels are proving inadequate to meet the substantial power requirements while maintaining environmental sustainability. In Chapter 4, we discussed the energy demands of AI systems, and nuclear energy has emerged as a compelling solution, offering carbon-free power generation capable of supporting the continuous operations characteristic of AI data centers.

Major technology companies are making significant strides in integrating nuclear power into their energy strategies. Google has formed a groundbreaking partnership with Kairos Power, announcing plans to develop small modular reactors (SMRs) that will provide up to 500 megawatts of carbon-free power by 2035. These SMRs have several advantages over traditional reactors including production at scale in a factory, cost efficiency, and enhanced flexibility in deployment. Similarly, Amazon Web Services has committed substantial resources to nuclear energy, planning to invest over $500 million in three SMR projects across Washington, Virginia, and Pennsylvania, demonstrating their commitment to supporting growing AI-driven energy needs while pursuing net-zero carbon objectives. Microsoft has taken a different approach by pursuing the rehabilitation of existing nuclear infrastructure. In September 2024,

CHAPTER 16 BEYOND LARGE LANGUAGE MODELS AND BLOCKCHAIN

the company entered an agreement to reopen a reactor at the Three Mile Island nuclear plant, which had been dormant since 2019. This strategic move, set to begin powering Microsoft's data centers in 2028, represents a significant step in repurposing existing nuclear facilities for AI operations. Meta has also joined this nuclear initiative, issuing an ambitious request for proposals seeking 1–4 gigawatts of new nuclear generation capacity to power its data centers and AI operations, with operations targeted to begin in the early 2030s.

However, the integration of nuclear power into data center operations faces several significant challenges. Regulatory approvals present a major hurdle, as nuclear projects must undergo extensive safety evaluations and secure multiple clearances, processes that can significantly extend project timelines and increase costs. Public perception remains another crucial challenge, as historical nuclear incidents have created lasting concerns about nuclear energy safety. This necessitates comprehensive public engagement strategies and transparent communication about safety protocols and risk mitigation measures. The management of nuclear waste continues to be a critical consideration in the implementation of these initiatives. Companies must develop and maintain robust long-term strategies for waste disposal and storage that ensure environmental safety and comply with strict regulatory requirements. This includes considerations for the entire lifecycle of nuclear materials, from initial use through final disposal, and the development of innovative solutions for minimizing and managing radioactive waste.

Despite these challenges, the movement toward nuclear power in AI data centers represents a net positive in sustainable energy solutions for the technology sector. As technology companies continue to invest and develop nuclear power, we can expect to see evolution in reactor design, safety protocols, and waste management techniques. The success of these initiatives could set important precedents for the broader adoption of nuclear energy in the technology sector and potentially influence energy policies and strategies across other industries as well

CHAPTER 16 BEYOND LARGE LANGUAGE MODELS AND BLOCKCHAIN

Sparks of AGI

Artificial General Intelligence (AGI) refers to an AI system that matches or exceeds human-level cognition across all domains of interest. Unlike narrow AI systems that excel at specific tasks, AGI would demonstrate human-like flexibility, transfer learning, and general problem-solving capabilities. The path to AGI remains hotly debated, with some researchers arguing that scaling current deep learning approaches could eventually lead to AGI, while others contend that fundamental new architectures or approaches are needed. The "Sparks of AGI" paper, published in 2023 by researchers studying GPT-4's capabilities, presented evidence of potentially emergent AGI-like behaviors in large language models. The research documented GPT-4's ability to perform complex multi-step reasoning, engage in strategic planning, and demonstrate zero-shot generalization to novel tasks. Perhaps most notably, the model showed signs of "theory of mind"—the ability to understand and reason about others' mental states and intentions. The researchers identified key capabilities like chain-of-thought reasoning, self-reflection, and task decomposition as potential building blocks toward AGI. To understand the degree of progress being made toward AGI, a few benchmarks have been developed:

1. The Abstraction and Reasoning Corpus (ARC-AGI), introduced by François Chollet in 2019, represents a fundamental shift in how we evaluate AI systems' generalization capabilities. Unlike traditional benchmarks that test pattern recognition within familiar domains, ARC-AGI challenges AI systems to solve novel problems without prior training on similar tasks. The benchmark's complexity is evidenced by its current highest score of 55.5%, achieved during the ARC Prize 2024 competition.

2. OpenAI's MLE-Bench introduces a novel dimension to AGI evaluation by focusing on AI systems' ability to engage in autonomous self-improvement. This benchmark comprises 75 sophisticated Kaggle tests, ranging from mRNA vaccine development to ancient scroll decipherment. The performance of OpenAI's "o1" model, achieving a bronze medal level on 16.9% of these tests, provides insights into the current state of autonomous machine learning engineering capabilities.

3. AGIEval takes a uniquely human-centric approach by utilizing standardized academic tests as a framework for evaluation. This benchmark has provided some of the most compelling evidence of AI progress, with GPT-4 demonstrating remarkable performance on standardized tests, including a 95% accuracy rate on SAT Math and 92.5% accuracy on the English portion of the Chinese national college entrance exam. These results suggest that in certain structured domains, AI systems are approaching average human performance.

4. The introduction of OlympiadBench in 2024 raised the bar significantly for AI evaluation. With its collection of 8,476 Olympiad-level mathematics and physics problems, this benchmark provides a rigorous test of advanced problem-solving capabilities. The relatively low performance of even sophisticated models like GPT-4V, achieving only 17.97% accuracy, underscores the significant challenges AI systems face in handling complex, multi-step reasoning tasks.

CHAPTER 16 BEYOND LARGE LANGUAGE MODELS AND BLOCKCHAIN

5. The GAIA Benchmark takes a more holistic approach to AGI evaluation by assessing AI assistants' capabilities in real-world scenarios. Its comprehensive evaluation framework includes 466 questions designed to test fundamental abilities across multiple domains, including reasoning, multimodal processing, web navigation, and tool utilization. The stark contrast between human performance (92% success rate) and GPT-4's performance with plugins (15%) highlights the substantial gap between current AI capabilities and true general intelligence.

6. Epoch AI's FrontierMath Benchmark represents the cutting edge in mathematical reasoning assessment. This benchmark is particularly significant as it tests not just computational ability but also the deeper understanding and creative problem-solving skills required for advanced mathematics. The benchmark's design reflects a sophisticated understanding of how mathematical reasoning relates to general intelligence, providing valuable insights into AI systems' capacity for abstract thought and logical deduction.

Artificial Super Intelligence (ASI) represents hypothetical future AI that would surpass human cognitive capabilities across all domains by orders of magnitude. The concept of an "intelligence explosion" or "recursive self-improvement" suggests that once AI reaches human-level intelligence, it could rapidly iterate and improve upon its own architecture, leading to exponential growth in capabilities. This could potentially result in intelligence far beyond human comprehension. Key technical challenges in ASI development include ensuring goal alignment, maintaining control, and addressing the "value learning problem"—how to imbue such systems with human values and ethics.

Recent technical developments that may contribute to progress toward AGI/ASI include advances in multimodal models that can process and reason across different types of data (text, images, audio), improvements in few-shot and zero-shot learning capabilities, and architectures that enable sophisticated reasoning. However, significant technical challenges remain, particularly around causal reasoning, commonsense understanding, and transfer learning. Current models still struggle with consistency, factual accuracy, and truly understanding the world in a way that enables reliable generalization to novel situations. The development of AGI/ASI in the future may require grounding provided by technologies such as distributed ledgers where integration of knowledge, consensus, and verifiability become necessary for intelligence.

Bibliography

Knoop, M., Chollet, F., Landers, B., & Kamradt, G. (2024). ARC Prize 2024: Technical report. Retrieved from https://arxiv.org/html/2412.04604v2

Glazer, E., Besiroglu, T., Amodei, D., Tao, T., Gowers, T., Borcherds, R., ... & Joseph, N. (2024). FrontierMath: A benchmark for evaluating advanced mathematical reasoning in AI. arXiv preprint arXiv:2411.04872. https://arxiv.org/abs/2411.04872

He, C., Luo, R., Bai, Y., Hu, S., Thai, Z. L., Shen, J., ... & Sun, M. (2024). OlympiadBench: A challenging benchmark for promoting AGI with Olympiad-level bilingual multimodal scientific problems. arXiv preprint arXiv:2402.14008. https://arxiv.org/abs/2402.14008

Bulletin of the Atomic Scientists. (2024, December 19). AI goes nuclear. https://thebulletin.org/2024/12/ai-goes-nuclear/

Goldman Sachs. (2025, January 23). Is nuclear energy the answer to AI data centers' power consumption? https://www.goldmansachs.com/insights/articles/is-nuclear-energy-the-answer-to-ai-data-centers-power-consumption

GT-RIPL. (2024). Awesome-LLM-Robotics: A comprehensive list of papers using large language/multi-modal models for Robotics/RL. GitHub Repository. https://github.com/GT-RIPL/Awesome-LLM-Robotics

Science Direct. (2024). Large language models for human–robot interaction: A review. https://www.sciencedirect.com/science/article/pii/S2667379723000451

Yao, Y., Liu, X., & Ge, B. (2024). Large language models for robotics: Opportunities, challenges, and perspectives. Science Direct. https://www.sciencedirect.com/science/article/pii/S2949855424000613

Duquenne, P. A., Schwenk, H., & Sagot, B. (2023). SONAR: Sentence-level multimodal and language-agnostic representations. arXiv Preprint arXiv:2308.11466. https://arxiv.org/abs/2308.11466

IBM Research. (2025, January 21). LLMs revolutionized AI: LLM-based AI agents are what's next. https://research.ibm.com/blog/what-are-ai-agents-llm

Zhao, A., Huang, D., Xu, Q., Lin, M., Liu, Y. J., & Huang, G. (2024). Expel: LLM agents are experiential learners. *Proceedings of the AAAI Conference on Artificial Intelligence*, 38(17), 19632–19642. https://ojs.aaai.org/index.php/AAAI/article/view/29936

Bubeck, Sébastien, Varun Chadrasekaran, Ronen Eldan, Johannes Gehrke, Eric Horvitz, Ece Kamar, Peter Lee et al. Sparks of artificial general intelligence: Early experiments with gpt-4. 2023. https://arxiv.org/abs/2303.12712

Index

A

Abridge, 376
Absolute positional embeddings, 293
Absorption, Distribution, Metabolism, Excretion, and Toxicity (ADMET), 365
Abstraction and Reasoning Corpus (ARC-AGI), 551
A/B testing, 511
Academic Endorsement Points (AEP), 412
Academic Endorsement System (AES), 412
Access control layer, 324
Accreditation criteria, 465
Actionable, 512
Activation functions, 167–169, 275
Active parameters, 435
Adapter modules, 80
Adaptive attention scaling, 439
Adaptive clipping mechanism, 437
Adaptive importance sampling, 432
Adaptive scheduling algorithms, 434
Adversarial fine-tuning, 177
Agent-based modeling, 305
Agentic AI
    autonomous system, 537
    components
        agent core, 538
        memory module, 538
        planning module, 538
        tools, 538
    platforms
        Amazon, 538
        Claude, 539
        CrewAI, 540
        Google, 539
        OpenAI Swarm, 540
AGIEval, 552
Aha moment, 449
AI-based reputation scales, 14
Aiberry, 381
AI doomers
    alignment research, 107
    amplification, 105
    existential risk, 107
    goal misalignment, 105
    intelligence explosion, 105
    recursive self-improvement, 105
    technological singularity, 106
AI-driven data analysis, 366

INDEX

AI-driven video generation
    methods, 133
AI-integration stack
    contract layer, 13
    decentralized marketplace, 11
    examples, 11
    interfacing layer, 12
    model deployment layer, 12
    model development layer, 13
    off-chain tracking layer, 15
    oracle layer, 14
    privacy layer, 15
    real-time market
        fluctuations, 11
    sourcing, 11
AI startups
    ASICs, 123
    business model canvas, 527, 528
    Butterfly Labs, 123
    capabilities, 532
    CoinTerra, 123
    cyclical process, 523
    data requirements, 532
    edge cases, 533
    explainability, 532
    factors
        data cleaning and
            management, 529
        ethics and responsibility
            frameworks, 529
        explainability and
            fairness, 531
        regulatory compliance, 530
        risk management, 531
        scaling considerations, 530
        technical infrastructure
            choices, 529
    feedback loops, 523
    HashFast, 124
    and investment opportunities,
        101, 102
    model accuracy vs. business
        value, 533
    MVP, 522, 524–527
    parameter depth, 522
    pre-training requirements, 522
    schemes, 124
    sentiment analysis, 523
Alibaba Cloud, 36, 488
Alignment research, 107
AlphaFold 1 (AF1), 357
AlphaFold 2 (AF2), 357, 358
AlphaFold 3 (AF3), 359, 360
Amazon, 538
Amazon CloudWatch, 484
Amazon Elastic Load Balancer, 4
Amazon Web Services (AWS), 9,
    484, 549
Amplification, 105
Analytics and monitoring
    system, 306
Anonymization, 404
Anti-arrhythmic drugs, 397
Antigen prediction, 365
Anti-money laundering (AML), 476
API layer, 5
Application Binary Interface (ABI),
    218, 219

INDEX

Application layer, 325
Application-Specific Integrated
    Circuits (ASICs), 120,
    123, 128
Approximate Nearest
    Neighbor (ANN), 175
A Robustly Optimized BERT
    Pretraining Approach
    (RoBERTa), 62
Artificial general intelligence (AGI),
    75, 283, 463, 551–554
Artificial intelligence (AI), 103, 185
    blockchain-based
        governance, 40–45
    CAI, 26, 27
    capabilities, 462, 463
    consensus algorithms, 46–48
    copyrights, 133–135
    ecosystem, 544
    energy crisis, 131–133
    foundational models, 1, 2
    guardrails, 24, 25
    hardware, 126–129
    infrastructures, 2
    integration, 104
    LLMs, 380
    memory considerations,
        129, 130
    open source models, 30–40
    paperclips, 106
    performance metrics,
        130, 131
    safety and responsible
        design, 16–24

SML, 28–30
startups, 522
traditional application
    stack, 3–6
Artificial Super
    Intelligence (ASI), 553
Asset allocation strategy, 310
Asset management, 305, 309
Asset metadata, 401
Asset-referenced tokens, 470
Asynchronous Byzantine fault
    tolerance (aBFT), 493
AthenaDAO, 326
Attention, 54, 57, 58
    context updating, 193
    data values, 188
    definition, 187
    feedback loop initiation, 192
    GQA, 191
    input reception, 191
    KVC, 188–190
    latency issues, 189
    LLMs, 190
    matrix-based approach, 188
    output delivery, 193
    post-processing, 193
    prefill/prompt phase, 192
    probability distribution, 190
    repetition, 193
    sequential prediction, 192
    termination check, 193
    token addition, 192
    tokenization, 191
    vectors, 187, 188

INDEX

Attention mechanisms
　embeddings, 161
　FFNN, 164
　linear transformation, 164
　multiple heads, 163
　NLP tasks, 161
　non-linear activation, 164
　scaled dot-product
　　attention, 162
　second linear
　　transformation, 164
　tokens, 161
　transformer models, 161
　vectors, 161
Attestations, 235
Attribute-based access
　control (ABAC), 486
Auction-managed AMMs
　(am-AMMs), 329
Auditing frameworks, 9
Augmedix, 379
Augmented reality (AR), 426
Augur, 412
Autoencoding, 355
Automated bridging
　mechanisms, 311
Automated market makers
　(AMMs), 328–330, 468
Automatic error detector, 286
Auto-regressive language
　model, 39, 287
Auto-regressive modeling, 355
Auxiliary-loss-free strategy, 38
Auxiliary loss functions, 436

AWS Generative AI Accelerator, 102
Aya family, 39, 40
Azure Active Directory (AAD), 485
Azure Kubernetes Service (AKS), 485

B

Back-end (server-side) layer, 3
Baidu's Wenxin Investment
　Fund, 102
Bank for International
　Settlements (BIS), 474
Batching techniques, 196, 197
Beacon chain, 233
　block proposers, 234, 235
　committees, 235
　function, 233
　managing validators, 234
　management, 233
　rewards/penalties, 235
Beam search, 433
BEnchmArk for COmprehensive
　RNA Task and Language
　Models (BEACON), 352
Benchmarking studies, 359
Bidirectional Encoder
　Representations from
　Transformers (BERT),
　55, 61, 62
Bidirectional self-attention, 61
BigScience Large Open-science
　Open-access Multilingual
　Language Model
　(BLOOM), 33

560

INDEX

Binary resources, 545
BioDAO, 326
BioGPT, 368
Bioinformatics, 338, 340
Biological language models, 338
Biomarker analysis, 365
BioMed Central, 395
Bitcoin, 48, 89, 92, 93
    consensus, 125, 126
    mining, 111
    mobile payments, 150
    network, 140, 150
    protocol, 202, 203, 205
    self-regulating system, 117
    startups, 123–125
    state channel, 236
BitDAO, 304
BitFit, 80
Black-box attacks, 29
Blob-carrying transactions, 246
Block builders, 248
Blockchain application stack
    AI integration stack, 11–16
    consensus layer, 6
    contract layer, 7
    definition, 6
    deployment layer, 9
    executable layer, 7
    explorer, 8
    foundation layer, 6
    front-end layer, 9
    identity layer, 9
    LLMs, 10
    loss function, 10
    MLLMs, 10
    players, 16
    regulatory layer, 10
    storage layer, 8
    tokenization layer, 8
Blockchain-as-a-Service (BaaS), 9, 202, 238, 239
    cloud-based architectural paradigm, 483
    decision tree approach, 494–500
    three-tier architecture, 483
    updates, 484–493
Blockchain-based ecosystem, 13
Blockchain-based governance components
    developers, 42
    maintainers, 42
    public/private interfaces, 43
    resource vendors, 43
    safety contract, 43
    computational resources, 45
    DAOs, 40
    open source community, 41
    perturbation techniques, 44
    proposed model, 46
    token types, 41
    trained model, 41
    ZKPs, 44, 45
Blockchain-based identity systems, 479
Blockchain-based reputation systems, 420
Blockchain explorer, 8, 151
Blockchain networks, 478

INDEX

Blockchain technology
    AI integration, 104
    application stack, 98
    definition, 139
    emerging landscape, 389
    forks, 156, 157
    frenzy phase, 459
    implications, 460
    institutional
        reconfiguration, 459
    irruption phase, 459
    ledger, 96
    parallel, 302
    properties and
        reproducibility, 390
    regulatory updates, 468–481
    technical challenge, 152
    timestamps, 96
    transaction list
        addresses, 150
        blockheight, 144
        change/change
            addresses, 145
        flash drive, 151
        inputs/outputs, 144, 145
        overview, 148, 149
        private–public keypairs,
            146, 147
        propogation, 147
        pseudonymity, 148
        purposes, 150
        script, 147
        tracking, 148
        unspent transactions, 144, 148
        UTXO, 144, 146
        wallets, 149–151
    transaction workflow
        block, 141–143
        components, 143
        principles, 140
        timestamp, 142
Blockheight, 144
BlueBERT, 373
Bridge protocols, 312, 423
BRUINchain, 415, 420
Business hypothesis
    experimentation, 510
Business model canvas
    components, 521, 522
        channels, 520
        cost structure, 521, 528
        customer relationships, 520
        customer segments, 519, 527
        key activities, 520, 528
        key partnerships, 521
        key resources, 520, 528
        revenue streams, 521
        value propositions, 519, 527
    definition, 519
Butterfly Labs, 123
Byte pair encoding (BPE), 158,
    338, 339
Byzantine fault tolerance (BFT),
    6, 496
Byzantine Generals Problem,
    93, 95, 139

INDEX

C

Caching layer, 4
Cambrian explosion phase, 140
Cancun-Deneb upgrade, 246
Candidate block, 113–115
Carbon footprints, 425
Category-weighted voting, 320
Center for Research on Foundation Models (CRFM), 2
Central bank digital currencies (CBDCs), 107, 460, 474
Central Processing Unit (CPU), 44, 126
CerebrumDAO, 326
Certificate authorities (CAs), 486
CFTC's jurisdiction, 469
Chain-of-thought (CoT), 100, 285, 442, 447
Chainshot, 225
Channel-based privacy, 488
Character-level tokenization, 159
Checkpointing, 83
Chinchilla scaling laws, 77, 78
Chunking strategies, 343
Clara, 383
Classification fine-tuning, 177
Claude, 539
Client-side layer, 3
ClinicalBERT, 367
Clinical-BigBird, 368
ClinicalGPT, 374
Clinical-Longformer, 368
Clinical-T5, 372
Clinical trials
    colored coin, 400, 401, 403, 404, 406
    data reporting, 398
    drug efficacies, 399
    implementations, 404
    innovations, 419, 420
    post-processing unit, 399, 406
    registration, 398
    workflow, 405
Coco framework, 239
CodeGemma, 35
Cognitive-behavioral therapy (CBT), 381, 383
CoinTerra, 123
Cold-storage wallets, 150
Collateralized debt obligations (CDOs), 91
Colored coins
    advantage, 400
    asset metadata, 401
    coloring scheme, 401
    implementation, 400
    interactions, 404
    rule engine, 401, 402, 406
    transaction, 401–403, 410
Coloring scheme, 401
Colosseum 355B, 375
Commercial off-the-shelf (COTS), 415
Commodity Exchange Act (CEA), 333, 469
Communication balance loss, 436

INDEX

Compiled contract, 218
Compliance costs, 467
Compliance system, 308
Compound's treasury management system, 310
Computational resources, 431, 452
Concept drift, 19
Confidential Consortium Framework (CCF), 485
Conflict resolution, 42, 44
Connectionist Temporal Classification (CTC), 378
ConPLex, 363
Consensus-based alignment, 46–48
Consensus layer, 6
Consensus of transactions, 141
Consensus rules, 156
Consensys Academy, 225, 490
Consortium-as-a-Service model, 492
Constitutional AI (CAI), 26, 27, 73
Consumer protection, 107
Contact map prediction (CMP), 352
Contemporary web-application stacks
   API layer, 5
   back-end (server-side) layer, 3
   caching layer, 4
   database layer, 4
   deployment layer, 5
   front-end (client-side) layer, 3
   monitoring layer, 5
   web server layer, 4

Content delivery networks (CDNs), 4
Context-free grammar (CFG), 290
Context management, 545
Contextual embeddings, 160
Continuous batching (in-flight batching), 197
Continuous integration/continuous deployment (CI/CD), 528
Contract layer, 7, 13
Contracts, 207, 211, 214, 218
Contract Validation Code in Creation, 250
Contrastive fine-tuning, 178
Convolutional sequence encoding (CSE), 350
Copilot apps, 99
Corda Distributed Applications (CorDapps), 491
Corti's emergency care, 379
Counterparty risk, 90
CrewAI, 540
Cross-border payment networks, 460
Cross-chain bridges, 474, 478
Cross-Chain Interoperability Protocol (CCIP), 312, 423
Cross-chain scientific infrastructure, 423, 424
Cross-chain verification mechanisms, 419
Cross-site scripting (XSS), 4

Cryptlets, 239
Crypto-asset service providers (CASPs), 480
Cryptographic hash functions, 94, 95
Cryptographic protocols, 22
Cryptography, 424
Customer discovery, 514, 523
Customer relationships, 520
Customer segments, 519, 527
   chasm, 517, 518
   early adopters, 517
   early majority, 517
   innovators, 516
   late majority, 517
Custom serialization schemes, 491

D

DAO-specific entity (DSE), 334
Data analysis tools, 9
Database layer, 4
Data center electricity consumption, 131
Data cleaning strategy, 529
Data contamination, 261, 264
Data Discovery Index (DDI), 396, 407
Data-driven decisions, 11
Data-driven translation methodologies, 54
DataGemma, 35
Data privacy requirements, 496
Data sharding, 82
Data sovereignty, 421, 422
Data version control (DVC), 529
Decentralized AI marketplaces, 104
Decentralized application (dApp), 6, 96, 202, 483
   backend calls, 241, 242
   blockchain, 242
   consensus-critical state, 240
   definition, 240
   ecosystem, 238
   Geth, 242, 243
   Mist, 243, 244
   mobile/web app, 240
   retrieve/download content, 242
   structure, 240
   Swarm, 240
   user interface, 240
   Whisper, 240
Decentralized autonomous corporations, 300
Decentralized autonomous organizations (DAOs), 40, 244, 416, 460, 472
   AMMs and RWA protocols, 328–330
   centralized authorities, 299
   definition, 300
   emergence, 299
   governance models, 316–323
   inception and collapse, 300–304
   regulatory challenges, 332–334
   technical foundations, 304–316
   traditional structures, 330, 332
   use case, 323–328

INDEX

Decentralized exchanges (DEXs), 246, 469
Decentralized finance (DeFi), 211, 327, 466, 468, 478
Decentralized identifiers (DIDs), 420, 423
Decentralized networks, 391
Decentralized science (DeSci), 391, 416, 417
　access control layer, 324
　application layer, 325
　decentralized storage layer, 324
　initiatives, 324
　intellectual property, 324
　micro-grants, 323
　ownership layer, 324
　use cases, biotech space, 325–328
Decentralized storage layer, 324
Decentralized Virtual Research Environment (D-VRE), 418
Decision-making process, 19
Decision tree
　business requirements, 494, 495
　compliance and governance, 499, 500
　infrastructure and integration, 497, 498
　operational considerations, 498, 499
　technical architecture requirements, 495, 497
　use case, 500
Decoder, 169, 170

Decoder-style transformers, 61
Decoding, 185, 186
Deep learning (DL), 128, 461
DeepLIFT algorithm, 19
DeepMind's AlphaProof system, 260
Deep neural networks, 10
DeepScribe, 378
DeepSeek architecture
　distillation, 450, 451
　FP8 quantization, 437, 438
　MLA, 438, 440
　MoE mechanism, 435, 436
　multi-token prediction, 440–442
　reinforcement learning and policy evolution, 444–446
　rejection sampling and supervised fine-tuning, 447, 448
　secondary reinforcement learning, 448, 449
　SFT, 442, 443
　stages, 435
　training costs, 452
DeepSeek family, 37, 39
DeepSeekMoE, 38
Delegated proof of stake (DPoS), 6
Denial of service (DoS), 4, 253
Dense retrieval models, 174
Dense vector retrieval, 175
Dependency graph, 283
Deployment layer, 5, 9
Description-based prompts, 364
Device-level balance loss, 436

INDEX

Device-limited routing (DLR), 436
Dialectical behavior therapy (DBT), 382
Diamond Reserve Club (DRC), 466
Differential network centrality analysis, 365
Digital assets, 423, 477, 480
Digital Currency Electronic Payment (DC/EP) system, 474
Digital economy, 332
Digital identity systems, 460
Digital Innovation Fund, 103
Direct dependency, 278
Directed acyclic graph (DAG), 20, 279, 493
Discrimination, 18
Disease biomarkers, 340
Dispute resolution system, 307
Distance map prediction (DMP), 352
Distillation, 35, 450, 451
Distributed ledger technology, 2, 493, 554
Distributed systems, 424
DNA language models
  computational resources, 343
  data preprocessing, 342
  ethical considerations, 343
  genomic and epigenomic regulation, 341
  genomic organization, 342
  innovations, 341
  multitask learning frameworks, 342
  overview, 343–346
  performance evaluation, 343
  technical optimization, 343
  training data, 341
Dokchain, 239
Double spending, 90, 93
Dreamers
  AI doomers, 104–107
  blockchain and AI integration, 104
  financial crisis, 89
  next generation, 99–101
  paradigm shift, 90–93, 101–103
  regulatory landscape, 107
  technology stack, 93–98
Dropbox ventures, 103
DrugAgent framework, 364
DrugChat, 364
Drug discovery, 363–365
Drug efficacies, 399
DrugLAMP, 363
Drug Supply Chain Security Act (DSCSA), 415, 420
Drug-target interaction (DTI), 363
DualPipe parallelism algorithm, 38
Dubai Financial Services Authority (DFSA), 471
Dumber approach, 288
Dynamic programming (DP), 295, 296, 433

INDEX

E

Economic activities, 426
Economic simulations, 305
EIP-1559, 249
EIP-3540, 249
EIP-3651, 245
EIP-3670, 250
EIP-3855, 245
EIP-3860, 245
EIP-4337, 247
EIP-4844, 246
EIP-4895, 244
EIP-5656, 247
EIP-6780, 246
Electronic cash system, 92
Electronic health records, 337
Electrum, 154
Embark, 224
Embeddings, 159, 160
Emergence, 2
E-money tokens, 471
Encoder–decoder architecture, 157
Encoder–decoder
    frameworks, 54, 59
Encoder-style transformers, 61
End-to-end request latency, 195
Enformer, 341, 344
Enterprise blockchain
    solutions, 460
Entropy-based metrics, 434
Environmental sustainability, 549
Epoch AI's FrontierMath
    Benchmark, 553

ERNIE-RNA, 348
Error correction, 288
Error detection, 288
Error handling, 314
Escrow mechanisms, 475
ESM-3, 356, 357
esmGFP, 357
Ethereum (ETH), 303
    account object values, 210
    accounts, 206, 207, 209
    block headers, 208, 209
    components, 201, 214
    DApps, 240
    data overload mechanisms, 212
    definition, 201
    ecosystem, 247, 303
    features, 203
    gas, 210, 211
    key issues, 202
    limitations, 212
    network, 212, 213
    network's security model, 308
    proposals, 252–254
    scripting language, 203
    smart contracts, 201
    spam prevention
        mechanism, 201
    state, 209, 210
    upgrades, 244–251
    validator/creator, 204, 214
    virtual stake, 204
Ethereum 1.0, 204
Ethereum 2.0, 232, 234

INDEX

Ethereum Blockchain as a Service (E-BaaS), 238
Ethereum Classic (ETC), 303
Ethereum Computer, 300
Ethereum Fee Market Upgrade, 249
Ethereum Improvement Proposals (EIPs), 244
Ethereum JavaScript API, 214
Ethereum Name Service (ENS), 314
Ethereum Object Format (EOF), 252
Ethereum Stack Exchange, 225
Ethereum Studio, 224
Ethereum Virtual Machine (EVM), 7, 201, 203, 211, 245, 249, 308
   arbitrary code, 215
   BaaS, 238, 239
   beacon chain, 232–235
   bytecode, 215
   code execution, 216
   contracts, 216
   cost, 215
   deterministic nature, 216
   developer resources, 224, 225
   nodes, 216, 217
   optimistic rollups, 230
   outcomes, 215
   plasma, 237, 238
   rationale, 218
   sharding, 231, 232
   solidity, 218–221
   state channels, 236, 237
   visualization, 217

Vyper, 222, 223
world computer, 215, 225–229
ZK-rollups, 230, 231
Ethical AI development, 529
Ethics committees, 23
Ethology theory of language models, 258
European Securities and Markets Authority (ESMA), 476
Event-driven interactions, 545
Evidence-based clinical sciences, 389
EVM Object Format (EOF), 249
Evo, 361–363
Exclusion criteria, 419
Executable layer, 7
Existential risk, 107
Expert-level balance loss, 436
Expiration rule, 401, 403, 407
Exploratory analysis, 23
Exponential backoff strategies, 434
External accounts, 206
Externally owned accounts (EOAs), 247, 252

F

Facebook AI Similarity Search (FAISS), 175
Fair Launch models, 467
Falcon family, 32
Fault tolerance, 95
Feature selection techniques, 365

INDEX

Federal Trade Commission (FTC), 123
Federated learning techniques, 47
Feedback loop initiation, 192
Feedforward neural network (FFNN), 161, 163, 164
Few-shot fine-tuning, 178
Few-shot prompting, 100
Field-Programmable Gated Array (FPGAs), 120
Financial Action Task Force's (FATF) Travel Rule, 472
Financial lucidity, 516
Financial Market Infrastructure (FMI), 474
Financial services, 495
Financial stability, 107
Fine-tuned preference model (PM), 27
Fine-tuning, 65, 271, 360
   adversarial, 177
   classification, 177
   contrastive, 178
   definition, 176
   few-shot and zero-shot, 178
   information bias and language-related issues, 179
   instruction, 176
   large language models, 179
   medical diagnosis assistant, 181, 182
   scenarios, 179
Fission-based reactors, 133
FlashAttention, 80, 82

Floating-point 8 (FP8) quantization, 437, 438
Floating-point operations per second (FLOPS), 130
Foundational models
   clinical use cases, 367–376
   definition, 1
   domains, 2
   emergence, 1
   features, 2
Foundation layer, 6
Front-end layer, 3, 9
Full Pay-Per-Share (FPPS), 121
Futarchy, 320

G

GAIA Benchmark, 553
Gated-interaction protocol, 25
GatedMLP, 275, 276
Gated recurrent units (GRUs), 54
GatorTron's architecture, 371
Gaussian Error Linear Unit (GELU), 164, 167
Gemma family, 34, 35
General Data Protection Regulation (GDPR), 404, 422
General Message Passing (GMP), 314
Generative adversarial networks (GANs), 133, 524
Generative AI, 102, 103, 134
Generative image editing, 99

Generative Pre-trained
    Transformer (GPT), 64
  contributions, 64, 65, 67
  definition, 63
  evaluation metrics, 68
  limitations, 66
  model architectures, 68, 69, 71
  multitask learning, 66
  phases, 64
  risks and limitations, 68
  task-specific instructions/
    labels, 66
  transformers, 64, 67
  zero-, one-, and few-shot
    learning, 67
Gener-RNA, 348
Genesis block, 97
Genomically Aware
    Transformer (GAT), 344
Genomic Native
    Attention (GENA), 346
Genomic-Scale Language
    Models (GenSLMs), 345
Geocentrism, 262
Geth, 242, 243
Goal misalignment, 105
Google, 539
Google Cloud Load Balancer, 4
Governance action execution, 313
Governance engine, 305
Governance frameworks, 10
Governance models
  category-weighted voting, 320
  emerging pattern, 323
  futarchy, 320
  holographic consensus, 318
  implementation, 323
  innovations, 323
  liquid democracy, 320
  multi-tiered governance, 319
  on-chain/off-chain, 322
  optimistic, 318
  permission-based voting, 321
  pod-based governance, 320
  quadratic voting, 317
  qualified majority voting, 321
  rage quit mechanisms, 321
  RBS, 317
  skin-in-the-game voting, 319
  time-weighted voting, 321
  token-weighted voting, 316
  trade-offs, 323
Governance outcome
    prediction, 305
Governance simulation
    system, 305
Governance token regulations, 477
GPT 2.0, 66
GPT-2 model, 281
GPT-2 vs. Llama, 275
GPT Stupid, 293
Gradient-based optimization, 432
Gradient problem, 165
Graphical user interface, 8
Graphics Processing Unit (GPU),
    44, 82, 83, 120, 126
Gray-box attacks, 28
Great depression, 89
Greedy methods, 291

INDEX

Green fluorescent
        proteins (GFPs), 357
Grounding Language in
        Demonstrations
        (GLIDE), 548
Group-based reward
        normalization, 446
Grouped query attention (GQA),
        31, 37, 191
Group Relative Policy
        Optimization (GRPO), 444
Guardrails, 24, 25, 42

H

HairDAO, 326
Hallucination, 290
Halting problem, 211
Hard fork, 157
Hard math problems, 278
Hardware-based privacy
        protection, 497
Hardware security module (HSM),
        474, 487, 490, 500
Harvest now, decrypt later
        (HNDL), 502
Hash-based signatures, 253
Hashcash, 94
HashFast, 124
Hash function, 114, 116
Healthcare and identity, 495
Hedera Consensus Service
        (HCS), 493
Hedera's token service (HTS), 493

Hellinger distance, 19
Hidden Markov
        models (HMMs), 53
High-bandwidth memory
        interface, 127
High-quality liquid
        assets (HQLA), 475
H-index, 413
Holographic consensus, 318
Homogenization, 2
Homomorphic encryption, 421
Howey Test, 465
Hugging Face Leaderboard, 99
Human cognition, 431
Humanoid robots, 548
Human Vaccines Project, 366
Hybrid governance systems, 322
Hybrid optimization approach, 433
Hybrid retrieval systems, 175
Hybrid validation systems, 329
Hyperledger fabric networks, 488

I

IBM Enterprise AI Venture
        Fund, 103
IBM's Blockchain Platform, 486
Identity and access management
        (IAM), 484
Identity and reputation
        systems, 313
Identity layer, 9
Image generation models, 34
Immutability, 390

Implicit bias, 101
Implicit computation, 279
Inclusion criteria, 419
Industrial Revolution, 457
Inference, 173, 183–185
Inference metrics, 193–196
Inference procedures, 287
Inference speed, 131
Influenza-like illness (ILI), 365
Information retrieval system, 174
Information-theoretic bits, 273
Infrastructure-as-a-Service, 238
Initial coin offerings
    (ICOs), 464–467
Initial DEX Offerings (IDOs), 467
Initial Exchange Offerings
    (IEOs), 466
Innovation, 107
Innovation Corps (I-Corps), 513
In silico protein language
    models, 357
Institutional adaptation, 462
Institutional adoption, 424, 425
Institutional review boards
    (IRBs), 23
InstructGPT, 72
Instruction fine-tuning, 74, 176
Instruction sampling, 73
Integrated development
    environment (IDE), 99, 202
Integrating version control
    systems, 423
Integration framework, 306

Intellectual property (IP),
    324, 418
Intelligence explosion, 105, 553
Interfacing layer, 12
Internal consistency, 140
International Atomic Energy
    Agency (IAEA), 132
International Mathematical
    Olympiad (IMO), 260
International tax reporting, 473
Internet Computer
    Protocol (ICP), 464
Internet of Things (IoT), 202
InterPlanetary File System (IPFS),
    8, 202, 404
Invariant Point Attention (IPA), 358
Investment contract, 465
Investment DAOs, 327
Investors
    AI startups and investment
        opportunities
    application builders, 101
    enablers, 102
    infrastructure builders, 101
    generative AI, 102, 103
IP as non-fungible tokens
    (IP-NFTs), 418
Istanbul Byzantine Fault Tolerance
    (IBFT), 490

J

JSON-RPC 2.0 specification, 546

INDEX

K

Kaleido, 492
Kaplan's scaling laws, 75–77
Karya's hierarchical attention architecture, 377
Kernel, 81
Key management service (KMS), 484
Key-query-value (KQV), 438
Key-value caching (KVC), 188–190
Key-value maps (KVMs), 210
Key vector, 162, 187
Kintsugi, 383
K-mer tokenization, 339
Knowledge augmentation, 265, 268–270
Knowledge capacity, 265
Knowledge extraction, 265, 266, 269
Knowledge graph–based approaches, 364
Knowledge manipulation, 270
Knowledge storage vs. extraction, 269
Know-your-customer (KYC) procedures, 469
Kraken's staking program, 470
Kullback–Leibler divergence, 19

L

LabDAO, 326
Label masking, 287
LaMPSite, 364

Language model (LM), 64
  bugs, 260
  data contamination, 261
  knowledge
    activation functions, 275
    attributes, 266
    augmentation, 265, 268
    bugs, 272
    capacity, 265, 275
    control experiments, 276
    CoT inclusion, 270
    data sizes, 266
    disclaimers, 275
    extraction, 265
    hyperparameters, 273
    major and minor celebrities, 268
    manipulation, 270
    memorization vs. extraction, 265
    parity test, 263, 264
    partial search, 272
    reversal, 271
    scaling laws, 273, 274, 277
    scenarios, 264, 276
    writing styles, 267, 268, 274
  laws of motion and gravity, 259
  laws of planetary motion, 260
  learning language structures, 290–296
  parity test, 261
  reasoning
    chain of thought, 285
    challenging, 280

comments, 288
dependency graph, 283
discovery, 286, 287
elements, 289
generation process, 286
goals, 277, 278
GPT-2 model, 281
GPT-4, 285
graphs, 278
ideas, 288, 289
internal states, 282
math problems, 282
mistakes, 283, 284, 287, 289
multi-digit arithmetic, 279
number of operations, 280
outcomes, 286
parameters, 279
problem description, 279
templates, 280
theory, 258, 259
universal laws, 263
Language model training, 445
Large concept model (LCM), 541–543
Large language models (LLMs), 10, 99, 174, 258
adaptations, 55, 340
AI capabilities, 462, 463
attention mechanisms, 54
BERT transformer, 61, 62
biological measurements, 340
biological modeling, 337
clinical disparities, 25
components, 340
computational biology, 337
developments, 55, 56
DNA, 341–346
domain-specific advantages, 339
drug discovery, 363–365
embeddings, 160
Evo, 361–363
financial and organizational structures, 461
foundational models, 367–376
frenzy phase, 461
genome sequences, 338
GPT, 63
hallucination-induced hidden biases, 25
hyperparameters, 257
inference, 190
integration, 547
irruption phase, 461
k-mer methods, 338
mental health services, 380–384
metadata, 339
model alignment research, 72–75
open source, 30
pre-training, 257
primary, 26
protein, 353–360
public health, 365, 366
reducing physician burnout, 376–380
regulatory frameworks, 462
RNA, 346–353

INDEX

Large language
    models (LLMs) (*cont.*)
  RNN, 57, 58
  scaling research, 75–83
  scGPT, 360, 361
  stages, 338
  statistical machine translation
      models, 53
  T5 architecture, 63
  transformer, 59, 60
Large learning rate, 82
Large planning concept model
    (LPCM), 542
Lattice-based cryptography, 253
Laws of planetary motion, 260
Layer 2 scaling architectures,
    474, 477
Layer normalization, 60, 165
Leader-based consensus, 6
Lean methodology
  AI startups, 522–524
  business hypothesis
      experimentation, 510
  customer segments, 516–518
  framework, 508
  MVP, 509, 513–516
  pivot, 509
  principles, 507
  product–market fit, 510, 518
  shorter product development
      cycles, 508
  validated learning, 512
Learnability theorems, 258
Learned update rules, 432

Learned value functions, 433
Learning language structures
  CFG, 290, 291, 295
  DP transition functions,
      295, 296
  goals, 290
  GPT Stupid, 293
  hallucination, 290
  physics, 296
  relative/rotary attention,
      292, 293
  rotary embeddings, 294
  uniform attention, 294
Learning rate scheduler, 82
Legal wrappers, 334
Life Active Factors (LAFs), 340
LIMFE algorithm, 19
Limited liability company
    (LLC), 331
Linear projection mechanism, 440
Linear transformation, 164
Liquidation management, 305
Liquid democracy, 320
Llama, 275, 281, 293
LLM-powered robotics, 547, 548
LncRNA-BERT, 350, 351
Local Interpretable Model-
    Agnostic Explanations
    (LIME), 526
Locking mechanism, 236
Long short-term memory
    (LSTM), 54, 57
Lookahead search, 433
Lower-rank matrix technique, 79

INDEX

Low-rank adaptation (LoRA), 79, 80, 355

M

Machine learning (ML), 2, 10, 15, 100, 296, 365, 444, 523, 526
MAIVeSS platform, 366
Mapping, 222
Markets in Crypto-Assets (MiCA), 467, 470, 480
Masked language modeling (MLM), 61, 62, 295, 346
Masked multi-head self-attention, 169
Mass spectrometry-based proteomics, 340
Mathematical correctness, 445
Mathematical theorems, 258, 259
Math reasoning, 278
Maximal extractable value (MEV), 245, 248
Medical context preservation, 377
Med-PaLM, 370
Membership interference breach, 29
Membership Service Provider (MSP), 486
Memorization vs. extraction, 265
Memory-aware attention mechanism, 82
Memory bandwidth, 129
Memory capacity, 130
Memory efficiency, 441
Memory hierarchy, 129
Memory latency, 130
Mempool, 112
Mental computation requirement, 285
Mental health services, 380–385
Merkle branch, 155
Merkle-Patricia trees, 201, 207–209
Merkle root, 141–143, 152–155
Merkle trees, 152–155, 209, 250
Message queue systems, 314
Message types, 546
Meta Platforms, 267
Meta's Llama models, 31
Metaverse platforms, 479
Micro-grants program, 324
Microsoft's Azure Blockchain Service, 485
Microtransactions, 8
Miners, 112, 113, 118, 119
Minimum publishing standards, 395
Minimum viable product (MVP), 509, 513–516, 522
   creating training data, 524
   early AI products, 526
   hybrid approaches, 526
   rapid AI prototyping, 526
   synthetic data, 524, 525
Mining
   block header, 113, 114, 116
   candidate block, 113–115
   cloud services, 121
   coinbase transaction, 116

Mining (*cont.*)
   concepts, 111
   hardware, 119–122
   hash function, 114, 116
   hash value, 116
   motivations, 111
   overview, 112
   participation, 118
   pools, 120
   PoW, 115, 118, 119
   stamp, 113
   target value, 116
   time, 117
   transaction pool, 112
   unpackaged transactions, 112
Minter rule, 401, 403
Mist, 202, 243, 244
Mistral, 31, 275, 281, 293
Mixed Treatment Comparisons (MTCs), 399
Mix-training, 270, 271
Mixture of Experts (MoE), 25, 32, 37, 38, 434–437
Mobile wallets, 150
Model alignment research
   AGI, 75
   CAI, 73
   InstructGPT, 72
   self-generated instruction, 73, 74
Model architecture, 277
Model confidence scores, 434
Model context protocol (MCP), 543–547
Model deployment layer, 12
Model development layer, 13
Model extraction, 30
Model FLOPS utilization (MFU), 196
Model inversion, 29
Model reconstruction, 29
Model View Controller (MVC), 96
Module Learning With Errors (MLWE), 503
Mohamed bin Zayed University of Artificial Intelligence (MBZUAI), 263
Monitoring layer, 5
Monte Carlo Tree Search (MCTS), 432
Multi-agent approach, 48
Multi-agent systems, 540
Multi-digit arithmetic, 279
Multi-head attention, 59, 163, 190
   encoder's output, 170
Multi-head attention (MHA), 35, 37
Multi-head latent attention (MLA), 38, 434, 436, 438, 440
Multi-hop payment routing, 475
Multi-hop reasoning capabilities, 176
Multi-Instance GPU (MIG) technology, 127
Multimodal LLMs (MLLMs), 10
Multimodal models, 463
Multimodal robotics, 547
Multi-omics analysis, 360

INDEX

Multi-party computation (MPC), 501
Multiple sequence alignments (MSAs), 339, 349, 357
Multi-signature schemes, 472
Multitask learning, 66, 342
Multitask Mixture of Denoising Autoencoders (MoDA), 63
Multi-tiered governance, 319
Multi-token prediction (MTP), 38, 272, 440–442

N

Nabla, 377
Nakamoto Consensus, 125
Namecoin, 203
Named entity recognition (NER), 377
National Institute of Standards and Technology (NIST), 425
National Institutes of Health (NIH), 396
Natural language processing (NLP), 53, 56, 140, 382, 523
Network-layer security, 502
Neural machine translation (NMT), 57
Neural networks, 128, 365, 461
Neural processing units (NPUs), 128
Neural retrievers, 175
New York Department of Financial Services (NYDFS), 475

Next sentence prediction (NSP), 61, 62
Node operators, 470
Non-fungible tokens (NFTs), 315, 324, 417, 418, 479
Non-linear activation function, 164
Notable Health, 379
Nothing-at-Stake problem, 501
Nuance DAX's platform, 378
Nuclear-powered data centers, 549, 550
Nuclear Regulatory Commission, 132
Nucleotide transformer, 345

O

Object-relational mapper, 4
Off-chain actions, 236
Off-chain governance, 322
Off-chain tracking layer, 15
OlympiadBench, 552
On-chain governance, 322
OpenAI's MLE-Bench, 552
OpenAI Startup Fund, 103
OpenAI Swarm, 540
OpenGenome dataset, 362
OpenMined, 13
Open-science innovation, 400
Open source AI models
    Aya family, 39, 40
    benefits, 30
    BLOOM family, 33
    DeepSeek family, 37, 39

579

INDEX

Open source AI models (*cont.*)
   Falcon family, 32
   fine-tuning, 30
   Gemma family, 34, 35
   meta's Llama models, 31
   Mistral family, 31
   performance gap, 30
   Phi family, 35
   Qwen family, 36
   stability AI, 34
OpenZeppelin, 12, 224
Optimistic governance, 318
Optimistic rollups, 230
Oracle Blockchain Cloud Service (OBCS), 487
Oracle Cloud Infrastructure (OCI), 487
Oracle layer, 14
Oracles, 314, 476
Ownership layer, 324

P

Paired Multi-Modal Attention (PMMA), 363
Pairformer module, 359
PaliGemma, 35
Paperclip maximizer problem, 17
Paradigm shift, 90–93, 99
Parameter-efficient finetuning (PEFT), 79, 80
Parity test, 263, 264
Partial payments, 475
PayPal Ventures AI Fund, 103
Pay-Per-Last-N-Shares (PPLNS), 121
Pay-Per-Share (PPS), 121
Peercoin, 204
Peer Data Availability Sampling (PeerDAS), 252
Peer selection algorithm, 502
Peer-to-peer network, 240
Peer-to-peer (P2P) communication, 7
Performance metrics, 47
Permission-based voting, 321
Personal health information (PHI), 380
Perturbation techniques, 44
PetaFLOPS (PFLOPS), 130
PGraphDTA, 363
Pharmaceutical drug tracking
   AR/VR technologies, 426
   BRUINchain, 415
   citations, 420, 421
   clinical trials, 419, 420
   cross-chain scientific infrastructure, 423, 424
   data sovereignty, 421, 422
   definition, 413
   DeSci movement, 416, 417
   environmental considerations, 425
   factors
      data retrieval, 414
      data timeliness, 414
      reliability, 414
   functionalities, 416
   institutional adoption, 424, 425

NFTs, 417, 418
and open science, 415
post-quantum world, 425
prescription, 414
reproducibility, 422
smart contracts, 418, 419
supply chain, 420
Phenotypes, 340
Phi family, 35
Pivot, 509
Plasma, 237, 238
Pocket-Guided Co-Attention (PGCA), 363
Pod-based governance, 320
Policy evolution, 444–446
Policy model, 26
Policy optimization, 444
Political decentralization, 300
Portfolio rebalancing, 305
Positional encoding, 59, 161
Post-analysis statistical methods, 406
Post-quantum cryptography (PQC), 425, 502, 503
PoW chain, 233
Power efficiency, 131
Prague-Electra (Pectra) upgrade, 252
Precision agriculture, 514
Prefill/prompt phase, 192
Prefill time, 194
Prescription drug monitoring programs, 413
Pre-training, 287

Privacy-by-design principles, 404
Privacy-centric architecture, 491
Privacy-focused blockchain networks, 476
Privacy layer, 15
Problem-solving skills, 280
Process reward models (PRMs), 433
Product–market fit, 510, 516
Professional investors, 467
ProGen, 354
Programming languages, 13
ProLLaMA, 355
Prompt engineering, 99
Prompting techniques, 22
Prompt tuning, 80
Proof of life, 142
Proof of stake (PoS), 6, 125, 204, 425, 501
Proof-of-work (PoW), 6, 94, 115, 118, 119, 125, 204, 425
Proportional rewards, 122
Proposal distribution, 432
Proposer–builder separation (PBS), 248
Protein Data Bank (PDB), 358
Protein language models
　AlphaFold, 357, 358, 360
　challenges, 354, 355
　context dependencies, 354
　ESM-3, 356, 357
　non-coding regions, 354
　nucleotides, 353
　three-dimensional structure, 354

Protein-level analysis, 340
ProtLLM, 355
Protocol DAOs, 327
Protocol-Owned Vault (POV) strategy, 309
Protocol-specific adapters, 315
Protocol standardization, 313
Proto-danksharding, 246
Proximal Policy Optimization (PPO), 444
Pseudonymization, 404
PsyDAO, 326
Public blockchain, 494
Public exchanges, 480
Public health, 365, 366
Public perception, 550
Publish and Evaluate Onchain (PEvO), 413
PubMedBERT, 369
PyTorch, 82

Q

Quadratic voting, 317
Qualified majority voting, 321
Quantum computing, 253, 425
Quantum-resistant technology, 254
Query construction, 174
Query vector, 161, 188
Queuing time, 194
Quorum Blockchain Service (QBS), 490
Qwen family, 36

R

R3's Corda, 491
RAFT consensus protocol, 484
Rage quit mechanisms, 321
Reality gap, 525
Real-time gross settlement (RTGS), 474
Real-world asset (RWA), 301, 328–330
REcoin, 466
Recomputation, 81
Recovery systems, 314
Rectified Linear Unit (ReLU), 35, 164, 165, 167
RecurrentGemma, 35
Recurrent neural networks (RNNs), 54, 57, 58, 157, 168
Recursive self-improvement, 105, 553
Reentrancy attacks, 501
Regulatory frameworks, 460
Regulatory layer, 10
Reinforcement learning CAI (RL-CAI), 27
Reinforcement learning from human feedback (RLHF), 35, 37, 47, 448
Reinforcement learning (RL), 18, 26, 38, 72, 438, 444–446, 448–450, 540
Reinforcement learning with AI feedback (RLAIF), 73

Rejection sampling, 432, 447, 448
Relational databases, 4
Relative attention, 292
Remix, 224
Remote procedure call (RPC), 243
Replication, 393
Replika, 382
Reproducibility crisis
    academia, 392
    clinical sciences, 391
    DDI, 396
    drug discovery, 392
    economic costs, 392
    erroneous research method, 393
    hypothesis testing, 394
    minimum publishing standards, 395
    negative data, 393, 394
    positive data, 393, 394
    project, 396
Reputation-based systems (RBS), 306, 317
Reputation system, 410
    colored coin transactions, 410
    DDI, 407
    evaluator function, 407, 409
    quality control, 407, 411
    rep_score, 408, 409
    scientific efforts, 411, 413
    sequential evaluation, 407
ResearchHub, 416
Residual connections, 60, 165
Resource allocation, 311, 517
Resource-constrained environments, 451
Response generation, 74
Retraction Watch, 392
Retrieval-augmented fine-tuning, 179
Retrieval-augmented generation (RAG), 103, 378
    advantages, 179
    components
        information retrieval system, 174
        LLM, 174
        query construction, 174
    cost efficiency and scalability, 179
    customer support knowledge base, 180, 181
    definition, 174
    hybrid retrieval systems, 175
    implementations, 175
    neural retrievers, 175
    re-ranking, 175
Revenue streams, 521
Reverse knowledge, 271
Reward-driven feedback mechanisms, 444
Reward model, 72
RiboNucleic Acid Language Model (RiNALMo), 347
Risk-adjusted return optimization, 305
Risk-adjusted threshold management, 311

INDEX

Risk management systems, 308, 310, 531
RNA language models
   advantages, 353
   applications, 347, 348, 350, 351
   BEACON, 352
   MLM, 346
   pre-training, 353
   transformer architecture, 346
RNA Multiple Sequence Alignment-based Language Model (RNA-MSM), 349
Rollback, 238
Rotary attention, 292
Rotary positional embeddings (RoPE), 34, 35, 361, 439
Rule engine, 401, 402, 406

S

Safe exploration techniques, 23
SafeMath libraries, 501
Safety and responsible design principles, 16, 17
   accountability, 21
   causal understanding, 19, 21
   explainability and interpretability, 19
   fairness and bias mitigation, 18
   human–AI collaboration, 21
   privacy and security, 22
   regulatory compliance and open standards, 24
   robustness and generalizability, 19
   safe exploration and ethical considerations, 23
   value alignment, 17
Salesforce Ventures Generative AI Fund, 102
SapBERT, 372
Scalability trilemma, 231
Scarcity, 402
scGPT, 360, 361
SCIENCE-index, 421
Scientific integrity, 390
Scientific reproducibility
   clinical trials, 398–406
   decentralization and democratic science, 391–397
   immutability and integrity, 390
   pharmaceutical drugs, 413
   reputation system, 407–413
   transparency and research verification, 390
Secondary structure prediction (SSP), 352
Second linear transformation, 164
Secure key management systems, 470
Secure machine learning (SML)
   breaches types, 29
   definition, 28
   limited-knowledge, gray-box attacks, 28

perfect-knowledge, white-box attacks, 28
poisoning *vs.* evasion attacks, 28
privacy breaches, 29
zero-knowledge, black-box attacks, 29
Secure multi-party computation (SMPC), 421
Securities and Exchange Commission (SEC), 465, 468
Security in BaaS, 500–504
Security Token Offerings (STOs), 466
Security vulnerabilities, 311
Self-attention approach, 10
Self-attention mechanism, 161
Self-generated instruction, 73, 74
Self-governance, 300
Self-reflective behavior, 449
Self-sovereign identity (SSI), 404, 422, 495
Self-sovereign platforms, 9
Self-supervised approach, 360
Self-supervised learning, 1, 2
Semantic-based prompts, 364
SentencePiece, 159
Sentiment analysis, 177
Sequence-to-sequence (Seq2Seq) models, 53, 54
Sequential Monte Carlo (SMC), 432
Sequential prediction (decode phase), 192
Server-Sent Events, 545
Service DAOs, 328
Shallow-and-wide model, 284
Shanghai/Capella upgrade, 244
SHapley Additive exPlanations (SHAP), 19, 531
Sharding, 231, 232
Sigmoid, 169
Simple Payment Verification (SPV), 139, 151, 152, 154
Simplified attention mechanism, 58
Single-cell RNA sequencing (scRNA-seq), 339, 360
Single-nucleotide tokenization, 339, 353
Single Secret Leader Election (SSLE), 253
Skin-in-the-game voting, 319
Sliding Window Attention (SWA), 31
Small language models (SLMs), 35
Small modular reactors (SMRs), 132, 549
Smart contracts, 7, 11, 13, 201, 227, 229, 247, 250, 301, 304, 322, 418, 419, 463, 464, 471, 483, 485, 496, 502
Smarter approach, 288
Smart-logging, 225

INDEX

Social inequalities, 100
Soft alignment, 57
Soft fork, 157
Softmax function, 162, 168
Softmax temperature scaling mechanism, 435
Solidity, 7, 218–221
Sparse parameters, 435
Spatial information processing, 356
Splice site prediction (SPL), 352
Split function, 301, 302
Split-testing, 511
Squeeze-Excitation Normalization (SENet), 81
SSL handshake, 403
Stability AI, 34
Stablecoins, 475
Starknet, 230
State channels, 236, 237
State space language model (SSLM), 33
State synchronization systems, 312
Static batching (naïve batching), 196
Static embeddings, 160
Statistical disclosure control, 29
Statistical machine translation (SMT), 53, 57
Storage layer, 8
Streaming processors/cores, 127
Structural equation models, 20
Structural score imputation (SSI), 352

Structured investment strategies, 310
Subscription fees, 8
Subword tokenization, 158
Suki's clinical context injection technique, 378
Supervised fine-tuning (SFT), 37, 38, 64, 72, 442, 443, 447, 448, 450
Supervised learning CAI (SL-CAI), 27
Supervised learning (SL), 26, 532
Supervisory model, 25
Supply-chain management, 389, 415, 420
Suspicious Activity Reports (SARs), 470
Swarm, 226, 240
Synthetic data, 524, 525
Synthetic knowledge, 273

T

T5 architecture, 63
Tail latency, 195
Talkspace, 381
Tanh (hyperbolic tangent), 168
Task management system, 307
Technical compliance, 473
Techno-economic paradigms, 458, 460
Technological revolution blockchain, 459

economic cycles and social
  transformation, 457
financial and production capital
  interface, 458
frenzy phase, 458
ICOs, 464–467
irruption phase, 458
leadership, 458
LLMs, 461–463
maturity phase, 458
smart contracts, 463, 464
synergy phase, 458
Technological singularity, 106
Technology Innovation
  Institute (TII), 32
Technology stack
  blockchain, 96
  cryptographic measures, 96
  cyberpunk community, 93
  data integrity and security, 98
  double spending, 93
  fault tolerance, 95
  features, 96
  Hashcash, 94
  MVC framework, 96
  one-way functions, 94
  suboptimal strategy, 95
Temperature parameter, 186
Template-based prompts, 364
Temporal-clinical attention, 377
Tennessee, 331
Tensor Processing Units (TPUs), 126
TeraFLOPS (TFLOPS), 130

TerraMiner IV, 123
Tess, 383
Test-time compute, 432–434
Text resources, 545
Theory of Computations (TCS), 258
Theory of mind, 551
Throughput, 195
Tiling, 80
Time-locked execution system, 313
Time Per Output Token
  (TPOT), 194
Timestamping research plans, 423
Time To First Token (TTFT), 193
Time-weighted voting, 321
Token distribution methods, 466
Tokenization, 8, 158, 159, 191,
  324, 338
Tokenomics system, 307
Token-weighted voting, 316
Tongyi Qianwen, 36
Top-k accuracy, 352
Top-k parameter, 185
Topological sorting, 290
Top-p/nucleus sampling, 185
Total Value Locked (TVL), 230, 330
Traditional AI agents, 540
Training speed, 131
Transaction workflow, 140–144
TransDTI, 363
Transferability, 65
Transformer architecture, 10, 55,
  59, 61, 63, 65, 67, 157,
  158, 360

Transformer modules, 440
Transformers, 274
Treasury management systems, 304, 311
Treasury monitoring, 309
Trial registration, 398
Troodi, 382
Turing test, 272

U

Ultra Light Nodes (ULNs), 312
Uncertainty quantification, 433
Unidirectional decoder model, 294
Unified Buffer, 128
Uniform attention, 294
Universal Sharing Framework, 301
Unlocking mechanism, 236
Unspent transaction outputs (UTXOs), 144, 209
Unsupervised pre-training, 64
Urgency detection system, 379
User accounts, 206
User experience (UX), 3
User interface (UI), 3
Utah, 332

V

Validated learning, 512
ValleyDAO, 326
Value alignment, 17
Value learning problem, 554
Value propositions, 519, 527
Value sensitivity analysis, 18
Value vector, 187
Verifier search, 433
Verkle trees, 250, 251
Virtual assets, 400, 476
Virtual machines, 233
Virtual Private Cloud (VPC), 489
Virtual reality (VR), 426
Visa GenAI Fund, 103
VitaDAO, 325, 416
Vote-escrowed tokenomics model (veCRV), 307
Vyper, 222, 223

W

Warm COINBASE, 245
Warm restarts, 83
Web3.js, 214
Web-scraping algorithm, 66
Web server layer, 4
WebText, 66
Whisper, 202, 225, 229, 240
White-box attacks, 28
Wikipedia, 266, 276
Woebot, 381
WordPiece tokenization, 159
Word tokenization, 158
World computer, 215, 225–229
Wyoming, 331
Wysa, 382

X

Xeon Platinum 8380, 127
xTrimoPGLM model, 354

Y

Youper, 383

Z

Zero-knowledge proofs (ZKPs), 2, 44, 45, 421, 474, 496
Zero-knowledge rollups (ZK-rollups), 230, 231
Zero-Knowledge Scalable Transparent Arguments of Knowledge (zk-STARK), 231, 247
Zero-Knowledge Succinct Non-interactive Arguments of Knowledge (zk-SNARKs), 230, 247, 503
Zero-shot fine-tuning, 178
Zero-shot learning, 65
Zero-shot prompting, 100

GPSR Compliance

The European Union's (EU) General Product Safety Regulation (GPSR) is a set of rules that requires consumer products to be safe and our obligations to ensure this.

If you have any concerns about our products, you can contact us on

ProductSafety@springernature.com

In case Publisher is established outside the EU, the EU authorized representative is:

Springer Nature Customer Service Center GmbH
Europaplatz 3
69115 Heidelberg, Germany